UNITED NATIONS CONFERENCE ON TRADE AND DEVELOPMENT
Geneva

THE LEAST DEVELOPED COUNTRIES 1995 REPORT

MID-TERM REVIEW
of the Programme of Action

Prepared by the UNCTAD secretariat

D1220599

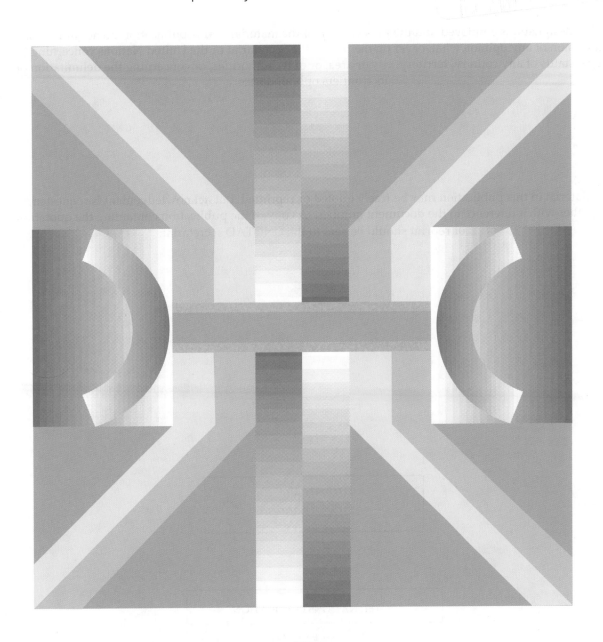

UNITED NATIONS
New York, 1995

NOTE

Symbols of United Nations documents are composed of capital letters combined with figures. Mention of such a symbol indicates a reference to a United Nations document.

*

*   *

The designations employed and the presentation of the material in this publication do not imply the expression of any opinion whatsoever on the part of the Secretariat of the United Nations concerning the legal status of any country, territory, city or area, or of its authorities, or concerning the delimitation of its frontiers or boundaries.

*

*   *

Material in this publication may be freely quoted or reprinted, but acknowledgement is requested, together with a reference to the document number. A copy of the publication containing the quotation or reprint should be sent to the UNCTAD secretariat.

HC
59.7
.L328
1995

TD/B/41/(2)/4

UNCTAD/LDC(1995)

UNITED NATIONS PUBLICATION

Sales No. E.95.II.D.2

ISBN 92-1-112370-4

ISSN 0257-7550

CONTENTS

LIST OF BOXES

LIST OF CHARTS

List of Text Tables

EXPLANATORY NOTES

The term "dollars" ($) refers to United States dollars unless otherwise stated. The term "billion" signifies 1,000 million.

Annual rates of growth and changes refer to compound rates. Exports are valued f.o.b. and imports c.i.f. unless otherwise specified.

Use of a hyphen (-) between dates representing years, e.g. 1981-1990, signifies the full period involved, including the initial and final years.

An oblique stroke (/) between two years, e.g. 1991/92, signifies a fiscal or crop year.

The abbreviation LDC (or LDCs) refers, throughout this report, to a country (or countries) included in the United Nations list of least developed countries.

In the tables:

Two dots (..) indicate that the data are not available, or are not separately reported.

One dot (.) indicates that the data are not applicable.

A dash (-) indicates that the amount is nil or negligible.

A plus sign (+) before a figure indicates an increase; a minus sign (-) before a figure indicates a decrease.

Details and percentages do not necessarily add up to totals, because of rounding.

ABBREVIATIONS

ACP	African, Caribbean and Pacific (Group of States)
ADF	African Development Fund
AIDS	acquired immune deficiency syndrome
AsDB	Asian Development Bank
BCEAO	Central Bank of West African States
BEAC	Bank of the Central African States
CBR	crude birth rate
CEMAC	Economic and Monetary Community in Central Africa
CFA	Communauté financière africaine
CFD	French Development Fund
CMEA	Council for Mutual Economic Assistance
CoV	coefficient of variation
DAC	Development Assistance Committee (of OECD)
DANIDA	Danish International Development Agency
DES	dietary energy supply
DRF	Debt Reduction Facility
ECA	Economic Commission for Africa
ECOWAS	Economic Community of West African States
EDF	European Development Fund
EFTA	European Free Trade Association
ESAF	Enhanced Structural Adjustment Facility
ESCAP	Economic and Social Commission for Asia and the Pacific (formerly ECAFE)
EU	European Union
FAO	Food and Agriculture Organization of the United Nations
FDI	foreign direct investment
GATS	General Agreement on Trade in Services
GATT	General Agreement on Tariffs and Trade
GDI	gross domestic investment
GDP	gross domestic product
GDS	gross domestic savings
GNP	gross national product
GSP	generalized system of preferences
HDI	Human Development Index
IBRD	International Bank for Reconstruction and Development
IDA	International Development Association
IGADD	Intergovernmental Authority on Drought and Development
IMF	International Monetary Fund
IPNS	integrated plant nutrition system
IPR	intellectual property rights
ISIC	International Standard Industrial Classification of All Economic Activities
ITU	International Telecommunication Union
KBO	Kagera River Basin Organization
LE	life expectancy
MFA	Multi-Fibre Arrangement
MFN	most favoured nation
MIGA	Multilateral Investment Guarantee Agency
MVA	manufacturing value added
NAM	Non-Aligned Movement
NARS	national agricultural research systems
NaTCAP	National Technical Cooperation Assessment Programme

NCTA	Northern Corridor Transit Agreement
NGO	non-governmental organization
NTM	non-tariff measure
ODA	official development assistance
ODF	official development finance
ODI	Overseas Development Institute
OECD	Organisation for Economic Co-operation and Development
OPEC	Organization of the Petroleum Exporting Countries
ORT	Oral Rehydration Therapy
PMAWCA	Port Management Association of West and Central Africa
PSRC	Parastatal Sector Reform Commission
PTA	Preferential Trade Area of Eastern and Southern African States
RAP	rights accumulation programmes
R and D	research and development
RCTD	road transit document
REER	real effective exchange rate
RMG	ready-made garment
RMI	Road Maintenance Initiative
SAF	Structural Adjustment Facility
SAL	structural adjustment loan
SAP	Structural Adjustment Programme
SATCC	Southern African Transport and Communications Commission
SDR	special drawing right
SECAL	sectoral adjustment loan
SITC	Standard International Trade Classification
SNPA	Substantial New Programme of Action for the Least Developed Countries for the 1980s
SPA	Special Programme of Assistance
SSA	sub-Saharan Africa
TFP	total factor productivity
TFR	total fertility rate
TIR	Transport international routière
TRIM	trade-related investment measures
TRIP	trade-related aspects of intellectual property rights
UDEAC	Central African Customs and Economic Union
UEMOA	West African Economic and Monetary Union (formerly UMOA)
UMOA	West African Monetary Union
UNCED	United Nations Conference on Environment and Development
UNCTAD	United Nations Conference on Trade and Development
UNCTC	United Nations Centre on Transnational Corporations
UNDP	United Nations Development Programme
UN/ECE	United Nations Economic Commission for Europe
UNEP	United Nations Environment Programme
UNICEF	United Nations Children's Fund
UNIDO	United Nations Industrial Development Organization
UPU	Universal Postal Union
VAT	value added tax
WTO	World Trade Organization

PREFACE

The group of Least Developed Countries (LDCs) currently comprises 48 countries with a population of more than 555 million. The LDCs are the poorest and most economically weak of the developing countries, with formidable economic, institutional and human resources problems, which are often compounded by geographical handicaps and natural and man-made disasters. The most recent additions to the group (General Assembly resolution 49/133) are Angola and Eritrea; Botswana graduated from the group of LDCs in 1994.[1]

To respond to the challenges faced by LDCs, the Second United Nations Conference on the Least Developed Countries, held in Paris from 3 to 14 September 1990, adopted the Paris Declaration and The Programme of Action for the Least Developed Countries for the 1990s. In these documents, the international community committed itself to urgent and effective action, based on the principle of shared responsibility and strengthened partnership, to arrest and reverse the deterioration in the LDCs' socio-economic situation and to revitalize their growth and development.

The Programme of Action entrusts UNCTAD with the focal role in the review and appraisal of the implementation of the Programme and its follow-up at the global level. The Declaration adopted by UNCTAD VIII, entitled "A New Partnership for Development: The Cartagena Commitment", reaffirms this mandate and provides for the Trade and Development Board to review the progress made in the implementation of the Programme of Action, during the spring segment of its annual sessions, using the Least Developed Countries Reports as background documents.

This year's Report, the eleventh in the series, will be, as in previous years, the main background document for the Trade and Development Board's annual review. It will also serve as the basic document for the High-level Intergovernmental Meeting on the Mid-term Global Review of the implementation of the Programme of Action scheduled for 26 September-6 October 1995. Consequently, this year's Report takes a retrospective look at the progress made in the implementation of the Programme of Action since its adoption in 1990 and analyses the difficulties encountered in sustaining development. Chapter I analyses LDCs' performance during 1990-1994, and reviews growth prospects for 1995 and 1996. It also assesses LDCs' economic and social progress since the adoption of the Programme of Action, documents the countries' experiences with the design and implementation of adjustment and reforms and draws policy conclusions. Chapter II, III and IV examine the experiences and performance of LDCs in the agriculture, manufacturing and infrastructure sectors, respectively. Progress in the implementation of international support measures in the areas of official development assistance (ODA), debt and external trade is discussed in chapters V and VI. The Report also contains an annex on Basic Data series on the Least Developed Countries. It should be noted that there is some variance in data coverage between some text tables and the Basic Data, due to different data sources used for analysis in the main text and, in some instances, to the different periods covered.

The UNCTAD secretariat expresses its appreciation to the Governments of States members of UNCTAD and to the international organizations that have provided valuable inputs and contributions to this Report. In particular, it is grateful to FAO, UNIDO and the World Bank for their useful contributions to the preparation of the Report.

---

[1]   Afghanistan, Angola, Bangladesh, Benin, Bhutan, Burkina Faso, Burundi, Cambodia, Cape Verde, Central African Republic, Chad, Comoros, Djibouti, Equatorial Guinea, Eritrea, Ethiopia, Gambia, Guinea, Guinea-Bissau, Haiti, Kiribati, Lao People's Democratic Republic, Lesotho, Liberia, Madagascar, Malawi, Maldives, Mali, Mauritania, Mozambique, Myanmar, Nepal, Niger, Rwanda, Samoa, Sao Tome and Principe, Sierra Leone, Solomon Islands, Somalia, Sudan, Togo, Tuvalu, Uganda, United Republic of Tanzania, Vanuatu, Yemen, Zaire and Zambia.

EXECUTIVE SUMMARY

This Report has been prepared keeping in mind the High-level Intergovernmental Meeting on the Mid-term Global Review of the Implementation of the Programme of Action for the Least Developed Countries for the 1990s, to be held from 26 September to 6 October 1995. In this context, it is fitting to recall that the Programme of Action inaugurated a new approach to development and international cooperation. In the Programme, development is regarded as a wider and more complex process that embraces a range of non-economic factors and objectives including, in particular, those relating to social development, respect for human rights and popular participation in the development process. At the same time, the Programme acknowledges the reality that economic growth in LDCs is indispensable to the achievement of these objectives. In this new approach, international cooperation for development is viewed as a matter of solidarity and partnership. Accordingly, the Programme of Action primarily emphasizes shared responsibility and strengthened joint efforts as the key to the successful achievement of the overriding objective of reactivating and accelerating growth and sustained development in LDCs.

The Programme was formulated against certain expectations including developments in the domestic and international economic environment and was predicated on the premise that further deterioration in the socio-economic situation of LDCs would be arrested. However, within a short time following the adoption of the Programme of Action, a number of LDCs were seriously affected by various problems, including man-made and natural disasters, while others were coping with the consequences of the Structural Adjustment Programmes (SAPs) and policy reforms that gave rise to certain short-term socio-economic difficulties and that were not always conducive to their long-term development. On the other hand, it was assumed in the Programme of Action that the increased global economic growth would permit a much strengthened external support to LDCs. However, the onset of a deep global recession following the Paris Conference had adverse consequences for the provision of external finance to LDCs. These unforeseen domestic and international developments that occurred in the immediate aftermath of the Paris Conference had important implications for the overall implementation of the Programme of Action during the first half of the 1990s. The High-level Intergovernmental Meeting on the Mid-term Global Review of the Implementation of the Programme of Action offers a unique forum for LDCs and their development partners to make an in-depth and comprehensive appraisal of the socio-economic developments in LDCs in the early 1990s and to consider and agree on concrete national and international measures and actions to accelerate the pace of the Programme's implementation.

The Meeting acquires even greater significance in view of the rapid pace of globalization of the world economy. For LDCs to break away from their marginalization and to participate more actively in the global economic processes, it is imperative that they and their partners devise policies and measures to widen and deepen the external orientations of their economies and, at the same time, address their domestic economic and social problems. This dual challenge will require strengthened national policies and international measures in favour of LDCs to ensure the timely and adequate implementation of the Programme of Action during the second half of the 1990s. LDCs will need to further strengthen their national development efforts which, as has been testified by those that have improved their performance, can make a difference.

However, without the benefit of sustained international support, LDCs will most probably become further marginalized as the process of globalization gains further momentum. Adequate external support is of particular significance since, without the cooperation of the international community, the prospects of greater participation of LDCs in the global international market-place will be highly uncertain. The improved economic performance by a number of LDCs and the successful transition to peace by others are an eloquent testimony to the importance of international support; these countries' achievements would not have been possible without the involvement of the international community. Therefore, it is imperative that the development partners continue to support LDCs with optimism and vigour and with a view to ensuring that the gains so painfully acquired over the past years are not lost.

The success of the Mid-term Review will depend to a significant extent on the adequacy of responses by LDCs and their development partners to these challenges. The spirit of international solidarity and partnership underpinning the Programme of Action must now be translated into vigorous, adequate and sustained national actions and international support measures on their behalf.

Socio-economic performance of LDCs in the early 1990s

LDCs' overall economic conditions continue to be bleak. Instead of reversing the economic deterioration in LDCs as a whole in the early 1990s, these years actually marked a period of decline following two decades of stagnation. The combined annual average growth rate of LDCs during 1990-1993 was 1.6 per cent and is estimated to be even lower for 1994 - at around 1.4 per cent. This trend is particularly disquieting because the situation is worse than in the 1980s, which was regarded as a lost decade for LDCs. Their performance is also in sharp contrast with the broad-based recovery of the world economy during 1994-1995.

However, although LDC economies face almost identical structural problems and are confronted by similar conditions of access to product markets and to external finance, their development experiences have become more heterogeneous over the years. So despite the overall bleak picture, as many as 12 LDCs (Bangladesh, Benin, Cambodia, Equatorial Guinea, Guinea-Bissau, the Lao People's Democratic Republic, Lesotho, Mozambique, Myanmar, Sao Tome and Principe, the Solomon Islands and Sudan) have improved their performance and most have had notable increases in their per capita output during the first half of the 1990s. A strong expansion of agricultural production, internal stability, strong government commitments, a sound political and regulatory framework for development, complemented by significant external support, among other factors, have contributed to raising economic growth rates. At the other end of the spectrum are several countries whose development experiences have been dominated by a range of non-economic factors. Thus, domestic and exogenous problems, such as civil conflicts, political instability, refugees and internally displaced persons, recurrent droughts, floods and devastating cyclones have had an adverse impact on these countries' socio-economic conditions.

The lack of progress made in improving the socio-economic performance of most LDCs in recent years is attributable to a set of factors which are summarized below.

Impact of policy reforms

Over the past several years, many LDCs have undertaken wide-ranging reform policies and measures. As they moved along the reform path, the reform objectives took on more complex and ambitious characteristics, shifting from the limited concerns of macroeconomic imbalances and stabilization to promoting development by a plethora of market-oriented reforms, including improving economic efficiency, curbing public-sector intervention, encouraging the private sector and liberalizing the external trade sector. The pace and scope of these reforms, which have been painful, contrast sharply with the meagre results achieved in most LDCs. While the need for reforms is not disputed, LDCs have been expected to implement policies not always designed to suit their conditions, and to accomplish too much, too soon - and with too few resources. So it is not surprising that, despite some positive developments in a few LDCs, the reform process has not lifted the structural constraints in many LDC economies nor improved their supply capacity.

A few important lessons can be drawn from the experiences of LDCs in this regard. First, reform measures must be designed to take better account of the structural characteristics, specific needs and level of development of each country as well as the importance of the expansion of supply capacity. Second, the roles to be played by the market, firms, States and institutions in structural transformation will be determined by each country's conditions. In addition, ensuring macroeconomic stability and consistency of policy formulation and implementation, maintaining realistic exchange rates and improving the public sector's efficiency are critical to the success of the reform efforts. The design of reform packages requires complementary efforts, particularly through mobilization of domestic financial and human resources. And finally, the degree of success will depend on the external economic environment, including adequate and appropriate external financing. It is particularly important to provide the requisite, quick-disbursing assistance to facilitate stabilization and short- to medium-term adjustment measures.

Political conflicts and civil strife

Another reason for the overall poor performance of several LDCs has been political conflicts and civil strife that have frequently led to armed hostilities, large-scale displacements of populations and a breakdown of the system of governance. The subsequent severe economic and social dislocations and output loss have created further impoverishment of people already at the brink of survival. As a result of these developments, the capacities of States to provide effectively the minimum requisites of a modern economy have been diminished. In view of this, greater emphasis will have to be given in the affected LDCs to rebuilding and strengthening these capacities to enable the States to perform essential functions. Bringing these conflicts to an early and peaceful conclusion is the most important precondition for reactivating the development process in these LDCs. This, in turn, will require multifaceted actions not envisaged at the Paris Conference.

Performance in the productive sectors

For most LDCs, the performance of the productive sectors (viz., agriculture, industry and infrastructure) has not been encouraging. During the early 1990s, agriculture was characterized by lags in production growth relative to that of the population, declines in terms of trade and loss of market shares for traditional agricultural commodities. Exogenous factors, including drought and sluggish world demand and prices, contributed to the poor performance. Moreover, years of domestic policy biases against agriculture - which, *inter alia*, suppressed real producer prices, taxed agriculture with overvalued exchange rates and cheap food imports, and neglected agricultural support services and investment - were important in shaping this sector's performance. A particularly disquieting trend in many LDCs is the growing incidence of man-made food emergencies arising from wars and related population displacements, which is the single most important cause of food insecurity in Africa. Enhancing food production and achieving food security remain a priority for LDCs and will require expansion and/or intensification of arable land and improved production through better provision of required inputs.

Notwithstanding the wide variation in the manufacturing growth rates among LDCs, the performance of the manufacturing sector has weakened in recent years. While some one-third of LDCs maintained a positive growth of manufacturing value added (MVA) in the 1980s and early 1990s, most LDCs experienced stagnation and even declines in manufacturing output. The average MVA growth rate for LDCs as a whole turned negative in the 1990s. There are many reasons for the failure of the manufacturing industry in the majority of LDCs. In addition to the problems arising from past policies and strategies, manufacturing activities were constrained by low investment, import compression and the policy environment, including the impacts of adjustment and reform. To revitalize the manufacturing activities, it is important to undertake selective interventions to remove constraints caused by structural deficiencies, market limitations, paucity of endowments and inadequate policies. The international community can play an important role in supporting LDC efforts to overcome these constraints and the difficulties created by external factors.

Lack of progress in establishing necessary physical infrastructure in LDCs continues to be a major handicap to providing the required services needed to support the expansion of the production base and the commercial sector in the LDCs. Insufficient physical infrastructure, particularly road transport and communications, is more evident in land-locked and island LDCs. Road density in most LDCs remains much lower than in many developing countries. Despite efforts to expand the road network in many LDCs, the lack of adequate and effective maintenance has led to a rapid deterioration of a significant part of the existing road infrastructure. Growth performance in the rail transport sector has been even more sluggish and the problem is compounded by lack of equipment and poor management. Inadequate communications systems in LDCs are a major bottleneck to providing required services to other sectors of the economy, particularly the commercial sector. The international community should support arrangements to help LDCs to benefit from the rapidly growing telecommunications technology. Further efforts should be undertaken in the area of air transport to encourage cargo pooling and the development of joint maintenance facilities at the subregional level.

Developments relating to social indicators

The persistent decline in human welfare in most LDCs and inadequate progress in mobilizing and developing their human capacity have adversely affected their development. As many as 42 LDCs were classified in 1994 in the low category of human development, as defined by UNDP. Despite the increasing attention being paid by LDC Governments, population growth rates are still generally higher, on average, than those in other developing countries. In African LDCs, in particular, the rate is accelerating. The Programme of Action adopted by the 1994 International Conference on Population and Development committed the international community to achieving quantitative goals in three mutually supportive areas of critical importance to other population and development objectives: education, reduction of mortality rates in infants, children and mothers, and universal access to family planning and reproductive health services. In the case of LDCs, a critical element in the achievement of these goals is the funding of population policies and programmes, which must be sustained and insulated from short-term budgetary pressures if they are to be effective.

It is important that priority be assigned to greater coverage and improved management for delivery of social services, including primary education and health care, as well as to improving their quality. Domestic resources alone will not be enough to meet the social sector expenditures, particularly in health and education areas. The role of external financing, therefore, continues to be particularly important. Donors will need to provide aid to the social-sector programmes and projects on a longer-term and predictable basis and to provide support for recurrent and local expenditures.

Social issues continue to be high on LDCs' development agenda. The forthcoming World Summit for Social Development and the Fourth World Conference on Women in Development present unique opportunities for the international community to agree on strategies and policies for these issues in favour of LDCs.

External environment and inadequacy of support measures

As the LDCs moved into the 1990s their share in both world exports and imports fell by one half and one third from the already meagre levels of 0.6 per cent and 1.0 per cent, respectively, in 1980. Moreover, the ratio of their exports to GDP fell from over 17 per cent to 14 per cent during the same period. This trend indicates that LDCs as a group have become further marginalized in the world economy in general and in international trade in particular. This intensifying marginalization, to a large extent, can be attributed to their continued reliance on the export of primary commodities. Sluggish external demand for those commodities and their falling world prices have adversely affected the export performance of many LDCs. While nominal dollar prices of many commodities recovered in 1994, there is always the apprehension that market sentiments could be quickly reversed.

Regarding the outcome of the Uruguay Round, a major concern for LDCs is that they will suffer erosion of preferential margins on most of their important exports to major markets, implying a loss of comparative advantage and, consequently, a loss in export market shares and export earnings. In addition, the net food-importing LDCs are likely to face higher food import bills, at least in the short-run, resulting from the agreement on agriculture. Thus, there is a compelling case for external support to mitigate possible adverse consequences on LDCs due to the Uruguay Round agreements, particularly through the provision of additional trade preferences, compensatory financing, ODA and debt relief.

As regards external financing, there has been little progress in the implementation of ODA targets adopted in the Programme of Action. According to preliminary estimates, ODA flows from DAC countries, and multilateral agencies mainly financed by them, to LDCs declined in absolute terms by almost $1.3 billion in 1993. The ODA/GNP ratio for DAC donors as a whole declined to 0.07 per cent in the same year. However, the donors' performance varies widely. Four DAC countries (Denmark, the Netherlands, Norway and Sweden) met the 0.2 per cent target, and two others (France and Portugal) the 0.15 per cent target in 1993.

The overall aid outlook continues to be uncertain. In this situation, LDCs must be given priority attention in aid allocations. Generous replenishment of the soft-term windows of the international financial institutions, as well as of grant-based multilateral programmes, will be of crucial importance. The possibility of tapping new sources of finance, such as special drawing rights (SDR) allocations and IMF gold sales, to help LDCs' development efforts should also be explored. ODA should be linked more closely to LDCs' long-term socio-economic objectives, and further improvements should be made in aid coordination and aid quality to enhance ODA's effectiveness.

Another important element in LDCs' external environment is the issue of debt. The external debt burden remains exceptionally high for most LDCs. At end-1993, their total debt stock stood at $127 billion, an estimated 76 per cent of their combined GDP. For almost half the LDCs, the size of the debt stock equalled or exceeded their respective GDP. The share of multilateral debt in total long-term debt, as well as debt service, has increased considerably in recent years. Effective reduction of other liabilities, such as official bilateral and commercial debt, coupled with increased ODA, will be required to bolster LDCs' capacity to service their growing obligations to the multilateral institutions.

Meeting future challenges

As noted above, the challenges LDCs face in the second half of the 1990s will require a broad range of actions aimed at strengthening national policies and external support measures. LDCs' national policies in the coming years should focus more on the following priority areas:

- Strengthened macroeconomic and sectoral policies, including improvements in designing, sequencing and management of policy reforms, as well as complementary efforts including the mobilization of domestic resources;

- Development of human resources, particularly through greater investment in education, training, health, nutrition and family planning;

- Poverty alleviation and sustainable development;

- Greater emphasis on the productive sectors, in particular agriculture, industry and infrastructure, to improve and diversify their supply capacity;

- Improved trade and investment policies for greater external orientation;

- Governance-related concerns including popular participation, the role of women, increased participation of the private sector and non-governmental organizations; civil service reform to strengthen national administrative and management capacity; and greater emphasis on the rule of law to assist in the avoidance and/or peaceful resolution of potential political and social conflicts.

These tasks are colossal and beyond LDCs' capacity to implement on their own. External cooperation - financial, technical and commercial - will be of critical importance in shaping the future growth and development of LDCs. Recent improvements in the economic performance of the major donor countries should lift the constraint on the provision of ODA. Donor countries are now in a better position to fulfil their commitments to provide substantially increased external financial support to LDCs. In particular:

- Donors should expeditiously fulfil their commitments to provide a significant and substantial increase in the aggregate level of external support to LDCs, keeping in mind the increased needs of these countries, as well as the requirements of the countries included in the list of LDCs following the Paris Conference;

- The quality of assistance needs further improvement; assistance should complement national efforts and be consistent with development priorities of the recipient countries; and adjustment and policy reforms in LDCs should be buttressed by adequate external financial support;

- New initiatives in the context of an international debt strategy should be launched to cancel LDCs' debt and allow them a clean start with regard to their external obligations;

- Priority should be given to operationalizing the Marrakesh Ministerial decisions in favour of LDCs and the net food-importing countries and to setting up "safety net" measures to enable LDCs to tide over possible unfavourable consequence of the Final Act of the Uruguay Round.

It is expected that the analysis and recommendations in this and previous annual Reports will be of value to Governments in conducting the Mid-term Global Review and in deciding on the policies and measures to be taken to ensure the full and effective implementation of the Programme of Action during the second half of the decade.

It is hoped that Governments will spare no efforts at the Mid-term Global Review to provide renewed impetus to the implementation of the Programme of Action and to ensure acceptable standards of living for the deprived millions of people in LDCs as they enter the next millennium.

I. An Assessment of Socio-Economic Developments and Policy Reforms in LDCs in the Early 1990s

A. Introduction

The early years of the 1990s were a period of severe economic and social difficulty for the least developed countries (LDCs). As a consequence, many are entering the second half of the 1990s with economies that are in several important respects in an even weaker state than when the decade began. This chapter reviews the socio-economic developments in LDCs in the early part of the 1990s in the context of achieving the objectives of the Programme of Action for the Least Developed Countries for the 1990s.[1]

Section B provides an account of LDCs' economic performance in 1994 (region-wise) and their short-term prospects in the context of the current world economic setting. Section C examines trends in their economic performance in respect of a range of key economic variables, which include real GDP and GDP per capita growth rates, gross domestic savings (GDS), gross domestic investment (GDI), foreign direct investment (FDI), consumer price inflation, fiscal deficits and overall current account deficits. Section D considers developments with regard to some selected social indicators. Section E evaluates LDCs' experience since the mid-1980s in implementing structural adjustment programmes (SAPs). Section F provides a summary and conclusions.

B. LDCs' economic performance in 1994 and their short-term prospects

The current world economic setting

After four consecutive years of poor performance, the world economy is well on its way to a broad-based recovery in 1994 and 1995 (table 1). The growth of 2.8 per cent forecast for 1995 suggests that world output will return to its trend rate of growth of the past two decades. World output in 1994 is estimated to have expanded by 2.2 per cent compared with 1.4 per cent in 1993, due mostly to robust growth in North America, the strength of the recovery in Western Europe and a return to positive growth rates in a majority of the transition economies of Central Europe. Prominent trends in the developing world in 1994 included an improvement in the performance of the African region, the continuing dynamism of the Asian developing economies and stable growth in Latin America. Following a marked slow-down in world trade

in the early 1990s, it is now expected to expand by over 7 per cent in 1994, one of the highest rates attained in the last two decades.

The rise in output of developed countries was estimated at 1.9 per cent in 1994, slightly more than half a percentage point higher than in 1993. Growth continued in North America with both Canada and the United States experiencing sharp upturns in levels of consumer spending, while Canada's economy also benefited from strong external demand and a rise in commodity prices. The recovery in Western European countries was particularly evident in Germany and France, where growth in consumer spending and the external sector contributed to GDP growth rates of 2.3 and 2.0 per cent, respectively. There are also some signs of recovery in Japan, fuelled by Government investment spending and private consumption, but the overall expansion of the economy remains weak and less robust than was anticipated at this point in the business cycle.

Table 1: Region-wise economic performance of LDCs in 1994 and prospects for 1995

(Percentage change of real output)

Country group	1994[a]	1995[b]
Least developed countries	1.4	2.3
of which:		
LDC Africa	-0.1	0.9
LDC Asia	3.5	4.2
LDC Other[c]	-1.0	4.5
Memo items:		
World	2.2	2.8
Developed market economies	1.9	2.4
Countries in Eastern Europe[d]	-6.4	-1.1
Developing countries	3.7	3.8

Source: UNCTAD secretariat calculations, based on national and international sources.
a   Estimates.
b   Forecast.
c   Pacific island countries and Haiti.
d   Including the former Soviet Union.

Growth in the developing world in 1994 is estimated at 3.7 per cent, slightly higher than the trend rate of growth recorded in the 1980s. In Latin America, the somewhat lower growth in a number of countries, including Brazil, has been offset by improved performance in other countries of the region. Asian developing countries are estimated to have expanded at a similar rate in 1994 as in 1993: growth in this region is supported by the continuing strong export performance in many of these countries. The African region's performance has been favourably affected by the recent positive developments in the primary commodities markets and by the recovery of the demand in European countries.

In contrast to the revival of world economic activity, there was no real improvement in the economic situation of LDCs as a group in 1994. Their growth performance is estimated to be around 1.4 per cent which is lower than the annual average rate for 1990-1993. Although Asian LDCs are estimated to attain GDP growth of 3.5 per cent, real output in African LDCs is estimated to have declined by -0.1 per cent and, as a consequence, real per capita incomes have continued to fall.

Certain external developments during 1994 point to several encouraging signs for a number of LDCs. For instance, higher current prices on world commodity markets helped many countries, especially African LDCs, to recover part of

their past losses. Additional aid and debt relief packages were set up for Franc zone economies to compensate them for the negative effects of the CFA franc devaluation in 1994 (see chapter VI) . These developments notwithstanding, LDCs' export performance continues to be depressed, and recovery in future aid flows to these countries, which dropped in 1993, remains uncertain.

Region-wise economic performance

This subsection provides an overview of LDCs' economic performance in Africa, Asia, the Pacific islands and Haiti during 1994 (table 1).

African LDCs

Economic conditions in African LDCs as a whole, which have been depressed for several years, deteriorated further in 1994 as real GDP is estimated to have declined by 0.1 per cent (compared with an annual average growth rate of 0.6 per cent during 1990-1993). This is due mainly to the impact of civil conflicts and political instability in several African LDCs and the unfavourable weather conditions which adversely affected agricultural production in some of the East African LDCs. Despite this overall bleak picture, economic performance was expected to have improved somewhat during that year in the countries that benefited from the rise

Box 1: World commodity prices

Non-fuel primary commodity prices recovered perceptibly in current terms since the beginning of 1994, but this upswing occurred after they had reached their lowest level, in real terms, in a decade during 1992-1993 (chart 1). Between 1980 and 1993, the commodity price index for developing countries in nominal terms declined by 28 per cent, with intermittent fluctuations, resulting in severe losses in export earnings and declines in government export tax revenues. The deterioration accelerated in recent years as global economic growth slowed forcing increases in commodity supplies to finance imports and service external debt obligations.

The volatility in prices led to policy changes in the early 1990s and discouraged investment decisions of developing countries' producers for using high-yield enhancing inputs. Sharp cut-backs in production capacity (by shifting to other crops) were necessary to counter adverse terms of trade, resulting in the depletion of world stocks of certain commodities. The consequences could be very serious for commodities, such as tree crops or minerals, where there is a long lag between the initiation of new capacity and the flow of new production. In other cases, such as coffee, there was an extended period of low prices since 1987. Then, the 1993 export-retention scheme and two severe frosts in mid-1994, which were followed by a prolonged drought in Brazil (the world's largest coffee producer) during the flowering season, sparked a rapid rise in prices in anticipation of substantial shortages. Even if no further production problems occur, significant production increases are not possible before 1996 and coffee prices are expected to remain high in both 1995 and 1996.

The recent price increase was due not only to a faltering supply *vis-à-vis* a strengthened demand induced by a recovery in the industrialized countries, but also to commodity-hedge funds and other speculative activities that contributed to the acceleration of price increases. After six years of gradual stock liquidation, cocoa prices also rose equally, as the 1993-1994 production estimate was lower than previously anticipated because depressed world prices made production largely unprofitable for many growers. Stocks of various crops, such as copra, cotton, edible oils and rice, are also relatively low compared with current consumption, and their prices have increased. A return to more moderate prices and comfortable stocks may be expected within one or two years. Prices for copra, an important source of income for many Pacific island LDCs, have fallen since 1984 with a huge cumulative decline of 58 per cent. Shortages resulting from natural disasters pushed copra prices upwards as from the third quarter of 1993. Cotton prices, which have been on a declining trend since 1991, fell by an annual average of 9 per cent, and rose in November 1993 because of poor crops caused by unfavourable weather conditions, and disease and insect problems in some major producing countries. With the general improvement in world economic activity and the gradual phasing out of the Multi-Fibre Arrangement (MFA), which will open some markets in industrialized countries, the demand for cotton will be sustained into 1995. Jute, which has been experiencing falling prices and demand since 1986, is now on the verge of making a comeback. In addition to its traditional uses as an environmentally friendly product, it is now being used for new industrial purposes. Higher world demand and tight supply of edible oils has boosted oil prices since the last quarter of 1993, with palm oil outperforming all other oilseeds. Japan's massive rice import requirements in the last quarter of 1993 put an end to the declining trend of rice prices since 1988 (except in 1991). Lower prices are expected with a good harvest, though the gap between high- and low-quality rice remains large. Tea prices seemed to stagnate in 1994, after increasing since 1988, because of sluggish world import demand, particularly from Middle Eastern countries and the former Soviet Union. In 1995, the demand for beverage crops, apart from tea, is likely to exceed supply.

After two years of decline in mineral prices (excluding crude petroleum) during 1992 and 1993, at an annual average 6 per cent, prices recovered as from March 1994 due to a rising world-wide demand for metals (particularly in the automobile and construction sectors), falling stocks, declining exports from certain countries because of production difficulties, and speculative purchasing of financial funds. The increases were particularly high for aluminium, copper and nickel. In the case of copper, the upward movement of prices had already started in December 1993. Besides industrial purchases, it was reported that a huge influx of capital helped to prop up prices to an artificially high level. Though there are many uncertainties surrounding the short-term outlook of copper prices, it is likely that prices will remain firm in 1995 due to growing world demand and expanded production flows which will take time to reach the market.

It is perhaps too early to say how long the recent improvements in non-fuel commodity prices will hold. As chart 1 shows, while the prices in current terms indicated significant volatility, the real prices suffered a clear downward trend. Available forecasts of the major commodities of interest to LDCs indicate that prices in real terms will either stabilize or decline somewhat in the medium term.[1] As a result, the pressure on external earnings of LDCs will most likely persist.

---

[1]   See, for example, The World Bank, *Global Economic Prospects and the Developing Countries* (Washington, D.C., The World Bank, 1994).

in world market prices for non-fuel primary commodities (box 1) and in some LDCs of the Franc zone following the devaluation of the CFA franc in January 1994 (on the impact of the CFA franc's devaluation, see chapter VI). Sufficient data are not yet available to accurately assess performance in each of the 32 African LDCs in 1994, but it is possible to discern some of the broad trends that emerged during 1994

and to make a preliminary assessment of their likely impact.

The rise in world market prices of primary commodities, and in particular tropical beverages, will provide some breathing space for many African LDCs to recover past losses. The nominal price of coffee doubled during 1994, while the average price of cotton was approximately 25 per cent higher than in the previous

**Chart 1: Primary commodity prices for developing countries
(excluding crude petroleum)[a], 1980-1994**

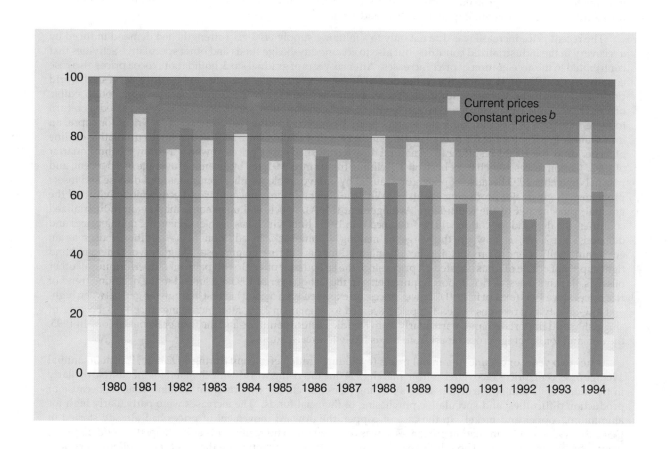

Source: UNCTAD secretariat calculations, based on United Nations, *Monthly Bulletin of Statistics*.

a   In current and constant 1980 dollars. Index numbers, 1980=100.

b   Deflated by unit value index of manufactured goods exported by developed market-economy countries.

year (table 2). Several LDCs are major coffee exporters, including Burundi, Ethiopia, Madagascar, Rwanda, Uganda and the United Republic of Tanzania. Cotton is a major export of Benin and Togo and of many of the Sahelian LDCs, including Burkina Faso, Chad, Mali and Sudan. The price of copper, a major export of Zaire and Zambia, rose by around one fifth in 1994 and the prices of other commodities of interest to African LDCs, such as cocoa and tea, also exhibited some buoyancy during the year.

The most immediate impact of the commodity price rises was an increase in foreign currency earnings for most of the major exporters noted above and therefore an improvement in their trade and balance-of-payment positions. Commodity price recoveries in sub-Saharan Africa (SSA) and elsewhere in the developing world are almost always temporary phenomena. Since past trends in commodity prices have been punctuated by recoveries and slumps, the latest price increases should not detract the

Table 2: World commodity prices, 1980-1994

A. By commodity group
(Percentage change)

Commodity group	1980-1990 (Annual average)	1991	1992	1993	1994ᵃ
All primary commodities	-1.9	-12.7	-1.4	-8.8	11.3
Food	-1.1	-3.4	2.4	-5.7	9.8
Agricultural non-food	0.0	-7.0	-2.2	-7.7	14.3
Minerals (excluding crude petroleum)	-0.1	2.0	-5.9	-5.3	12.2
Fuels	-2.7	-18.6	-3.5	-10.9	-4.1
Primary commodities (excluding crude petroleum)	-0.6	-4.3	-1.1	-5.6	13.2
Unit value index of manufactured goods exported by developed market-economy countries	3.1	-0.7	3.0	-2.2	-0.7

B. Commodities of export interest to LDCs
(Index numbers, 1980=100)

Commodity	1985	1991	1992	1993	1994ᵃ
Coffee	81	42	33	38	86
Copper	64	107	104	87	103
Copra	85	64	84	66	85
Cotton	75	88	68	65	81
Fish	77	122	125	118	130
Jute	140	95	80	74	85
Tea	112	128	150	200	203
Tobacco	129	131	132	128	119

Source: UNCTAD secretariat calculations, based on United Nations Monthly Bulletin of Statistics.
a   Estimates.

international community from providing the necessary external financial support and debt relief.

The most important sector of the economy in most African LDCs is rain-fed agriculture. Weather conditions have a crucial impact on the performance of this sector, and by implication, on the overall economy. Unfavourable weather conditions in East Africa reduced the output of food and export crops in several LDCs, including Sudan and the United Republic of Tanzania. Food production in Ethiopia was badly affected and resulted in serious shortages of food and the threat of famine. Drought also afflicted agriculture in parts of Mozambique and Zambia.

A number of African LDCs that have attained positive per capita GDP growth rates over the last few years (including, *inter alia*, Benin, Botswana, Cape Verde, Equatorial Guinea, Uganda and the United Republic of Tanzania) should have sustained this trend during 1994, particularly in view of the improved commodity prices. But for almost one quarter of African LDCs beset with political instability and armed conflicts, output growth rates are likely to have been negligible or negative. For many of these countries, effective Government has virtually ceased to exist, the modern sectors of the economy have collapsed and, in order to survive, large sections of the population have been forced to rely on emergency food provisions from NGOs and international donors. Despite emergency relief efforts, severe food shortages threatened the lives of vast numbers of people displaced by the conflicts in several LDCs in the region.

Besides the widely publicized human tragedy in Rwanda, the destructive effects of civil war have been most acute in Liberia, Somalia and Sudan, where conflicts have been ongoing for a number of years. The adverse effects of these conflicts have spread into neighbouring countries by large flows of refugees crossing international borders. At a less devastating level, civil strife and political instability have also threatened Burundi, Sierra Leone and Zaire. Efforts to revive the Togolese economy have also been affected by political uncertainty.

Fortunately, it appears that the long-running civil war in Mozambique finally ended with the successful completion of democratic elections in November 1994. The war left a legacy of refugees, destroyed infrastructure, social breakdown and a large stock of external debt. The Government is facing an immense task of rebuilding the economy and will require substantial support from the international community.

Asian LDCs

While there are variations in the economic performance of Asian LDCs, their overall performance has been significantly better in recent years, as compared with that of the African LDCs. During the 1990-1993 period, they were able to attain an annual average growth rate of 3.9 per cent. However, in 1994, their output growth was estimated to have slowed to 3.5 per cent, mainly due to increased instability in countries such as Afghanistan and Yemen. Some countries succeeded in raising growth rates or maintaining them at 5 per cent and more. This improvement reflects, in part, their relative success in implementing various development policies. A number of LDCs in the region have pursued a variety of structural and market-oriented policy reforms, of which fiscal measures have been a major component. Some made notable strides in attaining the main objectives of fiscal reforms, by a combination of expanding tax bases and lowering tax rates, and controlling the growth of current expenditures. In a number of countries, commercial banks have cut their lending rates and thus facilitated access to loans, while Governments have relaxed foreign-exchange regulations for external borrowing and permitted some firms to hold foreign accounts. The general trend of policy changes has been in the direction of reducing protectionism, increasing public-sector productivity, fostering private-sector development and revitalizing investment.

In some countries, policies and measures, such as reduction of tariffs on imports, greater incentives for exports, and depreciation of the national currency, have led to a shift in the product composition of exports towards more manufactured goods, though primary commodities continue to remain the principal exports of most Asian LDCs.

Though savings and investment rates have risen somewhat in recent years due in part to the declining trend of inflation, enhancing the level of investment, both foreign and domestic, remains a major concern of policy makers. Many Asian LDCs have taken a variety of measures, including the provision of tax incentives, to encourage foreign investments in order to expand the productive base, particularly in the export-oriented sectors. Moreover, the proximity of Asian LDCs to some of the most dynamic economies of the world is proving to be helpful. The newly industrializing Asian countries, such as the Republic of Korea, which previously enjoyed a comparative advantage in labour-intensive manufacturing, are relocating their industries to some of these LDCs. Bangladesh, Cambodia, the Lao People's Democratic Republic, Myanmar and Nepal have attracted the attention of investors from neighbouring countries.

Real per capita income contracted by an annual average of 2.6 per cent in Afghanistan during the 1980s, and, since January 1994, the situation has continued to worsen, with renewed and widespread fighting. In Bangladesh, the GDP was estimated to have grown by 4.8 per cent in 1994, compared with 4.5 per cent the previous year and an annual average of 4.2 per cent during the 1985-1990 period. While performance of the agricultural sector during 1994 was moderate, industrial output (which rose annually on average by over 8 per cent in recent years) continued to expand. Exports of ready-made garments have grown at a rapid pace since 1989 and accounted for over 57 per cent of total exports, which reached $2.5 billion in 1994. By the end of 1994, foreign reserves represented more than nine months of imports. In Nepal, the economy rebounded sharply in 1994, attaining a GDP growth of 7.7 per cent, after two years of slow growth caused by bad weather. Significant progress has been made in several areas, such as expanding exports, privatizing public enterprises, containing the fiscal deficit, controlling the inflation rate and expanding foreign reserves. Bhutan managed to grow on average by over 7 per cent in 1985-1990 and continued to maintain, on average, a 4 per cent annual increase in GDP up to 1994. Exports, in particular agro-industrial exports, have also increased in recent years. For the Maldives, GDP growth averaged 6.5 per cent in 1994 and 1993, compared with 7.0 per cent in 1992 and 1991.

Cambodia achieved an estimated growth rate of 4.5 per cent in 1994, despite renewed insurgency in the northern part of the country and the unfavourable weather conditions that caused a shortfall in rice production. Efforts are being made to tighten fiscal and monetary restraints. The Lao People's Democratic Republic attained an estimated output growth at around 7 per cent in 1994. The opening of the Mekong bridge in April 1994, linking the Lao People's Democratic Republic with Thailand, offered another boost to trade and investment, tourism expansion and economic cooperation with neighbouring countries. Increased industrial development contributed to rising exports, particularly garments and assembled motorcycles. In Myanmar, rapid rates of GDP growth were achieved in both 1992 and 1993, of 11.3 per cent and 6.0 per cent, respectively. Output growth resumed in most sectors, but was particularly strong in the

agricultural and construction sectors. Exports continued to expand, due mainly to enhanced border trade with neighbouring countries.

Yemen faced several adverse developments during the early 1990s, including the destruction caused by floods in 1992 and 1993 and the after-effects of the gulf war, the costs associated with the 1990 unification between North and South and the civil war in May 1994. Inflation, which was already running at over 100 per cent in 1994, continued to rise. The unemployment situation, which was aggravated by the return of expatriates after the 1991 gulf crisis, continued to worsen.

Pacific island LDCs and Haiti

LDCs in the Pacific display a number of similar characteristics. Small in size and population, the remote and scattered island economies are susceptible to climatic conditions and changes. Frequent cyclones disrupt the economic gains, cause serious damage to agriculture and entail high infrastructural rehabilitation costs. Manufacturing is generally limited and is restricted to the processing of agricultural products. With the exception of the Solomon Islands, exports are confined to a narrow range of primary commodities. Export earnings, with their associated impact on GDP growth, are heavily dependent on the world prices of these commodities.

Invisible earnings are important sources of external receipt items in all Pacific LDCs. While the countries of the region are giving renewed emphasis to the development of fishing, tourism has become a major foreign-exchange earner in recent years and provides many direct or indirect employment opportunities in several countries, such as Samoa and Vanuatu. In an effort to boost tourism revenues, Pacific nations joined forces recently to reorganize the island airlines and launch the "Visit South Pacific Year 1995" in many North American and European cities. Governments are funding road construction and actively promoting private-sector investment through tax incentives for hotel and resort developments. Latest available figures for tourist arrivals in the region show an increase of 25 per cent between 1987 and 1992. Revenues from offshore financial centres of Samoa and Vanuatu also contribute to economic growth. Measures are being taken to promote economic development through greater participation of the private sector with more incentives for businesses and foreign investors.

In 1994, the economy of Kiribati grew by an estimated 2.8 per cent, almost the same as on average in the preceding three years. The expansion of tuna fishing was achieved through joint ventures which facilitated the acquisition of technical and capital requirements. Economic activity in Samoa recovered partially during 1993 and 1994, after three consecutive years of devastating cyclones, and was estimated to have grown, respectively, by 3.5 and 3.0 per cent. The Solomon Islands recorded GDP growth rate of only 3.5 per cent in 1994 (as compared with an annual average growth rate of 5.7 per cent during 1990-1993), due partly to measures adopted for restructuring the economy.

In Tuvalu, economic growth slowed from 7.9 per cent in 1990-1993 to 3 per cent in 1994, reflecting not only a lower rate of expansion of the fishing sector, but also a curtailment of public expenditures to improve the budget situation. After two years of virtually no growth in Vanuatu because of severe cyclone damage, the economy picked up slowly with an estimated 2 per cent growth in 1994. Expansion has been retarded by the time-lag in the recovery of the main export product (copra), the cessation of round-log exports and ongoing political uncertainty.

Real per capita income in Haiti, which fell in the 1980s by a cumulative 25 per cent, declined further in 1992 and 1993 in consequence of the international economic embargoes imposed since 1991. The reinstatement of the first democratically elected president in September 1994 has helped to establish political stability, but the implementation of economic reforms and revival of growth pose major challenges for the future.

Short-term economic prospects

It appears that the sluggish growth that characterized the economic performance of African LDCs as a whole for most of the 1990s (the growth rate is estimated to have been negative in 1994) may give way to positive growth in 1995. However, its magnitude is likely to be very low - less than 1 per cent - and that too is based on the assumptions that weather conditions in most of the countries will remain favourable, that there will be no further deterioration in internal political conditions, and that peace will return in some key countries of the region. Consequently, a three-fold increase in growth than is presently forecast will be required to retain merely the current per capita income level, let alone to restore living standards to the level of the early 1980s.

The overall forecast, however, masks the fact that there are substantial differences in the growth prospects of individual countries. For example, prospects for Uganda's economy are looking increasingly brighter as they are for some African LDCs that are experiencing political stability. The higher international coffee prices, which are forecast to continue for at least two more years, will permit improvements in export receipts and a small current account surplus. A short-term forecast for Zambia suggests improved performance, both because of improvements in the mining sector and a return to agricultural output to normal levels. The rise of copper prices is likely to influence positively the trade balance with a small decline in current account deficit. Short-term prospects are also reasonably good for some of the Franc zone countries, particularly Burkina Faso, Niger and Togo. Further improvement of economic performance is expected in Madagascar, where tourism and industry are forecast to recover substantially, and also in Guinea, with its continuing strong activity in the mineral sector.

In Sudan, the economic performance is forecast to improve in consequence of better prospects for the cotton exports in 1995. However, the cost of civil strife and the absence of significant supplies of development assistance will affect the difficult economic situation and influence the pace of recovery. In the absence of progress towards resolving political conflicts, the economic conditions are forecast to continue to deteriorate in Liberia, Rwanda, Sierra Leone, Somalia and Zaire.

Assuming that normal weather conditions prevail in 1995, GDP growth of Asian LDCs should improve to 4.2 per cent, as against the estimated level of 3.5 per cent in 1994, though prospects will certainly vary between countries. Major Asian LDCs have, in the last few years, undertaken wide-ranging reform programmes with significant success in maintaining macroeconomic stability, which have led to the dismantling of many restrictive policies. The improvement in the policy environment is expected to have an impact on growth, savings and investment and trade in the short to medium term. The improved performance of these LDCs should generally be sustained in 1995.

The overall GDP growth of Bangladesh is likely to be over 5 per cent in 1995. An early agreement among political parties on modalities of future national elections may give further impetus to industrial output growth by boosting domestic and foreign investments. Ongoing efforts, such as further streamlining of bureaucratic procedures, combined with improved efficiency in the public sector, should help to establish a more timely implementation of the

Annual Development Programme and contribute to absorbing a larger amount of pledged aid. Short-term prospects in Nepal are mixed. While the encouraging results obtained in stabilizing the economy will probably help to contribute to an expansion of GDP, the recent decline in carpet exports to certain European countries may affect these prospects. In Bhutan, despite financial constraints hindering the implementation of development programmes, prospects for GDP growth in the short term remain good. The Maldives is expected to achieve a GDP growth rate of more than 7 per cent due to the envisaged increase in tourists.

While the Government of Cambodia is pursuing reforms, including strengthening the legal framework to improve the business climate, continued efforts are necessary to restore social and political stability. Only durable peace and security will attract a greater inflow of long-term commitments from foreign investors and an expansion of tourism. Industrial growth in the Lao People's Democratic Republic should be sustained in 1995, reflecting a strengthened domestic demand and heavy public investment in the expansion of hydroelectricity capacity generation and in infrastructure. In Myanmar, efforts to address persistent economic problems have started to show some results. The manufacturing sector, which is relatively small, may receive a boost in output from the increased capacity generation of the hydroelectricity power station, which was completed in December 1994, while exports should benefit from the recent agreements, including those for trade and transportation facilities, signed with neighbouring countries. Large reserves of off-shore natural gas discovered in the Gulf of Martaban have raised hopes for future gas exports.

However, as mentioned earlier, to the extent that the envisaged recovery of LDCs is influenced by the rise in commodity prices, which is almost always a temporary phenomena, it could prove to be difficult to sustain.

C. Trends in economic performance, 1990-1993

Output growth trends[2]

The economic performance of LDCs, measured in terms of growth of real output, deteriorated during 1990-1993. In contrast to the objective of the Programme of Action of achieving an acceleration of GDP growth rates, average real GDP growth decelerated significantly from the growth rates recorded during the 1980s. As a consequence of the fall in real growth rates, per capita output levels declined on average in LDCs; the rate of population growth exceeded that of output by a cumulative total of almost 5 per cent over this period. LDCs' poor performance contrasted with a marked improvement in economic growth rates among developing countries as a whole.

The real GDP growth rate of the 46 LDCs[3] for which data are available was 1.6 per cent per annum during 1990-1993, as compared with an annual average growth rate of 2.2 per cent during the 1980s (table 3). This is indicative of continued decline in output per capita since the 1980s leading to adverse consequences for living standards.

There was a marked regional difference in the growth rates recorded by LDCs, with countries in the Asian region attaining faster growth than those in the African region, although the slow-down in growth rates in relation to the 1980s was common to both regions (table 3). The nine Asian LDCs achieved an annual average real GDP growth rate of 3.9 per cent during 1990-1993, while the economies of the 32 African LDCs grew at an annual average rate of only 0.6 per cent. The real GDP of the four Pacific island economies, for which data are available, declined by an annual average rate of 1.4 per cent. Whereas the Asian LDCs attained an average per capita output gain of 1.4 per cent per annum in the 1990s, the African LDCs suffered a 2.3 per cent per annum fall. GDP per capita also declined in the Pacific island economies by 3.4 per cent per annum.

The growth performance of individual LDCs varied widely (table 4). Several countries, including Bangladesh, Botswana, Cambodia, Equatorial Guinea, the Lao People's Democratic Republic, the Maldives, Mozambique, Myanmar, Sao Tome and Principe, the Solomon Islands and Sudan, achieved per capita growth rates of 2 per cent per annum or more (which, if sustained, would almost double real income levels in two decades). Cambodia, Equatorial

Table 3: Real GDP and real GDP per capita growth rates,
1980-1990, 1990-1993
(Percentage growth per annum)

	1980-1990	1990-1993
LDCs:[a]		
real GDP	2.2	1.6
population	2.5	2.8
real GDP per capita	-0.3	-1.2
Regional breakdown:		
African LDCs:		
real GDP	1.9	0.6
real GDP per capita	-1.0	-2.3
Asian LDCs:		
real GDP	3.1	3.9
real GDP per capita	1.2	1.4
Pacific islands' LDCs and Haiti:		
real GDP	0.4	-1.4
real GDP per capita	-1.5	-3.4
Memo items:		
Developing countries:		
real GDP	2.7	5.0
real GDP per capita	0.3	3.0
of which:		
sub-Saharan Africa - real GDP	2.0	0.6
Asia - real GDP	6.8	7.5

Source: UNCTAD secretariat calculations, based on IMF, *World Economic Outlook,* May 1994; The World Bank, *World Tables, 1994;* IMF, *International Financial Statistics Yearbook, 1994;* the Asian Development Bank; and other international and national sources.

a   Data for 44 countries only (excluding Cambodia, Tuvalu and Yemen for which data are unavailable).

Guinea, the Maldives, Mozambique, Sao Tome and Principe and Tuvalu were able to attain per capita growth in excess of 4 per cent per annum during this period. In contrast, substantial falls in per capita GDP, amounting to more than 2 per cent per annum, were recorded in Afghanistan, the Central African Republic, the Comoros, Ethiopia, Haiti, Madagascar, Malawi, Niger, Rwanda, Samoa, Sierra Leone, Somalia, Togo, Yemen, Zaire and Zambia. Some countries that experienced a sharp contraction of their economies were afflicted with destructive civil conflicts.

Although there were several exceptions, the countries that recorded the highest growth rates among all LDCs during the 1980s continued to achieve positive per capita increases during the 1990s, while most LDCs that experienced a significant contraction of real per capita GDP in the 1980s had further falls in the 1990s. In reviewing their progress in the 1980s, the 1991 LDC Report classified LDCs according to their growth rates during the decade. Of the 11 LDCs in the high-growth rate group (defined as those countries that achieved an expansion of one third in real GDP and at least 10 per cent in GDP per capita over the course of the decade), seven LDCs continued to record positive per capita growth, although only the Lao People's Democratic Republic achieved an acceleration of growth. The economies of four members of this group (Burkina Faso, Burundi, Chad and Yemen) deteriorated to such an extent that they had falls in per capita output. The performance of Botswana, which is in the group of LDCs with higher growth rates, is particularly remarkable, in view of which the General Assembly in 1994 decided to graduate the country from the LDCs. Thus, Botswana was the first country ever to so graduate (box 2).

Table 4: Growth rates of real GDP, real GDP per capita and of populations in LDCs
(Percentages)

	Real GDP		Real GDP per capita		Population	
	1980-1990	*1990-1993*	*1980-1990*	*1990-1993*	*1980-1990*	*1990-1993*
Afghanistan	-1.9	-4.0[a]	-0.9	-8.2[a]	-1.0	5.6
Bangladesh	4.3	4.0	2.2	1.8	2.0	2.1
Benin	2.6	4.1	-0.3	0.9	3.0	3.2
Bhutan	7.6	3.0[b]	5.2	1.7[b]	2.3	1.1
Botswana	10.3	4.6	6.6	1.4	3.5	3.2
Burkina Faso	3.9	2.2	1.3	-0.6	2.6	2.8
Burundi	4.4	2.3	1.4	-0.8	2.9	3.1
Cambodia	..	6.3	..	3.1	3.3	3.1
Cape Verde	5.9	3.3	4.2	0.5	1.7	2.8
Central African Republic	1.7	-2.1	-0.6	-4.6	2.4	2.5
Chad	6.3	1.2	4.1	-1.4	2.2	2.7
Comoros	2.7	1.6	-0.8	-2.1	3.5	3.8
Djibouti	-0.4	1.6[a]	-6.4	-1.6[a]	6.4	2.5
Equatorial Guinea	1.9	7.2	-3.0	4.6	5.1	2.5
Ethiopia	1.8	-1.1	-0.8	-4.0	2.7	3.0
Gambia	3.4	2.6	-0.3	-1.4	3.7	4.1
Guinea	-1.2	3.4	-3.7	0.3	2.6	3.1
Guinea-Bissau	3.9	2.8	2.0	0.7	1.9	2.2
Haiti	-0.6	-4.0[b]	-2.5	-5.9[b]	1.9	2.0
Kiribati	0.7	2.0[b]	-1.4	-0.5[b]	2.1	2.5
Lao People's Democratic Republic	4.5	5.8	1.6	2.6	2.8	3.1
Lesotho	4.3	3.6	1.3	0.8	3.0	2.7
Liberia	-0.8[c]	..	-3.9[c]	..	3.2	3.4
Madagascar	1.1	-1.1	-2.2	-4.2	3.3	3.3
Malawi	2.8	1.1	-1.5	-2.8	4.3	3.9
Maldives	11.8	6.7	8.5	2.8	3.0	3.7
Mali	3.0	2.9	0.0	-0.3	3.0	3.2
Mauritania	1.7	3.1	-0.9	0.5	2.6	2.6
Mozambique	-0.2	6.6	-1.7	4.4	1.5	2.1
Myanmar	0.6	5.7	-1.5	3.4	2.1	2.2
Nepal	5.0	3.1	2.3	0.4	2.6	2.6
Niger	-1.1	-1.5	-4.3	-4.8	3.3	3.4
Rwanda	1.7	1.3	-1.3	-1.3	3.1	2.6
Samoa	1.0	-1.8[b]	0.8	-2.7[b]	0.2	1.0
Sao Tome and Principe	-0.4	19.3	-2.7	16.7	2.4	2.2
Sierra Leone	0.9	-0.8	-1.2	-3.2	2.1	2.4
Solomon Islands	6.6	5.7[b]	3.0	2.1[b]	3.5	3.4
Somalia	2.0	..	-0.6	..	2.6	1.0
Sudan	0.6	5.8[b]	-2.1	3.0[b]	2.8	2.7
Togo	1.8	-8.0	-1.2	-10.8	3.0	3.2
Tuvalu	..	9.5	..	7.9	1.2	1.5
Uganda	5.4	4.2	2.1	0.6	3.2	3.6
United Republic of Tanzania	2.9	3.9[b]	-0.3	0.8[b]	3.3	3.1
Vanuatu	3.1	1.5[b]	0.6	-1.1[b]	2.5	2.6
Yemen	..	-3.9[a]	..	-8.4[a]	3.2	5.3
Zaire	1.7	-8.9[b]	-1.5	-11.8[b]	3.3	3.3
Zambia	0.9	0.7	-2.6	-2.3	3.6	3.1
All LDCs	2.2	1.6	-0.3	-1.2	2.5	2.8

Source: UNCTAD secretariat calculations, based on data from the United Nations Statistical Office, The World Bank, the Asian Development Bank and other international and national sources.

a 1990-1991.   *b* 1990-1992.   *c* 1980-1989.

Box 2. Botswana: The first country to graduate from the LDC group - lessons for other LDCs

Botswana is the first country to graduate from the LDC group. This event is an eloquent testimony to the validity of the declaration of the international community at the Second United Nations Conference on the Least Developed Countries in 1990 that the socio-economic decline in LDCs is indeed reversible. Botswana was among the original 25 LDCs when the list of LDCs was first drawn up in 1971. At the time of its independence in 1966, it was one of the poorest countries in the world. Most of the country is arid or semi-arid and about two thirds of the land area is covered by the Kalahari desert. Until the early 1970s, livestock was its principal resource. Its small and largely uneducated population, land-locked position and distance from major international markets seemed to hold little hope for economic growth and development. The discovery of extensive mineral reserves soon after its independence and their subsequent exploitation have rapidly and profoundly transformed Botswana's economy. Substantial resources have been generated through exports of diamonds and copper/nickel (as well as beef). The country is currently the world's second largest producer of diamonds. It has grown to be one of the most prosperous economies in Africa - its national income in per capita terms second only to the richest oil-producing countries on the continent. In recent years, Botswana has consistently run surpluses on both the balance of payments and the Government budget, has accumulated substantial foreign exchange reserves and has had no external debt problems.

Botswana has also made substantial progress in the realm of social development, e.g. through expanded provision of health facilities and improved access to education. Of the total population, 86 per cent are within 15 kilometres of a health facility (78 per cent are within 8 kilometres); life expectancy and the infant mortality rate have much improved; enrolment of children of the relevant age group in basic education averages 83 per cent, and adult literacy is estimated at 74 per cent. The Government has also developed and demonstrated a good response capacity to the vulnerable population in times of disaster or suffering, as has been evidenced during the recurrent droughts.

Following these considerable achievements, and pursuant to a request from the Second United Nations Conference on the Least Developed Countries, the Committee for Development Planning reviewed the list of LDCs in 1991 and revised its criteria for identifying LDCs, retaining per capita GDP as a measure of relative levels of poverty as well as two composite indices, one for human resource development and another for economic diversification. On the basis of its review and the adoption of this new set of criteria, the Committee recommended Botswana's graduation from the list of LDCs. Subsequently, in 1991, the General Assembly decided to graduate Botswana following a transition period of three years, which was completed in December 1994.

What lessons can other LDCs learn from Botswana's accomplishments and development experience? Essentially, this may be the importance of careful economic management and of political and economic stability. Undoubtedly, Botswana has benefited enormously from the mineral wealth developed since independence. But its achievements in terms of economic growth and overall development are not simply a matter of good fortune. Botswana's good management of its resources is equally important. Much of the mineral revenue accruing to the Government has been well invested in social and economic infrastructure. Commitment to prudent economic planning and decision-making, and effective public management, has helped to shape its development. For instance, when the economy was affected by depressed mineral markets in the early 1980s and the budget and balance-of-payment positions turned to deficit, the Government reacted quickly by adopting and implementing a package of austerity and adjustment measures of its own. The country's strong democratic traditions, which are reflected in national goal-setting and the development planning process, should also be underlined. Since independence, the country has followed a multiparty system based on the rule of law and observance of the principle of separation of powers, coupled with traditional popular participation in discussions and decision-making, also at the local and village level.

But Botswana's development would have been impossible without foreign aid and investment. The basic infrastructure that made growth possible was paid for almost entirely by such external support in the period after independence; an important proportion of the development budget has continued to be dependent on aid; the debt service ratio has not reached critical levels because the Government has been able to obtain loans on concessional terms; and technical assistance is still vital because of the continuing shortages of skilled labour.

Thus, the key ingredients in Botswana's progress have been sound economic policies and management and the availability of substantial resources, including external support, over an extended time-span. However, its experience also shows that growing out of poverty is not an easy process; the country has not, as yet, been able to solve all its development problems. Outside the mining sector still lies an essentially rural economy, relatively poor, dependent on cattle and vulnerable to drought and environmental degradation. Rapid population growth is also straining resources. The relatively small domestic market, commodity-dependence of exports and consequent external vulnerability and the lack of skilled manpower still constrain economic development and will have to be overcome. Botswana's graduation comes at a time when the country is also facing new challenges and must prepare itself for significantly lower growth and seek new development options. The current National Development Plan, covering the years 1991-1997, is seen as a transition period during which a foundation should be laid that will help Botswana move from the exceptionally rapid expansion, which characterized its recent past, to a period of more moderate and sustainable growth, based on the diversification of its economic activities and the promotion of its private sector.

At the opposite end of the growth range during the 1980s were the 13 LDCs classified as having experienced severe decline, defined as a fall of 10 per cent or more in per capita GDP over the course of the decade. During 1990-1993, only four of these countries (Equatorial Guinea, Guinea, Mozambique and Sudan) were able to reverse the decline in per capita output and thus achieve positive per capita growth rates, while several countries, including Afghanistan, Haiti, Rwanda, Sierra Leone and Togo experienced an increase in the rate of decline of per capita output.

Between the categories of high growth and severe decline were 17 LDCs classified in either the medium growth or stagnation category in the 1991 LDC Report on the basis of their growth performance during the 1980s. Only five of these LDCs (Bangladesh, Lesotho, Myanmar, Uganda and the United Republic of Tanzania) were able to achieve marked improvements in growth rates (defined as an improvement of 1 percentage point or more) during 1990-1993, while the Central African Republic, Ethiopia, Mali, Samoa and Somalia experienced substantial deteriorations in growth performance.

Growth of exports

Export volume

The strength of the export sector in LDCs is crucial to the overall performance of their economies. Export earnings are a major contribution to foreign exchange earnings, to domestic incomes and demand, to savings and, in most LDCs, to Government revenues. The growth of export earnings for most LDCs, was weak during the 1980s because of the combination of slow rates of expansion of production and the decline of nominal export prices (valued in US dollars). The need to expand export earnings prompted many LDCs to implement policy reforms during the 1980s, such as devaluation and trade liberalization designed to improve incentives for export production.

For LDCs as a group, the growth of export during 1990-1993 was merely 0.2 per cent as compared with an average of 0.8 per cent during the 1980s and over 10 per cent during the 1970s. Moreover, the growth rate of purchasing power of exports declined consistently during the early 1990s, from 3.2 per cent in 1990-1991 to -1.5 per cent in 1992-1993. Overall, the share of LDCs in world exports in the early 1990s declined to 0.3 per cent, which is half of what it was a decade ago. Their poor export performance and their continued marginalization in world

trade reflected, *inter alia*, the fact that policy reforms in many LDCs have not succeeded in augmenting the supply of tradeable goods.

Export diversification

The diversification of export earnings by LDCs away from the excessive concentration on primary commodities was emphasized by the Programme of Action as one of the most important objectives for the 1990s. UNCTAD has prepared trade statistics that provide some indication of the degree of export concentration, in 1980 and 1991, in a sample of countries that includes 31 LDCs. These statistics include the number of products exported by each country at the three-digit Standard International Trade Classification (SITC) level and an index of export concentration.[4] The data suggest that LDCs as a group failed to diversify their exports between 1980 and 1991. Only 13 LDCs were able to increase the number of products they exported, while in 16 LDCs the number of exported products fell (there was no change in 2 LDCs). Furthermore, the index of concentration was higher in 1991 than in 1980 in 17 LDCs (i.e. their export earnings became more concentrated in a small number of products) and lower in 13 LDCs.

Most LDCs have made little progress in establishing viable non-traditional export industries. Notable exceptions include the garment and textile industries in Bangladesh and Nepal and tourism in the Gambia. Lesotho and Haiti have also established light manufacturing bases although progress in Haiti has been retarded by the political instability afflicting the country.[5] In general, however, manufacturing exports account for a very low proportion of exports. The import-substituting industries established during the 1960s and 1970s to serve domestic consumer markets have not been able to penetrate export markets successfully and there are few examples, outside the mineral sectors, of the successful processing of primary commodities for export. Many African LDCs export cotton but none has made the transition to the export of cotton textiles.[6]

The very limited extent of export diversification to date may reflect weaknesses in trade policy. Until the 1980s, many LDCs operated macroeconomic and trade-policy regimes that often discouraged exports in general (both primary and non-traditional products). With the adoption of policy-reform programmes, which included exchange-rate devaluation and trade liberalization, the domestic structure of relative prices has become more favourable to exporters in most LDCs, but the benefits so far have been confined mainly to the production of traditional primary commodities. While exchange-rate adjustments and the reduction of excessive levels of trade protection may have been necessary in these countries, these measures paid insufficient attention to export diversification. Policy measures to address critical supply-side constraints to the growth of non-traditional exports (which include weak technological capacities, deficiencies in the infrastructure and in the supply of appropriate forms of finance, and lack of marketing expertise) have not been given adequate attention in the formulation of policy-reform programmes.[7] Moreover, the success of LDCs' diversification efforts will also depend on international support measures in such areas as transfer of technology, improved market access, FDI and technical assistance.

Selected macroeconomic indicators

Savings and investment

Gross domestic savings (GDS) remained at very low levels in LDCs, averaging less than 1 per cent of GDP (table 5). This represents a marginal decline from the savings rates recorded in the previous decade and implies that LDCs relied almost entirely on resources generated abroad (foreign aid, remittances and capital inflows) to finance investment levels. Only Bhutan, Guinea, the Maldives, Myanmar, Nepal, Sierra Leone, the United Republic of Tanzania and Zambia were able to mobilize domestic savings in excess of 10 per cent of GDP. Several LDCs, including Chad, Guinea-Bissau, Lesotho, Mozambique, Sao Tome and

Principe and Somalia recorded substantial negative savings rates, probably reflecting the fact that either much of their national income was generated by migrant workers or that foreign aid was used to finance recurrent Government budgets.

During 1990-1992, LDCs attained a small rise in investment levels; the unweighted average amounted to 22.7 per cent of GDP, an increase of just over 1 percentage point. The increase in average investment levels was, however, mainly attributable to an expansion of investment in a handful of small countries with very high investment/GDP ratios. Investment as a percentage of GDP was generally higher in the countries with small populations than in those with larger populations: of the nine LDCs in which gross domestic investment (GDI) exceeded 30 per cent of GDP, seven have populations of less than two million, while investment in most of the larger LDCs with populations exceeding 25 million was less than 15 per cent of GDP.[8] When the investment levels of LDCs are weighted according to population size, the averages during both the 1980s and early 1990s are substantially lower than the unweighted figures indicate. Population-weighted average GDI amounted to 15.5 per cent of GDP during the 1980s and rose only slightly to 15.9 per cent of GDP in 1990-1992.

Investment levels varied considerably between individual LDCs during the 1990s as they had in the previous decade. Twelve countries - Lesotho, Maldives, Mozambique, Sao Tome and

Table 5: GDS, GDI and FDI in LDCs, 1980-1989, 1990-1992

	1980-1989	*1990-1992*
GDS % of GDP, unweighted average	1.0	0.6
GDI % of GDP, unweighted average of LDCs	21.6	22.7
GDI % of GDP, average of LDCs weighted by population size	15.5	15.9
FDI net inflows annual average per LDC: US$ millions; current prices	5.1	5.6
FDI net inflows annual average per LDC: US$ millions; constant 1980 prices	4.1	4.8
GDI % of GDP, all developing countries	23.5	26.2

Source: UNCTAD secretariat calculations, based on The World Bank, *World Tables, 1994.*

Principe, the United Republic of Tanzania, Vanuatu, Bhutan, Cape Verde, Equatorial Guinea, Guinea-Bissau, Samoa, and the Solomon Islands registered GDI levels of 25 per cent of GDP or above, with the first six of these countries raising GDI/GDP by more than 10 percentage points in comparison with the levels recorded in the 1980s. In 17 LDCs, investment levels were depressed: GDI was less than 15 per cent of GDP in Bangladesh, Benin, the Central African Republic, Chad, Ethiopia, Haiti, the Lao People's Democratic Republic, Madagascar, Myanmar, Niger, Rwanda, Sierra Leone, Sudan, Uganda, Yemen, Zaire and Zambia.

It is doubtful whether investment levels of the magnitude recorded in LDCs during the 1990s are adequate to support their developmental objectives. Although data on the depreciation of the capital stock are not available, depreciation rates are likely to be high; shortages of funds or foreign exchange have delayed essential maintenance and repairs in many LDCs, while the infrastructure has also been damaged by civil war in some countries. As such, the prevailing gross investment levels may have been able only to cover the replacement needs of the capital stock.

Foreign direct investment (FDI) experienced a small increase, albeit from the almost negligible volumes which had prevailed throughout the 1980s. Net inflows of FDI to LDCs, which augmented during 1990-1992, were about 10 per cent higher than those recorded during the 1980s. In constant 1980 prices, annual FDI flows during 1990-1992 were approximately 17 per cent higher than during 1982-1989. Despite the increase, the contribution of foreign investment to most LDC economies has remained marginal.

FDI was concentrated in a relatively small number of countries including Bangladesh, Liberia and Zambia. Although there are few data on the sectoral composition of this investment, it is likely that mining accounts for a large share, particularly in the African LDCs. Bangladesh and the Lao People's Democratic Republic have attracted foreign investment to the manufacturing sector. There are also indications that export-oriented manufacturing industries have been established by East Asian investors in several African LDCs, including Lesotho, Madagascar, Malawi and Mozambique.[9]

Fiscal deficit

Data on the overall fiscal deficit of the central Government is available for only 22 countries of the LDC group. Their fiscal position appears to have deteriorated with the overall deficit increasing from an average of 3.8 per cent of GDP during the 1980s to 5.2 per cent of GDP in the early 1990s (table 6).

This average has been pushed up by the very high deficits (in excess of 10 per cent of GDP) recorded in three countries - Madagascar, the Maldives and Zaire. In Zaire, a major cause of the deficit was the steep decline in mining production, which is one of the most important sources of Government revenue, while in Madagascar the deficit was exacerbated by strikes in the civil service which paralyzed revenue collection. Other factors that have contributed to a weakened fiscal position include the adverse impact of the decline in export commodity prices on Government trade-tax revenues (in many African LDCs), the effects of drought on both revenues and expenditures (as in Malawi and Mozambique), increased expenditures related to the political transition to elected Government (in Mali), war-related increases in expenditures (as in Rwanda) and the reduction of financial assistance from the former Soviet Union (in Cambodia).

Table 6: Annual consumer price inflation rates and overall fiscal deficits of LDCs, 1980-1989, 1990-1992

(Percentage)

	1980-1989	1990-1992
Annual consumer price inflation	10.8	11.5
Overall fiscal surplus/deficit (% of GDP)	-3.8	-5.2

Source: UNCTAD secretariat calculations, based on IMF, *International Financial Statistics Yearbook 1994,* and The World Bank, *World Tables, 1994.*

Of the 22 countries, 8 were able to reduce their overall deficits compared with the levels recorded in the 1980s, but the remaining 14 LDCs experienced a widening of the deficit. Only two LDCs avoided accumulating overall fiscal deficits during the 1990s: Botswana (whose overall surplus amounted to 12 per cent of GDP) and Burundi. While a fiscal deficit *per se* is not necessarily a cause for concern in a developing economy, the magnitude of the deficits incurred in many LDCs may be in excess of sustainable levels and necessitate some sort of fiscal re-trenchment in the near future. In 10 of the 22 LDCs, the overall deficit amounted to almost 7 per cent or more of GDP.

Consumer price inflation

Consumer price inflation registered a small increase compared with the previous decade. The median annual rate of inflation rose from 10.8 per cent during the 1980s to 11.5 per cent during 1990-1993.[10] Of the 45 countries for which data were available, 22 recorded an increase in the rate of inflation and 23 a de-cline. For about half the LDCs, inflation has not been a major economic problem; 22 coun-tries recorded average inflation rates of 10 per cent or less per annum. Most of these coun-tries were either small island economies (where rates of domestic inflation tend to be moderated by their openness to international trade) or members of the CFA monetary zone. Around one third of LDCs had annual inflation rates of 30 per cent or more.

Notable progress was made in reducing the rate of inflation in Guinea, the Lao People's Democratic Republic, Mozambique and Uganda, while there was a marked worsening of inflation in Afghanistan, Sudan and Zambia, and especially in Zaire, which has been afflicted with hyperinflation.

Current account deficits

LDCs accumulated current account deficits (excluding official transfers) amounting to about 9 per cent of GDP during 1990-1992, of which around two thirds was attributable to their trade deficits. The current account deficits, plus the accumulation of foreign reserves, were financed through official transfers and net external bor-rowing.

The information in this section does not clearly indicate the extent of macroeconomic stability achieved by LDCs during the early 1990s. Median inflation rates have increased slightly, overall Government deficits are higher, but the overall balance-of-payment position has improved with most LDCs accumulating sur-pluses. Given that the majority of LDCs have implemented trade and exchange-rate policy reforms (including devaluation) since the mid-1980s, it is not surprising that their external position has improved, but this may have merely shifted the impact of disequilibrium to else-where in the economy with the higher Govern-ment deficits financed by external and domestic borrowing.

D. TRENDS IN SOCIAL DEVELOPMENT INDICATORS

The Programme of Action recognized that the goal of strengthening the human capital base in LDCs requires particular emphasis in three crucial policy areas: reducing population growth rates, improving health and sanitation and enhancing education and training. This section briefly reviews the progress made by LDCs in attaining these social objectives.

Trends in the Human Development Index

UNDP's *Human Development Report* (HDR) presents a composite indicator of socio-eco-nomic development made up of indicators of income, life expectancy (LE) and educational attainment. Educational attainment is meas-ured through adult literacy and mean years of schooling: income is measured as GNP per capita on a US Dollar Purchasing Power Parity basis. The Human Development Index (HDI) is ex-pressed as a value between 0 and 1, with higher values signifying greater human development. Values between 0 and 0.5 represent low levels of human development, those between 0.5 and 0.8, medium levels and those between 0.8 and 1, high levels.

Given the limitations of HDI as an analysis tool for international comparisons, data should be interpreted with caution. Of the 45 LDCs for which an HDI was calculated in the HDR 1994 (the data pertained to 1992), 42 were classified in the low category of human development, i.e. their HDI was below 0.5. LDCs constituted 29 of the 30 countries ranked the lowest according to the HDI and were predominantly in Africa; 25 African LDCs were ranked the lowest of 30 countries. However, HDIs of three LDCs - Botswana, the Maldives and Samoa - placed them in the medium category. In 1992, the average HDI value of 45 LDCs for which data were available was 0.317, compared with an average for all developing countries of 0.54 and a world average of 0.61. Hence, the average HDI for LDCs was only 57 per cent of that of developing countries and only marginally more than 50 per cent of the world average - figures that indicate the enormous differences between levels of human development in LDCs and those elsewhere in the world.

United Republic of Tanzania had substantially higher HDI rankings than GNP per capita rankings.

Population policies

The demographic situation in LDCs has been reviewed in the 1992 LDC Report. It noted that despite some diversity, there are, with certain notable exceptions, some features typical to LDC demography. Their population growth rates are generally higher than those prevailing on average in developing countries and while many developing countries have reduced their population growth rates, those in LDCs are accelerating. However, significant regional differences

Table 7: Human Development Index, 1960-1992

	1960	1970	1980	1992
LDCs (31 countries)	0.147	0.190	0.236	0.293
LDCs (45 countries)	..	..	..	0.317

Source:UNCTAD secretariat calculations, based on UNDP, *Human Development Report, 1994.*

Although the majority of LDCs have remained in the low category of human development, as defined by UNDP, they have nevertheless made some progress as a group over the last three decades. For the 31 LDCs for which historical HDIs were provided in HDR 1994, the average HDI score rose by an average of 0.045 per year between 1960 and 1992 (table 7). However, even if the rate of progress of human development achieved in this period is maintained, it will be another 40 years before the average HDI value of this group of countries advances into the medium category of human development.

UNDP has ranked countries according to both their HDI values and GNP per capita. A comparison of the two rankings reveals the extent to which economic growth *per se* has not been reflected in broader human development (possibly because of large income differences), or conversely, some degree of human development has been attained without commensurate expansion of the economy. Several LDCs, including Botswana, Djibouti, Guinea, Mauritania and Vanuatu had an HDI ranking in 1994 that was more than 25 places below their GNP per capita ranking. In contrast, Madagascar, the Lao People's Democratic Republic and the

in the demographic features of LDCs have emerged since the 1960s. While population growth rates in Africa have accelerated, those in other LDCs have stabilized and have even marginally decelerated since 1980.

High population growth rates are attributable, as in other parts of the developing world, to a combination of continuing poverty and lack of education, health services and income-earning opportunities. Although medical advances have contributed to a marked fall in death rates (due largely to reduced child mortality) over the past 30 years, crude birth rates (CBRs) have remained persistently high, partly because parents are highly motivated to have many children who will provide additional labour, and security in their old age. Children are an investment for families that have few opportunities to acquire financial or physical assets. Fertility levels, as measured by the total fertility rate (TFR), average almost six births per woman in LDCs, almost twice as high as in other developing countries.[11]

The economic incentives for large families are exacerbated by the low status of women, low levels of educational attainment, especially among women, high infant-mortality rates and lack of access to, and information about, family-planning services. As a consequence, most LDCs are still in the earliest stages of the demographic transition to a state where there are both low death rates and low birth rates. Even when birth rates are reduced, the demographic structure created by a rapidly growing population (with a very high proportion of people yet to reach child-bearing age) ensures that population growth rates persist for a substantial length of time before population size begins to stabilize.[12] The total population of the 47 LDCs, which amounted to approximately 440 million in 1990, is projected to increase to 1,039 million by the year 2025.[13]

Reducing population growth rates requires advances across a broad spectrum of development aspects, to provide parents with both the incentives and the means to have smaller families. Improving women's education is considered one of the most effective long-term measures to reduce population growth. The most important factor in reducing fertility rates, however, is the increased availability and use of

Guinea, Madagascar, Mali, Niger, Rwanda, the United Republic of Tanzania and Zambia, had introduced national population policies in the 1990s. In addition to direct Government support for contraception and other family-planning services, population policies have, *inter alia*, raised the minimum legal age for marriage and developed educational campaigns to encourage longer spacing between births.[16]

For the 35 LDCs for which data are available, the CBR averaged 44.1 annual births per 1,000 population in 1992, having fallen only marginally since 1987 (table 8). Only seven LDCs - Bangladesh and Cambodia (which continued the progress made since the 1970s), Botswana, Lesotho, Sudan, the United Republic of Tanzania and Zambia - had significant reductions in their CBRs (i.e. three or more births per 1,000 population) during the 1987-1992 period. In several LDCs, the CBR actually rose: Afghanistan and Guinea recorded increases of three and four births per 1,000 population, respectively.

The average annual population growth rate rose further in the early 1990s to 3.0 per cent

Table 8: Population growth rates and crude birth rates (CBRs) in LDCs
1980-1989, 1990-1992

	1980-1989	*1990-1992*
Annual population growth rate %	2.7	3.0
CBR: annual births per 1,000 population	44.2[a]	44.1[b]

Source:UNCTAD secretariat calculations, based on UNICEF, *State of the World's Children, 1994*.
  a   1987.
  b   1992.

contraceptives.[14] Population policies that provide family-planning services are crucial in this area and increasing numbers of LDCs have been expanding these services in recent years.

In 1991 in Bangladesh, the contraceptive prevalence rate (the percentage of married women aged 15-44 who use contraceptives) rose to 31 per cent, compared with only 3 per cent in 1970. As a result, the TFR has fallen from seven births per woman to less than five in the space of 20 years.[15] Two other Asian LDCs, Myanmar and Nepal, have also had major reductions in TFRs since the 1970s. In most African LDCs, however, there have been no significant declines in TFRs although several countries in the region, including Burkina Faso,

from the 2.7 per cent recorded during the 1980s. Population growth rates had been steadily increasing during the second half of the 1980s. Although the average birth rate stabilized in the late 1980s and early 1990s as noted above, the momentum created by past increases in the CBR was sufficient to ensure that population growth rates continue to rise.

In the 1994 International Conference on Population and Development, the international community committed itself to quantitative goals in three areas that are mutually supportive and of critical importance to the achievements of other population and development objectives: education, reduction of mortality rates of infants, children and mothers, and universal access to family planning and reproductive health services. LDCs should be a prime focus of the international community in its efforts to reach these goals.

Education and literacy

The Programme of Action for LDCs called for the formulation of strategies to improve education and training, with particular emphasis on attaining universal primary education, and combating illiteracy especially among women. The 1993-1994 LDC Report, analysed the education sector and the progress made over the last 20 years. The Report noted that, although there was a large expansion of education during the 1970s and 1980s, as manifested in substantial increases in primary- and secondary-school enrolment ratios and adult literacy, the overall educational levels were low. In 1990, only two thirds of the relevant age group were enrolled in primary schools in LDCs, while net secondary-school enrolments averaged only 16 per cent. The enrolment ratios for girls were significantly worse than for boys; net primary- and secondary-school enrolment ratios for girls averaged 58 and 12 per cent, respectively, in 1990. Moreover, there was some evidence that progress in raising educational attainments had slowed during the late 1980s, with less public spending on education in many LDCs and a stagnation of enrolment ratios. Education services were adversely affected by the deteriorating economic conditions of the 1980s and early 1990s and in particular by the pressure on Governments to reduce fiscal deficits. In many countries, the real value of teachers' salaries has declined and there are acute shortages of books and other educational materials.

As indicated in table 9, the net primary-school enrolment ratio increased to 52.2 per cent in 1990 compared with 51.5 per cent in 1986-1988. The fact that progress in increasing primary-school enrolment has almost come to a halt is grounds for concern. The adult literacy rate rose from 41.1 per cent in 1985 to 47.7 per cent in 1992, and, with only three exceptions, all other LDCs raised their adult literacy levels over this period. This achievement reflects the resources devoted by many LDC Governments to adult literacy programmes, including the enlistment of volunteers in the local communities. Adult literacy campaigns have sometimes been combined with other development initiatives, such as health education and agricultural training.

Resources devoted to LDCs during the late 1980s for public education as a percentage of their GDP or GNP rose marginally. Public expenditures for education rose from 3.2 per cent of GNP/GDP in 1986 to 3.4 per cent in 1990, an increase which is not sufficient to ensure that educational expenditures in real terms keep pace with population growth.

Health and sanitation

The prevailing health situation in LDCs was reviewed in the 1993-1994 LDC Report. It noted that most LDCs continued to have high childhood mortality rates primarily caused by preventable diseases such as malaria, measles, acute respiratory infections, diarrhoeal infections and

Table 9: Indicators of educational attainments and expenditures in LDCs
(Percentage)

	1986-1988	*1990*
Net primary-school enrolment ratio	51.5	52.2
Adult literacy	41.1[a]	47.7[c]
Public expenditure on education (as %) of GDP/GNP	3.2[b]	3.4

Source: UNCTAD secretariat calculations, based on UNDP, *Human Development Report*, 1989, 1991 and 1994 editions.

a   1985.
b   1986.
c   1992.

neonatal tetanus. Poor sanitation and the lack of safe drinking-water supplies are major causes of the spread of some of these diseases, while immunity is weakened by inadequate nutrition. Maternal and infant health is also undermined by frequent pregnancies. AIDS has become a major cause of death over the course of the last decade in LDCs in Central and Southern Africa.

Armed conflicts are yet another threat to health in LDCs in several regions. Civilian populations have suffered large-scale casualties as a result of conflicts and civil wars. Refugees driven from their homes by civil wars have been especially vulnerable to a host of infectious diseases.

Aside from these effects of war, the unsatisfactory health conditions reflect, to a large extent, the underlying weaknesses of LDC economies: the lack of infrastructure and trained personnel to deliver health services and widespread poverty and malnutrition. The severe economic crises facing many LDCs since the start of the 1980s have further undermined the health of their populations. Living standards have fallen and health services have been cut back as a result of budgetary pressures, and foreign exchange shortages have affected the supply of imported medicines and other medical supplies.

Table 10 presents data on the evolution of a number of indicators of the health status of LDC populations during the late 1980s and early

1990s. There was no change in the LE indicator between 1987 and 1992 - the average LE for LDCs remained at almost 50 years. Some of the largest declines in LE (by between 3 and 10 years) occurred in Malawi, Rwanda, Uganda, the United Republic of Tanzania and Zambia, which have all been heavily afflicted with the AIDS pandemic during the last decade.

Child mortality rates in LDCs declined from 195 deaths per 1,000 live births in 1987 to 179 deaths in 1992. Impressive reductions in child mortality were achieved in Bangladesh, Burkina Faso, the Central African Republic, Ethiopia, the Gambia, Mali and Nepal. Unfortunately, the situation deteriorated in a number of other countries including Guinea-Bissau, Lesotho, Liberia, Uganda, Zaire and Zambia. As with adult mortality, AIDS most likely contributed to the regression of child health in some of these countries. The most likely cause of the overall reduction in child mortality is the increased immunization of children against major childhood diseases such as diphtheria, measles, pertussis, tuberculosis and polio. The increased use of Oral Rehydration Therapy (ORT) also contributed to reducing deaths due to diarrhoeal diseases, particularly in Bhutan, the United Republic of Tanzania and Zambia, where rapid strides have been made in promoting the use of this low-cost but highly effective technique.[17]

Public expenditures on health services as a percentage of GDP or GNP registered a small increase in the second half of the 1980s in the 30

Table 10: Indicators of the health status in LDCs

	1985-1989	*1992*
Life expectancy at birth, years	49.9[a]	49.9
Under-5 mortality: annual deaths of children under 5 per 1,000 live births	195.3[a]	179.4
Percentage of 1-year-olds immunized	56.5[b]	60.6
Access to safe drinking-water: % of population	48.1[c]	50.2[d]
Public expenditure on health as % of GDP/GNP	1.2[e]	2.5[f]

Source: UNCTAD secretariat calculations, based on UNDP, *Human Development Report*, 1991, 1993 and 1994 editions, and UNICEF, *State of the World's Children*, 1989 and 1994 editions.

a   1987.
b   1988-1989.
c   1985-1988.
d   1988-1991.
e   1986.
f   1990.

LDCs for which data were available. Health expenditures rose from an average of 1.2 per cent of GNP/GDP in 1986 to 2.5 per cent in 1990. Significant increases of 2 or more percentage points of GNP/GDP occurred in several countries including Benin, Burkina Faso, Chad, Haiti, Mauritania, Mozambique and Niger. Donor countries are beginning to give the health sector (along with education and other social sectors) greater priority in the allocation of their aid budgets, although the sector's share in official development finance (ODF) remains very low.[18]

Considerable progress can be made in improving health standards despite the constraints imposed by the overall low levels of economic development, as has been demonstrated in several developing countries:[19] first, by devoting a greater proportion of available resources - especially Government budgetary and overseas development resources - to health and related services (such as adequate sanitation and potable water), and second by concentrating health expenditures on the most cost-effective services.

E. Adjustment and policy reforms in LDCs: implementation, progress and constraints

In recent years, the majority of LDCs have carried out wide-ranging programmes of economic policy reforms, usually supported by the International Monetary Fund (IMF) and the World Bank. These are called Structural Adjustment Programmes (SAPs), although there are also various local names. The Programme of Action supported the need for policy reform but noted that the success rate of SAPs in the 1980s had been mixed, and it expressed its concern about deficiencies in their policy design and the amount of external finance available to support their implementation.

Structural adjustment in LDCs, as well as in other developing countries, has generated much controversy. Consideration of many aspects of this issue has begun to evolve towards a consensus. On the one hand, it is now widely accepted that reforms that allow greater freedom for market forces, promote private-sector development and maintain macroeconomic stability are essential. On the other hand, the World Bank and the donor community have recognized the need to incorporate into SAPs measures to address a broader (and longer-term) agenda including issues of structural transformation, poverty alleviation and environmental protection. The international financial institutions, bilateral donors and LDC Governments have all learnt from the experience of structural adjustment since SAPs were first adopted in the 1980s.[20] In returning to this issue, this year's Report aims to reflect the emerging experience of structural adjustment and to put forward proposals relating to the design and financing of SAPs that can command support from the international community.

Most LDCs began implementing SAPs during the middle or second half of the 1980s, although a few countries, such as Malawi and Togo, began earlier, and others, such as Burkina Faso, the Comoros, Ethiopia and Rwanda did not formally adopt SAPs until the 1990s. In a number of LDCs, including Sierra Leone, Sudan, Zaire and Zambia, adjustment programmes were begun but abandoned, although Sierra Leone and Zambia started new SAPs in the 1990s.

Most LDCs with these programmes have tried to implement policy reforms across a wide range of sectors despite financial, political and administrative constraints and a marked deterioration in the external trading environment and/or natural and man-made disasters.

The primary objectives of the reform programmes include short-term economic stabilization, restoration of sustainable rates of output growth and increased export production. The reforms have involved efforts to improve macroeconomic management and reduce direct Government involvement in, and control over, markets. These reforms were implemented as a response to the severe economic crisis that emerged during the first half of the 1980s, and in many countries was to intensify during the course of the decade. The crisis was manifested in the stagnation of output growth, the accumulation of chronic, balance-of-payment deficits and the unsustainable build-up of external debt. The genesis of the crisis lay in the combination of a sharp deterioration in the external economic environment facing these economies and inappropriate domestic policies.[21]

Nature and extent of adjustment and reforms

In implementing SAPs, three sets of policies have been used, namely: expenditure-reducing (monetary and fiscal) policies to lower inflation and balance-of-payment deficits; expenditure and production-switching (exchange rate and wage) policies to promote exports and import substitution; and supply-side, "growth-oriented" policies (e.g. trade and sectoral policies and public enterprise reforms) to remove the structural causes of macroeconomic imbalances and to raise the volume of investment while improving its efficiency.

As of June 1993, 32 LDCs had implemented adjustment reforms and received structural adjustment loans (SALs) or sectoral adjustment loans (SECALs) from the World Bank and/or loans from the IMF under the structural adjustment facility (SAF) or enhanced structural adjustment facility (ESAF), as indicated in table 11. The countries in receipt of adjustment loans include 28 of 32 African LDCs, 3 Asian LDCs (Bangladesh, the Lao People's Democratic Republic and Nepal) and Haiti.[22]

The evolving nature and extent of the reform effort are discussed in the 1993-1994 LDC Report.[23] The reform policy in SAPs varied between countries, but SAPs have typically involved a combination of fiscal and monetary

Table 11: LDCs in receipt of SAF/ESAF and/or SAL/SECAL loans[a]

Country	SAF/ESAF	SAL/SECAL
Bangladesh	1987	1987
Benin	1989	1989
Burkina Faso	1991	1985
Burundi	1986	1986
Central African Republic	1987	1986
Chad	1987	1988
Comoros	1991	1991
Equatorial Guinea	1988	-
Ethiopia	1992	1993
Gambia	1986	1986
Guinea	1991	1986
Guinea-Bissau	1987	1984
Haiti	1986	1987
Lao People's Democratic Republic	1989	1989
Lesotho	1988	-
Madagascar	1987	1986
Malawi	1988	1981
Mali	1988	1988
Mauritania	1986	1987
Mozambique	1987	1985
Nepal	1987	1987
Niger	1986	1986
Rwanda	1991	1991
Sao Tome and Principe	1989	1987
Sierra Leone	1986	1984
Somalia	1987	1989
Sudan	-	1983
Togo	1988	1983
Uganda	1987	1983
United Republic of Tanzania	1987	1986
Zaire	1987	1986
Zambia	-	1985

Source: UNCTAD, *The Least Developed Countries, 1993-1994 Report.*
a   The years refer to the dates of approval of each country's first SAF/ESAF and SAL/SECAL.

restraints to reduce aggregate demand, and market-oriented supply-side reforms, such as liberalization of trade, credit markets and agricultural marketing, the decontrol of prices and the reform or privatization of public enterprises, designed to enhance the efficiency of resource allocation. Efforts to raise domestic resource mobilization, often involving tax reforms and higher real interest rates, have also featured prominently in adjustment programmes. With the exception of SAPs implemented by the members of the CFA Franc monetary zone, they have also included exchange-rate devaluation in order to boost the competitiveness of the traded-goods sector and thus facilitate the reduction of external deficits.[24]

Impact of SAPs on LDCs' economic performance

The data in this section are drawn from the recent World Bank study on adjustment in Africa which covers 20 African LDCs.[25] Cross-country averages for the different variables are presented in table 12. A comparison is made between economic outcomes during 1981-1986 (which broadly corresponds to the pre-adjustment period for most of the countries covered here) and 1987-1991, a period in which all LDCs implemented SAPs, and provides a tentative indication as to whether the implementation of adjustment programmes has led to an improvement or a deterioration in their economic situation.

These data needs to be interpreted with caution; statistical associations of this nature do not prove that changes were attributable *per se* to SAPs (or adjustment lending). Other factors such as changes in the terms of trade, natural disasters, political instability, etc., could also have influenced the economy. Moreover, the implementation of SAPs has varied between LDCs in both the timing, intensity and consistency of the reform effort, which also impairs the validity of this type of analysis. In addition to

Table 12: Indicators of economic performance for African LDCs undertaking SAPs, 1981-1986 and 1987-1991
(Percentage)

	1981-1986	1987-1991
Real annual per capita GDP growth	-0.8	-0.4
Annual agricultural growth	2.9	2.9
Industrial growth	0.5	3.9
Manufacturing growth	1.7	6.4
Exports growth	0.9	2.3
GDS/GDP	3.8	3.6
GDI/GDP	16.5	17.6
Public investment/GDP	8.6	8.8
Public saving/GDP	-2.1	-1.2[a]
Overall fiscal balance/GDP (includes grants)	-7.5	-4.6[a]
Total Government revenue/GDP	16.2	15.6[a]
Total Government expenditure/GDP	27.0	25.4[a]
Inflation	20.0	20.6[a]
	(10.3)[b]	(8.0)[b]
Real annual interest rates for deposits	-5.1	0.5[a]
	(2.2)[b]	(3.0)[b]

Source: UNCTAD secretariat calculations, based on The World Bank, *Adjustment in Africa*, annex tables, 1994.
a   1990-1991.
b   Figures in parentheses are median.

methodological difficulties, empirical evaluation is impeded by the deficiencies of the available database. Many statistics are unavailable, and those that are available are unreliable and out of date. More time is needed before it will be possible to determine what impact structural adjustment has had on the course of economic development.

Bearing in mind the caveats noted above, the data in table 12 reinforce the conclusions of earlier LDC Reports that SAPs led to a small improvement in average economic performance. For some of the most important target variables, such as GDP growth and investment, the improvement was marginal and performance was far from satisfactory. For some variables, the improvement at the cross-country level is attributable to the strong recovery in only a small number of LDCs. In general, economic performance has differed greatly between countries, and in several LDCs economic conditions have deteriorated since implementing SAPs.

Real per capita GDP growth in the 19 African LDCs for which data were available registered a marginal rise from negative 0.8 per cent per annum during 1981-1986 to negative 0.4 per cent per annum during 1987-1991, which was insufficient to halt the decline in per capita output, let alone to generate growth rates that would contribute to raising living standards and reducing poverty. The goal of reviving sustainable per capita growth has yet to be achieved.

The rise in agricultural growth rates was not linked to the implementation of SAPs despite their policy emphasis on improving incentives for farmers. Agriculture grew at an annual average rate of 2.9 per cent during 1987-1991, as it did during 1981-1986. There was evidence of a revival in industry and manufacturing; industrial growth rates rose from 0.5 to 3.9 per cent per annum and those of manufacturing from 1.7 to 6.4 per cent. However, as chapter III points out, the performance of the manufacturing sector varied between countries. Those that had undertaken selective liberalization measures fared better than those with extensive liberalization. Exports recorded an acceleration in growth from 0.9 per cent per annum in 1981-1986 to 2.3 per cent in 1987-1991. Again, the export performance varied, and only a few African LDCs (e.g. Burkina Faso, Malawi, Mauritania and Niger) succeeded in raising their export growth sufficiently to make up for terms of trade losses.[26]

The savings and investment performance of the adjusting LDCs was not compatible with the objectives of sustainable growth and structural transformation. GDS actually fell from 3.8 to 3.6 per cent of GDP. GDI levels remained depressed, rising only to 17.6 per cent of GDP during 1987-1991 compared with 16.5 per cent of GDP in the pre-adjustment period.

Efforts to reduce macroeconomic imbalances produced varied results. As noted in section C above, Governments were able to improve public finances, mainly by cuts in public expenditure and increased grants, and hence lower overall fiscal deficits. Despite this, price inflation was resilient in several countries; the mean inflation rate rose marginally to 20.6 per cent per annum during 1990-1991, although there was a fall of 2.3 percentage points in the median rate of inflation to 8.0 per cent per annum.

Factors affecting adjustment performance

The salient factors explaining variations in economic performance among adjusting countries were analysed in the 1993-1994 LDC Report. These include:

- adjusting countries with higher growth rates had a better investment performance and more availability of official development assistance (ODA) and imports than the other adjusters;

- countries that undertook 'selective' trade liberalization have performed better than those undertaking across-the-board trade liberalization;

- manufacturing has been a dynamic force behind the growth and export performance of most LDCs with higher growth rates. Success or failure to augment manufacturing growth, in turn, is attributable to, *inter alia*, investments, imports, and the policy environment (see chapter III);

- other factors, such as structural and endowment-related constraints, country-specific conditions (e.g. political difficulties or natural calamities) and external conditions, partly explain the differential economic performance among adjusting countries;

- finally, the design and sequencing of adjustment and reform policies have been major determinants of performance. Problems inherent in policy design, particularly the neglect of structural conditions, including a low level of development, a small or marginal industrial base and an unfavourable external environment, etc., worked to retard, and even reverse, the momentum of reforms.

Limitations of SAPs and areas for possible improvement

LDCs' experience of structural adjustment provides few grounds for optimism that the prevailing strategy of macroeconomic restraint combined with market liberalization is sufficient to overcome the chronic economic problems that have afflicted these countries since the late 1970s. The LDCs undertaking SAPs that have managed to restore positive per capita growth rates and reduce external and internal imbalances could hardly make progress beyond that. The recovery that has taken place in these countries remains fragile, vulnerable to any downturn on world commodity markets or in the availability of external finance and to vagaries of weather. There is little evidence that the economies of the adjusting LDCs have emerged from the crises of the 1980s into a more dynamic and self-sustaining growth path capable of raising living standards and reducing poverty. Where a recovery in output has occurred, it has been based mainly on an expansion of traditional primary-commodity exports and low-productivity services, as well as on increased external flows in some cases. Positive structural changes, such as a strengthened industrial sector and diversified exports, have begun in just a few (mostly Asian) LDCs.

The fact that structural adjustment has not been an unequivocal success raises the issue of the changes that are needed in the current strategy to improve LDCs' economic performance and prospects. Although the experience of LDCs undertaking SAPs has not been uniform, there are three areas that are relevant to them: the adequacy of the external financing of SAPs; the time-frame in which adjustment policies are pursued and are expected to yield results; and the policy content of SAPs and, in particular, the overemphasis on market liberalization and the lack of investment in human and physical capital and the supply of vital public goods.

Financing structural adjustment

Structural adjustment entails intensive requirements for external financial support for two reasons. First, the process of structural adjustment itself generates demands for resources over and above what would be required in the absence of an adjustment programme: investment is needed to restructure production facilities and rehabilitate infrastructure, the recovery of production will raise demands for imported inputs, and financial and technical assistance is required to retrain workers, reform institutions and implement and manage adjustment reforms. Second, LDCs face severe domestic resource constraints: savings rates are low, Government revenues are limited, technical and professional skills are at a premium, and their foreign exchange earning capacities are insufficient and have been further undermined by declining export commodity prices.

The major sources of external finance to support structural adjustment are SAF and ESAF loans from the IMF, SALs and SECALs from the World Bank and ODA from the donor countries. Debt relief has also been extended from official bilateral creditors under enhanced concessional terms to countries in the Paris Club and from multilateral and non-official creditors under several other schemes. Although much of the initial adjustment lending from the IMF was on commercial terms with short maturities, this has largely been replaced by concessional and longer term SAF/ESAF loans. In addition, the funding made available to LDCs by the World Bank, by other multilateral creditors and from bilateral sources has been extended predominantly on concessional terms, with the bulk of bilateral finance in the form of grants.

World Bank estimates covering 17 African LDCs indicate that net transfers during 1987-1991 to these countries averaged 14.9 per cent of GDP.[27] However, this figure is somewhat distorted by the very large shares in GDP of net transfers to just two countries - Mozambique and the United Republic of Tanzania - which have very low levels of GDP per capita. When these two countries are excluded, net transfers fall to an average of 11 per cent of GDP for the remaining 15 LDCs.

Adjustment programmes in African LDCs have been supported with additional concessional finance, although the increase has not been large or uniform. Net external transfers to these 17 countries as a percentage of GDP were on average 3.9 percentage points higher during 1987-1991 than 1981-1986.[28] The median increase for this group of LDCs was 2.4 percentage points of GDP. The mean increase was, however, heavily influenced by very large rises in Mozambique and the United Republic of Tanzania. When these two countries are discounted, the mean increase was negligible, amounting to 0.3 percentage points of GDP. For six of the adjusting African LDCs, net transfers contracted. There are also concerns about the quality and appropriateness of some of this aid. Its value to the recipients is often diminished because it is tied to the purchase of specific goods or services from the donor country or to a particular project, whereas the priority for the adjusting countries is usually for balance-of-payment support in the form of untied programme aid.[29]

It is questionable as to whether the levels of external finance available to African LDCs have been sufficient to support their efforts to implement structural adjustment policies, reduce macroeconomic imbalances and revive growth rates. There are grounds for arguing that the external financing of adjustment has been inadequate and has contributed to the disappointing outcomes in terms of economic performance and, in several LDCs, has undermined the effort to sustain the reform process. There are three explanations to support this contention.

First, the losses of African LDCs that were due to declines in the terms of trade were not compensated by an increase in concessional external flows. These countries experienced a cumulative fall in the external terms of trade of about 15 per cent during the 1980s which was followed by further sharp falls in the early 1990s. By 1990, the fall in the terms of trade from 1980 levels represented an annual loss of 2.8 per cent of GDP.[30] Increases in the volume of ODA during the 1980s were not enough to compensate for the losses of the terms of trade incurred by most of these countries.

Second, as noted above, structural adjustment entails increased external financing requirements for imports, investment, rehabilitation of infrastructure and productive capacity and technical assistance, etc. The rise in debt-servicing requirements made additional claims on external resources during the late 1980s, that were due partly to the amortization of short-term IMF credits disbursed to support stabilization and/or adjustment programmes. Countries embarking on SAPs have been required first to clear all arrears outstanding to the IMF before they can become eligible for adjustment financing, which has further added to the burden of debt servicing. Also, in many LDCs, scarce external financial resources had to be used for rebuilding after civil wars or to provide relief food supplies following extensive drought.

Third, if adjustment is to be successful in the long term, a sustained revival of growth combined with structural transformation is required.

But vital expenditures in areas that are essential to attain these objectives, in particular investment and human resource development, have been constrained by shortages of funds, which could have been partly alleviated had a greater volume of concessional external finance in the appropriate form been made available.

Time-frame for adjustment

A lesson to emerge from the experience of implementing structural adjustment programmes is that successful adjustment involving sustainable growth of output, based on improved efficiency and expanded productive capacity, cannot be accomplished in a short time-frame. It has been argued that one of the shortcomings in the design of SAPs was the expectation that problems deeply embedded in the economic and political structure of adjusting countries could be solved quickly.[31]

Although it is possible, usually at high cost, to achieve a degree of stabilization based on expenditure compression in a relatively short time, supply-side reforms inevitably require more time to implement and to yield results. Successful adjustment in LDCs must be pursued in a medium- to long-term perspective for a number of reasons.

Policy reforms aim to stimulate output of tradeable goods, particularly exports. But a sustained rise in output usually requires an expanded supply capacity. In many LDCs, investment in the export sectors, especially in tree crops and mining, involves long gestation lags before new capacity can become productive. Furthermore, private-sector investment in the non-traditional export sectors, and in other industries, may only be feasible if the transport and communications infrastructure has been improved, which again entails substantial gestation lags.

Furthermore, a major aspect of adjustment programmes involves various institutional reforms: reforming the civil service, the tax system and state-owned enterprises; privatization; restructuring the banking system; and updating the legal and regulatory framework that governs the conduct of business and commerce. The need to strengthen the institutional framework of developing economies and its importance to the success of the overall adjustment programme has gained increasing recognition in recent years.[32] However, implementing these reforms makes heavy demands on highly skilled but scarce human resources. Institutional reform also involves retraining of staff which limits the pace at which these reforms can be undertaken and Governments may not have the resources to implement all the reforms at the pace required.

Greater emphasis should be placed on a broad range of supply-side reforms and less on orthodox demand restraint. Austerity programmes cannot be sustained indefinitely without straining fragile social and political structures. The costs of reforms, unlike most of the intended benefits, begin to accrue from the start of implementation. Unless Governments are provided with adequate resources to reduce these costs throughout the implementation process, political pressures may jeopardize the sustainability of the programme. In view of this, the sustainability of adjustment programmes becomes even more dependent on adequate external financing.

Policy content of SAPs

The failure of adjustment programmes in LDCs to substantially improve their economies is partly attributable to the composition of the policy reforms that form the core of most SAPs. The overriding emphasis in SAPs has been on relative price changes, such as exchange-rate devaluation, and the liberalization of markets from Government control. But many of the structural weaknesses that underlie the slow growth of production and contribute to the macroeconomic imbalances have not been adequately addressed, such as the rudimentary technology in the agricultural sector, especially in SSA; inadequate physical infrastructure, fragile and undeveloped financial systems; weak institutional capacity in public and private sectors; and the severe constraints due to poor human-resource development.

Structural weaknesses of this nature cannot be rectified without public intervention to overcome market failures and to supply goods and services that the private sector cannot be expected to supply in an optimal manner. Unfortunately, progress towards overcoming some of these constraints may actually have been impeded by the restraints on public expenditure that have played a prominent role in adjustment programmes and that have led to cutbacks in the supply of a range of public goods essential both to human welfare and as supplements to private-sector production. In addition, there has been an overly optimistic faith in the ability of the private sector to supply goods and services to markets from which the public sector has withdrawn. Rectifying the policy deficiencies of current adjustment programmes is crucial to achieving more rapid and sustainable rates of economic growth, to raising living standards and to reducing the extreme vulnerability of these economies to internal and external shocks.

Although the needs and priorities of individual LDCs differ, there are a number of policy areas that merit greater emphasis when adjustment programmes are formulated. Sustainable growth and structural transformation must be based on mobilizing and improving the productivity of domestic resources, which entails, in particular, boosting human capital and transforming the productive base, including the productivity of agriculture, the single most important sector in terms of employment (on agriculture, see chapter II). Given that LDCs have highly open economies that must import much of what they require for consumption and investment, developing a competitive export sector is also a priority. Import compression will prevent a sustained growth of output and undermine export performance. But there are diminishing returns from expanding production of traditional primary commodities because, given that LDCs in aggregate hold major world market shares of these commodities, supply increases drive down prices.[33] Hence, the long-term prosperity of the external sector requires export diversification.[34]

Export diversification

Export diversification has not been adequately addressed in current adjustment programmes but is an objective for which market-oriented reforms alone are insufficient except in a limited number of instances. The case for diversifying exports away from traditional primary products is well known and widely accepted.[35]

LDCs have the potential to compete in a range of non-traditional export markets, including horticulture and other agricultural products, wood products such as veneers, textiles and garments, and tourism, as some LDCs in the region have demonstrated.[36] An appropriate structure of incentives is necessary for non-traditional export industries to be viable (see chapter III). In addition, direct public intervention to overcome severe supply-side obstacles is required.

The supply-side obstacles that impede the growth of non- traditional export industries in African LDCs include the very weak technological capacities of domestic industry, attributable partly to the scarcity of managerial, engineering and other technical skills (see chapter III). Poorly developed infrastructure significantly raises the production and transport costs of industry and agriculture and thus erodes their competitiveness. With the exception of some of the major well-established companies, the access of most entrepreneurs to adequate supplies of credit, including trade credit and longer-term capital, is limited by the deficiencies in domestic financial systems. This problem is compounded because the domestic banks have little experience or expertise in evaluating loan proposals from entrepreneurs seeking to enter non-traditional markets. Potential non-traditional exporters also have difficulties in establishing marketing channels for their products in the world's major export markets.

Resolving these problems will not be easy. In some areas, such as improved infrastructure, an expansion of technical education, and the appropriate legal and fiscal framework to induce foreign investment in export industries, the way forward is clear although resources may not be available. In other areas - promoting entrepreneurship, provision of appropriate forms of finance, establishing marketing channels, transferring relevant technology, etc. - there are problems in formulating relevant and feasible policies and programmes, as well as in finding the resources to implement them. Progress depends on developing effective institutions to assist entrepreneurs with marketing, finance, training and technology.

In building a viable non-traditional export sector, donor assistance is needed to provide financial and technical support for export promotion, infrastructural development and technical education and to ensure that trade barriers do not exclude LDC exports from industrial country markets. Donor country Governments should also consider ways to provide incentives to firms in their own countries to establish commercial links with exporters in LDCs.

Investment

One of the most disturbing trends in LDCs that have adopted SAPs is the stagnation in capital investment, in many countries at levels that are barely sufficient to replace the depreciation of the existing capital stock. The mean level of GSI during 1987-1991 in 19 African LDCs undertaking SAPs was only 17.6 per cent of GDP, less than 1 percentage point higher than in 1981-1986, a period in which investment expenditures had been sharply compressed following the adverse terms of trade shocks at the turn of the decade.[37] Investment levels in these countries were almost 6 percentage points less than the average for developing countries and over 10 percentage points lower than the fast-growing Asian economies.

Fiscal retrenchment had already led to steep cut-backs in public investment expenditures during the first half of the 1980s. The intensified fiscal restraint under SAPs has not enabled public investment to recover. In 17 African LDCs for which data were available, public investment averaged 8.8 per cent of GDP during 1987-1991, only marginally higher than in the 1981-1986 period.[38] While there is a dearth of reliable statistics on private investment, it is probable that private investment also stagnated in the majority of adjusting LDCs. There is no evidence to suggest that any of these countries have enjoyed a boom in private investment - whether from domestic or foreign firms - since adopting structural adjustment policies.

Although the private sector has been the intended beneficiary of adjustment reforms, many of the policies that formed the core of SAPs have actually deterred private investment. The most important factor influencing private investment is usually the buoyancy of market demand; firms expand capacity or replace old machinery when they expect demand for their output to grow. Deflationary demand management policies, combined with import liberalization, has led to a stagnation or contraction in the markets for many companies, particularly in import-substituting manufacturing industries, which has proved a major disincentive to capital formation. The impact of weak domestic demand on investment has been accentuated by devaluation which raises the real cost of imported capital goods, by increases in interest rates which make borrowing for investment more expensive, and by tight controls over lending by domestic banks which have led to credit shortages. Lack of confidence in the sustainability of adjustment policies is also likely to have deterred private investment. The excessive levels of external debt in many LDCs are another factor undermining confidence, especially among foreign investors.[39] Several countries have taken steps to amend the legal, administrative and fiscal framework for investment, for example by removing bureaucratic licensing procedures and offering tax incentives. But until economic prospects improve, it is unlikely that private investment will recover.

Public investment in infrastructure is an essential complement to private-sector investment, particularly in economies characterized by severe structural constraints. The infrastructural facilities in most LDCs are so deficient in volume and quality as to be a major impediment to the viability of a whole range of industries. The condition of the infrastructure in many LDCs has been further eroded because of cuts in maintenance budgets.

Attention should also be focused on policies to promote private investment, although it is often difficult for public policies to exert a positive effect on private investment in poorly developed economies. The low levels of private investment are attributable partly to constraints, such as the small size of domestic markets, which are not amenable to policy change, at least in the short term. Nevertheless, there are a number of policy measures that would help to improve the climate for private investment. The remaining bureaucratic restrictions on investment should be eliminated and administrative controls over business minimized. The legal, fiscal and regulatory framework for business should be transparent and perceived as fair by all potential investors. Reforms in domestic financial markets are required to expand the supply of long-term finance. In many sectors of LDC economies, the exploitation of profitable opportunities for private investment is dependent on supporting public investment in infrastructure. As a consequence, an expansion of public investment may induce a complementary response from private investors. Business confidence is likely to be bolstered if the multilateral and bilateral donors are willing to demonstrate their own confidence in the adjusting economies by providing additional concessional finance and by granting external debt relief.

Human resource development

Human resource development was adversely affected during the 1980s in many African LDCs undertaking SAPs. The lack of progress in improving primary- and secondary-school enrolment ratios, which remains at levels well below those attained in other parts of the developing world, is particularly worrying.[40] Education and health budgets suffered in most adjusting countries as a result of pressures to reduce fiscal deficits. For example, the mean level of expenditure on education in a sample of 10 African LDCs undertaking SAPs, fell from 3.3 per cent during 1981-1986 to 2.6 per cent during 1987-1990.[41]

While structural adjustment policies do not share all the blame for the decline in social sector expenditures (the severe economic crisis facing these countries would almost certainly have forced some cut-backs in social expenditures even in the absence of adjustment reforms), the failure to protect health and educational budgets from general fiscal retrenchment was a serious policy error in the design of SAPs. Cut-backs of this nature inevitably have adverse consequences for social welfare and these in turn impinge on the economic productivity of human resources.

Unless the downward trends in social spending are reversed, the neglect of these sectors will negate the efforts under way to stimulate supply-side improvements in the economy. It will be impossible to achieve significant increases in labour productivity unless the health status and educational attainments of the current and future workforce improve.[42] Enhancing literacy and numeracy levels among the rural population, for example, is likely to facilitate the adoption of modern inputs in agriculture. Allocating a much greater share of available resources to public education and health care should become a major priority for LDCs and should be combined with changes in the intrasectoral allocation of expenditures. Within expanded social sector budgets, priority should be focused on projects and programmes that are the most cost effective and that yield the greatest benefits to the poorest sections of society. These include the provision of primary health-care services in rural areas and primary-school education.[43]

F. SUMMARY AND CONCLUSIONS

The LDCs as a group have not been able to meet most of the economic objectives set out at the Paris Conference. With only a few exceptions, there is little sign of a revival of LDCs economies and, instead of improvement, many indicators of economic performance registered a deterioration in the first three or four years of the 1990s. Of particular concern is the decline in growth rates of output to levels which, in more than half the LDCs, were insufficient to prevent a fall in real per capita incomes. By implication, living standards are likely to have been further eroded from the already low levels prevailing at the end of the 1980s. There has been only limited success in reducing the substantial macroeconomic imbalances and there is little evidence to indicate that much progress has been made in alleviating many of the deep-rooted structural deficiencies that impede growth and development in these countries, such as the lack of export diversification.

The Programme of Action attached considerable importance to the need to ameliorate social conditions, and, in particular, to reduce population growth rates, improve the education, training and health standards in LDCs. Although Governments in many LDCs have given greater priority to these objectives in recent years and have adopted a variety of policies and programmes to meet them, progress in these areas has been mixed.

The recent performance of a number of LDCs has also been affected by factors such as civil strife, political instability and natural disasters which have wrought havoc on their economies, destroying infrastructure, disrupting the delivery of vital public services and driving hundreds of thousands of farmers from their fields and creating fast movements of refugees. Other factors include policy shortcomings, problems associated with the design and implementation of SAPs and adverse external conditions, such as depressed commodity prices, difficulty of access to markets, heavy debt burden and lower than expected aid flows.

Despite the difficulties associated with adjustment reform, the need for policy reform, is not disputed in most of these countries, as was recognized in the Programme of Action. But LDCs have been expected to accomplish too much, too soon - and with too few resources. As such, it is not surprising that only limited benefits have accrued from the reform process. Reforms that aim to stimulate structural changes in production and expenditure patterns require time and adequate financing to achieve their intended results. The underfunding of SAPs by the international community has impeded reform efforts in LDCs and has also imposed excessive levels of austerity on some of the poorest people in the world.

The policy composition of SAPs has also reflected an overemphasis on pricing reforms such as exchange devaluation and liberalization, the efficacy of which is constrained by the severe structural weaknesses and low levels of human resource development that characterize LDCs. While the private sector should be given every encouragement to take advantage of liberalized markets, many crucial public goods and services can be provided only by the public sector. The need to strengthen public intervention in a number of crucial areas, such as agricultural research and extension services, has been neglected in the design of SAPs. Furthermore, in a minority of LDCs, the state's capacity to provide the minimum requisite of a modern economy has been eroded. Thus, much greater emphasis may have to be given to the rebuilding and strengthening of state capacities to perform essential functions if a market-oriented development strategy is to succeed. If policy reforms are to generate structural transformation, the important complementarities between public- and private-sector activities need to be recognized and incorporated into the design of SAPs.

There is a strong case for improving the policy content of SAPs in the areas of agricultural and manufacturing development, export diversification, investment and human capital formation. If resources are to be directed towards attaining these objectives, macroeconomic policies will almost inevitably have to accommodate a more expansionary stance: i.e. given that there are few areas of expenditure from which resources could be drawn, overall expenditure will have to increase. This will only be possible if the international community is prepared to support adjustment programmes with more financial assistance than before.

In advocating a change of emphasis in structural adjustment policies, the strengths of existing SAPs should be recognized and consolidated. First, maintaining macroeconomic stability is crucial if the adjustment programme is to retain credibility among economic actors. Second, it is important to establish and maintain realistic real exchange rates; these are essential (although not necessarily sufficient on their own) to the competitiveness of export production. Third, the efforts made so far to improve the efficiency of public expenditure and to broaden the Government's revenue base need to be consolidated and extended to enable the public sector to maximize its own contribution to development in countries where resources for both public and private sectors are scarce. Most important, however, is the need to maintain consistency in policy implementation. The attainment and sustainability of policy consistency by LDCs has a vital counterpart in the provision of adequate external support. The issues relating to international support are taken up in chapters V and VI.

NOTES

[1]   The Programme of Action for the Least Developed Countries for the 1990s, adopted by the Second United Nations Conference on the Least Developed Countries, held in Paris from 3 to 14 September 1990 (A/CONF.147/Misc.9/Add.1 and Corr.1.

[2]   A detailed assessment of performance in sectors of key importance to LDCs, notably agriculture, manufacturing and transport and related infrastructure, is given in chapters II, III and IV, respectively.

[3]   Tuvalu is excluded from these figures because of unavailability of data.

[4]   UNCTAD, *Handbook of International Trade and Development Statistics, 1993*, table 4.5, pp.241-244. The number of products exported includes only those which exceeded $50,000 in 1980 or $100,000 in 1991, or are more than 0.3 per cent of the country's exports.

[5]   See the articles by Kirkpatrick and Weiss on African LDCs, and by Madhur on Asian LDCs in the forthcoming UNCTAD publication, *Trade Diversification in the Least Developed Countries*, UNCTAD, New York and Geneva, 1994.

[6]   Jorg Mayer "Diversification Experience in Least Developed Countries", UNCTAD Commodities Division, 1993 (mimeo).

[7]   This issue is addressed in more detail in section E on structural adjustment programmes.

[8]   This may partly be explained by two factors. First, several types of investment projects, especially the infrastructural projects which often constitute a large share of the total investment in LDCs, are characterized by economies of scale and indivisibilities and therefore tend to be large scale. Projects such as these are likely to account for a relatively high proportion of total expenditures in small economies. Second, a large proportion of investment expenditures in LDCs is financed by external capital and aid. Many of the smaller LDCs receive a higher volume of external finance as a percentage of GDP than do the larger countries.

[9]   Colin Kirkpatrick and John Weiss, "Trade Diversification in African Least Developed Countries: Efforts, Results and Constraints", UNCTAD, 1994 (mimeo).

[10]   In assessing trends in inflation among a multicountry sample, such as the LDC group of countries, the median is a more appropriate indicator than the mean because the mean is sensitive to extremely high levels of inflation in one or two countries.

[11]   *The Least Developed Countries, 1992 Report*, p.16.

[12]   In 1990, 44 per cent of the LDC population was estimated to be under the age of 15; *ibid.*, p.15.

[13]   United Nations Department of Economic and Social Development, *Report on the World Social Situation 1993*, p.3.

[14]   *Ibid.*, pp.4-6.

[15]   UNICEF, *State of the World's Children, 1994*, p.30.

[16]   *The Least Developed Countries, 1992 Report*, pp.16-20.

[17]   UNICEF, *op.cit*, pp.7 and 15.

[18]   *The Least Developed Countries, 1993-1994 Report*, pp.146-150.

[19]   According to the *Report on the World Social Situation, 1993*, p.38, public sector health initiatives have played a major role in reducing infant mortality in Chile, China, Costa Rica, Cuba, Malaysia, Mauritius, Panama and Sri Lanka, which all have infant mortality rates below those of other developing countries with similar income levels.

[20]   For example, see: Robert Cassen, "Structural Adjustment in Sub-Saharan Africa", in Willem Van Der Geest (ed.), *Negotiating Structural Adjustment in Africa*, James Curry, London, 1994.

[21]   Ibrahim A. Elbadawi, Dhaneshwar Ghuru and Gilbert Uwujaren, "World Bank Adjustment Lending and Economic Performance in Sub-Saharan Africa in the 1980s", World Bank Working Papers WPS 1000, Washington, D.C., 1992, provides a review of the competing structuralist and neoclassical explanations of the economic crisis in SSA and a synthesis of the two views.

[22]   LDCs that have not implemented SAL/SECAL and/or SAF/ESAF supported SAPs have not done so for a variety of reasons. The economies of countries such as Botswana, Cape Verde, the Maldives and some of the Pacific island LDCs have been strong enough, especially in regard to external performance, not to require official adjustment support from the IMF or the World Bank. Several other LDCs, including Afghanistan and Liberia, may have been unable to implement SAPs (and access adjustment loans) because of the severity of the domestic political instability afflicting these countries.

[23]   *The Least Developed Countries, 1994-1994 Report*, Part One, chap.II. Also, The World Bank, *Adjustment in Africa: Reforms, Results and the Road Ahead* (New York, Oxford University Press for The World Bank, 1994).

[24]   The CFA franc, which had been maintained at a fixed rate against the French franc, was devalued by 50 per cent in January 1994.

[25]   The World Bank, *Adjustment in Africa, op.cit.*

[26]   UNCTAD, *Trade and Development Report, 1993*, pp.99-102.

27 "African LDCs' experiences with structural adjustment", The World Bank, 1994, annex table 20 (mimeo).

28 The World Bank, *Adjustment in Africa, op.cit*, p.258.

29 UNCTAD, *Trade and Development Report, 1993*, UNCTAD, pp.102-104.

30 The statistics refer to 16 African LDCs that have contracted adjustment loans and are taken from G.K. Helleiner, "Trade, Aid and Relative Price Changes in Sub-Saharan Africa in the 1980s", mimeo, Dept. of Economics, University of Toronto, p.3.

31 For example, see: Robert Cassen, "Structural Adjustment in Sub-Saharan Africa", in Willem Van Der Geest (ed.), *Negotiating Structural Adjustment in Africa*, James Curry, London, 1994; and G.K. Helleiner "Structural Adjustment and Long-Term Development in Sub-Saharan Africa", paper presented at the workshop on Alternative Development Strategies in Africa, 11-13 December 1989, Queen Elizabeth House, Oxford.

32 Stanley Please, "From Structural Adjustment to Structural Transformation", in Willem Van Der Geest (ed.), *Negotiating Structural Adjustment in Africa*, James Curry, London, 1994.

33 UNCTAD, *Trade and Development Report, 1993*, pp.98-102.

34 G.K. Helleiner "Structural Adjustment and Long-Term Development in Sub-Saharan Africa", paper presented to the workshop on Alternative Development Strategies in Africa, 11-13 December 1989, Queen Elizabeth House, Oxford.

35 See the forthcoming UNCTAD publication, *Trade Diversification in Least Developed Countries*.

36 For example, garments and other light manufactured products have been exported from Chad and Lesotho, tuna fish products from Cape Verde and the Gambia and Botswana have developed successful tourist industries.

37 The World Bank, *Adjustment in Africa, op.cit.* pp.250-251.

38 *Ibid*, pp. 250-251.

39 Ibrahim A. Elbadawi, Dhaneshwar Ghuru and Gilbert Uwujaren, "World Bank Adjustment Lending and Economic Performance in Sub-Saharan Africa in the 1980s", World Bank Working Papers WPS 1000, Washington, D.C.

40 *The Least Developed Countries, 1993-1994 Report*, Part Two, chap.I, pp.101-102.

41 The World Bank, *Adjustment in Africa, op.cit.*, p.173.

42 The economic benefits arising from education and health expenditures were examined in *The Least Developed Countries, 1993-1994 Report*, Part Two.

43 Giovanni Cornia and Frances Stewart, "The Fiscal System, Adjustment and the Poor", UNICEF International Child Development Centre Innocenti Occasional Papers, No.11.

II. Agriculture in LDCs

A. Introduction

Agriculture is the main productive sector in LDCs and is central to their economic development. It supplies, on average, about 40 per cent of their GDP, one third of export earnings and employment for 70 per cent of the labour force. But far from serving as an engine of growth and transformation, the performance of the sector has been a source of considerable macroeconomic disequilibrium. In over two thirds of these countries, there have been decades of decline in per capita production, and this decline has continued into the early 1990s with little prospect of a decisive reversal; the goal to achieve food self-sufficiency is becoming increasingly more remote while food dependency on exports is on the rise.

Against this background, sections B and C review LDCs' agricultural performance, as well as commodity prices and export trends. The implications of production performance for food security are assessed and measures for expanding production are discussed. Section D deals with recent agricultural policy reforms and assesses the progress made in reforming incentives for producers and in marketing structures. The final section (E) draws together some broad strategies for the transformation and revival of the sector's growth.

B. Overview of Agricultural Performance

As the main productive sector in LDCs, agriculture will face enormous challenges over the next several decades, in particular in meeting the food demands of a fast-growing population. This will not be an easy task given that its performance has declined for nearly a quarter of a century. Since the 1970s, agricultural output has experienced declining growth rates, a trend that has persisted through the 1980s and early 1990s (table 13). During the period 1980-1989, real agricultural value added for LDCs as a group grew by no more than 1.5 per cent per annum. This performance not only compares unfavourably with the previous decade's record (1.8 per cent per annum), but is also substantially below the annual 2.7 per cent agricultural growth achieved by developing countries in the same period. Agricultural growth has, moreover, fallen increasingly short of population growth (2.7 per cent per annum) particularly since the early 1990s; the outcome has been one of accelerated falls in per capita agricultural and food output with an increasing number of countries participating in the decline (table 14). The worsening production trends have been accompanied by falls in food self-sufficiency, rising food imports, and the contraction of export growth and world market shares of major agricultural exports.

This poor production performance has been matched by an equally disappointing export performance which has deteriorated in the last decade, as indicated in table 13. The share of LDCs' agricultural exports in world exports has consequently fallen sharply, with most commodity exports, except copra and jute, participating in the decline (table 15).

The impact on the balance of payments of the loss of world market shares has been magnified by declines in the international prices of agricultural commodities that are of export interest to LDCs. After rising by about 60 index points over the 10 years to 1980, the unit price of LDCs' agricultural exports fell by 30 index points between 1980 and 1993 (table 16). Prices of most

Table 13: Key indicators of agricultural performance growth rates
(Annual average)

	1970-1980	*1980-1989*	*1989-1993*
Total agricultural production[a]	1.8	1.5	1.5
Per capita agricultural production[a]	-0.7	-0.7	-1.4
Per capita food production[a]	-0.5	-0.8	-1.3
Agricultural exports[b,c]	9.1	-0.5	-3.0[d]
Net food imports[b]	7.4	11.6	22.5[d]

Source: Calculations based on UNCTAD database.
a   In constant terms.
b   In current terms.
c   Including fishery and forestry products.
d   1989-1992.

major agricultural commodities exported by LDCs were part of the general decline; the sharpest drop in prices was for coffee and cocoa, which collectively accounted for 10 per cent or more of the export earnings of 14 countries. Between 1970 and 1993, the net barter terms of trade of agricultural exports (i.e. the ratio of the export unit value index to the import value index), declined by about 56 per cent, while the income terms of trade lost about 63 per cent of its value.

Overall, the value of agricultural export earnings from crops, livestock and fisheries fell by 0.5 per cent annually between 1980 and 1989 and by a sharper 3 per cent in the three-year period to 1992. The broad average, however, conceals uneven country performances. More than two fifths of the 47 LDC countries, among them relatively large exporters such as Bangladesh, Ethiopia and Uganda, experienced negative export growth. Of the large exporters, only Myanmar achieved positive growth. In contrast, a number of smaller agricultural exporters (i.e. Comoros, Gambia, Guinea, Guinea-Bissau, Kiribati, Lao People's Democratic Republic, Maldives, Solomon Islands and Zambia) achieved buoyant growth in their agricultural exports.

To offset the impact of long-term structural declines in market prospects for traditional exports, a number of LDCs has embarked on trade policy reforms, an important component of which has been to undertake vertical and horizontal diversification. Equatorial Guinea, for example, reduced its share of commodity ex-

ports, mainly cocoa, from 96 per cent in 1979-1981 to 70 per cent in 1988-1990, while raising its share of its semi-processed exports, mainly timber, from virtually zero to 8 per cent during the same period. Benin has diversified from cocoa beans to cotton lint; Madagascar from coffee beans to shellfish and sugar;[1] Sierra Leone and Mozambique are emphasizing the development of fisheries, while others (e.g. Ethiopia, Lesotho, Malawi, United Republic of Tanzania and Uganda) are targeting their efforts, *inter alia*, on increasing production of high value-added, income-elastic exports of horticultural products.

For the majority of LDCs, the general trend has been one of either unchanging or increased agricultural commodity dependence. The share of three main agricultural commodities (coffee, cotton, tea) in LDCs' total agricultural exports, which was around 40 per cent in 1970, remained virtually unchanged (39 per cent) by 1993.[2] Dependence on these three commodities, in fact, increased to about 47 per cent in the mid- and late 1980s. Among the impediments to diversification are the constraints on skills and investment resources and the difficulties of penetrating new export markets. Potential for diversification into non-traditional, highly perishable products, such as fruits and vegetables, is constrained in many countries by logistical factors, such as packaging, transport and storage and handling costs (box 3). Restraints on public expenditure in many LDCs have also confined investments to the rehabilitation of facilities for traditional commodities which is less resource intensive than the creation of new facilities for

Table 14: Annual growth rates of per capita agricultural and food production: 1980-1989, 1989-1993

(Percentage)

	Per capita agricultural production		Per capita food production	
	1980-1989	*1989-1993*	*1980-1989*	*1989-1993*
Afghanistan	-2.1	-5.2	-2.1	-5.6
Bangladesh	-	-1.3	-	-1.4
Benin	2.9	-0.2	2.5	-0.5
Bhutan	-2.2	1.8	-2.3	1.8
Botswana	-2.5	-6.9	-2.5	-6.9
Burkina Faso	3.7	2.7	3.5	2.9
Burundi	-	-0.3	-	0.5
Cambodia	2.7	-1.9	2.4	-2.2
Cape Verde	8.1	-6.7	8.1	-6.6
Central African Republic	-0.5	-1.2	-0.5	-0.8
Chad	0.7	0.6	0.5	1.5
Comoros	-1.3	-1.9	-1.3	-1.9
Ethiopia	-1.8	-1.8	-1.7	-1.9
Gambia	-1.5	-6.4	-1.5	-7.7
Guinea	-0.7	-1.7	-0.8	-1.6
Guinea-Bissau	0.6	-0.6	0.6	-0.6
Haiti	-0.7	-10.7	-0.5	-10.9
Lao People's Democratic Republic	0.4	-1.8	0.4	-1.9
Lesotho	-1.7	-9.6	-1.5	-10.1
Liberia	-1.1	-14.3	-0.7	-10.0
Madagascar	-1.4	-1.9	-1.4	-1.7
Malawi	-2.9	-2.6	-3.5	-3.1
Maldives	-0.9	-3.1	-0.9	-3.1
Mali	-0.3	-0.8	-0.6	-1.2
Mauritania	-0.4	-4.7	-0.4	-4.7
Mozambique	-0.9	-6.5	-0.8	-6.1
Myanmar	0.5	1.9	0.6	2.0
Nepal	1.8	-2.7	2.0	-2.6
Niger	-3.1	2.2	-3.1	2.2
Rwanda	-2.0	-3.2	-2.5	-3.2
Samoa	-0.8	-4.8	-0.8	-5.0
Sao Tome and Principe	-3.1	-4.5	-3.1	-4.5
Sierra Leone	0.4	-4.3	-0.2	-4.3
Solomon Islands	-1.7	-1.7	-1.7	-1.7
Somalia	-0.4	-19.6	-0.4	-19.6
Sudan	-2.7	7.7	-2.8	9.0
Togo	0.5	-1.0	-	-1.7
Uganda	-0.5	-0.3	-0.5	-0.3
United Republic of Tanzania	-0.9	-3.6	-0.8	-3.7
Vanuatu	-1.4	1.7	-1.4	1.7
Yemen	-1.4	-3.3	-1.4	-3.4
Zaire	-0.6	-1.8	-0.6	-1.7
Zambia	0.4	-2.5	0.3	-2.6
All LDCs	-0.7	-1.4	-0.8	-1.3

Source: UNCTAD secretariat calculations, based on data from FAO.

Table 15: LDCs' share in world agricultural exports value

	1970	1980	1989	1993
Agricultural exports[a]	4.2	2.1	1.5	1.0
Coffee	13.7	11.7	12.4	8.2
Cocoa	4.5	5.1	2.3	1.8
Copra	14.7	24.1	25.4	31.8
Jute	75.3	83.6	68.0	80.0
Rice	10.0	3.9	0.8	0.8
Cotton	14.4	7.4	9.3	10.9
Tea	14.4	6.9	5.0	5.7

Source: UNCTAD secretariat calculations, based on FAO, Agrostat database.

a   Excludes forestry and fishery products.

Table 16: Volume and terms of agricultural trade
(1979-1981 = 100)

	1970	1980	1993
Export volume index	117.9	103.9	100.0
Export unit value index	38.7	99.0	69.7
Barter terms of trade	119.0	93.4	52.5

Source: UNCTAD secretariat calculations, based on FAO, Agrostat database.

non-traditional exports. This poses a particular problem for diversification when physical and other supporting infrastructures have been geared to serve traditional commodities. For example, successful diversification into highly perishable horticultural products places a premium on timely and reliable deliveries to export markets. The problems are further aggravated by the lack of knowledge for engaging in the complex challenges of penetrating new and highly competitive export markets.

Agriculture's poor performance must be seen in the context of unfavourable international prices, backward technologies and, in many countries, continued exposure to periodic episodes of drought. Agricultural performance has also suffered from the deterioration of agricul-tural support systems, i.e. roads, storage and communications systems, inspection facilities for graded products (e.g. coffee), consequent to lack of investment. This has led to prohibitive costs for transportation and commercialization (box 4).

The Green Revolution technologies, widely adopted in many parts of the Asian developing region, have largely bypassed most LDCs, particularly those in Africa. Two examples serve to illustrate this. The importance of technological innovations cannot be overemphasized. In Bangladesh, for example, widespread use of high-yielding rice varieties, improved farming and irrigation methods, and more efficient application of fertilizers have contributed to food grain self-sufficiency.[3] Ethiopian cotton had tradi-

---

Box 3: Development of horticulture in the United Republic of Tanzania

The horticulture industry in the United Republic of Tanzania is completely in the hands of the private sector which controls all production and marketing. Like other sectors of the economy, horticulture has suffered from the compression of public expenditures which resulted in a reduction of financing opportunities for maintenance as well as for the repair and development of key infrastructural facilities, such as roads, cold storage at ports and airports and telecommunications. This has seriously hampered the growth of agricultural exports. The lack of post-harvest handling and quality-control assistance, together with insufficient research and development, means that exports of fresh fruits and vegetables are often of poor quality. The situation is made worse by inferior packaging materials which do not meet international requirements. Perhaps the single biggest barrier to exports is the lack of air freight and storage space for exporters at the two main airports, Kilimanjaro and Dar-es-Salaam.

Nevertheless, the horticultural sector has benefited from structural adjustment reforms, particularly successive devaluations which resulted in a strong supply response from the private sector. Export revenues from horticultural products have increased steadily from $410,000 in 1986 to $2.6 million in 1992. Recent reforms in the investment code have, moreover, attracted a number of foreign joint ventures to the horticultural sector.

Box 4: Reforming the tea sector in Uganda

During the 1970s, the tea industry in Uganda lost virtually all its regulatory, infrastructural, technical, managerial and marketing capacity because of political instability. With the return of normalcy in 1986, the sector has been rehabilitated and liberalization policies have been implemented. Tea production reached 11,695 tons in 1993, about 2.5 times the level in 1989, and export earnings over the same period trebled to $9.2 million.

Since the late 1980s, export marketing of tea was liberalized along with foreign exchange regulations; now, plans are to completely privatize the sector by 1998. Despite the sector's improved performance in recent years, it continues to have high production costs as a result of a deficient infrastructure, and also quality problems. Most roads are impassable during the rainy season and the feeder road network needs urgent rehabilitation. There are also shortages of electricity, which require most producers to rely on costly generators, which add to production costs. Credit shortages have undermined the rehabilitation of tea factories established in the 1930s but neglected since 1972. The absence of research since 1978, following the collapse of the East African Research Institute, has resulted in current yields of 900 kilograms of mate tea per hectare - some 70 per cent below the level of the 1960s.

---

tionally been of very fine quality. Exports had reached 8,000 tons in the early 1980s, but ceased in 1985, and in recent years the country has become a net importer of cotton. To revitalize this sector, the Government is emphasizing the improvement of cultivation practices in existing production areas including variety replacement. Because of the long and repetitive use based on the same parent source, the cultivar 1516/70, used since 1974, has degenerated. The authorities are planning to replace it initially with a similar but purer variety to enhance yields. As almost all production is on irrigated land, expansion of rain-fed production could also be helpful. However, improvements could best be obtained by increasing irrigated production areas.

Comparisons with successful regions and countries both, within and outside the LDC group, suggest that a yearly agricultural growth rate of 3.0 to 3.5 per cent is a feasible target for many LDCs. But this will require a high prioritization of agriculture along with the appropriate policy conditions. These include: satisfactory producer prices; high-yielding technologies; more arable land; improved marketing; more effective research and extension; and more investment in infrastructure. In certain cases, environmental concerns would also need to figure explicitly in the formulation of policy priorities (box 5). Many of these issues will be dealt with in the discussions that follow.

Box 5: Solomon Islands - when the traditional farming practices get lost....

There is growing awareness in the Solomon Islands of the importance of environment conservation and protection, brought about in part by the undesirable result of extensive and rapidly expanding logging activities throughout the country. A revival in logging operations began in the early 1960s and picked up momentum during the last 10 years with over 10 species being exploited (compared to one - the Kauri - in the early days). In 1992, some 10,000 hectares of tropical forest were logged -- double the average of the previous five years. At this rate, the commercially exploitable forests of the Solomon Islands will be exhausted by the end of the first decade of the next century. Frequent increases in log prices make more areas commercially viable, seriously affecting the potential for the sustainable management of these resources.

There is a common misconception, however, held both by outsiders and the local authorities, that logging operations alone are having a direct adverse effect on the environment. In fact, local agricultural developments and practices, which are being encouraged individually throughout the country, are among the major factors that encroach on the environment.

Since the introduction of modern agricultural practices, heavy emphasis has been placed on a cash economy; people have discarded their traditional farming practices, which had preserved the environment through careful land allocation closely related to the various soil types. Crops are now growing in unsuitable areas. Arable land once used for village food gardens is being used by coconuts or cocoa plantations; drinking-water for villagers has been fenced-in by cattle projects. Indiscriminate farming has led to the general lowering of water levels in some rivers; there is also evidence that the water table in the soil has been lowered.

The country has not benefited from a coherent agricultural policy although efforts are under way to implement one. Crops are sometimes promoted for local farming, regardless of whether such crops could be successfully adapted to local conditions. Large areas of land, including virgin forests - some of them among the best forest stands in the country - have been wasted through such practices. Furthermore, little research has been undertaken on traditional food crops, which are naturally suited to local climatic conditions, to determine their potential for exports. Recently, nali nuts, which provide high-quality oils, have been found to be very suitable for cakes. They are now an exportable commodity, at a time when most of the trees have been cut down to clear land for cocoa, coconut and cattle farms.

It is unfortunate that discussions on the environment are limited to considerations of virgin forests, probably because logging activities have an immediate and visible impact. Their effect on local communities, however, is less than what is experienced in agricultural development. The destruction caused in this field through environment degradation is felt heavily by rural communities. Lack of understanding of environmental issues, coupled with inappropriate legal instruments, is a contributing factor to this situation. A better appreciation of traditional environment management should be encouraged. The knowledge thus acquired could provide a solid basis for assessing new and present development programmes in relation to the impacts they have, or could have, on other rural communities and their environment.

C. FOOD PRODUCTION AND FOOD SECURITY[4]

Per capita daily dietary energy supplies (DES) for LDCs was 2050 kilocalories in 1988-1992, the same low level as in 1980-1982. This is in sharp contrast to developing countries as a whole where aggregate food supplies increased significantly during the same period. Using the 2300 kilocalories mark as a rough measure of the required level for normal body growth, about 80 per cent of LDCs for which data are available had, on average, inadequate food supplies. Since the available food in a country is rarely distributed equally, these figures indicate that a significant proportion of the population in these countries does not have adequate access to food supplies.

Food production increased in 31 countries, but growth rates in excess of 3 per cent - which is roughly the pace of population growth - occurred in only 15. In addition, annual average rates of growth in food production were lower in the 1980s than in the 1970s in the majority of LDCs. Cereal production increased by 1.5 per cent and roots and tubers by 1.7 per cent during the 1988-1993 period. However, since these aggregate trends were dominated by the production changes of a few major producers, growth rates for the majority of countries were low. Total food imports grew at a compound rate of 2.2 per cent during 1980-1992. In addition, the share of export earnings spent on food imports increased in a number of countries. Large increases, over 5 percentage points per annum, were registered in Ethiopia, the Gambia, Liberia, Mozambique and Rwanda.

To sum up, food supplies continued to be grossly inadequate in LDCs as a whole because of inadequate production and low import capacity with resultant compression of consumption levels.

Instability in domestic cereal production and aggregate food supplies

Cereal production in LDCs varies greatly from year to year. This is the result of drought and has been reflected in the growing number of food emergencies. For the period 1980-1993, the index of instability, measured in terms of the coefficient of variation (CoV) of cereal production for LDCs was around 10 per cent.[5] Shortfalls in production were excessively high in some years. For example, the production shortfall in cereals was over 50 per cent in Liberia during 1990-1992, close to 50 per cent in Sudan in 1987, 1989 and 1990, and over 40 per cent in Botswana in 1985-1987 and 1992. Moreover, production variability in the 1980s increased significantly compared with the 1970s. At the individual country level, many LDCs had a CoV of 20 per cent or more in the 1980-1993 period. In seven countries, notably Angola, the Central African Republic, Chad, Liberia, Somalia, Sudan and Uganda, the CoV increased by over 10 percentage points in the second period. In contrast, a significant drop in variability was noted only in the Gambia and Mauritania.

In view of the large amount of cereals in the diet of LDC populations and their inadequate import capacity, variable cereal production translates into unstable volumes of food supplies, leading in turn to variable consumption patterns. Any shortfall in consumption of more than 5 per cent, in terms of aggregate food supplies, could have serious food and nutritional consequences. A shortfall of this magnitude has been experienced by many LDCs in various years during the 1980s.

Apart from lack of access to sufficient food, the overall nutrition and health situation remains poor as a result of both food and non-food factors. An increased household food supply is important but does not in itself solve the problem of poor nutritional status. Equally necessary prerequisites are improved health services, better hygiene and education which contribute to improved care. For example, a study based on sample data from Rwanda[6] notes that protection from infection by parasitic worms could reduce stunting by the same degree as could doubling household calorie consumption from 1500 to 3000 kilocalories per adult-equivalent, while a clean latrine would have twice this impact.

Recurrent food emergencies

LDCs, especially in Africa, are prone to recurrent food emergencies, caused by both man-made and natural factors, which not only affect the vulnerability of individuals, households and nations, but render the entire socio-economic infrastructure more fragile and less productive over time. Although the economic and social losses as a result of such hardships cannot be precisely quantified, there is no doubt that they take an extremely large toll on development.

By and large, experience has shown that it is relatively easier to fend off potential food emergencies resulting from natural causes. For example, countries in Southern Africa experienced an unprecedented decline in staple food production during their 1991/92 growing seasons, largely on account of drought, which put at least 18 million lives at risk. Mechanisms to deal with the large-scale relief operations that were necessary to alleviate hunger did not exist. Yet the capacity of "the world food security system" to act in a timely and effective manner during all phases of the response process was remarkable. Human suffering was kept to a minimum and losses of production capacity and capital, so essential for a speedy recovery, were minimized.

A very disquieting trend, however, has been the growing number of man-made food emergencies that have led to a large number of food-insecure households. Wars and related factors have become the single most serious cause of food insecurity for LDCs in Africa, often producing large urban concentrations of displaced persons. For example, in the Intergovernmental Authority on Drought and Development (IGADD) region, some 45 million people (nearly half the population) were estimated to be subject to food insecurity in 1990. Of these, some 45 per cent had been affected by war and were classified as refugees. In general, food aid and other resources have been used as needs dictated. However, the international community is often faced with tragedies of proportions that far outstrip the means available to deal with them.

Opportunities for increasing food production

According to FAO estimates, increased crop yield will be the major contribution to the rise in crop production in LDCs during the next two decades. Other contributions will be additional arable land and crop intensity. These factors place considerable demands on all major sources of production: area expansion, increased yield and technology adoption, and an intensification of production, which will have implications, *inter alia*, for the management of both irrigation and soil fertility.

How to increase the use of fertilizers is a major policy issue, particularly since its use has remained virtually unchanged since 1985, after a slow-down in growth in the early 1980s. The adoption of improved crop-management practices, which can help solve this problem to some extent, has so far been slow. Approaches such as integrated plant nutrition systems (IPNS), which integrate and optimize the effects of organic manure, and increased biological fixation are being advocated, but they have not been tested on farms. If adopted, they may eventually make some contribution, but a significant turn around in food production is not likely unless chemical fertilizers are made accessible, both physically and economically, to the large number of small-holders.

Partly as a result of their colonial heritage, agricultural strategies, as well as resources for agricultural research, have been biased in favour of export crops at the expense of indigenous food crops. Efforts to reverse these strategies have been painfully slow. At the same time, most African staples (millet, sorghum, cassava, yams, cowpeas, bananas and plantains, and traditional vegetables) have received little attention from advanced research institutions elsewhere. As a result, African LDCs have lagged behind most other developing regions in generating improved varieties and technologies adapted to local conditions. Increasing research efforts in this direction will be one of the major challenges of the future.

Stabilizing food production and consumption

As discussed above, most LDCs have large fluctuations in output, both seasonally and from year to year, because of weather-induced variability and other factors. The implications for food production are particularly serious for countries that already devote a large share of foreign exchange to food imports. At the national level, apart from influencing food-import capacity in an unpredictable manner, weather-induced variability complicates planning in a number of areas, such as investments in infrastructure for food imports and their distribu-

tion, and necessitates large expenditures for stockholding and consumer price subsidies. Price instability is a particularly serious problem for the poor in view of their low purchasing power.

Reducing variability in production is both a long- and short-term concern. For the long-term, a number of measures could be pursued. First, the large variability in cereal production can be addressed by developing varieties of drought-resistant crop. Current research efforts in this area, as noted above, are far from adequate. Second, assured access to irrigation provides a sound buffer against weather-induced variability. There is considerable unexploited potential in many LDCs in terms of water-conservation measures and the development of small-scale, farmer-managed irrigation schemes. Third, indigenous drought-resistant crops, such as sorghum, millet and cassava, have always been an effective cushion against shortfalls in other crops. The development of such indigenous crops needs to be given higher priority: several countries in Southern Africa initiated programmes with this objective following the 1991/92 drought.

The short-term response to production instability is to vary the level of imports and/or to draw upon domestic stocks. Over the recent past, a majority of countries has implemented policies aimed at increasing the efficiency of parastatals and reducing Government outlays towards stockholding and consumer subsidies, as part of economic restructuring (see discussions in section D). The costs and benefits of building and utilizing food reserves or relying on the world market for food supplies need to be carefully weighed.

Overall, a number of lessons can be drawn from these experiences. First, stabilization schemes should be administratively simple and transparent. Second, other mechanisms, such as crop insurance schemes and forward and future markets could be explored before implementing fully fledged supply stabilization schemes. Third, Governments should carefully weigh the costs of schemes that require the public sector to perform such activities as procuring, storing and distributing stocks. They should determine whether these functions could be more efficiently contracted out to the private sector. Fourth, sharing crop production risks among neighbouring countries through regional stockholding schemes provide cost-effective protection against production variability.

D. POLICY REFORMS IN THE AGRICULTURAL SECTOR

Until the early 1980s, many LDC Governments intervened extensively in all spheres of agricultural activity through controls on production, marketing and agricultural pricing by parastatals. Price interventions were exercised directly through producer price fixing and taxing agricultural inputs and exports and were also implicit in trade protection and exchange-rate policies. Inefficient price intervention in many countries served to discriminate against agriculture. Producer prices paid to farmers were depressed by direct taxes and marketing-board costs. Agriculture was also indirectly taxed through overvalued exchange rates and the protection of industry which turned the domestic terms of trade in favour of manufacturing at the expense of agriculture. Such interventions reduced farm prices in some LDCs by at least 30 per cent[7] while Government support of agriculture through its investment programme, far from compensating for this taxation, was biased against agriculture and the smallholder sector. In extreme cases (e.g. Zambia), direct and indirect taxation of agriculture was estimated to have accounted for more than 50 per cent of the value of the sector's output. Prohibitive taxation of agriculture, particularly of exportables, resulted in a shift by producers away from export crops, which, combined with the decline in world commodity prices, accelerated the collapse of export earnings and import capacity. Price distortions were exacerbated in many African LDCs by inefficient interventions and, in some cases, the malpractices of state-marketing boards. The accumulation of policy biases against agriculture not only reduced the overall growth in agricultural production and exports, but also encouraged the shift from commercial to subsistence farming while at the same time increasing parallel market activity.

Agricultural reforms have been high on the priority agenda for LDCs given the size of the sector and its implications for Government revenues, food, income and employment. In general, the reforms in the agricultural sector, which have usually been carried out in the context of multilaterally supported structural adjustment programmes, have sought to reduce the Government's role in production, pricing and marketing of agricultural inputs and outputs and to remove historical price and non-price disincentives to agriculture in ways that promote a more efficient use of resources. Attempts to achieve this general objective have relied on a variety of policy instruments, including agricultural input and output pricing and trade and institutional reforms. The discussion in the following sections concentrates on two aspects of agricultural reforms: producer price incentives and decontrol of marketing.

Reform of producer price incentives[8]

Reform of producer incentives to increase farm returns has encompassed a number of different measures including: liberalizing or raising the share of administered prices in border prices; lowering export taxes; passing on to exporters a greater share of the local currency proceeds which result from currency depreciation; reducing marketing costs or decontrolling marketing completely.

Restoring producer incentives has posed a major challenge for many LDC Governments, since the export prices of many commodities have fallen at a time when Governments are attempting to align domestic producer prices closer to their export parities. However, the results of these attempts are so far mixed. Available data on 18 African LDCs show that while 8 countries[9] managed to increase real producer prices of agricultural exports between 1981-1983 and 1989-1991, for the remaining countries, real producer prices declined, exceeding 20 per cent or more in 6 countries and in Guinea-Bissau, Sierra Leone and Zambia exceeding 40 per cent.[10]

With regard to changes in implicit and explicit taxation of the agricultural sector, available data[11] indicate that 11[12] out of 18 LDCs succeeded in reducing the overall tax burden on their agricultural sectors during the 1980s. For the rest, the overall tax burden on agriculture actually rose and was particularly significant in Guinea-Bissau and Zambia where it exceeded 50 per cent. Where implicit taxation rose as a result of currency overvaluation, attempts were made by most countries to offset the loss of export competitiveness through a reduction in explicit taxation, i.e. export taxes, subsidization of producer prices and/or reduction in the profit margins of marketing boards.

Agricultural price reforms involve not only raising prices for agricultural output, but also simultaneously entail the removal of producer support, such as subsidies for fertilizers and credit. This raises production costs and thus has an offsetting effect on incentives. An issue that has sparked some controversy concerns the elimination of fertilizer subsidies. The subsidization of fertilizers is usually justified on the grounds of their prohibitive costs due to limited procurement quantities and high shipping, handling and domestic transportation charges that are associated with inefficient marketing and deficient infrastructure. Supporters of subsidies argue that, by lowering costs and encouraging use, subsidies stimulate agricultural innovation and their elimination would undermine the use and production of fertilizer. Those who oppose subsidies claim that subsidized fertilizers tend to benefit large farms at the expense of smaller ones; they argue, moreover, that funds are better spent on improving agricultural support systems including research and dissemination of more fertilizer-responsive crop technologies.

Notwithstanding the ongoing debate, 11 out of 17 LDCs[13] known to have greatly intervened in the marketing and pricing of fertilizers had, by late 1992, completely eliminated fertilizer subsidies, in addition to liberalizing their distribution systems. Three countries (Sierra Leone, Uganda, United Republic of Tanzania) liberalized fertilizer marketing but still retained some subsidies or enforced price controls; other LDCs, such as Benin and the Central African Republic, freed prices but the state retained control over its distribution. But sustaining such reforms has not always been easy when other production costs have been rising as well. Malawi, for example, was obliged to reverse earlier policies and reinstate subsidies in the late 1980s to cushion the impact on production costs of increases in transport charges and the costs of inputs from currency devaluation. While there is insufficient evidence as yet to draw firm conclusions, anecdotal evidence[14] suggests that higher prices may not have constrained fertilizer use. Fertilizer sales to smallholders in Malawi more than doubled from 49,000 tons to 107,000 tons between 1980 and 1991 in spite of substantial increases in their official prices and the stagnation of producer prices for smallholders. Similarly, in the United Republic of Tanzania the reduction in fertilizer subsidies by 50 per cent between 1989 and 1993 does not appear to have affected fertilizer use in the Southern Highlands, a major recipient of subsidized fertilizers.

In any event, the general effect of the removal of subsidies on agricultural inputs is to turn the terms of trade against farmers. When this coincides with high interest rates and overall restraints on credit, the potential for significant reductions in input use cannot be dismissed. Hence the structural adjustment objective of correcting relative prices could be in conflict with the goal of increasing agricultural output and exports. In such circumstances, the removal of subsidies may have to be phased with targeted credit programmes to maintain input use. Credit subsidies are often discouraged in adjustment programmes and when this is combined with monetary restraint and high interest rates, their effect can be quite debilitating in agriculture. In the short run, higher interest rates can offset the effect of higher producer prices. Over the longer term, however, higher real interest rates can stimulate the mobilization of national and rural savings and generate new sources of credit for farmers. Financial liberalization may, however, facilitate the growth of private trading and marketing to the extent that it encourages equal access to credit by both the public and private sectors. Historically, preferential access to subsidized credit by state entities placed these entities at an unfair advantage *vis-à-vis* private traders, who not only had difficulties accessing credit but who were also often obliged to pay higher interest rates. To the extent that credit constraints limited the scale and quality of marketing services provided by the private agents, the convergence (as a result of liberalization) of the terms of credit access for the public and private sectors could stimulate the growth of private marketing. In practice, however, the transfer of preferential credit away from the politically powerful may not be easy to sustain.

Since price reforms affect both the pricing of agricultural inputs as well as outputs, whether incentives actually accrue to producers, will depend on their net return per unit of output. Even assuming that the net return to farmers is positive, it is now widely acknowledged that while the responsiveness of the production of individual agricultural commodities to price incentives may be high, in the short and medium term it is likely to be low for agricultural output as a whole, due to aggregate resource constraints (such as land, labour, infrastructure). The supply response to price signals will, moreover, tend to be muted in LDCs where there is a predominance of subsistence farming by producers who have little or no contact with markets. The exposure of agriculture to repeated shocks, such as climatic hazards, moreover, makes farmers more risk averse and hence more prone to emphasize subsistence and survival objectives. This in turn may discourage a response in the short run to changes in market signals.

In the long run, price incentives, however important, cannot, on their own, increase supply elasticities without complementary "non-price" measures, particularly in countries with structural barriers in research capacity, extension services, marketing, transport, storage, etc. It has been estimated that the aggregate supply response to prices in agriculture will only become significant in 10 to 20 years when public investments in infrastructure, technology and education are made.[15] With the benefit of experience, the approach to policy reform has changed over the years and much more emphasis is now being given to assist countries to improve agricultural infrastructure and to deal with problems of environmental and resource degradation. Supplying public goods is one important area where Government intervention can help with structural change. Pricing issues are just as important in the provision of public goods (e.g. electricity, irrigation, etc.). Unless "fair" or "cost recovery" charges are applied to the use of such resources (e.g. water), their burden on public budgets will undermine the capacity for maintenance and rehabilitation and encourage the wasteful use of the resources.

Success in raising price incentives has sometimes proved to be self-defeating due to the low price elasticities of demand of many commodities of export interest to LDCs. Aggressive exchange-rate policies and outward-oriented trade strategies in the developing countries during the 1980s have had an adverse impact on world prices of traditional and even non-traditional raw materials.[16] For demand inelastic commodities, export prices fall when the volume of aggregate supply increases. Consequently, the increase in export revenues is usually less than commensurate with export volumes, in which case it may not be possible to recover the costs of the additional output. This may be the case for cocoa and coffee, two agricultural exports on which many LDCs are heavily dependent.

Marketing reforms[17]

The agricultural marketing systems in LDCs, particularly those in Africa, have historically been controlled by state entities that were simultaneously agents of economic development and conduits of the Government's welfare and social policies. Characteristically, marketing parastatals served wide-ranging commercial and non-commercial objectives beyond those of marketing. Their mandate often included the stabilization of producer and consumer prices, managing related buffer-stock operations (for food security), internal distribution of food supplies and provision of agricultural inputs and credits to farmers. Very often the parastatals were endowed with social functions that were in direct conflict with commercial objectives: for example, state entities were sometimes required to finance and/or subsidize buffer-stock operations out of their own resources, an operation that would undermine the finances of even the best-run corporation.

Marketing parastatals, not unsurprisingly, tended to perform poorly; far from achieving their prescribed objectives, they proved to be a key constraint on agricultural growth in many countries. Typical weaknesses included late payments to farmers, inadequate and untimely supplies of production inputs, poor quality control and unreliable access to marketing facilities. Parastatals even managed in some countries to destabilize producer prices and incomes (see section D). High operating costs, incompetence and political favouritism have commonly figured among the causes of the operational inefficiencies of marketing boards.[18] The large financial losses generated by the parastatal sector in many countries has been a major source of the public deficit. Reform and the closure of marketing boards have consequently usually been at the centre of stabilization measures aimed at reducing the fiscal deficit.

Since the early 1980s, measures to increase the efficiency of agricultural marketing has featured prominently in LDC policy reforms. The main features of these reforms have involved the dismantling and/or demonopolization of marketing boards to allow private traders to compete and managerial and operational reforms of marketing boards to cut costs. Most LDCs have embarked on at least partial liberalization of marketing of both export and food crops. Of 13 LDCs[19] that have intervened strongly in the marketing of food staples prior to the institution of reforms, all but two countries - Malawi and Zambia (both producing maize) - had by 1992 confined their intervention to the operation of food security stocks. In other LDCs where intervention was initially much less extensive or non-existent (e.g. Burundi, Chad, Mauritania, Sierra Leone), state control of the marketed surplus was in any case marginalized because of widespread diversion of trade into unofficial channels in response to more lucrative prices. In such cases, marketing reforms served no more than to formally endorse unofficial private trading. Countries that have in recent years abolished or demonopolized their marketing boards include Burundi (coffee), the Central African Republic (coffee), Guinea-Bissau (palm kernels and non-traditional products), the Lao People's Democratic Republic (rice exports), Madagascar (all export crops), Myanmar (rice exports), Niger (groundnuts and cowpeas), Uganda (cotton, tobacco, tea and coffee) and the United Republic of Tanzania (cashew nuts).

Despite the trend towards liberalization, marketing parastatals are likely to continue to play an important, albeit reduced, role in many LDC economies. Areas most likely to require continuing Government involvement include imports of food aid and closely related commercial imports of food, the management of buffer stocks for food security interventions, and price stabilization through acting as buyer and seller of last resort. When private traders are either unwilling or unable to maintain sufficient reserve stocks, the state is likely to continue to intervene in the management of strategic food crops in the interest of assuring access of supplies to vulnerable groups most at risk in times of food shortages. Withdrawal of state intervention in some countries has in fact worsened access to food as a result of hoarding and the speculative activities of private traders.[20] The desirability of dismantling state monopoly marketing structures is, moreover, open to question in small countries where the scope of efficiency gains from competitive market structures is likely to be limited by the size of the market.

Experience in restructuring commodity marketing boards,[21] moreover, suggests that state entities may need to intervene in providing support services i.e. dissemination of market intelligence, agricultural research and extension and maintenance of quality-control standards. Unfortunately, reforms aimed at improving the financial position of marketing boards have often involved a reduction in staff and thus a cessation of support activities. This is not without economic costs since the private sector is often not in a position to fill this vacuum, either because of the lack of capabilities or of the appropriate legal framework. The importance of support systems is illustrated by Madagascar's loss of coffee exports when its quality was compromised by the lack of enforcement of quality control when the coffee marketing board was dismantled.

Marketing reforms have raised many difficult policy dilemmas for LDCs. For consumers, higher food prices that result from the removal of parastatals' price subsidization functions not only have implications for the welfare of vulnerable groups because their access to food is reduced, but also have political implications for Governments. The issue of food subsidies is particularly sensitive when real incomes are at, or below, subsistence levels. The removal of food subsidies, which is often a component of

stabilization programmes, can become a politically explosive issue particularly when it coincides with loss of jobs and incomes as a result of austerity-induced cuts in wage and staff levels in the public sector. The challenge thus is to find ways to reform food subsidization which protects vulnerable groups and is economically efficient.

For producers, marketing reforms impose two types of risks.[22] First, the removal of marketing parastatals that perform price stabilization functions means that producers are exposed to more unstable prices. Second, producers face a higher degree of marketing insecurity as private traders may not have a purchasing network of the same density as that of the Government. Market insecurities undermine the incentives to increase investment and production and upgrade product quality, which is necessary if producer prices and returns are to be raised. Improving quality standards is becoming an increasingly stringent requirement in international trade. For many traditional (e.g. coffee), as well as non-traditional agricultural products (e.g. fruits and vegetables), only the market for prime quality products is still expanding.

Decontrol of marketing has inadvertently led to the fragmentation of markets. Deregulation of competition has given rise to a proliferation of small traders who are usually inexperienced, have restricted access to credit, and, because of their lack of knowledge and small size, are at a disadvantage in using modern marketing techniques (e.g. countertrade) and in international trade negotiations. The fragmentation of marketing activities coincides with the intensification of competition and the growing complexity of international commodity trade that places a premium on access to, and capacity to use and evaluate, market intelligence.

Lessons learned from policy reforms[23]

LDCs' reform experiences in general as well as in regard to agriculture suggest that while emphasis has so far been placed on the removal of barriers to private enterprise, less attention has gone to providing support services. LDC Governments must intensify efforts in the following areas:

- ensuring dissemination of market intelligence;

- defining and maintaining quality standards;

- strengthening the legal system to enforce contracts;

- developing procedures to provide access to credit and foreign exchange;

- providing adequate infrastructure and institutional and administrative support to encourage competition;

- defining and establishing clear rules for owning property.

The conclusions of a recent workshop[24] on the structural adjustment experiences of African countries noted that the "right of private individuals to acquire land and secure right of tenure is fundamental if farmers are to have an incentive for taking good care of the land." Participants also emphasized that licensing and registration procedures facilitate rather than complicate the activities of the private sector. They also recommended an implementation of a code of business standards to sanction unethical business behaviour and thus raise export credibility in international markets.

Success in carrying out reforms also depends on closer cooperation between the public and private sectors. In providing public goods, for example, the modalities, institutional organization and relative roles of the public and private sectors may differ depending on the types of public goods. In the research area, an activity with significant externalities, public-sector support may be necessary to ensure an optimal level of research by private firms. If left to the market, firms may not have enough incentives to invest in developing new technologies given that they may capture only a small part of the benefits. The provision of other types of public goods, such as irrigation facilities, might require public sector support because of the complexity of management and large financing requirements, and also the involvement of villages and local communities in their construction, design and operation. Technical assistance from the international community is also indispensable to help countries to increase their marketing knowledge and meet the challenges of new and more complex marketing techniques and systems.

Recent experience has also shown that where there is a history of limited private-sector involvement in marketing and distribution activities, the private sector may not step forward to cover the vacuum left by the state's withdrawal, notably in the area of agricultural parastatals in marketing, storage and processing of inputs and outputs. Governments may be well advised to carefully scrutinize the options for the reform of their marketing boards. While there are probably valid grounds in most countries for rationalizing their functions, proposals for their outright dismantling will warrant critical appraisal on a case-by-case basis. In countries where the private sector is dormant, the emphasis should be placed on improving the efficiency of parastatals. This will involve streamlining their operations, limiting their development functions (e.g. as employer of last resort), cutting costs, imposing more stringent demands on accountability through better operational and financial targeting of their performance, and improving management, for example, by linking remuneration incentives to performance. Experience with privatization in other countries shows that where the complete elimination of parastatals is not immediately feasible, increasing competition and accountability are pragmatic steps towards improving efficiency.

As a result of these experiences, a number of positive elements is emerging in policy and programme formulation. For example, more emphasis is being given by international funding institutions and donors to assist countries to improve the factors that help to reduce aggregate resource constraints, thus enabling production to respond to incentives. These factors include agricultural infrastructure, education and health, alleviating poverty and implementing measures to deal with environmental and natural resource degradation. Since many of these investments have the character of public goods, this emphasis reinforces the role that the state ought to play in development, though in a different form - namely, away from direct intervention in production and distribution and towards the provision of public goods and the creation of an environment conducive to competitive growth.

The scope for food security interventions in LDCs is enormous, both in order to meet the needs of chronically food-insecure people and to provide emergency relief. In principle, food-security interventions should be targeted towards the poorest and most food-insecure people, particularly those who do not benefit from economic growth: households short of labour (especially those headed by women), vulnerable groups like pregnant and lactating women, children, the elderly, the disabled and, often, people living in marginal areas. In practice, however, through implicit, hidden taxes and subsidies for different groups, many national food systems benefit the rich and the urban population rather than the poor, rural and marginalized households. This has increased the political support for such interventions in

Africa - and also their cost. Yet targeting is difficult because of the heavy demands it puts on local administration. Another challenge is to find ways that limit conflicts between social security and growth, a danger which always exists when apparently unproductive social expenditures are allowed to spiral at the expense of productive investment.

E. AREAS FOR PRIORITY ACTION[25]

LDCs have made little progress in the past three decades towards improving their food security situation. Indeed, in terms of average aggregate per capita food availability, LDCs are worse off now than in the past. Aside from the numbers of chronically food-insecure people, which are projected to increase, the numbers of refugees and displaced persons are also growing. Immediate emergency needs are absorbing a considerable volume of national and international resources at the expense of longer-term development.

The scale of food insecurity and poverty underscores the importance of economic growth, particularly agricultural growth in view of LDCs' great dependence on agriculture. A growing and productive agricultural sector should be the driving force for their economies, providing food, jobs, savings and markets for goods from the industrial sector. As noted earlier, most LDCs have considerable untapped potential for increasing agricultural and food production. Exploiting this potential should be their first priority and calls for concrete agricultural and food-policy initiatives, some of which are summarized below.

Focusing on potential areas

A production-oriented strategy to improve LDCs' performance in their agricultural and food sectors requires that priority be given to high potential areas. The thrust of such a strategy should be to create an infrastructure and a policy environment that would allow growth in productivity and increased output for those commodities where countries have a comparative advantage. Attention should also be given to less endowed areas, but not at the expense of overall growth. Increasing food availability at the national level may not automatically ensure food security, but food entitlements are meaningless without adequate supplies.

Strengthening capability for technology generation and dissemination

In order to exploit LDCs' agricultural potential, there is an urgent need to strengthen the capacities of the national agricultural research systems (NARS) in adaptive research. As Asia's experience with the Green Revolution demonstrated, a strong national research system is essential if new technologies generated at the international centres are to be transferred immediately to potential users. Priorities include: increasing the budgetary allocation of resources commensurate with agriculture's role in the economy; achieving a balance in the relative allocation of resources based on an objective analysis of the potential contribution of commodity disciplines to food production and food security; maintaining funding stability, including external sources; and investing in personnel training to facilitate the transfer and adoption of technology. In addition, extension systems need to be strengthened if the benefits of available technologies are to be extended to farmers. Special action programmes, initially as pilot projects, should be launched to demonstrate the technical feasibility and economic viability of new technologies at the farm level.

Preventing further environmental degradation

A growth-oriented strategy concentrating on high potential areas should be supplemented with measures that address the problems of resource-poor households, which are usually concentrated in environmentally degraded areas. Moreover, continued population growth, when it occurs where there is inequality of access to land and other resources, tends to push the rural poor to extend their farming into ecologically fragile areas, risking a vicious cycle between increasing poverty and resource degradation. Various strategies may be needed to reverse such trends, particularly new ways to generate growth in resource-poor areas, for example through small-scale irrigation works, soil conservation and reforestation activities. Sustainable solutions will depend on making extensive use of the untapped human resources in these rural communities by providing the poor with adequate resources to secure their livelihood.

Enhancing efficiency of food systems

Efficient food markets have become increasingly important in LDCs, as more people become dependent on food markets, either as consumers or as food producers. Agricultural policy should ensure remunerative prices to farmers by correcting exchange-rate distortions, reducing taxes and improving the efficiency of marketing organizations. Equally important is that due consideration be given to "non-price constraints" such as infrastructure, technology, credit, transport, storage and marketing services, which have often been ignored in the past.

Improving agricultural statistics and food information systems

These are essential prerequisites for all actions. The following should receive priority: national databases on natural resources should be improved (climate, soil and terrain conditions, water resources, vegetative cover), including their actual and potential use; these data should be collated at the subregional level to facilitate international and national agricultural research efforts; more precise assessments at national and subnational levels of the extent and seriousness of land degradation, such as that caused by "soil mining", desertification and deforestation, are needed as a basis for land rehabilitation and conservation schemes; and national and regional capabilities for early warning assessments and analysis should be strengthened because of the continued acute food problems that require constant monitoring.

Managing variability in export earnings

The volatility of international markets makes the management of risk associated with commodity price variability a high priority issue. Various schemes, such as international commodity agreements, compensatory financing and domestic price stabilization schemes have in practice met with limited success. More effective measures will be needed for stabilizing exports and revenues by improving these schemes or introducing new ones.

The international environment

Equally critical for improving food security in LDCs is the broader international environment. LDCs will continue to depend on the world market for a high share of their food requirements, both in commercial and concessional terms. Financial and technical assistance from the international community will be needed, but, above all, developed countries should make efforts to expand the opportunities for LDC exports and provide an overall environment that will enable countries to transform their economies and proceed to self-reliance. The agricultural policy reforms of major food-exporting countries and the broader trade-liberalization developments, as a result of the Uruguay Round Agreement (see chapter VI), provide the basis for a better trade environment for both exporting and importing countries. However, there is room for more efforts from the international community, including:

- ensuring that the world food market continues to be a dependable and stable source of supplies; in particular, developments in the world food market should be closely monitored and adequate global food stocks be ensured, perhaps by maintaining small public-sector food-security reserves and by encouraging stockholding by the private sector;

- providing food aid or other forms of assistance to countries that may be adversely affected if world food prices are substantially increased;

- further liberalizing trade barriers and internal taxes on agricultural commodities exported by developing countries and supporting compensatory financing and other mechanisms that would help ensure greater stability of earnings and better terms of trade for these exports;

- taking into consideration the impact of regional trade blocs and environmental policies on the export interests of developing countries; as regards environmental problems, there is a need to ensure that environmental policies do not become a new form of disguised protectionism; and

- ensuring a continuation of financial and food assistance as well as setting priorities for using scarce development resources, focusing on alleviating poverty in the food-insecure countries by promoting growth in agricultural and food production as sources of employment and income.

NOTES

1   UNCTAD, *Trade and Development Report, 1993*, p.100.

2   Calculations based on UNCTAD database.

3   UNCTAD, "Analysis of Ways and Means to Improve Market Opportunities for Commodities in the Medium Term, with Emphasis on the Examination of the Best Ways of Achieving Diversification, taking into Account Competitiveness, Market Trends and Opportunities" (TD/B/CN.1/24, p.15).

4   The question of food security in LDCs was addressed in detail in *The Least Developed Countries, 1991 Report*; in this section (C) a number of recurring themes on this subject is covered in the broader context of an analysis of the agricultural sector.

5   FAO, "Food Security Problems & Issues in Africa South of the Sahara and Priority Action". Paper presented at regional conference for Africa in preparation of the 1996 World Food Summit (Rome, FAO, 1994).

6   IFPRI, "Commercialisation of Agriculture under Population Pressure: Effects on Production, Consumption and Nutrition in Rwanda", *IFPRI Research Report* No.85, Washington, D.C., 1991.

7   Henk-Jan Brinkman and Alberto Gabriele, "Problems in Agricultural Development in Sub-Saharan Africa", Department of International Economics and Social Affairs (DIESA), Working Paper No.17, January 1992.

8   *The Least Developed Countries, 1991 Report*, chap.V, pp.33-38.

9   The eight countries are: Benin, Burkina Faso, Madagascar, Mali, Mozambique, Niger, Togo and United Republic of Tanzania.

10 The World Bank, *Adjustment in Africa, Reform, Results and the Road Ahead*. Oxford University Press for The World Bank, 1994, p.78, fig.3.3.

11 The World Bank, 1994; *op. cit.*, fig.3.4.

12 The 11 countries are: Burkina Faso, Burundi, Central African Republic, Guinea, Madagascar, Malawi, Mali, Rwanda, Togo, Uganda and United Republic of Tanzania.

13 The 17 countries are: Benin, Burkina Faso, Burundi, Central African Republic, Chad, Gambia, Guinea, Madagascar, Malawi, Mali, Mauritania, Niger, Sierra Leone, Togo, Uganda, United Republic of Tanzania and Zambia. See The World Bank, 1994, *op. cit.*, p.88, table 3.4.

14 The World Bank, 1994, *op. cit.*, p.89, box 3.6.

15 The World Bank, 1994, *op. cit.*

16 UNCTAD, "Adjustment and Stagnation in sub-Saharan Africa", *Trade and Development Report, 1993*, chap.II.

17 *The Least Developed Countries, 1991 Report*, Part One, chap.V, pp.33-36.

18 Keith Marsden and Thérèse Bélot, *Private Enterprise in Africa, Creating a Better Environment*, World Bank Discussion Papers, No.17, Washington, D.C., July 1987.

19 The World Bank, 1994, *op. cit.*, table 3.3.

20 FAO, "Structural Adjustment and Agriculture, A Review of the Issues," *The State of the World's Food and Agriculture*, Rome, FAO, 1991.

21 See again UNCTAD, TD/B/CN.1/24.

22 Janet Farooq and Lamon Rutten, "The Challenge of Marketing Commodities from Developing Countries," in B. Hartartyo and H.P. Smit (eds.), *International Commodity Development Strategies* (Amsterdam, VU University Press, 1993).

23 *The Least Developed Countries Reports*, 1991 and 1992.

24 UNCTAD/CON/47, "Commodity Export Policies and Strategies in African Countries in a Process of Structural Adjustment: Cotton, Tea and Horticultural Products", 8 November 1994.

25 The policy conclusions in this section draw to a large extent on *The Least Developed Countries, 1992 Report*, chap.II.

III. THE MANUFACTURING SECTOR OF LDCs: PERFORMANCE, ISSUES AND POLICIES

A. INTRODUCTION

The Programme of Action for the Least Developed Countries for the 1990s views the development of an industrial base as one of the key aspects of LDCs' efforts to produce essential goods and services to meet the needs of their people, generate employment, enhance the domestic value added and overcome the difficulties inherent in the monoculture of their economies.[1] Upon gaining independence, the leaders of these countries viewed industrialization and, in particular, the rapid growth of domestic manufacturing, as important ways of departing from the earlier pattern of production that had perpetuated dependence on imports for intermediate and final manufactured items. The manufacturing sector in those LDCs with a longer history of industrialization has since evolved through the broad and overlapping phases shown in box 6.

This chapter focuses on three distinct areas as regards the manufacturing sector of LDCs, namely: its recent performance and the principal determinants thereof; the implications of structural adjustment and policy reforms for manufacturing; and, finally, policy options for removing the constraints on manufacturing development. This chapter is confined to the formal manufacturing sector.

B. OVERVIEW OF RECENT PERFORMANCE

Salient trends in manufacturing value added

A major characteristic of the manufacturing sector in LDCs is its very narrow base (box 7). The manufacturing value added (MVA) accounts for less than one tenth of the combined GDP of LDCs, as compared with nearly one quarter in the developing countries as a whole. In the early 1990s, LDCs' share in total MVA of developing countries amounted to less than 1.5 per cent; in 1990, for example, the combined MVA of Chile and Colombia exceeded that of all LDCs together. In per capita terms, the MVA of LDCs in 1991 stood at slightly more than $30, as compared with $240 for developing countries as a whole.

Besides its small size, the relative importance of manufacturing in LDC economies has diminished in recent years. Thus, the contribution of the manufacturing sector to their GDP declined during the 1980s, from 10 per cent in 1980 to 9 per cent in 1991. This decline is also manifest in the annual average growth rates of

MVA for all LDCs: the annual average MVA growth dropped from 6.4 per cent during the 1970s to 2 per cent during the 1980s; it turned negative in the early 1990s and during 1990-1991 stood at -5.3 per cent. Notwithstanding the good performance of several countries, this decline was traced to deindustrialization[2] in certain LDCs and the failure of other LDCs to strengthen or maintain manufacturing growth.

In terms of their recent manufacturing performance in the latter part of the 1980s and the early 1990s, three groups of countries are identified: group A countries with a positive per capita MVA growth, 3 per cent and above; group B countries, with a generally positive MVA growth rate, but below 3 per cent; and group C countries, with a generally negative MVA growth. The LDCs for which data are available are listed in these three groups in table 17.

As the table shows, some one third of LDCs (16) has maintained positive per capita MVA growth since the mid-1980s (group A). Their individual performance, however, has varied

---

Box 6: Periodization of manufacturing development

Period	Phase	Main characteristics
1960s to early 1970s	Initiation of the manufacturing process	- Heavy Government interventions through import protection and other subsidies in favour of investment in import-substitution (and frequently large-scale) manufacturing. - Nationalization policies in many LDCs.
Mid-1970s to 1980s	Manufacturing crisis	- Stagnation and/or contraction in manufacturing output.\ - Inefficient manufacturing parastatals rendering Government budgets unsustainable.
1980s to 1990s	Adjustment and reform	- Market-oriented macroeconomic and sectoral reforms.

---

greatly. Thus, at one end of the spectrum are countries like Bhutan, the Lao People's Democratic Republic, Lesotho and Maldives which enjoy high MVA growth while, at the other end, MVA growth in countries like the Comoros and Mali could barely keep pace with population growth. In Cape Verde and Mali, MVA growth has picked up greater momentum in recent years after years of depressed performance.

In group B are 10 LDCs which exhibited slow MVA growth. Of these, the Central African Republic, Nepal, Samoa, and Sao Tome and Principe experienced decelerated MVA growth rate in recent years, while Mauritania, Niger, Sudan and the United Republic of Tanzania were able to improve their performance in the early 1990s, the latter quite significantly.

Finally, as many as 13 LDCs (group C) experienced negative MVA growth on average since the mid-1980s. The most severe losses have been incurred by Zaire and Zambia, experiencing -21.5 and -10.6 per cent MVA growth rates, respectively, in 1991. The collapse of manufacturing in this group of countries has been a major source of the disappointing performance of the manufacturing sector of LDCs as a whole during the early 1990s. Salient factors affecting recent performances of manufacturing are discussed in section C.

Sectoral composition of MVA and the diversification of the manufacturing base

Two primarily consumer-oriented subsectors, viz. food processing and textiles and clothing, command the lion's share of the manufacturing value added in LDCs. Table 18 shows the subsectoral share of MVA for 1990, based on two-digit ISIC code for a selected number of LDCs for which recent data are available. These two subsectors together account for two thirds of their combined MVA. Food processing alone contributes to nearly half of LDCs' MVA taken together. For five LDCs (Burkina Faso, Burundi, the Central African Republic, Sudan and Yemen), this subsector accounts for some three fifths of their respective MVAs, while its share for Ethiopia, the Gambia, Togo, Zaire and Zambia is over 40 per cent.

Next in importance is textiles (including garments and leather). Like food processing, it is a subsector close to final demand, with few backward and forward linkages with other sectors. For Bangladesh, Madagascar and Mali, textiles represent the largest manufacturing activity, while for Ethiopia and the United Republic of Tanzania each it accounts for around one fifth of the total MVA. On the other hand, its share in manufacturing is extremely low in the Central

---

Box 7: Characteristics of the manufacturing sector in LDCs - Sierra Leone

As in many other African LDCs, Sierra Leone's attempt at industrialization started with an import-substitution strategy although for many years the country did not have a well-articulated long-term industrial policy. The industrial scene was predominated by state-controlled initiatives. The nature of the incentives, namely, tax holidays, duty-free importation of machinery, equipment and even raw materials, did not encourage the growth of resource-based industries. The lack of strategic industries such as steel, machine tools, electronics, etc., was a restraining factor in industrial growth. In response to the import-substitution strategy, however, some consumer industries were established using capital-intensive technology. Thus, Sierra Leone has industries producing cigarettes, beer, beverages and confectionaries. A few firms are engaged in assembly-type operations based on imported components rather than on local production of parts.

First, in terms of overall structure, the manufacturing sector in Sierra Leone is characterized by a relatively small urban-based modern enclave of medium- and large-scale enterprises. There is also a dispersed subsector embracing small-scale and informal manufacturing activities. A key feature of these medium- and large-scale industries is that they operate as single-unit monopolies. Examples include industries that produce beer, cigarettes, plastic-wares, nails, sugar, etc.

Second, these enterprises employ capital-intensive technologies and thus have a limited role in terms of employment. They have very little backward and forward linkages both at the firm and sectoral levels. They always press for generous protection and high tariffs in order to avoid competition. Furthermore, both the medium- and large-scale enterprises demonstrate very low export awareness.

Another important feature of the modern manufacturing sector is the key role of foreigners, including multinationals. They own or have majority shares in most medium- and large-scale enterprises. The average capital investment is about $100,000.

In terms of geographical distribution, over 70 per cent of the industries are located in the western area of the country.

As regards performance, although adequate and updated data are not available, it appears that manufacturing output has remained depressed for quite some time. Significant declines have taken place not only in output but also in employment and capacity use. Between 1980 and 1985, for example, the total number of enterprises decreased from 210 to 194, while three enterprises employing more than 100 people completely ceased operations. Overall, the contribution of the manufacturing sector to the GDP decreased from 6 per cent in 1980 to 4 per cent in 1990.

Source: Information provided by the United Nations Industrial Development Organization (UNIDO), in response to an UNCTAD questionnaire.

African Republic (2.1 per cent) and in Yemen (4.0 per cent).

For a number of LDCs, the chemicals subsector is of considerable importance. In Bangladesh, Malawi and the United Republic of Tanzania, it accounts for one sixth or more of total MVA, while it comprises nearly 10 per cent or more of MVA in Sudan and Zambia. Non-metallic machinery and equipment are the two other notable subsectors. In Ethiopia and Yemen, non-metallic manufacturing activities account for one fifth of their respective MVAs. In five LDCs (Mali, Sudan, the United Republic of Tanzania, Yemen and Zaire), machinery and equipment contribute at least 8 per cent to their re-

spective MVAs. However, in almost all these LDCs, this subsector produces very simple tools and equipment rather than capital goods. Overall, the subsectoral distribution of MVA points towards a concentration of manufacturing in a few activities that are close to the final demand.

Moreover, the lack of dispersion of MVA across a wide range of manufacturing activities indicates that LDCs made only limited progress in diversifying their manufacturing bases. According to UNIDO findings, the countries with highly skewed manufacturing sectors were Burundi, Equatorial Guinea, Lesotho, Mauritania and Sierra Leone.[3] On the other hand, a few other countries (e.g. Bangladesh, Haiti, Malawi,

**Table 17: Classification of countries in terms of
levels of MVA growth rate, 1985-1993**

Group A[a]	Group B[b]	Group C[c]
Bangladesh	Central African Republic	Equatorial Guinea
Benin	Djibouti	Guinea
Bhutan	Ethiopia	Guinea-Bissau
Burkina Faso	Mauritania	Haiti
Burundi	Nepal	Kiribati
Cape Verde	Niger	Liberia
Comoros	Samoa	Madagascar
Lao People's Democratic Republic	Sao Tome and Principe	Myanmar
Lesotho	Sudan	Rwanda
Malawi	United Republic of Tanzania	Sierra Leone
Maldives		Somalia
Mali		Zaire
Solomon Islands		Zambia
Togo		
Uganda		
Vanuatu		

Source: Based on UNCTAD data.

a   MVA growth rate above 3 per cent.
b   Positive MVA growth rate but below 3 per cent.
c   Negative MVA growth rate.

Uganda and the United Republic of Tanzania) made some strides to diversify their manufacturing base. Significant gains by the chemicals subsector helped Bangladesh to diversify its manufacturing and to disperse more widely the manufacturing activities in Malawi and the United Republic of Tanzania. The latter also witnessed the machinery and equipment subsector obtaining an increasing share of MVA. In Haiti, the machinery and equipment subsector came to command a substantial share of MVA.

These findings, however, need to be interpreted with caution. For example, statistical findings on a number of LDCs do not point to a strong correlation between diversification and economic progress. Thus, while the manufacturing sector in Lesotho and Burundi display lack of dispersion on the one hand, they experienced relatively strong MVA growth in recent years on the other. This, however, does not imply that diversification as an objective of the development of the manufacturing sector should be abandoned. It only indicates that diversification itself is not a sufficient condition for manufacturing progress. Moreover, the smallness of subsectoral activities can also have implications for the relative importance of each subsector within the manufacturing sector and, thereby, for diversification. Smallness is especially relevant in an LDC setting where manufacturing is carried out by a handful of enterprises, and the entry or exit of enterprises within a subsector can significantly change the degree of dispersion of activities. This is well illustrated by the experience of the textile and clothing subsector of the Central African Republic, where the closure of one single factory led to a virtual disappearance of this subsector's contribution of more than 30 per cent to the overall MVA in the early 1980s.

Utilization of capacity and resources

Data on manufacturing capacity utilization in LDCs at the sectoral, subsectoral and plant levels are either unavailable or incomplete. A 1991 survey by UNIDO[4] of 20 LDCs found that capacity underutilization is a widespread phenomenon in these countries. It concluded that:

• at the sectoral level, for about half the countries covered by the survey, the overall manufacturing capacity utilization was very low (below 20 per cent), while in five

**Table 18: Share in total MVA of manufacturing
subsectors in selected LDCs, 1990**

(Percentage)

Country	Food	Textiles	Wood	Paper	Chemicals	Non-metallics	basic metals	Machinery & equipment	Others
Bangladesh	19.4	37.8	1.1	3.5	18.2	9.1	4.0	6.0	0.7
Burkina Faso	66.0	18.9	1.5	0.5	0.5	1.9	1.5	1.9	7.3
Burundi	80.7	6.4	..	0.9	3.7	1.8	4.6	..	..
Central African Republic	60.4	2.1	20.8	4.2	6.3	-	-	4.2	2.1
Ethiopia	46.7	20.2	1.6	2.9	3.4	20.9	2.7	1.6	-
Gambia	53.8	..	7.7	..	..	..	..	..	23.1
Madagascar	26.5	46.3	..	4.1	6.1	10.2	2.7	2.0	..
Malawi	34.6	17.3	2.3	7.5	21.1	9.8	3.8	3.8	-
Mali *a*	26.5	51.7	0.1	1.2	2.7	1.2	0.0	16.6	0.0
Sudan *a*	58.1	12.9	0.4	3.8	9.5	1.3	4.9	8.8	0.2
Togo	55.9	15.7	2.0	2.9	4.9	15.7	2.9	-	-
United Republic of Tanzania	28.7	20.7	3.4	5.7	16.1	10.3	8.0	8.0	..
Yemen *a*	66.7	4.0	-	-	-	20.0	-	9.3	-
Zaire	50.0	12.5	2.1	1.0	8.3	3.1	6.3	8.3	9.4
Zambia	41.0	13.9	4.8	3.4	10.7	10.1	8.8	7.5	0.1

Source: UNIDO, *Industry and Development, Global Report 1993-94; Industry in the Least Developed Countries: Structure and Development* (UNIDO publication No.V.92-57643, January 1993).

  a Data for 1989.

countries (Bangladesh, Comoros, Myanmar, Sudan and Yemen) it varied between 20 and 40 per cent. Only Ethiopia and Malawi reported more than 60 per cent capacity utilization at the time of the survey;

• at the subsectoral level, capacity utilization was very high (around 80 per cent) in agro-based industries with ample supplies of raw materials from domestic sources (e.g. food, beverages, textiles, wood and paper processing). Nearly half of all food-processing industries in these case countries operated at 60 to 80 per cent of their capacity. In contrast, capacity utilization rates in other manufacturing subsectors were very low (less than 20 per cent).

Capacity underutilization of manufacturing can be traced to a number of factors. The policy-related factors include the consequences of earlier stress on large-scale manufacturing development which led to the establishment of units with high capital intensity; management inadequacies, such as lack of maintenance of machinery and equipment, rent-seeking tendencies, etc.; and limited (and at times adverse) impact of adjustment and reform measures.

Among the endowment-related or structural factors contributing to low-capacity utilization are the following: shortages and/or delays in supplies of imported raw materials and spare parts; cash-flow problems; difficulties in obtaining external investment funds; small size of the domestic market; weak technological capability and the related low level of human-resource availability, particularly that of engineering, entrepreneurial and management skills, and weak infrastructure (e.g. power cuts, transport bottlenecks, etc.).

The persistence of the above factors has also affected the efficient use of various production factors. An indication of this is provided by the total factor productivity (TFP) which aggregates the partial productivities of individual inputs in the production process. The available information on changes in TFP in a few LDCs points to a limited or declining efficiency of factor utilization. Thus, in Zambia, a World Bank study estimates that during 1965-1980, the total factor productivity growth of the manufacturing sector as a whole declined uniformly at an annual average rate of 3.8 per cent.[5] Out of a total of 17 subsectors, 14 experienced declines in TFP growth. Another estimate for Bangladesh indicates that out of a large sample of manufacturing activities, only 35 per cent of establishments demonstrated a positive growth of TFP during 1976-1984, and that TFP for the country's manufacturing as a whole declined during the early 1990s.[6] These declines in resource use resulted mainly from stagnating or deteriorating labour productivity, coupled with falling capital productivity as investment outpaced output growth.

Changes in TFP have important implications for the manufacturing sector. On the one hand, falling TFP implies rising production costs. Improvement of TFP, on the other hand, can have multiplier effects on the supply-side by raising MVA growth. Thus, a study on three African LDCs concluded that an increase in TFP growth by 1 per cent would result in an increase in MVA growth rate of 1.8 per cent for Sierra Leone, 1.36 per cent for the United Republic of Tanzania, and 1.15 per cent for Ethiopia.[7] While an improvement in TFP is certainly desirable, the specific mechanisms for improvement vary from one country to another. However, improved skills, investment in research and development and enhanced technological opportunities are of particular significance in this regard and are discussed in section D.

C. FACTORS AFFECTING RECENT PERFORMANCE

Longer-term factors such as weak inter- and intrasectoral linkages (box 8), poor skills, underdeveloped infrastructure and technological bases, and market imperfections continue to affect LDCs' manufacturing performance. In certain countries, a number of exogenous factors affected the performance of the manufacturing sector: for example, in several LDCs, the sharp contraction in manufacturing output resulted from the disruption caused by civil conflicts, while in some other LDCs, natural calamities, including droughts which led to shortages of agricultural raw materials, adversely affected performance. These long-standing and exogenous factors have been reinforced in recent years by the impact of several other factors which are discussed below.

Demand conditions

Manufacturing performance is considerably affected by the levels of aggregate demand. An indication of demand conditions can be conveyed by the trends in overall income and, in particular, by agricultural performance as most people in LDCs are dependent on this sector for living. Barring a few exceptions, LDCs with higher MVA growth tend to be those with good overall growth.[8] Thus, almost all LDCs of group A (i.e. with positive per capita MVA growth rate during 1985-1993; table 17) have also been the ones registering average annual GDP growth rate during 1980-1991 that was higher than the average for LDCs as a group. Moreover, most of the countries of this group enjoyed growth of agricultural production higher than the average for LDCs during this period. On the other hand, group C countries suffered economic stagnation or decline during the 1980s and the early 1990s.

External demand conditions can also play a major role in shaping the performance of particular activities in the sector, as exemplified by the impressive growth of the ready-made garments (RMG) manufacturing in Bangladesh in recent years. As an LDC, Bangladesh could benefit from the quotas under the Multi-Fibre Arrangement (MFA), which made it attractive to foreign buyers in the early 1980s. From a handful of manufacturing units in the 1970s, the number of registered RMG production units soared to over 1,600 in 1993, and the earnings from RMG export exceeded 50 per cent of the total export earnings of the country that year as compared with less than 2 per cent a decade ago.

Investment

Two important determinants of manufacturing supply capacity in LDCs are investment and imports. Investment assumes greater salience in augmenting productive capacity in LDCs than in other developing countries owing to the former's narrow supply base. Besides MVA growth, growth of investment, as well as that of the share of investment in GDP, can provide some indications of the state of supply capacity.[9] It would thus be appropriate to look at the trends in investment in manufacturing in LDCs.

However, sectorally disaggregated data on investment in LDCs are not available. An alternative could be to use total investment as a proxy for manufacturing investment. Table 19 shows the share of investment in GDP for group A countries during 1980-1985 and 1986-1993. It is apparent that, in general, these countries also invested a higher percentage of GDP throughout the 1980s than the average for LDCs as a whole. Moreover, many of them were able to

---

Box 8: Inter- and intrasectoral linkages of the manufacturing sector in LDCs

There are serious gaps in the availability of relevant data on manufacturing linkages in LDCs, particularly input-output statistics. However, available country-level evidence points to a number of broad observations.

First, linkages between the various subsectors within the formal manufacturing sector are weak. A major reason for this is the paucity of domestically produced intermediate goods reflecting the lack of linkage industries. The resulting dependency of LDC manufacturing on imported intermediate goods, including spare parts and machinery, remains high. Except for a small number of subcontracting arrangements (e.g. knitting and shoe manufacturing in Lesotho or ready-made garments in Bangladesh) backward or forward linkages within manufacturing is very limited. However, while interindustry linkages are lacking in the formal sector, transactions do occur between the formal and informal sectors, as reported by the World Bank.[1] Two typical forms of such linkages are the utilization of the waste of the formal-sector enterprises by the informal ones, and the use of savings from formal-sector employment to finance informal-sector activities.

Next, while intramanufacturing linkages are not well developed, those between manufacturing and some other sectors appear to be stronger. Regression analysis between the growth rate of manufacturing and other sectors of the economy (including agriculture, mining, utilities, construction, trade and services, and transport) for 44 LDCs for the period 1985-1988 indicated that the trade and services sector played an important role in manufacturing growth.[2]

The high share of food processing in the overall manufacturing value added point to a significant interdependence between manufacturing and agriculture. Moreover, food-processing subsectors tend to have very low import dependence and strong backward linkages to the economy. The textiles subsector, on the other hand, displays a variety of situations. For example, in the United Republic of Tanzania, it is based mainly on the locally produced cotton and sisal, whereas in Bangladesh it is heavily dependent on imported raw materials.

Finally, manufacturing linkages to mining and quarrying in LDCs are limited by the fact that mining activities require highly specialized equipment and inputs which are not feasible to produce in these countries. The contribution of mining to manufacturing is also low, except in the case of non-metallic minerals (e.g. limestone, clay stone, sand and aggregates) which are largely used by domestic industry, particularly as building materials.

---

[1]   The World Bank, *Sub-Saharan Africa - From Crisis to Sustainable Growth, A Long-term Perspective Study* (Washington, D.C., The World Bank, 1989).

[2]   UNIDO, Linkages between manufacturing and other sectors of the economy in the LDCs (UNIDO, ID(WG.515/1(SPEC)).

---

sustain a stable share of investment in GDP and a few others were able to improve it, although in the late 1980s and early 1990s their ability to maintain higher levels of investment came under pressure owing in part to financing difficulties. On the other hand, as for LDCs in groups B and C, the majority either invested less as a percentage of GDP than the average for LDCs, or experienced sharp falls in the investment-GDP ratio during the 1980s and the early 1990s. The overall socio-economic and policy environment, availability of industrial financing and the ability to import critical raw materials and spare parts were among the key factors influencing investment in recent years.

Import capacity

The heavy dependence of LDC manufacturing on imports renders the performance of this sector vulnerable to changes in the level of imports. As regards the role of imports in shaping the recent performance of their manufacturing sector, the following broad conclusions can be made:

- first, the ability of most of the group A countries to contain import compression in the second half of the 1980s and the early 1990s may have helped them to perform better. While for 8 countries of the group, the import growth rate in real terms decelerated over 1980-1992 as compared with the average level during 1970-1980; for seven others it was higher during the latter period. Moreover, several of these eight countries (e.g. Benin, Burkina Faso and Mali) could significantly improve their real import growth performance during the late 1980s and the early 1990s;

- second, 9 out of the 13 countries that registered negative MVA growth rate (table 17, group C) experienced negative import growth rate during 1980-1992, and all but one country did so during 1985-1992;

- finally, the situation with regard to group B countries (table 17) is mixed. Out of 10 countries in this group, 6 experienced lower import growth rate during 1980-1992 than during 1970-1980, of which 2 were able to improve their performance during 1985-1992.

Policy environment

Since the early 1980s, an increasing number of LDCs has adopted adjustment and policy reforms under the sponsorship of the World Bank and the IMF.[10] In so far as the manufacturing sector is concerned, the impetus to adjustment and reform was provided by a number of considerations arising from the pre-adjustment period.[11] First, distorted incentives accorded by overvalued exchange rates, high effective protection, and policies in the areas of pricing, credit, etc., had allowed an expansion of manufacturing capacity that outstripped the ability to obtain imported inputs as well as the demand for manufacturing output. Second, the structure of incentives also created a bias towards capital-intensive technology, and the resulting high import and capital intensity of manufacturing investment went well beyond the capacity of these countries to earn foreign exchange. Third, public ownership of manufacturing entities often far exceeded the Government's ability to ensure efficient management and financial operations. Finally, the type and pattern of industrialization, such as overinvestment in import-substitution industries and, in the final stage, consumer goods, also contributed to a poor performance.

LDCs' response to deteriorating manufacturing performance has been through adjustments of macroeconomic policies and instruments and sectoral measures to augment manufacturing output and efficiency. Macroeconomic reforms have mainly revolved around "big prices" (e.g. exchange rates and credit), as well as commercial policy measures (e.g. trade liberalization). At the sectoral level, a reorientation of the incentive structure and changes in institu-

Table 19: Share of investment in GDP for group A countries
(Percentage)

Country	Share of investment in GDP	
	1980-1985	*1986-1993*
Bangladesh	14	12
Benin	17	13
Bhutan	39	35
Burkina Faso	19	21
Burundi	17	16
Cape Verde	55	33
Comoros	30	20
Lao People's Democratic Republic	7	12
Lesotho	43	69
Malawi	20	18
Maldives	31	60
Mali	17	22
Solomon Islands	30	30
Togo	26	22
Uganda	7	13
Vanuatu	26	44
LDC average	16	15

Source: UNCTAD secretariat calculations.

tional policies and regulatory arrangements have been the highlights of reform. Overall, these reforms reoriented the thrust of public policy towards a "market-friendly" approach.

As regards the impact of these policies on manufacturing performance, the following broad conclusions can be made.

Exchange policies

The consequences of exchange adjustment for MVA levels in LDCs was discussed in the LDC 1993-1994 Report.[12] The main conclusion was that the available evidence did not point to any clear association between movements of the real effective exchange rate (REER) and the rate of growth of MVA share in GDP. Countries with mild real depreciation registered better MVA/GDP growth than those with massive real devaluation. The latter group in fact fared worse than those with REER appreciation. The implications of the 1994 devaluation of the CFA franc for the manufacturing sector of the Franc zone LDCs are taken up in chapter VI.

Trade liberalization

As regards the impact of trade liberalization on the manufacturing sector, it is pertinent to examine to what extent trade liberalization measures induced a structural shift in favour of the manufacturing sector. One approach, although imprecise, is to look at the change in the share of MVA in GDP during the 1980s for countries that undertook extensive liberalization ("high" liberalizers), weak liberalization ("low" liberalizers) and those in between ("medium" liberalizers).[13] The percentage point changes in the MVA/GDP ratio between 1980 and 1990 for African LDCs in these three groups are portrayed in chart 2. It appears that the countries that liberalized least extensively have also been the worst performers in terms of the growth of MVA share in GDP (box 9). This conclusion is further reinforced by the fact that, barring a few exceptions, countries of this group registered negative real MVA growth in the late 1980s and early 1990s. On the other hand, both high and medium liberalizers were able to increase their MVA share in GDP over the 1980s, although the medium liberalizers fared better in this respect. However, the overall experience of medium liberalizers among African LDCs needs to be clarified, since the performance of individual countries varied substantially. For example, while Lesotho saw a doubling of the contribution of MVA to GDP during the 1980s, there was no increase in Botswana in the same period. Nevertheless, it can be broadly concluded that LDCs which implemented fairly

extensive trade liberalization measures also experienced a shift towards the manufacturing sector

Financial sector policies

The main thrust of the financial sector policy of LDCs undertaking structural adjustment has been the restructuring of financial systems to enhance efficiency by moving towards a market-oriented system with decreasing reliance on administrative controls. As concerns the manufacturing sector, measures such as abolishing interest subsidy and curbing inflation through tight monetary control were advanced as a means to promote efficiency, as a high cost of credit would enable only the profitable ventures in operation and price stability would prevent domestic currency from being overvalued. Moreover, it has been argued, such an approach would help correct earlier bias in favour of capital-intensive technology by raising the cost of capital, and higher interest rates would increase the level of liquidity of financial institutions which could, in turn, be used for productive investment.[14]

Whether these measures led to a higher level of manufacturing investment remains doubtful as the developments with regard to industrial financing indicate.[15] Industrial investment in LDCs, as in many other developing countries, used to be financed mainly by specialized financing institutions.[16] The lending operations of these institutions were not always efficient particularly in such matters as choice of projects, delivery and recovery of loans, accounting practices, etc.[17] The reversal of markets in the 1980s exposed further the weaknesses of official industrial financing, as the number of company bankruptcies rose. This, in turn, led in many cases to a virtual collapse of industrial financing institutions, resulting in a widespread decline in the volume of credit distributed through this channel. The commercial banks also have not yet proved to be an alternative source of financing for the manufacturing sector as they usually offer short-term credit to finance the bottom of a company's balance sheet, and generally refrain from tying up their funds to long-term, high-risk ventures (on issues relating to financing manufacturing development, see box 10). Finally, external financial assistance to LDCs' manufacturing also appears to have dwindled in recent years. As table 20 indicates, in 1988, the share of manufacturing in the overall flow of official development finance (ODF) to all LDCs was 6 per cent. Since then it has declined steadily and in 1992 stood at 2 per cent. This trend reflects the low priority that donors now assign to the manufacturing sector in their aid programmes.

Institutional policies

Institutional reforms of LDCs' manufacturing sector have two objectives, namely, reforming and/or limiting the public sector and promoting private ownership. Privatization, in particular, has been an important mechanism in this exercise. LDCs' recent experience with privatization is summarized below.

Privatization has an important place on the current policy agenda of a large number of LDCs. It represents a substantial policy reorientation away from earlier extensive reliance on the public sector (brought about either by high levels of public sector investment in manufacturing or nationalization of private enterprises, or both) towards a transfer of ownership of enterprises to the private sector. For example, in Bangladesh and Ethiopia, extensive nationalization of private-sector enterprises took place in the 1970s. As a result, over 90 per cent of total value added of Ethiopian enterprises employing 10 or more workers accrued from the public sector, and over 90 per cent of the total fixed assets in the formal manufacturing sector in Bangladesh was brought under public-sector ownership through nationalization. In Guinea, massive public-sector investment and the proliferation of parastatals resulted in a near-complete domination of the manufacturing sector by public enterprises. In the United Republic of Tanzania, public-sector enterprises came to account for over two thirds of industrial employment and 60 per cent of value added. In most cases, over the years, the public-sector manufacturing enterprises witnessed substantial erosion of the equity base, accumulated vast losses and could remain afloat only with credit financed through bank overdrafts - a situation that could hardly be sustained.

LDCs have tried to cope with this situation by implementing a combination of three types of measures: privatization of state-owned enterprises, reforming public enterprises (including corporatization) and, to a limited extent, allowing greater private sector entry into hitherto restricted areas to increase the efficiency of public-sector entities. As regards privatization, it has not only been seen as a way to achieve better economic efficiency and to redress fiscal imbalances by offloading loss-making enterprises, but also as a means to encourage private-sector participation.

Some LDCs had started the process of privatization well before structural adjustment and policy reforms became fashionable. In Bangladesh, for example, privatization began as early as 1975 when the Government embarked on a policy of denationalization of enterprises that had been brought under the public sector in the early 1970s. There have already been several phases of privatization, and under the Industrial Policy of 1991 the Government narrowed the areas reserved for the public sector to airlines, railways, electricity and defence industries only and decided to privatize public-sector enterprises in all remaining areas. Nepal also began its privatization programme in the 1970s. In Uganda, the legal framework for returning nationalized entities to their previous owners was put in place in 1982. Privatization gained further momentum in these LDCs and has been adopted by an increasing number of others in recent years in the context of adjustment and reform efforts. In 1990, Togo began its first phase of privatization of public enterprises in manufacturing (totalling 26) and has implemented several phases of the process. In the Lao People's Democratic Republic, a major reorientation of economic policies began in 1985, and by 1990 more than half of the public manufacturing companies were privatized. In Zambia, a privatization law was approved by its Parliament in 1992, which defined the modalities, framework and time-table for the divestment of some 130 state-owned enterprises. During the same year, the Government of the United Republic of Tanzania set up the Parastatal Sector Reform Commission (PSRC) to execute privatization.

Despite policy pronouncements, enactment of legal provisions and setting up institutional frameworks by many LDCs in favour of privatization have so far met with, at best, limited results as is illustrated by the experience of countries that have attained a modest degree of success in this regard. In Bangladesh, the various phases of privatization since the mid-1970s did little to change the importance of the public sector. The process of privatization has been slow: for example, in early 1993, the Government decided to privatize at least 32 industrial units, but by the first quarter of 1994 only three units were transferred to the private sector. In the United Republic of Tanzania, by mid-1994, only 24 out of 400 parastatals were privatized. Such slow progress can be attributed to factors such as the Government's uncertain commitment to privatization; institutional inadequacies and bureaucratic delays; dearth of local entrepreneurs; lack of financing; poor financial conditions of enterprises offered for privatization which make them unattractive to the private sector; and concerns about possible ad-

Chart 2: Trade liberalization and change in MVA/GDP in African LDCs, 1980-1990

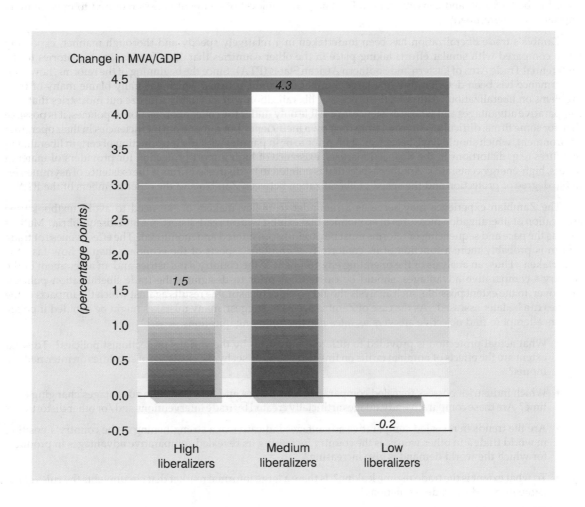

Source: Based on The Least Developed Countries, 1993-1994 Report, p.58.

Note: High liberalizers: Benin, Burkina Faso, Chad, Gambia, Guinea, Malawi;

        Medium liberalizers: Botswana, Burundi, Central African Republic, Lesotho;

        Low liberalizers: Djibouti, Ethiopia, Madagascar, Mali, Mauritania, Niger, Rwanda, Sierra Leone, Somalia, Sudan, Togo, Uganda, Zaire, Zambia.

verse social repercussions. In the end, the success of the privatization programmes will need to be judged not merely by the number of enterprises privatized, but against such considerations as output and efficiency gains, enhancement of competition (rather than simply converting public monopolies into private ones), skill development, improvement in technological and managerial capabilities, contribution to domestic savings and investment, etc.

In sum, structural adjustment measures and policy reform processes have had at best a mixed and limited impact on LDCs' manufacturing sector. The particular constraints faced by manufacturing in LDCs (section D) suggest that the "market-friendly"-type measures advanced under adjustment policies are not enough to revitalize and expand the manufacturing base.

Box 9: Trade liberalization and industrialization - lessons from Zambia

After approximately two decades of experimentation with import-substitution policies, in the second half of the 1980s Zambia initiated a process of trade liberalization aimed at improving the competitiveness of the economy and of exports. Import-substitution policies have left behind a legacy of inefficient industries that apparently never ceased to be "infants" and consequently did not acquire the level of competitiveness required to operate in an unprotected environment.

Zambia's trade liberalization has been undertaken in a relatively speedy and thorough manner, especially when compared with similar efforts taking place in the other countries that, like Zambia, are signatories to the Preferential Trade Area of Eastern and Southern African States (PTA). Since the beginning of the reforms, however, performance has been deteriorating in a large number of Zambian firms, which generally blame many of their problems on liberalization. Although the process of liberalization will inevitably squeeze out industries that lack comparative advantages and whose existence is possible only under the cover of protectionist policies, it is possible that, for some firms, difficulties stem not from their own inefficiency but rather from inefficiencies in their operating environment, which should have been dealt with prior to or in parallel with the introduction of certain liberalizing measures (e.g. distortions in the financial markets, existence of high import protection for providers of material inputs, high-energy costs, etc.). Another aspect that is pointed to by distressed firms is the existence of asymmetries in the degree of protection and the speed of liberalization between Zambia and the other members of the PTA.

The Zambian experience may serve as a reminder to policy makers of the need to avoid textbook-type application of liberalization measures in economies that exhibit widespread distortions and disequilibria. Matters such as the pace and sequencing of reforms must be carefully considered and monitored. The effectiveness of trade reform is probably more a function of its conformity with other aspects of the economy than of how fast it is undertaken. Thus, an analysis of the operating environment of the country's industries and an assessment of the country's comparative advantages, should be carried out prior to designing the trade liberalization policies. Moreover, to the extent possible, such analysis should produce measurable results against which the impacts of the policies can be later assessed. As the case of Zambia seems to suggest, many mistakes might be avoided if policy makers attempt to find objective answers to, *inter alia*, the following questions:

- What actual protection is provided to different industries by the various protectionist policies? To what extent are the effects of nominal tariffs on finished goods offset by the existence of subsidies on intermediate inputs?

- Which industries possess revealed comparative advantages and how are these advantages changing over time? Are these comparative advantages artificially created by trade interventions and/or other distortions?

- Are the trends in revealed comparative advantages indicative of a strengthening of the country's position in world trade? In other words, is the country increasing its revealed comparative advantages in products for which the world demand is also increasing?

- To what extent is the trade regime leaking? Is there a large informal market that circumvents the rules of the game imposed by trade regulations?

- What would be the effects of eliminating certain measures, such as subsidies to Government-controlled companies that provide intermediate inputs, in industries that use such inputs?

- Are the country's trade partners also undergoing trade liberalization? If so, what is the pace of their programmes? Would opportunities for the triangulation of non-originating goods appear as a result of non-synchronization with the trade policies and reforms in countries with which special trade arrangements exist?

Attempts to obtain meaningful answers to these questions by applying quantitative tools of analysis, such as the calculation of the rate of effective protection or the determination of revealed comparative advantages, in the context of developing countries, can be frustrating exercises because of the lack of credible and readily available data. However, it is often possible to find appropriate proxies and to carry out analyses and surveys that could provide useful information.

In conclusion, it is important to look at trade liberalization as a process within the wider economic context and whose implications cannot be isolated from the effects of distortions existing elsewhere in the economy. Furthermore, the impact of trade liberalization can be adequately assessed only if a benchmark for comparing its consequences is established.

Box 10: Issues in financing manufacturing development - the United Republic of Tanzania

During the socialist period many industries in the United Republic of Tanzania made large investments financed with hard currency loans from abroad. The currency devaluation and the sector's poor performance made it impossible to pay back these loans and the industry is heavily indebted, especially the parastatals. This is a major obstacle to the privatization process. The possibilities for these enterprises to get further loans are very limited in the absence of further financial help from the Government, which seems unlikely under the present budget constraints and pressure from donors.

The current sources for finance are found in five major groups: public banks; private banks; specialized national financial institutions, viz. Tanzania Investment Bank (TIB), Tanzania Development Finance Ltd. (TDFL); Tanzania Venture Capital Fund (TVCF); international financial institutions; and informal money markets, which are the most important source of finance for small-scale and informal sector ventures.

The banking system is dominated by the National Bank of Commerce (NBC), a public bank that had no competition for a long time. The lending to industries during the socialist period was not based on assessments of risk and return, but more on political decisions. The Central Bank covered the enormous losses by supplying more money which fuelled inflation. The institutional weakness of the credit system was seen in the poor services offered. The NBC eventually became practically bankrupt and its lending for industrial investment is limited.

With the liberalization of the financial system, four international banks have recently entered the scene. These banks are limiting their credit to export/import activities, and so far have had little impact on credit possibilities for industrial investments.

The specialized financial institutions offer the best opportunities for loans for industrial investments, and TVCF is a new fund established with donor assistance. However, the funds have a target group of projects with above average growth and it is difficult to get access to these loans.

The liberalization of imports and the devaluation of the shilling under the Structural Adjustment Programme has created an environment with high nominal interest rates which encourage speculative, high-return, short-term activities, mainly in trading.

Some of the current problems concerning both long- and short-term financing of industrial development are:

- inadequate liquidity in the banking system due to poor servicing of outstanding debts;

- overcautious and lukewarm support of the external financing institutions to finance the local industries due to their past performance;

- complicated procedures for financing and lending are guided by subjective considerations rather than by the merit of the projects;

- absence of sound industrial projects since investors prefer the trading sector which gives a faster and higher rate of return;

- inadequate policies to stimulate and mobilize domestic savings for use by the banking sector.

Given the above difficulties, organizing financing for small-scale enterprises is not only difficult but also expensive, with the main credit institutions for rural credit and small-scale credit facing serious financial problems. Some donors are addressing the situation by setting up credit schemes for small-scale industries, but these efforts are far from adequate. The financial question remains one of the biggest constraints to the development of the manufacturing sector.

Source: Information provided by the United Nations Industrial Development Organization (UNIDO) in response to an UNCTAD questionnaire.

Table 20: Official development finance (ODF) for the industrial and manufacturing sectors in LDCs, 1988-1992

	1988	1989	1990	1991	1992
Aggregate flows to LDCs ($ million)					
1. Total ODF, gross	14,524	14,272	14,056	13,552	11,162
2. ODF to the industry sector	882	547	335	481	251
(2) as % of (1)	6	4	2	4	2
3. ODF to manufacturing sector	801	467	256	208	209
4. (3) as % of (1)	6	3	2	2	2
Share of ODF to industry in selected countries (%)					
Bangladesh	14	7	6	1	0
Burkina Faso	5	4	1	1	0
Chad	3	0	0	2	17
Ethiopia	0	6	..	3	2
Madagascar	9	2	1	4	2
Mali	9	1	5	3	10
Mozambique	5	3	2	0	0
Myanmar	3	2	1	..	..
Nepal	0	..	1	0	2
Niger	3	3	..	1	5
Sudan	2	1	..	6	..
Uganda	2	32	3	2	5
United Republic of Tanzania	6	4	1	4	2
Zaire	15	4	1	1	..
Zambia	3	4	16	4	1

Source: Data provided by OECD.

D. POLICY OPTIONS FOR REMOVING CONSTRAINTS ON MANUFACTURING DEVELOPMENT

The salient constraints faced by LDCs' manufacturing sectors can be categorized in four broad groups, namely:

- *market-related constraints*, such as product and factor market failures, limited domestic markets and restricted access to external markets, etc.;

- *policy constraints*, such as inappropriate macroeconomic framework, policy bias against small- and medium-scale manufacturing and against agriculture, excessive regulation, administrative inefficiency, inadequate legal framework, etc.;

- *structural and endowment-related constraints*, such as low level of entrepreneurial, managerial and engineering skills, excessive dependence on imported raw materials, restricted capacity to reap economies of scale in production and distribution of manufacturing goods, inadequate physical infrastructure, etc.; and

- *country-specific constraints*, such as political difficulties, susceptibility of natural calamities, transit and transport-related constraints, remoteness of island countries from external markets, etc.

The experience of the more successful LDCs as well as of other developing countries that have created a competitive manufacturing base, and the level of progress and characteristics of manufacturing in LDCs point towards the importance of policies and measures, both functional and selective, to overcome these constraints. Market imperfections in LDCs inhibit efficient resource allocation, which provides a strong economic justification for functional interventions to redress market failures.[18] Removing market distortions are not, however, enough to inspire a particular group of activities (e.g. small-scale enterprises) or discourage others (e.g. environment-unfriendly activities). Selective interventions are required to promote specific activities. Appropriate functional and selective interventions should be seen as measures towards the creation of an enabling environment for enterprises rather than an end in themselves.

Moreover, there is no standard recipe for development. The choice of policies and measures depends on the situation of individual countries. For some countries, especially certain small-island LDCs, widespread manufacturing development may be neither desirable nor feasible. Moreover, national actions clearly do not suffice to foster manufacturing development in LDCs: there is considerable need and scope for external support. The following paragraphs outline the salient elements of national and international actions in removing constraints on manufacturing development.

National policies for manufacturing

Removing market-related constraints

Correcting market failures: LDCs are in the early stages of manufacturing development and are more susceptible to failures in both product and factor markets that lead to distortions of allocation of investment among competing activities. In general, distortions in the product market can arise from differences in learning periods and in costs associated with manufacturing technology, economies of scale and external economies or "diseconomies", while in the factor market these can be caused by imperfections in the markets for skills, capital, information and technology.[19] Together, such distortions raise the cost of entry into manufacturing activities, especially the more complex and difficult ones. This is particularly relevant for LDCs that have had very limited manufacturing experience.

The critical question here is how to reduce entry costs for enterprises and at the same time ensure efficiency. An approach in this regard could be to create an enabling environment through a combination of specific incentive and competition measures. To improve financing of

manufacturing, for example, the provision of directed and subsidized credit will need to be revitalized. Facilitating female entrepreneurs' access to credit will be important in integrating women into the process of manufacturing development (box 11). At the same time, the development or strengthening of capital and financial markets will be needed to eventually phase out the need for such credit. Skill and entrepreneurship development should be high on the agenda, which calls for non-selective measures, such as general vocational education and training, as well as selective measures such as specialized tertiary education and upgrading specific skills through retraining (discussed below). This should be buttressed by the development of national technology infrastructure through investments in local research and development capabilities.[20] Moreover, a development-oriented competition policy needs to be pursued with a view to diversifying the manufacturing base. This can be accomplished by promoting the entry of enterprises into manufacturing activities that entail more complex technologies, more risk and a longer learning period through selective import protection, and by simultaneously exposing firms with simpler processes and shorter learning periods to more external competitions.

It should, however, be pointed out that subsidization and protection policies could work either way: a judicious and highly selective mix of support policies that are periodically monitored against performance criteria can go a long way in reducing market distortions for firms. Across-the-board use of subsidy or protection, on the one hand, can lead to further aggravation of different types of market failure and, therefore, prove to be inefficient and wasteful. Thus, policies and measures to correct market failures need to be formulated and implemented with utmost care.

Market expansion: To obviate the constraints imposed by the small size of domestic market for manufacturing goods, LDCs need to consider a three-pronged approach: enhancing rural income, fostering regional cooperation and increasing external orientation of manufacturing. An agricultural strategy that emphasizes food production, encourages production of selective export crops and promotes incomes and capacities of peasant farmers will go a long way in increasing consumer demand for small and rural manufacturing and foster backward linkages in such areas as food processing.[21]

Greater regional and subregional cooperation can also help expand product and factor markets. So far, the experience with such coop-

Box 11: Improving female entrepreneurs' access to credit

In LDCs, female entrepreneurs are engaged predominantly in small and micro-enterprises, frequently in food-processing activities, which in many cases are informal-sector enterprises. A major constraint to their activities is the very limited access to funding, particularly to formal-sector financing. The reasons are rather well known. The activities that female entrepreneurs are involved in are perceived by formal banking institutions as being associated with high risk, offering inadequate collateral and involving high processing costs. Many of these activities are temporary, and the accounting and record-keeping are either weak or non-existent. Legal impediments, such as registering property in the names of the male members of households in certain countries, and the widespread lack of education, training and information on the part of women, constitute further barriers to obtaining formal sector funding. Frequently, the banking procedures and regulations, such as the requirement of a male co-signatory, are detrimental to female entrepreneurs.

Despite the above difficulties, a number of approaches have emerged in recent years to cater to the needs of female entrepreneurs. These include:

- specific credit schemes within formal banks, including development finance institutions (e.g. the Agricultural Development Bank of Nepal has a department that deals with loans to women);

- poverty-focused banks with group collateral schemes (e.g. the Grameen Bank of Bangladesh);

- women's indigenous finance institutions (e.g. the *tontines* of West Africa);

- intermediary programmes, such as Women's World Banking, which provide an opening to formal-sector financing for women;

- provision of venture capital (e.g. *Fonds de Participation* in some countries in West Africa).

The above approaches suggest that it is indeed possible to tailor the formal sector credit to the needs and requirements of female entrepreneurs. Policies and measures in this regard need to focus mainly on institutional and regulatory reforms within the banking sector, adjustment of interest policies, legal reform, and provision of information and training to women. In particular, it is important to:

- develop and strengthen credit institutions that address the requirements of female entrepreneurs;

- simplify banking regulations to enable women to obtain loans;

- provide appropriate interest subsidies;

- create intermediary credit institutions and programmes in the management, marketing and entrepreneurship training and product quality standardization intended to enable female borrowers to obtain formal-sector funding;

- undertake legal reforms to remove inequalities in the status and rights between men and women;

- initiate appropriate reforms of property laws to widen women's access to credit.

eration arrangements in which LDCs participate has not been encouraging, as very little has been achieved in terms of the expansion of intraregional trade, rationalization of production structures and promoting specialization. Scope for regional and subregional cooperation in the area of manufacturing is currently limited by factors such as the production of competing items by the participating states, poor economic prospects of certain subregions, lack of response from external donors and foreign private investors, etc. Progress in interstate cooperation at the regional and subregional level for manufacturing development will be slow and will require, among other things, identification of areas of critical supply constraints; improvement in investment climate through well-designed incentive schemes for regional or subregional operators in those areas; formulating trade policies and instruments that favour subregional or

regional transborder exchanges of manufacturing goods; cooperation in the areas of skill development and expansion of technological capacities. Strong and sustained commitment of participating Governments are a key factor for the success of regional and subregional cooperation.

Seeking external markets warrants an outward-looking approach. The relevant measures in this area are:

- trade promotion and liberalization measures (e.g. removal of quantitative restrictions, selective adjustment of tariff structure to reflect economic objectives, liberal foreign exchange regime, export promotion measures, etc.);

- micro-economic measures (such as export performance benefit schemes; duty-drawbacks; duty rebates on the import of capital goods and spare parts; bonded warehouse facilities; export financing schemes, etc.); and

- institutional measures (such as simplified procedures and documentation; quality control; mechanisms for dissemination of information on external markets, etc.);

However, national actions by LDCs themselves are not enough to improve external market prospects. International support measures, which are discussed below, have an important role in this regard.

Removing policy constraints

Macroeconomic framework: As the recent experience of many LDCs indicates, macroeconomic reforms do not automatically lead to economic regeneration. However, a stable macroeconomic framework, along with policies to correct market failures, can augment growth and enhance efficiency. In so far as the manufacturing sector is concerned, policies and measures for macroeconomic adjustment should take into account the structural rigidities and changing domestic and external circumstances of individual LDCs; linkages between manufacturing and other sectors of the economy, as well as intrasectoral linkages within manufacturing; the interface between macroeconomic goals and sectoral and subsectoral restructuring within manufacturing; the implications of the mix and sequencing of macroeconomic policy instruments for the manufacturing sector; external financing requirements, particularly quick-disbursing type of aid for necessary imports of raw materials and spare parts.

Small-scale manufacturing: Import-substitution industrialization strategies in many LDCs led to a bimodal structure in manufacturing with some large modern enterprises at one end of the spectrum and a large number of microenterprises at the other end, with very few middle and small enterprises in between. However, considerations such as the factor (including skill) endowments of LDCs, the predominantly rural nature of their economy, microefficiency, income distribution, better availability of raw materials from domestic sources and improved intersectoral linkages, etc., make a strong case for policies and measures favouring the development of small manufacturing enterprises, particularly in rural areas. Past bias against small-scale manufacturing should give way to well-targeted measures to promote small-scale manufacturing. These measures need to

aim simultaneously at attracting informal sector activities to the formal sector with a view to strengthening the linkages between them.

The *demand-side* measures for promoting small-scale manufacturing should include:

- selective product reservation schemes, whereby entry into particular product markets is restricted to small enterprises;

- encouraging subcontracting;

- sales promotion, which includes improved marketing techniques, increased Government purchases, and dissemination of market information.

The above should be accompanied by a number of *supply-side* measures, such as:

- targeting budgetary, fiscal and financial instruments to promote small-scale ventures, including improved access to credit for small enterprises (e.g. through specialized financing institutions, as well as innovative financing mechanisms such as the Grameen Bank of Bangladesh), tax holidays for new enterprises, simplified tax collection procedures, etc.;

- allocating a specific share of foreign exchange to meet the import needs of small enterprises;

- providing infrastructural and other support services, including well-conceived small estate facilities, and identifying and enabling acquisition of appropriate technology and upgrading existing processes through research and development;

- providing entrepreneurial and vocational training facilities.

Governance and manufacturing development: The importance of governance in the context of policies, strategies and instruments for the development of the manufacturing sector arises from a number of considerations. First, the discretionary use of promotional instruments may give rise to rent-seeking behaviour. Second, there is a need for Government intervention to move away from regulation to promotion. Third, as indicated above, across-the-board protection and subsidy should give way to highly selective incentives, which need to be constantly monitored against well-defined performance criteria. Consequently, administrative efficiency, accountability and transparency are of critical importance for the success of policies and instruments.

An improved governance warrants implementing clearly defined roles and functions of Government bodies and augmenting their capacity and skills, and limiting Government intervention to activities for which it has financial, managerial and technical resources. This should be accompanied by simplifying and streamlining procedures (e.g. genuine one-stop type services) to reduce entrepreneurs' start-up costs, formulating rigorously defined performance criteria against which to constantly monitor enterprises' implementation of incentive measures; improving quality control; and elaborating supportive legal framework and ensuring fair and speedy litigation.

Improved governance should be matched by responsible private-sector behaviour. For instance, private-sector entrepreneurs will need to undertake a variety of self-assessment exercises in order to avoid creating fake projects, and to ensure scheduled repayments of bank loans; ensure product quality (particularly of export items); and adhere to legal obligations (e.g. labour laws, environmental standards, etc.). Associative bodies of private entrepreneurs (e.g. chambers of commerce and industry) could institute measures to enforce self-assessment through random checks and by penalizing defaulters. Moreover, public- and private-sector cooperation are important for the formulation of appropriate policies, designing incentive or punitive measures, promoting skill development, product improvement and technological upgrading, and disseminating information relating to products, technologies and markets.

Resolving structural and endowment-related constraints

Skill development: Paucity of entrepreneurial, managerial and technical skills is a major endowment-related constraint on LDCs' manufacturing development. Appropriate intervention in the skill market, complemented by supportive measures by enterprises themselves, can go a long way in ameliorating skill-related market failures. Such interventions need not involve massive allocation of financial resources over an indiscriminate range of activities, which is neither efficient nor sustainable. What is needed are well-defined, appropriately targeted and demand-driven measures.

The *demand-side* measures can include, first, identification of areas of critical skill shortages,

and second, assessment of current and prospective demand for various skill categories. The latter, however, is a difficult task, as future skill structure would depend on the pattern of manufacturing growth, which is not easy to anticipate given the general uncertainty of development in most LDCs. Nevertheless, a well-targeted intervention warrants a minimum degree of precision regarding prospective demands for different types of skills, rather than a general indication of requirements. This is an area where LDCs can benefit from external help, particularly technical cooperation from more advanced developing countries.

On the supply side, the following actions can be useful: rationalizing, modernizing and decentralizing existing training facilities towards improved client orientation, better quality of service, cost efficiency, and a greater focus on rural and small enterprises; establishing cost-effective and selective training facilities targeted to specific skill demands; treating skill development as a major criterion for providing subsidy or protection to private-sector enterprises; and reducing gender gaps by promoting the development of women's skills.

Overall, skill-development measures should be treated as an integral part of manufacturing policy and should take into account such factors as new and emerging technologies, product quality requirements, responsiveness to domestic and external market changes, environmental considerations and the need for efficiency and demand orientation.

Physical infrastructure: Manufacturing-sector policies will need to be complemented by measures to maintain and develop physical infrastructure, including roads, railways, waterways, communication systems and physical facilities for housing manufacturing enterprises. Within the limits of public resources, LDCs should strike a careful balance between new investment in infrastructure and the maintenance of existing facilities. At the same time, it is important to examine ways and means to promote private-sector participation in this area. In this context, it is necessary to identify those services that are strictly "public goods", which are not likely to be provided by the private sector, and to devise strategies and measures to promote private-sector entry into the non-public goods activities. The issues and policies concerning infrastructure, particularly transport and communications, are addressed in detail in chapter IV.

International support measures

External financing

Official development finance: While official development finance in recent years appears to be largely bypassing the manufacturing sector, aid flows can nonetheless play an important role in the rehabilitation, promotion, expansion and deepening of the manufacturing sector in LDCs (box 12). A number of broad approaches is suggested in this regard:

- providing adequate quick-disbursing types of fund to the manufacturing sector to help tide over short-term difficulties that arise during the process of adjustment and reform (e.g. meeting the critical import needs of the sector to facilitate adjustment and restructuring and cushioning the possible adverse consequences of liberalization);

- substantially increasing the volume of aid to the manufacturing sector, as well as improving the quality of such aid with a view to removing structural impediments and improving the supply capacity in the medium to long run;

- tying a part of aid to promote greater intra-LDC procurement of manufactured goods;

- providing well-designed and appropriately targeted technical assistance, particularly in the areas of skill development and technological capacity building.

International private-sector finance: LDCs encounter tremendous difficulties in attracting external private-sector finance. In 1990, they received only 3 per cent of the total private flows to the developing countries. Their lack of access to such funds is caused by a perception of risk arising from the high stock of debt and the level of debt servicing, poor economic performance and prospects, domestic political circumstances, natural disasters, etc.

Increasing private flows is a daunting task for LDCs. However, those LDCs that have succeeded in recent years in registering good economic growth in general, and improved manufacturing performance in particular, could make efforts to improve their knowledge about, and make use of, the various financial mechanisms in the international markets, including

---

Box 12: External assistance for industrial development in Cape Verde

External official development financing for the industrial sector in Cape Verde is focused on assisting the Ministry of Tourism, Industry and Commerce (MTIC) in setting up new institutions and instruments for entrepreneurial development, reorganization and the consolidation of institutions and services aimed at framing industrial sector activities and undertaking necessary basic studies. Following are the major areas of external support:

- institutional support to the Institute for Support to Entrepreneurial Development (IADE), which includes: upgrading its technical and financial capacity; assisting in the creation and the management of an industrial development fund; reinforcing national capacity in the preparation of pre-investment studies and assistance/advice to companies;

- support to the local private sector (co-financing pre-investment studies, study tours and technical assistance activities, and training activities; direct financing of projects/entrepreneurial activities);

- development of micro-enterprises (promotion of the informal and artisanal sector; set-up of a support unit for micro-enterprises at IADE with branches in the different municipalities; definition of the legal framework and an adequate support system; definition and implementation of a support programme for micro-enterprises with a technical-assistance and financial-support component);

- development of entrepreneurial capacity (training entrepreneurs, technicians, workers and future trainers);

- valorization of mineral resources (review of existing studies and complementary geologic documentation; overview of economically important mineral resources).

Representatives of the local private sector often regard the above donor activities as inadequate and too narrowly focused on assisting governmental entities. Such criticism is partly valid owing to the fact that projects and programmes financed by external official aid are addressed either to the Government or to companies that have obtained Government endorsement for their request for assistance. Nevertheless, much remains to be done in developing the necessary legal and institutional framework to underpin the development of the manufacturing sector. This is a major reason why donors often prefer to support the upgrading of existing services to financing manufacturing ventures.

Source: Information provided by the United Nations Industrial Development Organization (UNIDO), in response to an UNCTAD questionnaire.

**Box 13: Towards an enabling environment for foreign investment
in the Lao People's Democratic Republic**

The Government of the Lao People's Democratic Republic began serious attempts to attract foreign investment from mid-1988. A new Foreign Investment Code or Law was issued in March 1989, which authorized three forms of investment: business by contract, joint ventures and wholly foreign-owned companies. It also offered tax holidays for periods of up to four years, exempted reinvested profits from taxation, and provided guarantees against nationalization of assets and for repatriation of profits. More specifically, it allowed repatriation of capital, dividends and after-tax income of foreign employees provided that the foreign exchange earnings of the company covered the last two.

At the same time, an Investment Oversight Board was established to consider and approve investment proposals. It was chaired by the Prime Minister and included representatives from the Ministry of Commerce and the Ministry of External Economic Relations (MEER). Within MEER, the Foreign Investment Management Committee (FIMC) was charged with implementing the Foreign Investment Code and issuing licences for foreign investors.

FIMC plays a role to fill the "information gap" in respect of "the new development approach" being pursued by the Government of the Lao People's Democratic Republic and related opportunities. One encouraging development is the success of the garment industry, to which a large number of foreign enterprises have been attracted and licensed within a short space of time, which is likely to exert a positive demonstration effect abroad. One stated objective is to achieve geographical diversity in its investment sources, to avoid dependence on a single source (as existed in the past) and to secure the most up-to-date technology.

Significant levels of investment began in 1989 when investments of some $65 million were licensed: by 1992 the annual figure was $160 million. The number of approved investments has continued to increase in 1993, 79 having been approved in the first half year, compared with 102 in 1992 and 69 in 1991. Investments up to the end of 1992 were about equally divided between joint ventures and wholly foreign-owned enterprises.

Although a large proportion of the investments was quite small (216 out of 280 were below $1 million) and a good many were very small (62 were below $100,000), investment was still dominated by the 64 largest investments, these having a mean value of $6.76 million and accounting for almost 90 per cent of the total invested. The mean values in the other categories by comparison were $330,500 and $48,300, respectively.

Over half the investments made during 1988-1992, about 35 per cent of the value invested, was in manufacturing. Within the manufacturing sector three sectors stand out in terms of numbers of projects. In garment-making, there were 48 projects, 35 of these in the last two years. There were also 27 investments in agri-business and 22 in wood products, both resource-based industries.

As regards the geographical sources of new investments, the former Soviet Union has ceased to be a major source, accounting for no more than 4 per cent of the total invested in 1992. The most striking feature is the dominance of Asian investment, amounting to 64 per cent of the total. Out of this, as much as 39 per cent (110 out of 294 projects) were from Thailand, although there is a broad spread of Asian countries showing concrete interest, including China, Hong Kong, Malasia and Taiwan Province of China.

The rising influence of the East Asian countries can be gauged by the fact that they accounted for 82 per cent of the value in 1991 and 1992. This may presage a progressive incorporation of the economy of the Lao People's Democratic Republic into a regional market.

Source: United Nations Industrial Development Organization, *Lao People's Democratic Republic: Industrial Transition* (Vienna, April 1994).

---

portfolio investments, debt-equity swaps, transnational venture capital, leasing, counter-trade, etc.

Foreign direct investment

While many LDCs have improved the policy framework for foreign direct investment (FDI) and some have achieved a degree of success (box 13), their overall experience so far indicates that attracting increased flows of such investment is not an easy task. LDCs need to emphasize policies that are investment-friendly, promote human and infrastructural capacity, and create a stable economic environment with a view to positioning themselves well for increased inflows of FDI.

The Governments of the home countries of FDI could help to improve the flow of FDI to LDCs by such measures as supporting and improving investment guarantee schemes in order to underwrite some of the financial risks associated with investing in LDCs, as well as providing fiscal and other incentives for investing in LDCs. The various instruments or facilities promoted by multilateral financial institutions - such as the World Bank's Expanded Co-financing Operations (ECO) and the Multilateral Investment Guarantee Agency (MIGA) - can offer important scope for LDCs in augmenting FDI flow. It would be particularly helpful for LDCs if they were offered more flexible conditions for ECOs and exempted from making financial contributions to MIGA.

Improved market access

Better access to external markets can help LDCs in lifting the constraints imposed by small domestic markets, initiating new lines of manufacturing activities and reaping economies of scale in production and distribution. Manufacturing of ready-made garments, as noted earlier, well illustrates this point. However, recent developments in the international trade policy environment, particularly the Final Act of the Uruguay Round, has heightened the concerns as regards external market prospects of LDCs. For example, in the area of textiles, the favourable treatment that a number of LDCs have been receiving under MFA would be phased out under the Final Act, leading to liberalized access to all producers. The ensuing intensified competition among producers would have important consequences for LDCs in terms of market share, FDI and technology transfer. Considerations of manufacturing diversification and LDCs' access to improved external markets make a strong case for implementing external support measures by providing additional trade preferences, particularly through the GSP, and financial and technical support, and by offering technical assistance for the development, diversification and marketing of manufacturing exports.

In particular, significant improvements in the provisions of GSP schemes for LDCs and their utilization by LDCs are called for. In the main, these schemes should provide unrestricted entry for LDCs' export items into the markets of the preference-giving countries. This topic is taken up in detail in chapter VI.

Strengthening technological capacity

International support measures in favour of building technological capability in LDCs can play a key role in the structural transformation of their manufacturing sector. Such actions could include the following:[22]

- provide LDCs with the freest and fullest possible access to technologies whose transfer is not subject to private decisions, and facilitate access to technologies whose transfer is subject to private decisions, *inter alia*, by providing incentives to private enterprises and institutions in the technology-exporting countries to encourage such transfers to LDCs;

- assist LDCs to make the fullest possible use of the transition period accorded to them in respect of the application of the Uruguay Round Agreement on Trade Related Aspects of Intellectual Property Rights;

- support and/or participate in LDCs' national programmes for developing human skills and institutional infrastructure for research on, and development of, technology;

- strengthen support for technical assistance programmes for LDCs in such areas as: formulation and implementation of technological policies and programmes; information and training to technology users, including support of intra-enterprise cooperation between LDCs and the technology-exporting countries; evaluation and negotiation of transactions involving technology transfer; and technology transfers to LDCs from other developing countries.

To conclude, the development of the manufacturing sector is an area where there is a strong need for national efforts to be complemented by external support measures. For instance, domestic measures for providing credit to entrepreneurs can be strengthened by making available appropriate external financing. Market expansion efforts can be facilitated by improved access to the markets of their major trading partners. Financial and technical support can help augment returns from LDCs' actions to expand skill and technological endowments. Specific external measures can enhance the effectiveness of national policies to attract foreign direct investment.

For the large majority of LDCs, manufacturing development represents an important means to enhancing growth and improving participation in the world economy. A strengthened partnership and collaboration between LDCs and their development partners can provide the required impetus for realizing the potentials offered by this sector towards creating and expanding the linkages between LDCs' economies and the global economic processes.

NOTES

1   *Programme of Action for the Least Developed Countries for the 1990s*, part V, "Development, particularly expansion and modernization of the economic base".

2   "Deindustrialization" is understood in the narrow sense of persistently negative MVA growth rates.

3   UNIDO, *Industry in the Least Developed Countries: Structure and Development*, pp.21-22 (UNIDO publication No.V.92-57643, January 1993).

4   *Ibid.*, pp.23-25.

5   The World Bank, *Industrial Adjustment in Sub-Saharan Africa* "The Pattern of Industrial Development in Zambia" in G.M. Meier and W. F. Steel, (Oxford University Press, 1989), pp.64-65.

6   Reported in S.H. Rahman, M.S. Emran and M. Rahman, "Trade and Industrialization in Bangladesh Reconsidered", paper presented at the UNU/WIDER Conference "Trade and Industrialization Reconsidered", Paris, July 1991.

7   T. Fukuchi, "Development Strategy for sub-Saharan countries", in *Industrial Development*, No.33 (UNIDO, Vienna).

8   This point is also made in *The Least Developed Countries, 1993-1994 Report*, Part One, chap.II, sect.C.

9   *Ibid.*

10 For an analysis of implications of these reforms, *ibid.*, Part One, chaps.II and III.

11 W.F. Steel and J.W. Evans, "Excess Capacity", in G.M. Meier and W.F. Steel (eds.), *op. cit.* Also, Howard Stein, "Deindustrialization, Adjustment, the World Bank and the IMF in Africa", *World Development*, vol.20, No.1, 1992.

12 *The Least Developed Countries, 1993-1994 Report*, Part One, chap.II, pp.57-59.

13 *Ibid.*, p.55, for a definition of these groups of liberalizers.

14 Stein, *loc. cit.*

15 For a review of industrial financing in LDCs, see UNIDO, "Financing the Industrial Action Programme for the LDCs: A Challenge for the 1990s" (PPD. 254 (SPEC), 1993).

16 A large share of the capital of the industrial financing institutions was held by the state, while bilateral institutions such as Caisse Française de Développement and the German KFW (Kreditanstalt Für Wiederaufbau, bank for reconstruction) were major participants in certain cases.   These national industrial financing institutions also established credit lines with donor institutions such as the World Bank.

17 On the role of the industrial financing in LDCs, see, for example, UNCTAD, *Report of Round Table on Promoting Indigenous Private Enterprises in the Asia-Pacific Least Developed Countries*, part D (UNCTAD/RDP/LDC/60, November, 1991).

18 For a discussion on the role of interventions to promote industrialization, see S. Lall, "Industrial Policy: The Role of Government in Promoting Industrial and Technological Development" in *UNCTAD Review, 1994*.

19 S. Lall, *ibid.*

20 The Programme of Action, in part V, identifies actions in the areas of strengthening the scientific and technological bases in LDCs.

21 G.A. Cornia, R. Vander Hoevan, and T. Mkandawire, *Africa's Recovery in the 1990s: From Stagnation and Adjustment to Human Development* (New York, St. Martin's Press for UNICEF, 1992).

22 For some of these points, see *The Programme of Action for the Least Developed Countries for the 1990s*, *op. cit.*, chap.V, sect.B.

IV. Transport and Communications Infrastructure and Services

A. Introduction

The Programme of Action for LDCs in the 1990s provides the framework and guidelines for addressing the issues of transport and communications infrastructure and services. It stipulates that "the improvement of the transport sector is vital for the expansion of all productive sectors and essential social services, for the delivery of humanitarian and emergency relief, as well as for facilitating subregional and regional cooperation and integration". This chapter provides an overview of the recent developments in this sector and of the strategic policy and operational initiatives taken to improve it. Some key conclusions and policy recommendations for future action are highlighted.

B. Some overall observations

Development of the transport and communications infrastructure is crucial for improving a country's economic performance. Benefits of an efficient transport infrastructure are generally more wide ranging than those elaborated in economic cost-benefit analyses. At the local level, transport is a vital aspect in the production of tradeables and, at the international level, is important to LDCs in order for them to avoid marginalization and maintain a competitive edge.

LDCs and their development partners acknowledge the importance of the development of the transport and communications infrastructure by allocating to it higher shares of Government funds and official development assistance (ODA). About 10 per cent of ODA, and up to 20 per cent of Government funds, are spent on this sector, with the largest proportion usually allocated to roads. Within most LDCs, the regional distribution of these resources has been uneven. Transport and communications in rural areas, where over 80 per cent of LDC populations live, have been neglected until recently and despite the fact that most LDCs still rely on their agricultural resources for most of their production and value added in their national economy.

Another important dimension of infrastructure development is the deterioration of the physical infrastructure due to poor maintenance and outdated equipment, which has serious consequences for roads in Africa where most LDCs are located. About 50 per cent of the paved roads and 80 per cent of the unpaved main roads are in poor condition,[1] which reflects a trend in overall poor planning and coordination and is addressed in more detail below.

A discussion of specific issues is difficult because of LDCs' varied geographical characteristics, which range from the mountainous countries of Bhutan, Lesotho and Nepal, to desert countries, such as Botswana, Chad, Mali and Niger. Some LDCs, notably Chad, Mali and Niger, have large areas with small populations, but others, such as Burundi and Rwanda, have small areas with large population densities. Furthermore, 19 of the 47 LDCs are land-locked and 11 are islands. Except for Madagascar, the island LDCs are small and many are remote and thus isolated from world markets.

The limited resources of the 19 land-locked LDCs are used not only to develop an internal transport and communications infrastructure, but also to maintain external transport services through transit countries. These activities create additional transport costs which are yet another financial burden. Available data for 1992 indicate that payments to foreign carriers for transport services comprised 57 per cent of exports of goods and services in Uganda, 50 per cent in Malawi, 49 per cent in Chad, 47 per cent in Mali, 32 per cent in Burundi and 27 per cent in the Central African Republic. The average payments to foreign carriers for all developing countries were only about 6 per cent.[2]

The high costs and inadequacies of both domestic and international transport and communications services hinder the economic development of the 10 small-island LDCs. These costs are high because the distances from mainland ports and major shipping lines, and the low demand for cargo and passenger loads, make their ports of call unattractive to long-haul air or shipping lines, particularly in the Indian and Pacific Oceans. Importers are obliged to accept larger than usual consignments and to stockpile goods in the event that delivery may be delayed because of unreliable transport, poor management and/or bad weather.

Some coastal LDCs provide transit transport services to land-locked countries. But these services overburden their congested ports and transport systems. Coastal LDCs may also incur financial losses when land-locked countries divert their transit cargo to more accessible ports.

C. RECENT DEVELOPMENT TRENDS

Road transport

Expansion of the road network

Roads are the most important mode of transport in most LDCs. Although the paved road network was greatly expanded during 1980-1990, its rate of expansion varied: Botswana, Burkina Faso, Burundi, Lesotho and Mali recorded rates of kilometre increase of over 90 per cent; in Bangladesh, Chad, Niger, Rwanda and Yemen, the rates ranged between 40 and 80 per cent; and in Haiti, Madagascar, Mauritania, the United Republic of Tanzania and Zambia, they were below 10 per cent.[3] The share of paved roads in the total road network also varied: in 1990 it was over 30 per cent in 8 LDCs, between 15 and 30 per cent in 17 LDCs and below 10 per cent in 10 LDCs. Available data also indicate that 19 LDCs had a road density of less than 60 km paved roads per 1,000 km[2] in 1990 (annex table 41), which is much lower than in many developing countries.

These road networks have been supported by increased investments in LDCs, largely by the donor community. National programmes in Asia and Africa have been supplemented by regional projects. The Southern African Transport and Communications Commission (SATCC) road rehabilitation and expansion programme in Southern Africa has attracted donor support. The programmes of the United Nations Transport and Communications Decade in both regions have also earmarked significant resources for roads. The Trans-African Highways projects, for example, now cover 31,519 km and the feeder-road links a total 43,066 km.[4]

Development patterns and strategies

There is more emphasis on building district and feeder roads (including paths and tracks) whose standards vary widely. Studies done in West Africa[5] estimate that to connect a village to a road by converting a footpath to a vehicle track had a greater gross benefit than if the same length of vehicle track had only been upgraded to a gravel road. Greater priority is being given to rehabilitation and maintenance. More local labour and labour-based equipment-supported methods are being used, especially for district and feeder roads. For example, of the 1,462 km of bitumen roads started or completed during the Botswana Sixth National Development Plan (1985-1986 to 1990-1991), 736 km were built by local workers, and local and unconventional materials were used to reduce costs. These low-cost methods are particularly suitable for LDCs.

Some LDCs are also turning to the private sector, instead of to the Government, to help finance additional transport infrastructure. This includes raising revenue through the introduction of road tolls.[6]

Large LDCs with dispersed populations find it financially difficult to build and maintain an adequate road system because of the distances involved. LDCs in the Sahelian region, such as Mali, Mauritania, Niger and Sudan, have some of the lowest road densities in the world. In the Central African Republic a "priority network" is used, i.e. roads that carry about 20 vehicles a day are maintained, and roads with 50 vehicles or more a day are rehabilitated.[7]

In LDCs with difficult terrain, the road network is limited unless the population is relatively small and clustered, as in Bhutan. In Nepal, the lack of road transport links is one reason for the steady migration from the hills to the plains and urban fringes. Nepal's difficult terrain and bad weather increases the costs of building and maintaining roads and so the Government can maintain only less than 25 per cent of its roads: in 1992 about 50 per cent of the road network was in poor condition and 25 per cent in only fair condition. The donor community is now focusing its support on rehabilitation and maintenance of roads.[8]

Rail transport

Expansion of the rail network

Several LDCs have no internal rail connections. Where they do exist, there has been sluggish expansion, poor management and equipment shortages. The data available for 20 LDCs show that during 1980-1990 the railroad tracks were expanded in 8 countries only: Burundi (100 per cent), Guinea (42 per cent), Madagascar (17 per cent), Myanmar (7 per cent), Togo (16 per cent), Uganda (8 per cent), Zaire (13 per cent) and Zambia (18 per cent). In 1990, 13 countries had less than 1,000 km of rail track; Madagascar, Uganda and Zambia had less than 2,000 km. In contrast, Mozambique, Myanmar, Sudan, the United Republic of Tanzania and Zaire had rail routes of 3,150, 4,664, 4,784, 2,600 and 5,088 km, respectively.[9] The railway network density in LDCs is well below that of the developing countries, as illustrated by the following: it is less than 2 km per 1,000 km^2 for 8 LDCs, and less than 5 km per 1,000 km^2 for 19 LDCs (annex table 41).

During the last 10 years, the donor community has been supporting a number of national and subregional programmes to rehabilitate and provide equipment for the rail network. Some of these programmes are: the Railway Restructuring Programme to rehabilitate the rail link between Uganda and Mombasa (Kenya), which is being supported by the World Bank; the multi-donor supported railway rehabilitation programmes in West Africa; the scheme in India to convert all metre gauge to broad gauge, which will facilitate access to Nepal; and the multi-donor supported railway projects to rehabilitate the railroad links to the ports of Lobito (Angola), Beira, Maputo and Nakala (Mozambique), Walvis Bay (Namibia) and Dar-es-Salaam (United Republic of Tanzania). However, despite donor support, investments to expand the rail networks remain inadequate.

Development opportunities

For many land-locked LDCs, railways are vital for international trade. The network linking Botswana with South Africa, Zimbabwe with ports in Mozambique, and Zambia with the port of Dar-es-Salaam is a major route to ports in the Indian Ocean. Uganda's railway to Kenya and the United Republic of Tanzania provides access to the ports of Mombasa and

Dar-es-Salaam, and Burundi and Rwanda also have rail and road connections to Dar-es-Salaam. Many LDCs in West and Central Africa have rail access to the ports of Benin, Cameroon, Congo, Côte d'Ivoire, Dakar, Nigeria and Togo.

These development opportunities are still hampered by the lack of equipment and other facilities needed for railway operations. In addition, seasonal traffic irregularities have increased operational costs and reduced the railway's competitiveness. Because of the poor quality of rail services, particularly for short-haul deliveries, and with the increasing competition of road transport services, shippers tend to prefer the latter, which accounts for the lack of profitability of most African railways.[10] All these factors have seriously undermined many LDCs' ability to expand their railway networks and to maintain their tracks and equipment. The limited progress made has been largely donor supported.

Progress in transport interface development

For land-locked LDCs, the interface between different modes of transport creates a bottleneck that leads to delays, damage and loss of cargo. Modalities to resolve these problems are being developed based on intermodal transport technology. The increasing use of containers is also playing a major role because of, *inter alia*, reduced handling costs and increased security. By using through bills of lading, land-locked LDCs have reduced the costs and delays that occur during customs clearance in the transit countries. Plans are being made, some of which are attracting private funds, for "inland" or "dry" ports designed to promote containerization, in order to capitalize on intermodal transport and to move the customs procedures from the border to a more central point so that the through-transport system will not be disrupted.

There has been significant progress in Southern Africa. A UNDP-funded and UNCTAD-executed transit transport project carried out some feasibility studies on establishing dry ports in all the land-locked countries, including the land-locked LDCs of Botswana, Lesotho, Malawi and Zambia, with follow-up actions under way in Botswana and Zambia; there were similar projects undertaken in Burkina Faso and Uganda. The dry port facilities at the rail-lake terminal in Kisumu, Kenya, and the railroad terminal in Isaka, the United Republic of Tanzania, will assist in the speedy and streamlined movement of the transit cargoes of Uganda and Rwanda, respectively. To support these efforts,

UNCTAD prepared a handbook on the operation of dry ports. It outlines the benefits, planning, legal and institutional framework, operational procedures and management of dry ports. The handbook has also been used as an orientation tool in workshops, which UNCTAD organized, on the development and management of dry ports, and has attracted interest from both the public and private sectors.

Port and inland water transport

In recent years, investment in LDC ports has been made mostly to rehabilitate and replace equipment in countries affected by conflict: Djibouti, Asab in Eritrea, the Mozambican ports, especially Maputo, and Mogadishu in Somalia. In some other LDCs, many general cargo berths have already been converted to container berths. New container berths and purpose-built bulk handling berths have been, or are being, developed in several LDCs in West and Central Africa and in the United Republic of Tanzania.

Many major ports of entry of coastal LDCs have special facilities to store and handle transit cargo. In Dar-es-Salaam, a private shipping company operates a facility of this kind according to the terms of the Belbase agreement between Burundi, Rwanda, the United Republic of Tanzania and Zaire, which provides for, *inter alia,* negotiations on tariffs and arbitration. (Plans are being made to review the agreement, which dates back to the colonial period.) Other facilities are the Nepal Transit and Warehousing Company and, in West Africa, the Entrepôts Maliens (EMS) which include EMASE in Dakar, Senegal, EMACI in Abidjan, Côte d'Ivoire, and EMATO in Lomé, Togo. The Central African

Republic and Chad have also been given land to construct similar facilities outside the port of Douala in Cameroon.

The increasing size of international container ships creates problems in many LDC ports. Few can provide or maintain adequate port facilities for these ships, especially for loading, unloading and handling equipment that these new vessels require. Regional hubs are being developed in small and remote island LDCs where cargo is decanted into feeder vessels. But the low volume of individual shipments, an imbalance between import and export volumes, delays and extra handling procedures result in higher transport costs. Archipelagic LDCs, where the links between the main ports and other islands are inadequate, are at even more of a disadvantage. Port planners have to find ways to strengthen their weak competitive position: improve productivity; reduce staff; increase mechanization for handling containers; and make better arrangements for interfacing with inland transport (box 14).

The Governments of some land-locked LDCs, e.g. Burundi, the Central African Republic, Malawi and Uganda, have, for several years, been supporting inland water transport which is a part of the transit system. In Burundi, where the waterway on Lake Tanganyika connects the capital with the Tanzanian rail-head, many changes have been made to increase the capacity of the lake vessels and to modernize the lake-rail interface infrastructure. Uganda and the United Republic of Tanzania have cooperative management arrangements for a transport system on Lake Victoria. The Danish International Development Agency (DANIDA) has an assistance programme to rehabilitate the physical

---

Box 14: Port sector development in West and Central Africa

The Port Management Association of West and Central Africa (PMAWCA) was created in 1972 by the United Nations Economic Commission for Africa, and since 1977 has served as a specialized body on maritime transport for the West and Central Africa States Conference. It has 19 regular and 8 associate members along the 9,400 km of coast between Angola and Mauritania. PMAWCA is primarily concerned with the improvement and modernization of port operations and shipping administration in member countries. Its objectives are to: improve, coordinate and standardize procedures, equipment and services of ports and harbours for increased efficiency; ensure the coordination and development of its members' activities; establish and maintain relationships with other bodies; and provide a forum for members to exchange views on current problems.

The Association's fields of activities and study have included the collection of standardized data and performance indicators, harmonized tariff setting, costing and accounting techniques, port maintenance and security, navigational assistance and sea pollution, containerization and transport modes. It also facilitates programmes of South-South technical assistance. The Association is urging greater autonomy of ports and an expansion of their roles in commercial and industrial activities.

facilities for lake operations. This programme is supplemented by advisory services, provided by UNCTAD, to establish an institutional and legal framework for these operations. A draft agreement for lake transport is being considered by the Governments of Kenya, Uganda and the United Republic of Tanzania.

Since 1989, the waterway services on Lake Malawi have been used more frequently since its outlet to the sea via Mozambique was closed following the prolonged civil strife there. The waterway is an integral part of the so-called "Northern Corridor" lake-road-rail route linking Malawi with Dar-es-Salaam. An UNCTAD transit transport project in Southern Africa has provided technical assistance for these operations along this transport corridor. A lake route links the Central African Republic with the seaport of Pointe Noire in the Congo. Recent efforts to improve the river operations, where water levels vary seasonally, include building a dam that ensures a more stable river navigation.

Air transport

Air transport has a number of advantages over land transport: speed, security, flexibility and point-to-point service. It is appropriate for freighting high-value/low-weight commodities, particularly where land routes transit several countries, change modes, and/or cross hazardous or difficult terrain, but it is capital intensive, technically complex and relatively expensive. For land-locked and island LDCs, it is often justified at low cargo values/weight once delays and losses are included in the costing of surface transport. However, while LDC import commodities often reach this value threshold, their export cargoes do not move on a steady year-round basis as do import cargoes, which results in a low use of aircraft capacity.

Most international airports have good runways, but some have restricted time slots for take-off at maximum weight. At times, there are weight constraints, even on taxiing, due to the poor physical condition of the runways. Many runways and taxiways were first built in the 1950s and were extended or replaced in the 1970s. Age and wear and tear have affected the structures and the ancillary equipment; even where the equipment is in reasonable condition, it may not be to modern standards. The surface distribution systems also are still inadequate.

Increasing competition in the air industry has limited the expansion of air transport operations. Of the 31 LDCs for which data are available, 23 recorded international freight volumes of less than 10,000 tonnes and only 8 recorded 10,000 tonnes or more in 1990. Some 14 of 33 LDCs had less than 100,000 international passengers. In 1990, of the remaining 19 LDCs, none exceeded the level of 1 million passengers (annex table 41). These growth levels are significantly lower than in many other developing countries.

The prevalent institutional problem in air transport is that its development does not take into account the traditional cost-benefit analysis usually administered outside the mainstream transport and works environment. For example, there is some interest in funding air transport in land-locked LDCs to allow them greater independence, and in Asia and Africa several donors are supporting air transport projects to help develop alternatives to land transport.

Growth patterns in the communications sector

Telecommunications network

Some external services in the telecommunications systems are adequate, but urban, interurban and rural services are poor. Available data indicate that in 1980, there were 2.4 telephones per 1,000 inhabitants in LDCs and 20.8 telephones in all developing countries. In 1992, LDCs as a group had only 3.1 telephones per 1,000 inhabitants as compared with 32.6 in all developing countries. The Maldives, with 37.0 telephone densities, and Samoa with 40.6, are the only LDCs that exceeded the average for all developing countries in 1992. That same year, the number of telephones per 1,000 inhabitants in 22 LDCs was below the 3.2 average for LDCs as a group. Most LDCs that have more than 10 telephones per 1,000 inhabitants are geographically small and have small populations and many are island countries (annex table 40).

The central facilities and international telecommunications services for some LDCs have been improved by electronic digital systems, microwave and fibre-optic transmission and satellite technology, but the demand for telecommunications, including facsimile and data transmission, is increasing faster than facilities can be provided. In Botswana, domestic calls nearly trebled from 1986 to 1990 and international calls quadrupled, while the number of subscribers only doubled (from 10,000 to 22,200). In Mali, only about 16 per cent of the demand for telephones can be met. Furthermore, the benefits have not spread uniformly throughout the more remote areas and much of the telecommunications infrastructure and modern services is still concentrated in the capital cities. In Mali, which has one of the lowest telephone densities in LDCs, 68 per cent of the telephones are in Bamako. Chad's master-plan for telecommunications proposes extensive development in its interior and envisages that 72 per cent of all telephones will still be in N'djamena in the year 2000.

With satellite technology, land-locked LDCs need not depend on the surrounding countries' networks. But in small-island LDCs, and in the more remote areas of large LDCs with thinly spread populations, satellites are frequently not economic. The problem is most acute where there are dispersed populations, mountainous terrain and no roads or electricity. These factors make ground-based transmission systems impractical. Bhutan, for example, still does not have a unified national network with digital microwave and digital radio systems, but it does have access to the international satellite network through one earth station.

As systems become more complex, the weak institutional capability, shortage of skilled staff and lack of training programmes become more serious. These deficiencies are most apparent in telecommunications and, result in, *inter alia*, poor maintenance.

At its 1994 Buenos Aires Conference, the International Telecommunications Union (ITU) recognized LDCs' special status and adopted policies for them. The development of rural telecommunications was accepted as a priority, as well as human resource development, maintenance, planning and reform and restructuring of the telecommunications sector. In its latest action plan as a target for the year 2000, the ITU recommended that main lines be provided, which will require an investment of about $4,300 million during 1994-2000, mostly in urban areas.

Extension of postal services

Available data for 41 LDCs indicate that, between 1980 and 1992, the expansion of the urban postal services was minor, and that there was, in fact, a slight decline in their number. In 1992, there were 6.1 post offices per 100,000 inhabitants in 45 LDCs, as compared with 12.6 per 100,000 inhabitants for all developing countries. A pattern of their expansion has been their increased concentration in rural areas. In 1980, about 90 per cent of post offices per 100,000 inhabitants in 30 LDCs were in rural areas. In 1992, similar available data indicate that the share of rural post offices in 42 LDCs was 85 per cent. Also in 1992, 29 LDCs recorded a total number of rural post offices per 100,000 inhabitants that was below the average for all LDCs. The highest number of post offices per 100,000 inhabitants was in Madagascar (71), the Solomon Islands (35), Samoa (28) and Nepal (21) (annex table 40).

The Universal Postal Union (UPU) had a special action programme in the 1980s which concentrated on three areas: establishing post offices and training middle- and junior-level staff especially in rural areas; and securing funds for postal transport. Particularly in countries with dispersed populations, postal services are hampered when the post office has to use passenger or freight transport services to carry the mail. The UPU initiatives for 1991-1995 address these problems.

Despite action at the national level, and UPU's resource mobilization efforts, donor support is still limited. UPU has had a disappointing response from donors to its requests for funds for postal transport, which is non-profit making.[11]

Development of broadcasting services

Broadcasting networks still play a complementary role in supporting telecommunications services. Available data show that the number of radio receivers per 1,000 inhabitants for all LDCs increased from 52 to 95 during 1980-1991, which was an annual growth rate of some 4 per cent. In all developing countries, there were 115 radio receivers in 1980 and 175 in 1991, i.e. an annual growth rate of some 5.5 per cent. The numbers of radio receivers in each LDC also vary. Twenty-one of all LDCs had a below average number of radio receivers per 1,000 inhabitants; 12, between 100 and 200; and 13, over 200.

D. SOME KEY POLICY AND OPERATIONAL CONSIDERATIONS

Road maintenance measures

The World Bank estimates that "timely maintenance expenditures of $12 billion would have saved road reconstruction costs of $45 billion in Africa in the past decade".[12] Inadequate and deferred maintenance eventually causes seasonally or permanently impassable roads and the costs then to repair them are often beyond LDCs' financial means. The sustainability of highway investment projects depends on funds and human resources. Routine maintenance protects the investments in highway infrastructure and avoids rehabilitation and vehicle operating costs.

Maintenance needs have to be taken into account from the planning and design stages and should include guidelines for supervising construction and rehabilitation. Routine maintenance of drainage structures is also essential for roads and can be accomplished with unskilled workers and few tools. Yet even with these minor costs, maintenance may have to be foregone because of lack of finances or management systems. Poor design and substandard construction methods and materials also contribute to the further deterioration of roads at a faster than average rate.

Overweight vehicles deteriorate roads by damaging the pavement and the underlying structures, including culverts and bridges. Most countries impose a limit on axle loads but it is rarely measured and more rarely enforced because LDCs have, at best, only one weighbridge, which is usually located at the port in coastal LDCs, and on the main access route in land-locked LDCs. The trucks most likely to be weighed are large tractor-trailer or semi-trailer units with four or more axles, yet trucks with only two or three axles can cause greater damage than the larger trucks.

Limits on axle loads are being established and harmonized between neighbouring countries. In 1991, the Preferential Trade Area of Eastern and Southern African States (PTA) agreed to limit axle loads to 8 tonnes but there have been frequent violations by road haulers. Actions at the national level to enforce axle weight limits have had varied results. In 1990, the PTA also drew up an agreement to harmonize road transit charges, which went into effect in January 1992. Malawi and Zimbabwe are already implementing the agreement, and Uganda and the United Republic of Tanzania are levying charges close to the agreed amounts.

Revenue from payments will be used to improve and maintain highway links. It is encouraging to LDCs that maintenance is being given greater importance by donor agencies.

For example, in Zambia, road haulers have taken steps to curtail overloading by appointing unpaid Road Traffic Commissioners at weighbridges, who have the authority to impound overloaded vehicles and arrest the drivers. The haulers have also recommended that the Government impose fines on overweight vehicles so as to reduce the incidence of overloading. The road haulers themselves benefit from the protected pavement and from the removal of unfair competition, particularly of foreign operators on international routes.

Road network management requires a reform of the institutional base, with defined responsibilities and more public accountability. The proposals of the World Bank's African Road Maintenance Initiative (RMI) are based on this reform (box 15). Inadequate management and planning skills, especially at the local level, are often blamed for poor road maintenance and equipment and lack of materials, etc. Specialized training and close supervision, good management systems and training manuals[13] are being introduced for labour-based road maintenance, which is advocated because of the spin-off of additional income and skills acquisition for the local population.

Legal and institutional framework for transport operations[14]

The most important of the international conventions on international transport are: the Convention on Transit Trade of Land-locked States (1965); Article V of the GATT Agreement; the United Nations Convention on the Law of the Sea; the TIR Convention (1975) (Transport international routière); the Kyoto Convention; the International Convention on the Harmonization of Frontier Controls of Goods (1982); the Customs Convention on Containers (1972); the International Convention concerning the Carriage of Goods by Rail (1961); and the Convention on the Contract for the International Carriage of Goods by Road (1956). Two reasons for the limited adherence to these conventions is that their benefits and implications are not always apparent and international agencies have not promoted them sufficiently. Many LDCs have not signed or ratified them.

Box 15: The World Bank's African Road Maintenance Initiative[1]

Under the World Bank's Road Maintenance Initiative (RMI), four policy initiatives aimed at solving the problems of inadequate funding for road maintenance, are being implemented in nine target African countries, including five LDCs -- Madagascar, Rwanda, Uganda, the United Republic of Tanzania and Zambia.

The first reform deals with ways to involve stakeholders in decisions on road management. Benin, the Central African Republic, Mozambique, Rwanda, Sierra Leone, the United Republic of Tanzania and Zambia all have road boards, some with members from the private sector. The legislation of most anglophone countries provides for the establishment of these boards. They begin in a purely advisory capacity, but should eventually evolve into an executive board directly responsible for managing the road network.

The second reform aims at establishing a stable flow of funds. The nine African countries are introducing road tariffs (licence fees and fuel levies) and depositing the proceeds in a road fund. Other countries are introducing the same system which is already in place in the Central African Republic. In the United Republic of Tanzania, a fuel levy of $0.10 per litre, plus an average heavy goods vehicle licence fee of $120 per heavy goods vehicle, will pay for all routine maintenance costs and 10 per cent of rehabilitation requirements. This compares with fuel levies of $0.06 in the United Republic of Tanzania (c.f. $0.09 in the Central African Republic and $0.11 in Rwanda).

The third reform focuses on establishing an organizational structure to manage main, urban, district and community roads. The simplest model is a highway authority which can devolve responsibility, under contract, to local Government agencies or to other bodies such as private contractors -- a system that is used in Sierra Leone. Conversely, in Zambia, each level of Government has its own highway authority. This has inherent pitfalls, as most rural district councils lack the financial and technical capacities to manage road networks.

Fourthly, the private-sector members of road boards will seek a more commercial approach: improved systems and procedures, better attitudes towards setting priorities and more emphasis on autonomy and accountability which will lead to greater transparency and efficiency. Benefits derived from more autonomy are the payment of market wages, instead of the depressed civil service wages that create numerous shortcomings.

---

[1]   Heggie, I., Commercializing Africa's Roads: Transforming the Role of the Public Sector, Sub-Saharan Africa Transport Policy Program Working Paper No. 10, Environmentally Sustainable Development Division, Technical Department, Africa Region, The World Bank, 1994; and Heggie, I., Management and Financing of Roads: An agenda for reform, SSATP Working Paper No. 8, Environmentally Sustainable Development Division, Technical Department, The World Bank, 1994.

There have been several initiatives, with varied success, to establish a legal and institutional regime to regulate transport operations. There are bilateral trucking agreements that stipulate that quotas have been negotiated, especially in Africa. In West Africa, bilateral arrangements have been made to divide transit cargo between national road haulers in land-locked and coastal LDCs on a two-thirds to one-third basis and are in effect in Burkina Faso, the Central African Republic, Mali, Niger and their transit neighbours, but it has not yet been determined if they actually improve transit operations. Efforts are being made towards greater liberalization. UNCTAD and the World Bank have made several recommendations to ensure freedom of choice to shippers and freight forwarders.

LDCs have put in place legal and institutional frameworks to regulate international transport, e.g. in the treaties establishing the Economic Community of West African States (ECOWAS); the Preferential Trade Area; and the Northern Corridor Transit Agreement (NCTA) covering Burundi, Kenya, Rwanda, Uganda and Zaire. Several other bilateral agreements between LDCs, particularly for land-locked LDCs and their coastal LDCs, have not been too successful because there are no mechanisms to monitor and enforce them.

In Southern Africa, where the road haulage industry is dominated by South Africa, similar initiatives have been taken to increase the participation of the land-locked LDCs of Botswana and Lesotho, as well as Swaziland, in road transport operations between them and commercial centres and ports in South Africa. UNCTAD was instrumental in drafting a multilateral agreement outlining the modalities for these initiatives. Success will depend, however, on these countries' operational capability to build up their road haulage industry so that they can offer cost-effective competitive services.

Transport logistics for humanitarian and emergency relief

Calls for emergency assistance have increased dramatically during the last decade and require large scale ad hoc transport arrangements. Most calls are due to the large displacements of populations who need to be supplied with basic staples. Many of these events occur outside the national borders of the affected populations, for example, Rwandan refugees who move into Burundi, the United Republic of Tanzania and Zaire. Refugees tend to encroach onto the agricultural land and settlements of the resident population, but the aid agencies try to resettle them into camps outside the populated and production areas. Supplies therefore have to be distributed to different sites in previously unpopulated areas, where road access is often poor. Shortages of time and money preclude improvements in transport infrastructure except if there is a specific bottleneck, for example, a small ferry that is being replaced by a bailey bridge (e.g. in the United Republic of Tanzania during the Rwandan emergency). In longer-term programmes, repairs may be done to counteract wear and tear, for example, filling potholes in Zaire during the rainy season to keep the Goma-Bukavu road open for the Rwandan refugees.

Airlifting is an expensive alternative to shipping and trucking, but is often used in the early stages of a relief operation when speed is crucial and especially when access from ports to roads is long and difficult. Unlike roads, airstrips are often available, even in remote areas and especially in Africa. Aircraft are tailored for these operations, but aid agencies have at times improved airstrips for even larger aircraft to be used when the relief operations have ceased.

Host Governments can rarely provide infrastructure or transport services for most relief operations since they themselves are developing countries or LDCs, with inadequate services for their own people, and also are not usually prepared for emergencies.

Many natural disasters like tropical cyclones, volcanic eruptions, earthquakes and landslides, have caused havoc in many small-island LDCs. Many of the relief efforts are carried out by the Governments, with aid agencies often on hand at an early stage. Again, speed is of utmost importance and best use has to be made of existing resources. There is no time to improve the infrastructure except to temporarily replace damaged bridges, etc. Donor support plays a key role here. National and regional disaster preparedness plans are being promoted to deal

with these events. Many LDCs, left on their own, cannot provide the required transport infrastructure.

Arrangements for regional and subregional cooperation

Cross-border collaboration for infrastructure development and maintenance is crucial for international transport operations for landlocked LDCs and their transit neighbours. Landlocked LDCs have high transport costs because they must transit through neighbouring coastal states and have to cooperate with their neighbours to harmonize procedures, facilities, sector policies and laws and regulations. Customs procedures cause delays and high costs at ports and border crossings. They include late arrival of documents at transit ports, extended warehouse storage that incurs high charges, losses and pilferage, costly customs security bonds and low capability of clearing and forwarding agents. The bilateral, subregional and international conventions, referred to above, provide a framework for addressing these problems.

At the subregional level, the PTA and the Northern Corridor Transit Agreement have also agreed to collaborate to facilitate the movement of cargo by road and rail. International transit documents, such as the road transit document (RCTD) and the rail consignment note, are being promoted to this effect. In West and Central Africa, the UDEAC (l'Union douanière et économique en Afrique centrale) was set up under the 1964 Treaty of Brazzaville as part of a long-term plan for economic union. It is a group of six countries (Cameroon, Chad, Central African Republic, Congo, Equatorial Guinea and Gabon) whose prime objective is to facilitate the movement of international cargo. It also aims to improve transit conditions for the land-locked member countries and the land-locked provinces of other members through a common transport and transit policy.

Other subregional organizations, like SATCC and the Kagera River Basin Organization (KBO), also have several projects that promote coordination and planning of the transport network as a basis for longer-term economic integration schemes. They are designed to enhance regional integration in other areas such as trade, industry, agriculture and energy. They are supported by the Economic Commission for Africa's Transport and Communications Decade programme and various donors. In Asia also, similar projects involving several LDCs are under way, assisted by ESCAP and the donor community. The Asian Development

Bank's (AsDB) Regional Technical Assistance to the six countries of the Greater Mekong Subregion also has projects for transport between these countries, which will facilitate the transport system of the Lao People's Democratic Republic.

Economies of scale in long-haul international air services can also be achieved by jointly owned, regionally based airlines. One successful example is Air Afrique, which was set up in 1961 by a treaty signed by 11 countries (Benin, Burkina Faso, Central African Republic, Chad, Congo, Ivory Coast, Mali, Mauritania, Niger, Senegal and Togo), and another is a regional airline established by South Africa, Uganda and the United Republic of Tanzania. The largest successful regional shipping operation, the Pacific Forum Line, owned by and serving, *inter alia*, Kiribati, Samoa, the Solomon Islands and Tuvalu, is supported by Australia, New Zealand and the European Union.

E. POLICY CONCLUSIONS AND RECOMMENDATIONS

Investment planning in the transport and communications sectors should take account of wider cross-sector development benefits. It should be carried out within a national transport and communications plan in which the distribution of funds between and within the subsectors is considered. Furthermore, duplication of efforts must be avoided when planning international transport corridors for land-locked LDCs. Alternative outlets to the sea must be maintained without incurring unjustified costly investments. In order to support the above strategy of the transport and communications sectors, the following key actions need to be given high priority.

Road transport

- Funding for maintenance through viable road funds, a good network management system with greater accountability of highway authorities, and cost-reduction methods should also be accorded high priority.

- In funding highway rehabilitation projects, the donor community should insist on a maintenance schedule financed by road-user charges.

- Regulations on vehicle and axle weights are needed to protect the highway infrastructure and reduce maintenance costs and should be established and enforced.

- Private sector participation in major new construction and rehabilitation schemes, still limited, should be promoted.

- Road transport operations can become more competitive through carefully planned deregulation and privatization, but the benefits derived from the more regulated environment, especially driver and vehicle standards that affect public safety and cargo security, should be preserved.

- Bilateral and subregional agreements to facilitate intercountry movement of road freight with respect to customs documentation and procedures should be implemented and institutional mechanisms established. Countries must be encouraged to adhere to international road transport conventions.

Rail transport

- Railways are capital intensive and expensive to maintain and therefore need better management systems and more sophisticated tariffs. The long-term wide-ranging benefits of the railways, especially for long-haul cargo traffic, should be considered in the plans for investment or cut-backs in railway systems. Some railways, like roads, are showing the effects of age, but it is mostly poor maintenance that damages their infrastructure. Maintenance programmes should therefore be supported by appropriate policies.

- The introduction or re-introduction of rail links into ports, industrial estates and other cargo-intensive areas should be considered by LDCs and the donor community, in the light of the wider benefits that accrue from what are often only short additional rail lines.

- Equipment shortages are often responsible for poor service and need to be addressed by railway administrations. There is also a lack of operational planning capacity and of a system to locate wagons and motive power units. Asset tracking systems should therefore be introduced on complex railway networks. Donors should give priority to these areas.

- Efficient through-running of rail services between neighbouring countries is crucial for land-locked LDCs. They and the donor community should develop bilateral and subregional agreements and arrangements for payment procedures for hired equipment and services provided in wagon interchanges, conditions for using wagons on foreign tracks and consultation and arbitration procedures.

Transport interface

- There are still problems inherent in changing transport modes, particularly in land-locked LDCs. With the support of the private sector, LDCs should encourage containerization as a way to improve cargo flows and the operation of block trains. Containers and other intermodal transport systems require further development, especially in Africa, with the necessary handling equipment and infrastructure in place.

- Intermodal systems can simplify bilateral and international facilitation procedures. Coastal LDCs serving land-locked LDCs should modify their international transport procedures for greater efficiency. With international technical assistance, problems of container verification procedures and cargo handling in ports and at road/rail heads can be resolved.

Port and inland water transport

- Overstaffing and poor management and equipment maintenance are more serious problems for LDC coastal ports than is infrastructure. Many port authorities are profitable and attract funds for new development (for example, Dar-es-Salaam). Port charges are under competitive pressure and profitability of some ports may not continue, especially in Southern Africa where there is a proliferation of port facilities.

- Ports of the transit neighbours of land-locked LDCs should provide special facilities and services to minimize the losses, costs and delays due to port handling and storage.

- Unlike the coastal states, small-island LDCs have an inadequate port infrastructure to deal with large ships that handle international cargoes. Regional ports should be designated and developed and be given facilities for transhipment of containers and other cargo from trunk shipping routes to the smaller island LDCs. Regional facilities for ship repair should be promoted through regional funding.

- Improvements to facilities in the outer islands of the archipelagic LDCs should be planned as part of the transit system for the islands as a whole. Small-island LDCs should standardize the types of vessel used on inter-island and intraregional shipping routes in order to minimize operating and maintenance costs.

- Regional training institutions should promote professionalism and technical skills, tailored to local conditions. The ongoing UNCTAD training programmes in the marine sector, such as TRAINMAR, are relevant for small-island and coastal LDCs.

- National regulations are needed to govern inland water transport operations. Lack of up-to-date, enforceable legislation concerning safety of life, protection of property and environment, control and prevention of marine pollution and liability in case of major accidents or disasters on lakes and rivers calls for immediate action, and uniform legislation for safety and carriage of goods is recommended.

- LDCs involved in marine service operations should improve, standardize and maintain navigational aids on lakes and rivers, most of which are inoperative or ineffective. There should be a uniform system of ship-to-ship and ship-to-shore radio communication for emergencies and search-and-rescue operations.

Air transport

- In view of the high cost of air freight operations and the increasing competition between carriers, LDCs should continue their efforts with their neighbours to enter into regular pooling air freight arrangements that permit economies of scale.

- The trade-offs between service quality and operating costs of the newer types of aircraft, and the capital costs of new equipment and runway improvements, as well as the cost of the aircraft themselves, should be analysed. Technical assistance to LDC airlines usually focuses on aspects important to the carrier, but a broader view of national expenditure and benefits is needed.

- Land-locked LDCs should capitalize on the greater benefits of air freight by providing storage facilities, handling equipment and airport infrastructure and efficient ground-distribution systems to facilitate air cargo movement and attract more foreign carriers.

- Where tourism is developing, airport charges and investment policies should be devised and external technical assistance is required.

- Regional cooperation arrangements for air freighting can provide opportunities for small-island LDCs. Furthermore, seaplanes could be used where difficult terrain or shortage of land preclude building airfields that can accommodate larger aircraft.

Communications

- Further donor funding and technical assistance are needed in the communications subsector if the benefits of information technology are to be realized. For land-locked and small-island LDCs isolated from sea ports and international markets, telecommunications, postal services and broadcasting can help to alleviate this isolation and provide services for LDCs with dispersed populations. Donors should take these factors into account in their assistance programmes. Regional and subregional schemes (with LDC participation) to improve communication services should be supported.

NOTES

1. UNTACDA II (Second United Nations Transport and Communications Decade for Africa), Road sub-Sector Working Group Strategy Paper, December 1990.

2. UNCTAD, *Handbook of International Trade and Development Statistics*, 1993.

3. The World Bank, *World Development Report, 1994*, table A.1.

4. ECA, Facilitation of International Traffic in the Field Road Transport, Transcom/232, November 1988.

5. Hine, J.L. and J.D.N. Riverson, The impact of feeder road investment on accessibility and agricultural development in Ghana; Conference on Criteria for planning highway investments in developing countries, London, 1982.

6. Yates, C., *Toll Roads in Argentina*, to be published in New World Transport, Sterling Publications Ltd., London, 1995.

7. Ministry of the Economy, Finance, Planning and International Cooperation, Central African Republic, 1990.

8. The World Bank, "Nepal: Road Maintenance and Rehabilitation Project", Staff Appraisal Report, Energy and Infrastructure Operations Division, Country Department 1, South Asia Region, 1994.

9. The World Bank, *World Development Report, 1994*, table 1a.

10. Heggie, I. and M. Quick: *A Framework for Analysing the Financial Performance of the Transport Sector*, The World Bank, 1990.

11. Universal Postal Union, Report of the Executive Council on the Action of the UPU in favour of Least Developed Countries, Washington Congress, 1989.

12. Heggie, I., Commercializing Africa's Roads: Transforming the Role of the Public Sector, Sub-Saharan Africa Transport Policy Program Working Paper No. 10, Environmentally Sustainable Development Division, Technical Department, Africa Region, The World Bank, 1994.

13. One such handbook for foremen and workers is an updated and expanded version of the 1982 popular United Nations Economic Commission for Africa series, prepared with funding from the United Kingdom's ODA -- The International Road Maintenance Handbook.

14. For a more detailed discussion, see UNCTAD/LDC/92, Legal and Institutional Framework for Transit Operations: current situation and proposals for improvement, 1994.

V. INTERNATIONAL SUPPORT MEASURES: EXTERNAL RESOURCES AND DEBT

A. INTRODUCTION

LDCs traditionally rely on ODA for most of their external financing, and in the early 1990s became increasingly dependent on aid from DAC donors, as other financing sources dried up. In a situation where there seems to be few prospects for significant expansion in total ODA, at least over the next few years and perhaps beyond, special attention must be given to focusing available aid resources on LDCs in order to meet their external capital and other assistance requirements (box 16), and to measures to provide further debt relief to help ease financing constraints. The net transfer of resources to LDCs during the early 1990s would in fact have been substantially lower had there not been a significant accumulation of external arrears (with many LDCs unable to fully service their heavy debt burden), and had creditors not extended debt relief to these countries. In this respect, there is an important trade-off between debt relief and additional financing; without the latter, LDCs' payment problems and needs for debt relief are likely to subsist or further increase in the near future.

Recent trends in ODA contributions and aid flows to the LDCs are reviewed below in section B. This section also deals with the potential contribution of non-ODA financing, with the role of consultative and aid groups and the round-table process in mobilizing external support for LDCs, and with related issues of aid conditionality and aid effectiveness. LDCs' external debt situation, measures taken to alleviate their debt burden and further debt-relief requirements are reviewed in section C.

B. EXTERNAL RESOURCES FOR LDCs

Aid targets and trends in ODA and other resource flows to LDCs

General trends affecting resource flows to LDCs

Since the adoption of the Programme of Action in 1990, major changes have taken place in the global economy and in the setting for aid and pattern of resource flows to the developing countries. Economic recession in the OECD area, budgetary constraints and widespread cuts in aid budgets and programmes, have affected the supply of ODA resources from DAC member countries. At the same time, there has been a sharp decline in assistance from other traditional donors (OPEC and former CMEA countries), leaving the OECD/DAC countries as the only major source of concessional assistance to LDCs. On the demand side, pressure on resources has increased, stemming from the emergence of new claimants for aid, from massive emergency and relief needs related to multiplying crisis situations, as well as from increased attention to global concerns, such as the environment, and to requirements for sustainable development. In this general context, LDCs are now facing sharper competition for increasingly scarce aid resources.

Positive developments that have taken place in the world economy in the early 1990s have been the reform efforts undertaken by a number of developing countries, followed by better economic performance. In response to the improved conditions and growth prospects in these countries, there has been an upsurge in external resource inflows, in particular private capital flows. In 1993, the total net flow of resources to developing countries reached a new record level, with virtually all of the expansion since the beginning of the decade attributable to the growth in private capital flows, which have overtaken official financing in importance. But the increase in resource flows has been unevenly distributed. It is mainly the more advanced and some larger low-income countries that have been able to attract private financing, whether in the form of capital market financing or foreign direct investment. As discussed below, LDCs have so far benefited little, if at all, from this increase in external resources.

In contrast with the expansion of private capital flows, official development finance[1] on which LDCs traditionally rely, stagnated over 1991-1992 before taking a downturn in 1993. ODA provided by DAC countries declined sharply in 1993, and the share of overall ODA (to all developing countries) in DAC members' GNP fell from 0.33 per cent in 1992 to 0.30 per

Box 16: External capital requirements of LDCs

According to most recent estimates, net capital flows to LDCs will need to increase very substantially if these countries are to achieve accelerated growth during the current decade, even assuming strong efforts by LDCs themselves to mobilize domestic savings and use resources efficiently. These requirements have been calculated under: (i) a baseline scenario assuming a growth rate in real GDP of 3 per cent annually on average for LDCs as group during the second half of the 1990s, resulting in 2.2 per cent growth for the decade as a whole (below the current rate of population increase); and (ii) an "accelerated growth" scenario assuming a boost in real GDP growth to 6 per cent on annual average during 1995-2000, raising the growth rate for the decade as a whole to 3.9 per cent.

Under the accelerated growth scenario, LDCs' annual external capital requirements are calculated to reach some $37 billion in 1990 prices by the year 2000. Debt-servicing payments have been projected to not exceed one-fifth of export earnings. This implies exceptional financing in the form of debt relief, or continued accumulation of payment arrears on external obligations. Unless appropriate provisions are made for debt relief, LDCs' assistance needs would grow further. As discussed later in this section, ODA must be expected to meet most of the external resource needs of LDCs during the current decade.

These projections of LDCs' external capital requirements call for two observations. First, even under the baseline scenario - which implies only a slight increase in per capita income for LDCs as a group over the second half of the decade, and no improvement over the decade as a whole - ODA inflows would need to increase by the year 2000 to a level some 50 per cent in real terms above current levels. Under the accelerated growth scenario which, in turn, implies only a modest growth of per capita income during the current decade, ODA requirements at the end of the 1990s amount to two and a half times the current volume. While it is clearly unlikely that this "accelerated growth" could be achieved during the remainder of the decade, it nonetheless illustrates the exceptional magnitude of the task involved in attaining the primary objective of the Programme of Action. Second, the addition of new countries to the list of LDCs have further enhanced the external capital requirements. They are about 23 per cent higher for the 48 countries included in the list at the outset of 1995 (including Angola and Eritrea) than for the 41 countries which were on the list in 1990 when the Programme of Action and its aid targets were adopted. This raises the issue of the needed adjustment of the aid targets, to cover the resource requirements under the expanded list of LDCs. The ODA requirements could have been lower if it were possible for them to implement successful export-oriented strategies and to receive significantly improved flows of private investment - a scenario which is not quite likely for the great majority of LDCs in the next few years. Consequently, their present near-total dependence on concessional financing will continue.

Overall, the projections put into stark light the massive external capital requirements of LDCs and the necessity to enhance ODA and other external resource flows to them in order to permit even a modest improvement in the economic welfare of more than a half billion people living in these countries.

Note: The projections are based on a methodology similar to that employed in *The Least Developed Countries, 1992 Report*, chap.IV, sect.A.

---

cent in 1993, the lowest level recorded for two decades.

The fall in overall DAC ODA in 1993 also led to a significant decline in aid to LDCs. The share of ODA to LDCs in DAC members' GNP, which had been 0.09 per cent in 1990 (and throughout most of the previous decade), had already shrunk to 0.08 per cent in 1991 and 1992, and fell further to 0.07 per cent in 1993. According to preliminary estimates, disbursements under bilateral aid programmes and from multilateral agencies mainly financed by the DAC countries dropped by almost $1.3 billion in 1993 from the previous year's level (chart 3.A).

The GNP share of aid and corresponding disbursements measure the support extended to LDCs in two different ways. The GNP share is calculated on the basis of donors' contributions (aid provided bilaterally plus imputed contributions to multilateral agencies, e.g. through capital subscriptions). The disbursement figures measure the actual flow of aid to recipient countries (bilateral aid plus paid-out expenditure by the multilateral agencies in these countries).

Contributions to multilateral agencies entering into the measurement of the GNP share of aid tend to show important year-to-year variations (notably through the bunching of capital subscriptions to financial institutions.) The aid outcome in 1993 for LDCs in terms of the share of DAC donors' GNP was thus affected by lower contributions to multilaterals in that year. In the past and as also observed in the first years of the 1990s, despite variations in the GNP share, the actual flow of aid (paid-out expenditure) to LDCs from DAC countries and multilateral agencies mainly financed by them nevertheless held up, supported by the continued expansion of multilateral disbursements. This was no longer the case in 1993.

Although there may be a certain evening-out effect on the actual provision of aid over time through a steadier flow of disbursements, a declining GNP share of aid over the longer term must affect resource availability for LDCs. In

Chart 3: The flow of external resources to LDCs, 1983 - 1993

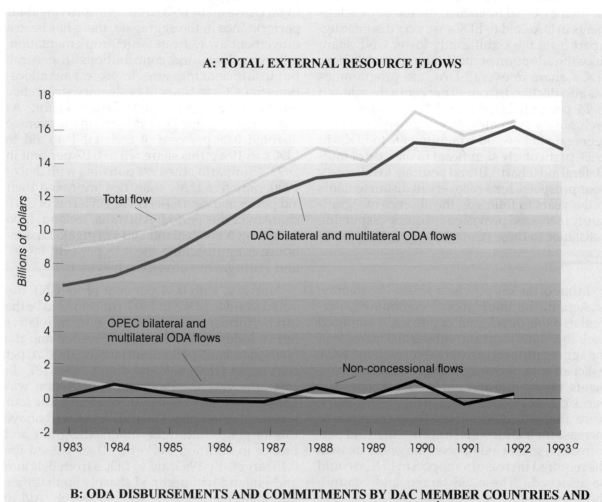

A: TOTAL EXTERNAL RESOURCE FLOWS

Total flow

DAC bilateral and multilateral ODA flows

OPEC bilateral and
multilateral ODA flows

Non-concessional flows

Billions of dollars

1983 1984 1985 1986 1987 1988 1989 1990 1991 1992 1993ᵃ

B: ODA DISBURSEMENTS AND COMMITMENTS BY DAC MEMBER COUNTRIES AND BY MULTILATERAL AGENCIES ᵇ

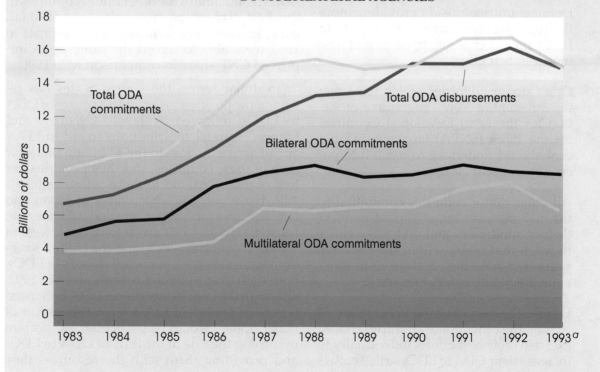

Total ODA
commitments

Bilateral ODA commitments

Total ODA disbursements

Multilateral ODA commitments

Billions of dollars

1983 1984 1985 1986 1987 1988 1989 1990 1991 1992 1993ᵃ

Source: UNCTAD secretariat, based on OECD data.
a Preliminary estimates.
b Multilateral agencies mainly financed by DAC member countries.

view of this and of LDCs' now near-total dependence on aid from the DAC group of donors
for their external financing, the recent developments in DAC aid to LDCs are very disquieting.
Apart from the significantly lower GNP share
since the adoption of the Programme of Action,
LDCs' share in overall DAC aid programmes
has also declined, from 29 per cent a decade ago
to 24 per cent in 1992 and 1993.[2] Moreover,
preliminary estimates show a downturn in the
aggregate in new aid commitments to LDCs in
1993, particularly significant in the case of multilateral aid (chart 3.B) and pointing to relatively
poor prospects for a recovery in disbursements
in the years to follow in the absence of significantly increased provisions of quick-disbursing
assistance to these countries.

Implementation of aid targets

In one of the key provisions in the Programme
of Action, the international community, particularly the developed countries, committed
itself to a significant and substantial increase in
the aggregate level of external support to LDCs.
A set of alternative aid targets and commitments, taking into account the aid policies and
performance *vis-à-vis* LDCs of different donors,
were adopted to encourage these countries to
increase their efforts and improve their aid performance, so that aid flows commensurate with
the required increase in support to LDCs would
be achieved. These aid targets and commitments merit to be recalled:

- Donor countries already providing more
  than 0.20 per cent of their GNP as ODA to
  LDCs should continue to do so and also
  increase their efforts;

- Other donor countries which have met
  the Substantial New Programme of Action for the Least Developed Countries
  for the 1980s (SNPA) target of 0.15 per
  cent should undertake to reach 0.20 per
  cent by the year 2000;

- All other donor countries committed to
  the 0.15 per cent target should reaffirm
  their commitments and undertake either
  to reach that target within the next five
  years or to make their best efforts to accelerate their endeavours to reach it;

- During the period of the Programme of
  Action, the other donor countries should
  exercise their best efforts individually to
  increase their ODA to LDCs so that collectively their assistance to these countries
  will increase.

Implementation of the aid targets set in the
Programme of Action has, however, been weak.
In fact, instead of DAC donors improving their
performance in the aggregate, there has been a
movement away from target implementation,
following lower aid contributions in general.
But insufficient measures to protect aid allocations to LDCs in times of budgetary stringency
must also be seen as a contributory factor. As
noted above, while DAC donors on the average
devoted 0.09 per cent of their GNP to aid to
LDCs in 1990, this share fell to 0.07 per cent in
1993. Comparing the 1993 outcome with that of
1990, only five DAC countries improved their
aid performance *vis-à-vis* LDCs in terms of GNP
share over this period: Australia, Ireland, Luxembourg, New Zealand and Portugal. Luxembourg is approaching the 0.15 per cent target,
and Portugal has already achieved it.

Norway, with 0.44 per cent of its GNP devoted to aid to LDCs in 1993, continued to be the
top performer among DAC donors in relative
terms, followed by Denmark, Sweden and the
Netherlands, all of them surpassing the 0.20 per
cent target (chart 4.A and annex table 18). In
1990, the year the Programme of Action was
adopted, a total of five DAC countries (the four
just mentioned plus Finland) were well above
this target, while three others (Belgium and
France in addition to Portugal) surpassed the
0.15 target. By 1993, aid to LDCs from Belgium
and Finland had declined sharply so that they
no longer met the 0.15 per cent target. Aid to
LDCs from some of the other donor countries in
this best-performing group also tended to fall
back, so that only Denmark and Portugal in
1993 were able to record the same or an improved GNP share in comparison with 1990.

In dollar terms, the United States has re-
gained the position as the largest source of ODA
to LDCs, followed by Japan, Germany and
France. Annual contributions to aid to LDCs
are all above or close to the $2 billion mark for
each of these countries, and they provide over
half of total DAC aid to these countries (chart
4.B). However, the GNP shares of Japan and
United States (at 0.05 per cent and 0.03 per cent,
respectively, in 1993) are among the lowest of
the DAC countries. Italy and the United Kingdom have also been major aid donors to LDCs,
both with over $1 billion contributions in 1992,
although they fell below this in 1993. Enhanced
efforts in favour of LDCs from this group of
major donors would be particularly important
in turning the tide in the flow of ODA to LDCs
and providing them with the resources they
need.

Chart 4 : ODA to LDCs from DAC member countries, 1983 and 1993

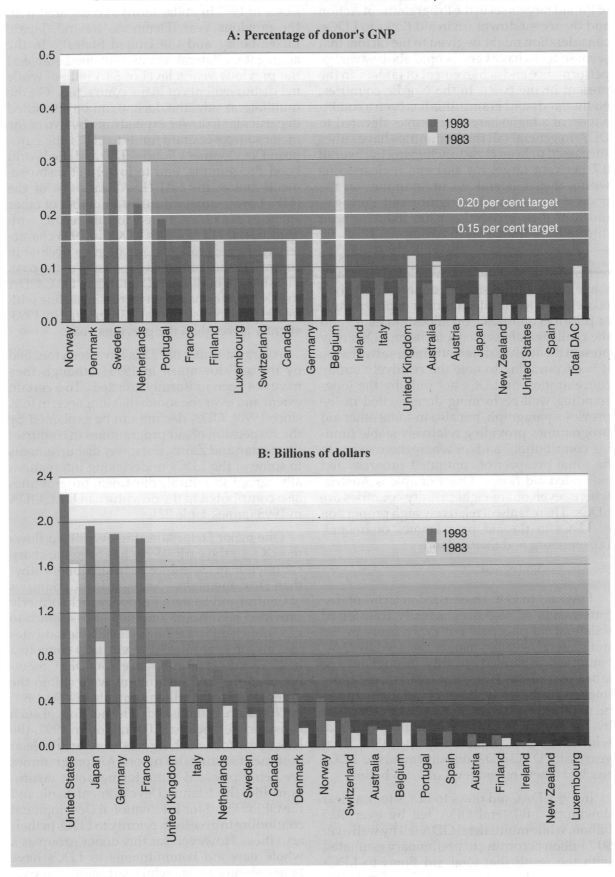

A: Percentage of donor's GNP

1993
1983

0.20 per cent target

0.15 per cent target

B: Billions of dollars

1993
1983

Source: UNCTAD secretariat, based on OECD data.

In view of the weak overall implementation of the aid targets set in the Programme of Action and the recent downturn in aid flows to LDCs, consideration might be given to the factors that seem so far to have been behind above-average performance and achievement of targets, in the present or the past. In the Nordic countries, Netherlands and France, this has been a combination of a high share of resources devoted to ODA in general (all these countries have either surpassed or been close to achieving the overall 0.7 per cent target for aid) and a clear focus within their bilateral aid programmes on the poorest countries. In Belgium and Portugal, much of their bilateral aid has likewise been directed to a few LDCs in Africa.

Aid programmes of the largest donors in terms of volume tend to have global coverage, while many of the smaller donors direct their bilateral aid to a limited number of programme or priority countries. Aid allocation issues and the challenge of keeping a focus on LDCs may present themselves differently in these two cases. It is encouraging to note the relatively strong concentration on LDCs not only by the long-standing well-performing donors cited in the previous paragraph, but also in some other aid programmes providing relatively stable funding contributions and/or where there seems to be some prospect of continued progress and expanded aid flows. One example is Austria, where seven out of eight priority countries are LDCs. There is also a relatively high proportion of LDCs in the aid programmes of Ireland, Luxembourg and Switzerland.

Trends in ODA flows

DAC aid to LDCs measured in terms of disbursements or resources actually transferred (bilateral aid plus paid-out expenditure by the multilateral agencies mainly financed by DAC countries) expanded steadily throughout the latter part of the 1980s, but trends were more uneven in the early 1990s. Variations in the bilateral aid flow were, however, largely offset by the steady expansion of multilateral aid, which increased continuously up to 1992. That year, total DAC ODA disbursements to LDCs reached a new record level of $16.3 billion.

In 1993, DAC aid flows to LDCs took a clear downturn. Bilateral ODA fell by over $0.5 billion, while multilateral ODA fell by well over $0.7 billion according to preliminary estimates, with the result that total aid flows to LDCs declined markedly to under $15 billion, below the level achieved in 1990. Funding provided under most bilateral aid programmes contracted, in some cases significantly. Only five

donor countries increased their bilateral aid to LDCs in 1993 in dollar terms as compared with the previous year (Denmark, Ireland, Japan, Luxembourg and the United States). In the aggregate, bilateral grants remained stable at the previous year's level of $8.4 billion, while net disbursements of loans contracted. On the multilateral side, the decline can be attributed in particular to lower expenditure by two of the major sources of grant funds to LDCs, the European Development Fund (EDF) and the World Food Programme, and to lower net disbursements under the SAF/ESAF facilities of the IMF. Lower expenditure by a number of other agencies also contributed to this result, with multilateral aid flows to LDCs in 1993 characterized in general by stagnation or decline in contrast to the continued expansion of the past. The share of multilateral funding in DAC ODA to LDCs, which had been increasing in line with this expansion, settled at 43 per cent in 1993, slightly lower than the previous year.

A large number of LDCs have been touched by the aid downturn in 1993, although they have not been uniformly affected. To a certain extent and over the somewhat longer term (e.g. since 1990), ODA decline can be explained by the suspension of aid programmes in countries like Sudan and Zaire. But lower disbursements to some of the LDCs undertaking internationally agreed structural adjustment programmes also contributed to the downturn in DAC ODA in 1993 (annex table 22).

One major factor affecting overall aid flows to LDCs in the early 1990s has been the sharp contraction in assistance from aid donors other than DAC members. As regards the countries of Central and Eastern Europe, which formerly provided significant amounts of assistance to LDCs, such information as is available indicates that aid programmes have virtually come to a halt. Concessional assistance from OPEC member countries and institutions were still in the order of $0.5 to 0.6 billion annually in 1990-1991, but has since diminished. The net flow of such assistance fell below $100 million in 1992, the latest year for which figures were available at the time of writing this report. Aid programmes are being pursued with, for instance, institutions like the Islamic Development Bank and the OPEC Fund for International Development continuing to give high priority to LDCs in their activities. However, for this donor group as a whole new aid commitments to LDCs have fallen significantly, while substantial repayments on past loans are reducing the net flow of assistance.[3]

Non-concessional flows

Non-ODA flows play a relatively marginal role in the external financing of LDCs as a group. For instance, the total net inflow of non-concessional official funds and of private capital to all 47 LDCs in 1992 was at about the level of bilateral funding provided to this group of countries under the Danish aid programme alone. While some LDCs have, over the past, occasionally been able to attract relatively significant non-ODA flows, on the whole the pattern of such financing has been erratic, and there has been no steady inflow of resources other than ODA and grants from non-governmental organizations (NGOs). As with ODA, OECD/DAC countries remain the main source of other official and private capital to LDCs.

While there was a net inflow of non-concessional official resources to LDCs over most of the past decade, net financing on private export credit account has been negative. Other private flows have tended to be very small for most LDCs, with annual variations in the flow in and out of a few countries largely determining aggregate figures for LDCs as a group. In 1990, for example, the total of non-concessional financial flows to LDCs reached a record level of $1 billion, due in large part to official flows to Zaire and private capital going to Liberia. In 1991-1992, non-concessional official flows and direct investment from DAC sources shrank. The net result of these various capital movements was an outflow of resources on non-concessional account from LDCs as a group of $0.3 billion in 1991, and an inflow of similar magnitude in 1992 (annex table 15).

The exceptionally high volume of financing on non-concessional terms in 1990 raised the total net flow of external resources to LDCs to $17.2 billion. Total flows contracted by $1.4 billion in the following year, before partially recovering to $16.7 billion in 1992, close to the ODA level. (These figures exclude NGO grants, currently estimated to be in the order of around $1.5 billion annually for LDCs.) With relatively low interest payments made by LDCs (in the broad order of $2 billion) and declining, the net transfer of resources to LDCs has remained largely positive over this period.

Other official (non-concessional) and private flows have played a more important role in some LDCs. In nine, such flows accounted for more than 10 per cent on average of total financial inflows over the period 1987-1992. Apart from Zaire and Liberia, already mentioned, these were Botswana, characterized by exceptional economic performance, Gambia, Lesotho and Sierra Leone (with relatively significant private financing inflows) and a few of the island LDCs (Maldives, Solomon Islands, and Vanuatu) (annex table 23).

In discussing the potential role of non-concessional financing for LDCs, a distinction must be made between loan financing and non-debt-creating flows (direct and portfolio investment). With many LDCs severely debt distressed and their economic and export prospects bleak, there seems to be relatively little scope for new borrowing on non-concessional terms. In fact, many have adopted a restrictive policy with regard to such borrowing as part of their adjustment and debt-management efforts. Over the short to medium term, only a few among the most advanced and less-indebted LDCs might be able to seek recourse to market financing, and, in general, non-concessional financing should be envisaged only for carefully selected projects with high rates of return, assured to yield benefits covering corresponding debt-servicing obligations.

The Programme of Action drew particular attention to the need for supportive action to expand private non-debt-creating flows. LDCs in all regions have of late shown keen interest in attracting such financing, in particular direct investment, and have adopted more liberal FDI policy regimes and set up programmes for investment promotion. By mid-1994, 31 LDCs had signed the Multilateral Investment Guarantee Agency (MIGA) Convention, and some (such as Bangladesh, Uganda and the United Republic of Tanzania) benefited from guarantees and other activities undertaken by that agency. Many donor countries also have schemes for promoting private-sector development and direct investment flows to developing countries, although they have few special provisions for LDCs. Some have more of a regional focus, e.g. the French agency for promotion and participation in economic cooperation (PROPARCO). Institutions and programmes such as the Centre for Industrial Development working with African, Caribbean and Pacific (Group of States) (ACP) countries and the African Project Development Facility are also of particular relevance for LDCs.

LDCs still capture a very small part of worldwide investment flows. Their share of such flows was 0.3 per cent in 1993 (0.7 per cent of FDI flows into all developing countries (table 21). LDCs continue to face many handicaps in competing for FDI, including political and economic instability and a range of structural problems which may take long to resolve. Thus, it is probably not realistic to expect any large-scale

Table 21: Foreign direct investment inflows to LDCs, 1981-1993

| | Annual average | | | | |
	1981-1985	1986-1990	1991	1992	1993
$ million					
Total developing countries	12733	25244	39632	52249	70179
LDCs	242	547	389	396	518
African LDCs	206	499	302	271	348
Asian LDCs	22	22	30	72	116[a]
Percentage shares					
Share of LDCs in total developing countries	1.9	2.2	1.0	0.8	0.7
Share of African LDCs in total LDCs	85	91	78	68	67
Share of Asian LDCs in total LDCs	9	4	8	18	22[a]

Source: UNCTAD, Division on Transnational Corporations and Investment database on foreign direct investment. Figures given here differ from those on direct investment in the annex tables, which reflect flows from OECD/DAC countries only.

    a Excluding LDCs from West Asia.

FDI inflow to LDCs as a group over the short to medium term, although individual countries should certainly be encouraged to exploit possibilities in this area and donor countries should give all possible support to such efforts. Substantial ODA will be needed to bring about conditions conducive to increased FDI in LDCs, *inter alia*, to build up requisite physical and institutional infrastructures and for entrepreneurship and skills development.[4]

Outlook and policy issues

Will ODA to LDCs continue to contract as it did in 1993, or is there hope of recovery in aid flows in the years to come? It seems that no significant expansion in total ODA can be expected over the next few years, whether from DAC member countries or other traditional donors. Information available on DAC members' plans and programmes still suggests that the fall in the overall ODA/GNP ratio in 1993, directly reflected in the implementation of the aid targets for LDCs, may have been in the

nature of a temporary setback. According to this assessment, recovery in 1994-1995 will be possible for some DAC countries as they emerge from recession.[5] On the other hand, as long as unemployment in these countries remains widespread and financing deficits linger, restrictive fiscal policies will very likely persist and aid budgets continue to be under pressure.

The cyclical nature of multilateral replenishments which affected the 1993 aid outcome for LDCs in terms of share of donors' GNP, does point to the possibility of a better result again in 1994, or at least no further backsliding in this ratio, provided contributions to multilateral agencies pick up again. Other factors that speak for a possible recovery in aid efforts in favour of LDCs over the short to medium term are their continued adjustment and reform efforts and for some an improved policy environment, the stated commitment of donors to provide aid and debt relief to reforming countries (including promised support to the countries in the CFA zone following the devaluation of the CFA franc in early 1994), and increasing emphasis on poverty-reduction policies. The flow of bilateral grant aid from DAC donors already held up fairly well in current dollar terms in 1993. On the other hand, as noted above in the discussion of general trends affecting resource flows to LDCs, preliminary estimates show a downturn in aggregate new aid commitments to LDCs in that year. Much will depend on what happens to multilateral aid. All in all, there are reservations about prospects for a turn-around in current trends and a substantially enhanced aid flow to LDCs in the near future, until there are firmer indications of donor plans and intentions and of the outcome of multilateral replenishment exercises.

The fact remains that the ODA provided to LDCs is far below the level of resources foreseen under the aid targets and commitments set out in the Programme of Action. And donors' performance would be even lower if measured in terms of aid provided to the 41 countries belonging to the group of LDCs when the Programme of Action was adopted, and for which the targets were originally set.

In order to reverse current trends in ODA to LDCs, overall aid flows must be sustained and the necessary focus be given to the poorest countries within the aid programmes. In this context, progress towards the overall 0.7 per cent target would obviously be important as a means to provide more resources to LDCs. In reporting on measures taken to implement the Programme of Action, donor countries have reaffirmed their adherence to the 0.7 target (although in some cases as a longer-term objective or without a set timetable) or corresponding national targets, as well as their continued commitment to the objectives and subtargets set for aid to LDCs.[6]

In the current situation, however, until such time as growth prospects for overall ODA improve, the question of improving aid allocations to LDCs must be confronted. As proven over the recent past, other developing countries have been able to attract private capital and their inherent capacity to raise such funds and to service debt is very much stronger. LDCs are the countries with the weakest internal-savings capacity and are also the countries least likely to have access to non-official financing flows (and least able to afford borrowing on market terms.) Against this background, donor countries must give priority to LDCs in allocating aid. They will need to consider concrete measures to ensure that LDCs receive the necessary ODA resources and review their aid strategies, programming and budgetary planning mechanisms to this

end. Some of the donor countries have emphasized their geographical concentration policies as being a critical factor in safeguarding assistance to LDCs in times of budgetary stringency. However, where volumes of ODA have fallen significantly, this does not always seem to have been the case in practice. In aid programmes with global coverage and activities in many countries around the world, LDCs are from the outset subject to another degree of competition for resources, and different measures (e.g. national subtargets incorporated in budgetary planning mechanisms) may be required to ensure that their needs are given sufficient priority.

Ensuring the resource base and funding capacity of multilateral agencies and financial institutions is also of critical importance for sustaining aid flows to LDCs in the future. These institutions in general allocate a remarkably high share of their resources to LDCs, much higher than the average in DAC bilateral aid. This share is as high as between 40 and 50 per cent in a number of agencies. The significant decline in disbursements and commitments to LDCs from these agencies in 1993 is thus of special concern. An enlarged ESAF became operational in early 1994, and should ensure continued IMF support to LDCs' adjustment programmes over much of the remaining decade. However, there are a number of other ongoing or upcoming replenishment exercises, including the eleventh replenishment of the International Development Association (IDA), the outcome of which will be particularly important for future resource availability for LDCs. Attention will also have to be given to sufficient funding of the United Nations grant-based agencies. Failure to provide sufficient resources to the multilateral institutions could seriously impair their later disbursement capacity and their ability to support programmes and projects in LDCs over the medium term.

An important unresolved issue is also that of the adjustment of ODA targets and commitments in view of the addition of new countries to the list of LDCs since the adoption of the Programme of Action, which have substantially enhanced the resource requirements of LDCs as a group.

Country-review meetings and their role in mobilizing external resources

Coverage of the review process

In the Programme of Action, country review mechanisms such as the UNDP-sponsored round-table process and the World Bank consultative and aid groups were assigned a key role in mobilizing resources for the development programmes of individual LDCs. These follow-up arrangements have been further strengthened during the early 1990s with additional countries joining or rejoining the country-review process and meetings taking place more frequently and on a more regular basis. Compared with the early 1980s, when only a few such groups for LDCs were in place, there is now much closer monitoring of policy developments and resource needs at the country level. In all, close to 60 full-scale consultative or aid groups and round-table or similar meetings were arranged from the adoption of the Programme of Action until the end of 1994 (table 22). In addition, a large number of ad hoc meetings and sectoral and other follow-up meetings have been arranged as part of the process. This must be recognized as a major effort undertaken jointly by LDCs, the lead agencies (UNDP and the World Bank) and the donor community for the effective implementation and follow-up of the Programme.

Seventeen of 47 LDCs have World Bank-sponsored consultative or aid group arrangements. Not all these groups are currently active, but in the main they are well established and meet regularly; full-scale meetings were convened for 11 of these countries since September 1990, when the Programme of Action was adopted, until the end of 1994, with notably the consultative group for Ethiopia meeting in 1992 for the first time in almost two decades, and a new group established for Sierra Leone in 1994.

Virtually all other LDCs have adopted the round-table process, with UNDP as the lead agency. By the end of 1994, 16 LDCs had convened main round tables with donors following the adoption of the Programme of Action. This process has already been established on a regular basis in a number of Asian LDCs (e.g. Bhutan, Lao People's Democratic Republic and Maldives) as well as in some African countries (for instance, Burkina Faso and Gambia). In others, meetings have been much more irregular. In some, round-table meetings have only recently been convened for the first time or after a long interval, or preparations are still ongoing. The complexities of political reform initiated by many LDCs and difficulties in drawing up and implementing economic adjustment programmes in this context have been important factors in delaying formal consultative meetings. In yet other LDCs, consultative group and round-table countries alike, civil strife and political instability have stopped or blocked this process.

Activity under the country-review process is not restricted to formal full-scale meetings. For instance, the World Bank in 1994 arranged an informal donors' meeting for Haiti, in anticipation of the resolution of that country's constitutional crisis, as well as a special meeting for Burundi. Other special meetings have also been held to deal with emergency situations. Sectoral consultations again form an essential part of the round-table process sponsored by UNDP, and play an important role in following up the main round tables and formulating strategies and mobilizing finance for the development of specific sectors.

Recent policy developments and scope for further strengthening

Since the mid-1980s, there has been increasing emphasis on policy discussions not only in consultative and aid groups but also in round-table meetings. Indeed, the Programme of Action defined the country-review process as the principal means of policy dialogue and coordinating the aid efforts of development partners with LDCs' development programmes. Adoption of internationally approved structural adjustment programmes has become a virtual precondition for the convening of formal country-review meetings. Most of the countries that have arranged consultative or aid group meetings or round tables since the Paris Conference have had ongoing SAF/ESAF programmes (although notably some Asian LDCs did not have any formal arrangements of this kind). Donors' concerns with governance, democratization, and human rights have also increasingly come to the fore and have been reflected in the outcome of meetings. In a number of cases, donor support at significant levels has been pledged following endorsement of economic reform programmes and progress towards democratization. Bangladesh and Zambia in the first years of the 1990s can be seen as cases in point. On the reverse side of the coin, perceived lack of progress on economic and political reform may lead to withdrawal of donor support. This has been illustrated by the experiences of Haiti (suspension of aid programmes after 1991) and Malawi (fall in commitments before political reform), and by the suspension of the consultative group process and lower aid flows in Myanmar, Sudan and Zaire.

These conditionalities in the country-review process reflect the increasing linking, in general, of the provision of aid with economic and political reform in recipient countries, and also more concerted conditionality (e.g. bilateral donors taking into account policy performance

Table 22: Consultative and aid group and round-table meetings, 1985-1994

Country and type of meeting	*Date of meeting[a]*

Consultative and aid group arrangements

Bangladesh	**Annually**
Ethiopia	**1992, 1994**
Guinea	1987, 1990
Haiti	1986, 1987, 1988, 1990, **1991, 1992[b], 1994[b]**
Madagascar	1986, 1988
Malawi	1986, 1988, 1990, **1992, 1993, 1994**
Mauritania	1985, 1988, 1989, **1994**
Mozambique	1987, 1988, 1989, **1990, 1991, 1992, 1993**
Myanmar	1986
Nepal	1986, 1987, 1988, **1990, 1992**
Sierra Leone	**1994**
Somalia	1985, 1987, 1990
Sudan	1987, 1988
Uganda	1987, 1988, 1989, **1991, 1992, 1993, 1994**
United Republic of Tanzania	1986, 1987, 1988, 1989, **1991, 1992, 1993**
Zaire	1986, 1987
Zambia	1986, 1988, 1990, **1991, 1992, 1993, 1994**

Round table and other arrangements

Afghanistan	No meetings
Benin	**1992**
Bhutan	1986, 1988, **1992**
Burkina Faso	**1991, 1993**
Burundi	1989, **1992**
Cambodia[c]	**1992, 1993, 1994**
Cape Verde	1986, **1992**
Central African Republic	1987, **1991, 1994**
Chad	1985, 1990
Comoros	**1991**
Djibouti	No meetings
Equatorial Guinea	1988
Gambia	**1990, 1992, 1994**
Guinea-Bissau	1988, **1994**
Kiribati	No meetings
Lao People's Democratic Republic	1986, 1989, **1992, 1994**
Lesotho	1988
Liberia	No meetings
Maldives	1986, 1989, **1991, 1994**
Mali	1985, **1994**
Niger	1987
Rwanda	**1992**
Samoa	1986, 1988, 1990
Sao Tome and Principe	1985, 1989, **1992**
Solomon Islands	1988
Togo	1985, 1988
Tuvalu	1990, **1991**
Vanuatu	1988
Yemen	**1992**

Source: Information from UNDP and The World Bank.

a   Meetings held since the adoption of the Programme of Action in September 1990 are in bold type.

b   Caribbean Group for Cooperation in Economic Development.

c   Ministerial Conference on Rehabilitation and Reconstruction of Cambodia, co-chaired by UNDP (1992) and the International Committee on the Reconstruction of Cambodia (1993 and 1994).

under IMF agreements in making their own decisions on aid programmes and commitments). The emerging policy conditionalities of donors and their implications have been discussed at more length most recently in the LDC 1993-1994 Report.[7]

Once meetings have been held, financing requirements under well-prepared economic programmes have, in general, been adequately covered. Individual country experiences vary, however, and resource mobilization has not been equally successful in all cases. In some, promised funding has even exceeded requests, while in others financing gaps have remained to be filled. Commitments over the last two to three years have also been affected by constraints on donors' overall budgets and general trends in aid flows discussed above.[8]

Besides amounts of aid pledged, there are other factors that affect the subsequent flow of aid. Issues of expediting programme and project implementation, accelerating disbursements and needs for quick-disbursing assistance have been raised at a number of recent meetings. They have also brought up requirements for flexibility in donor programmes to enable the reallocation of funds and the provision of new resources to meet emerging priority needs, e.g. responding to emergency situations and filling financing gaps. This could also involve shifting aid resources from investment to essential recurrent expenditure, supporting debt and debt-service reduction programmes, and lifting procurement and technical assistance recruitment restrictions (untying). All this forms part of coordinating the aid efforts of development partners with LDCs' development programmes.

Part of the effort to strengthen the country-review process in recent years has been the attempt to link these arrangements more closely to national policy-making and programming. The "ownership" of the process has been identified as a crucial issue in this regard, just as ownership of economic programmes is of critical importance for the effective use of aid. Consultative and aid groups and round tables so far seem to have been to a large extent donor-driven, the reason being the weak analytical and planning capacities of many LDCs.[9] There are exceptions, including some recent ones where recipient involvement in the preparation of meetings was stronger and where Governments assumed an active role in the process (Bangladesh, Ethiopia, Gambia, Guinea-Bissau, Maldives and Mali are all examples). In this respect, the World Bank/IMF Development Committee at its meeting in October 1994 noted

that consultative groups and round-table meetings are more effective when preceded by the active involvement of the recipient Government. With respect to the agenda of consultative groups, the Development Committee suggested that they should address issues of development strategy, aid utilization, aid coordination, and technical assistance, in addition to mobilization of financial resources.[10]

On the whole, progress in strengthening the country-review process has undoubtedly been made, although it has been accompanied by stronger conditionalities, and gaps which are not easily addressed remain in the country coverage. Some relaxation of the rules currently governing the convening of formal meetings (in line with some of the ad hoc meetings which have recently taken place) might contribute to more comprehensive country-level review and monitoring of socio-economic developments and related resource needs of LDCs. There is also scope for further strengthening, notably with regard to "ownership" and to the overall coordination function assigned to these groups. Ensuring that the documentation prepared for the meetings draws on local participation as much as possible and that it forms a useful part of the country's aid strategy could contribute to the former. Moreover, in a situation where external debt-servicing obligations are a binding constraint on many LDC economies, full integration of debt issues into the agenda of consultative and aid groups and round-table meetings, and their closer coordination with Paris Club proceedings seem particularly called for and would strengthen overall coordination.

With respect to the role of a country-review process in the mobilization of resources for LDCs' development programmes, in particular the element of additionality in pledges and commitments announced at specific meetings is difficult to assess. It is not likely that a single event such as a meeting in itself would lead to increased availability of resources and enhanced aid flows. The role of consultative and aid groups and round-table meetings in resource mobilization may need to be seen more over the longer term, as an element in fostering LDC-donor relations, informing donors about resource requirements and helping meet those needs, *inter alia*, by identifying and filling financing gaps and contributing to making aid more effective. This role should become even more important over the rest of the decade as the aid supply is likely to remain limited, and competition for those resources among aid claimants strong.

Aid modalities and effectiveness

Special aid provisions for LDCs

The Programme of Action set out a number of recommendations concerning modalities and the effectiveness of aid to LDCs. It stipulates, *inter alia*, that further steps should be taken by the development partners to provide bilateral ODA to these countries in the form of grants and/or to provide loans on highly concessional terms, and that the timeliness and the terms of aid should correspond to LDCs' short-term and long-term needs, including the growing requirements of their adjustment efforts.

With respect to specific measures taken by donors in favour of LDCs, most OECD/DAC donors have now shifted to a grant basis in their aid programmes with LDCs. As a result, the grant element of bilateral ODA further increased in the early 1990s. It rose from 93 per cent of new ODA commitments to LDCs from DAC member countries in 1990 to 97 per cent in 1993 (annex table 20). Most multilateral funding to LDCs is also on highly concessional terms. A large part is provided in grant form (United Nations agencies, the EDF). IDA, the most important single source of loan funds to LDCs, provides credits with maturities of 40 years, including a grace period of 10 years and a service charge of 0.75 per cent on the disbursed and outstanding amount of credits; principal repayment is at the rate of 2 per cent per year from the 11th to the 20th year and at 4 per cent a year thereafter. Most other multilateral lending to LDCs is on similarly soft terms.

Relatively few other special provisions for LDCs within DAC donors' aid programmes have been reported although they have to some extent benefited from, e.g., more flexible rules with regard to local cost financing and procurement. The general picture seems to be that LDCs tend to benefit alongside other aid recipients as donor approaches are developed and adaptations in aid modalities and procedures undertaken, possibly with a margin of preferential consideration but with special treatment and concessions accorded more on a case-by-case basis than as part of an LDC-specific approach. Donor countries have stressed, for instance, poverty-reduction policies and programmes and various forms of technical assistance as being particularly relevant for their implementation of the Programme of Action.

Priority areas: adjustment support, capacity-building and social development

LDCs' adjustment and development experience during the early 1990s has again underlined the needs for adjustment support on sufficient scale and in appropriate forms, as well as needs for capacity-building and better capacity utilization, and the imperative to utilize aid more effectively in view of the increased scarcity of such resources. Poverty reduction and social development have also become increasingly important concepts in development cooperation.

The previous UNCTAD report on LDCs attempts to assess the donor response to the special needs and circumstances of LDCs, including the support given to their policy-reform process.[11] It underscores that donor support can play a critical part in enhancing the implementation of adjustment and reforms, particularly by enabling countries to make urgent imports, facilitating liberalization of certain controls, such as that of foreign exchange, and helping to avoid drastic cuts in critical public expenditure. A main conclusion of the report is that the volume of ODA that has been forthcoming to underpin adjustment has been inadequate. To help LDCs in implementing policy reforms in a sustained manner, it would be important to provide a substantially increased volume of aid; make available requisite quick-disbursing assistance to facilitate stabilization and short- to medium-term adjustment measures; link ODA more closely to long-term socio-economic objectives of LDCs; promote their ownership of adjustment programmes; provide support to mitigate the social consequences of adjustment; further improve donor-recipient coordination; and enhance aid quality by avoiding procurement tying, supporting capacity building and leaving the management of counterpart funds to LDCs.

Two initiatives first developed during the latter half of the 1980s that address these issues and have particular relevance for LDCs are the Special Programme of Assistance (SPA) for low-income, debt-distressed countries of sub-Saharan Africa sponsored by the World Bank, and, with respect to technical assistance, the National Technical Co-operation Assessment Programme (NaTCAP) initiated by UNDP. Of 29 countries covered by SPA in 1994, 24 were LDCs. Asian LDCs have not so far benefited from any similar aid coordination and co-financing exercise. It is also mostly African countries that have taken advantage of the NaTCAP programme.

The primary aim of the SPA is to assist eligible countries in strengthening their policy-reform programmes and structural-reform efforts. Priorities and objectives of the ongoing third phase of the Programme, which covers the years 1994-1996, are to achieve higher growth rates and alleviate poverty, supplement policy-reform programmes with more investment in human resources and infrastructure, raise the level of domestic savings and private investment, place greater emphasis on ensuring that benefits of growth are directed at reducing poverty and strengthen local economic management and institutional capacity. Besides mobilizing resources to these ends, a key objective is also to improve the quality of donors' adjustment assistance. For this purpose, guidelines have been adopted for simplifying and harmonizing donors' procedures for disbursing balance-of-payment support, and for donor financing of civil service compensation. Discussion is continuing on sector-wide approaches to donor financing aimed at improving aid coordination and effectiveness. The SPA's role would be to serve as a catalyst to encourage donor support for integrated sector programmes, to monitor outcomes, and promote the harmonization of donor procedures.[12]

The sustainability of economic reforms very much hinges on building requisite national capacity. One of the instruments for this is technical cooperation. NaTCAP exercises are intended to provide a basis for developing a recipient policy on technical cooperation, to formulate national policy framework papers in this area and to introduce a programming process for technical cooperation. Over half of the LDCs have already initiated NaTCAPs.[13] Recent innovations in UNDP's technical cooperation, such as the notion of the programme approach, the priority attached to national execution, and greater use of national expertise, are also advances towards reform for enhanced capacity-building. In addition to technical cooperation, education and training and civil service reform have been other traditional policy tools for developing and strengthening national capacities. Capacity utilization has also emerged as an important concept. There is recognition that new approaches are needed in all these areas, but more effective ways to promote capacity building and utilization are still being sought.[14]

The Programme of Action already strongly emphasized participatory approaches to development, noting that mobilization and development of human capacities are a crucial factor in promoting sustained and increasingly self-reliant socio-economic development. Since the Programme's adoption, increased attention has been given in donors' programmes to a poverty-focused framework for aid. For instance, poverty alleviation has been set as a priority for the World Bank and poverty assessments are being carried out to provide the basis for collaboration between the World Bank and its active borrowers on the best way to reduce poverty. These assessments have for their objectives the identification of the policy, public expenditure and institutional issues that constrain effective poverty reduction and the recommendation of an agenda for reform. To date, 13 such poverty assessments have been completed for LDCs.

In the context of a poverty-focused framework for aid, assistance to sectors such as education, population, health and nutrition and other social sectors and programmes take on heightened significance. A major challenge for the LDC-donor partnership is also to ensure that LDCs' concerns and requirements are adequately taken into account in the follow-up to the 1994 International Conference on Population and Development, as well as in the preparations for and follow-up to the World Summit for Social Development and the Fourth World Conference on Women to be held in 1995.

Improving the effectiveness of aid

Donors have over the recent past devoted a great deal of attention to issues of aid effectiveness and development results. These issues are particularly relevant for poor, aid-dependent countries such as LDCs, with many of these countries characterized by political and economic instability and weak institutions.

Increasingly, donors have come to emphasize such questions as stability, the nature of the policy environment, as well as the need for national "ownership", as critical to the effective use of aid. Perceptions of effective aid use are also likely to be an important factor in maintaining public support for aid in the donor countries. This creates something of a dilemma for the LDC-donor partnership. First, LDCs need assistance although conditions may be difficult and initially less conducive to successful aid efforts. If the donors "(do) nothing while waiting for a propitious environment and local demand to manifest themselves, the result may be continuing deterioration which will further complicate later development efforts".[15] Second, LDCs in general have limited national capacity and skills are scarce - but, precisely, weak administrative and institutional capacity has been identified as a major barrier to the effective use of aid. If donors direct their aid according to criteria where aid is most effectively used and to where programmes and projects are easier to implement, this may add another constraint on aid to LDCs. In this situation, enhancing aid effectiveness and capacity-building and institutional development become key elements in sustaining aid flows to these countries. LDCs and donors both must do their utmost to remove bottlenecks in this area.

Work undertaken so far on these issues, e.g. by OECD/DAC and within the World Bank (box 17), points to aid being most effective in countries that have strong institutions and have policies and procedures that lead to economy-wide efficient use of resources, and in particular have a sound budgetary process. To create conditions for effective use of aid, LDCs must pursue their efforts to formulate and implement appropriate domestic policies. Donors for their part should support more participatory approaches to development and help recipient countries develop critical policies and institutional capacities to use their resources efficiently. Donors can also ensure that their own practices and procedures, including approaches to coordination, make the most of the available resources and do not undermine the efforts of recipient countries.

Box 17: Issues in aid effectiveness

During the second half of the 1980s and the early 1990s, the OECD/DAC developed a number of principles for effective aid, intended to provide policy orientations and operational guidance for its members, and addressing such diverse themes as aid coordination, technical cooperation, environmental impact assessment, women in development, and evaluation, as well as project appraisal, programme assistance and good procurement practices. First collected and published in one volume in 1992,[1] these principles have since been augmented by the adoption of DAC Orientations on Participatory Development and Good Governance (December 1993) and Orientations on Cooperation in Support of Private Sector Development (June 1994). DAC members have undertaken to review and adapt their aid practices against these standards and have requested the DAC to monitor their implementation. These principles are also seen as a basis for dialogue and cooperation with developing countries in order to improve the overall effectiveness of resource use.

Aid effectiveness issues were also addressed by the World Bank/IMF Development Committee at its October 1994 meeting. The Development Committee set out a number of guiding principles for recipients and donors alike for effective aid, summarizing findings of recent work on these issues which include the following:

- The best conditions and policies for aid cannot substitute for strong ownership by the recipient Government and good governance. Donors and recipients must collaborate to make this the basis for effective aid.

- Donors should support participation by relevant "stakeholders" (especially women, the poor and other disadvantaged groups); this helps to improve project design and ensure that the projects are properly implemented and operated.

- Technical assistance is likely to be most effective when it responds to clearly defined needs and the absorptive capacity of the recipient. It should work within and, if necessary, seek to strengthen the institutional environment.

- Aid programmes should be consistent with the country frameworks being put in place for macroeconomic and structural policies fostering the private sector and strengthening public-sector management, and with the recipient country's own development priorities.

- Efforts to coordinate and simplify donor-aid procedures should be accelerated. Aid operations should be made more transparent to improve accountability. Donors should avoid setting up mechanisms that are inconsistent with the recipients' own efforts to manage their budgets and implement aid. (Efforts should also be undertaken to reduce the use of tied-aid credits, and to minimize the additional costs associated with trade-distorting tying of aid.)

- Recent efforts to improve aid effectiveness, focusing on development impact and on field results, need to be sustained and extended. Particular attention should be given to factors such as shifting the focus from projects to country programmes; strengthening evaluation and disclosure policies; streamlining procedures; and addressing urgently the adequacy of field office networks.[2]

---

[1]   OECD, *Development Assistance Manual. DAC Principles for Effective Aid* (Paris, 1992).
[2]   Development Committee of the IMF/World Bank, October 1994 (OECD press release SG/NR(94)56), paras. 4 to 5.

Mobilizing external support to LDCs: conclusions

LDCs' dependence on aid is not likely to lessen during this decade. The basic policy issue that the donor countries must address in the current climate of budgetary stringency and ODA scarcity is how to improve aid allocations to the group of LDCs so as to make progress towards the aid targets adopted in 1990 and to ensure that these countries' external financing needs are met and that their adjustment and development efforts receive adequate support. In view of the weak implementation of the relevant provisions of the Programme of Action so far, donor countries will need to consider specific measures to incorporate the targets and commitments set out in the Programme more explicitly into national aid strategies and budgetary planning mechanisms. The possibility of tapping new sources of funds, such as special drawing right (SDR) allocations and IMF gold sales, to help support LDCs' development efforts should also be explored.

In view of the important role of multilateral funding in aid flows to LDCs, particular attention will have to be paid in the near future to generous replenishment of IDA and the soft-term windows of the regional banks, as well as of EDF resources, all major sources of financing to LDCs.

The country-review process (consultative and aid groups and round-table meetings) will continue to constitute an essential element in the development partnership and in sustaining aid flows to LDCs over the rest of the decade, through focusing attention on LDCs' financing requirements and directing resources to them. Efforts to link these arrangements more closely to national policy-making and programming in LDCs and to strengthen their involvement in the review process, as well as to achieve more comprehensive coverage of countries and is-

sues (in particular with respect to external debt) should be pursued.

The recommendations in the Programme of Action on aid modalities and effectiveness remain valid and efforts to implement them should continue. In particular, LDCs will continue to require substantial adjustment support on a timely basis and on terms adapted to their special needs and circumstances, as well as support for poverty reduction and social programmes. Measures should be taken to extend SPA-type approaches and the benefits of technical cooperation programming to all LDCs. Also, in order for the aid effort to become truly successful, much more needs to be done to strengthen LDCs' administrative and institutional capacity in general, and to promote ownership by LDC Governments and participation by the stakeholders in these countries' development.

Although the role of ODA must be expected to remain dominant in the provision of external resources to LDCs, other types of financing still have a role to play. Even modest improvements in this area, e.g. marginally enhancing such flows so that there would be a steady net inflow of resources with a larger number of LDCs benefiting (among those able to attract/afford financing on non-concessional terms), would be welcome and help ease overall financing constraints. Too high hopes should perhaps not be pinned on obtaining significantly increased non-ODA flows until there is a definite improvement in LDCs' economic fortunes and external performance and their debt problems are resolved.[16] Still, special efforts to promote FDI and to develop capital markets with a view to attracting portfolio investment should be pursued. Moreover, implementation of debt-relief measures to eliminate repayment obligations on the overhang of export credits contracted in the past, and stop the current drain on resources on this account, will be very important in this context.

C. LDCs' EXTERNAL DEBT: THE UNCOMPLETED AGENDA

The Programme of Action identified the debt overhang of LDCs as a major hindrance to their development plans, making economic adjustment with growth extremely difficult and threatening to undermine the essential political commitment to reform. In spite of the debt-relief measures taken in LDCs' favour since 1990, this constraint has not since been removed or even eased in any significant way. Levels of indebt-

edness remain dramatically high (the stock of outstanding debt equals or exceeds GDP in almost half the LDCs), and they continue to confront heavy external debt-servicing obligations, while their debt-servicing capacity weakened significantly in the early 1990s. Dealing with the debt burden and repeated reschedulings also drain scarce economic management capacities. External debt remains an overriding problem in most LDC economies and needs to be addressed more decisively and in a more comprehensive manner.

Ways to eliminate LDCs' debt overhang must be a major area of focus in the mid-term review of the Programme of Action. The aim should be to allow them a clean start in this respect, so that aid and export receipts and economic management capacities no longer need be diverted in large measure to debt servicing, but available resources, instead, can be directed at meeting essential rehabilitation and development needs.

Overall debt situation

Trends in debt stock, composition of debt and debt-service payments

The stock of LDCs' outstanding external debt continued to grow steadily in the early years of the 1990s. Their external indebtedness increased from a level of $114 billion at end-1990 to $122 billion at end-1992, corresponding to an estimated 76 per cent of their combined GDP in 1992. This ratio, which had been decreasing since 1987, took an upwards turn in 1992. Preliminary estimates indicate a further increase in their indebtedness in 1993 to $127 billion, implying a more than 10 per cent increase in LDCs' total external debt since the adoption of the Programme of Action (table 23 and chart 5).

This continued growth in LDCs' debt stock is explained partly by increased lending (mostly on concessional terms) from the international financial institutions in support of LDCs' adjustment and development efforts. In all, LDCs' multilateral debt grew by an estimated $8 billion from end-1990 to end-1993. Debts due to non-OECD creditor countries also increased by an estimated $9 billion over the same period. Meanwhile, a trend towards a levelling-off or even a slight decline has been confirmed as regards their indebtedness to OECD countries. Changing financing patterns and debt relief extended to LDCs by the group of OECD creditors have brought down outstanding obligations by an estimated $3 billion, some 10 per cent of LDCs' total debt due to the OECD countries.

Most of LDCs' external debt is long term, and around 70 per cent of outstanding long-term debt stems from borrowings on concessional terms. In 1992, some 60 per cent of LDCs' long-term debt was due to official bilateral creditors or officially guaranteed, with the international financial institutions holding another 38 per cent, and the rest, less than 2 per

cent, constituted by borrowings from financial markets.

Debt-service payments by LDCs peaked at a level of $5.4 billion in 1989, corresponding to 28 per cent of their export earnings in that year, and then declined markedly in the early 1990s. In 1992, debt-service payments amounted to $3 billion. The aggregate debt-service ratio for the group of LDCs as a whole fell to only 16 per cent in 1992. As discussed below, this is more an indicator of LDCs' weak economic and external performance and their low debt-servicing capacity than of any easing of the debt-service burden as such. While debt forgiveness and rescheduling of obligations also contributed to lower payments, massive accumulation of arrears seems to have been the main explanatory factor. The bulk of debt-service payments continue to go to OECD countries and international financial institutions (chart 5). Well over half of the debt service paid relates to non-concessional debts.

The decrease in debt-service payments and in the debt-service ratio in the early 1990s does not signify a decline in LDCs' debt-servicing burden in terms of obligations. These figures show actual payments, as opposed to payments due, and as already discussed in the previous UNCTAD report on LDCs,[17] the trends observed in the early 1990s largely reflect LDCs' financial distress and inability to meet their contractual obligations. During 1991-1992, when aggregate payments fell steeply, LDC economies grew little (their combined GDP increasing no more than 1 per cent or below in each of these years), and export earnings declined for the group as a whole. LDCs also had to meet urgent import needs out of low and dwindling external receipts. The internal budgetary difficulties that many LDCs faced in the early 1990s have also contributed to acute debt servicing problems.

A large number of LDCs consequently continued to accumulate arrears on both principal and interest payments during the period under review, some of them subsequently rescheduling their obligations. Available data indicate that payments due in 1992 and 1993 by the LDCs as a group, before debt relief, were on the order of $7 billion annually, well over twice the amounts actually paid in those years. Had the LDCs paid their contractual obligations for 1992 in full, avoiding arrears and rescheduling, external debt-servicing would have absorbed as much as one third or more of their export earnings. This figure doubtless gives a better indication of the actual debt-servicing burden of LDCs than the debt-service ratio calculated on payments. However, a true measurement of LDCs'

Table 23: Total debt and debt service of LDCs, 1984-1993
(Billions of dollars)

	1984	1985	1986	1987	1988	1989	1990	1991	1992	1993[a]	1992[b] (%)
Debt											
Total long-term	54	63	73	90	94	97	104	109	113	118	92
Concessional	32	38	45	58	63	67	70	77	81	..	66
OECD countries	8	10	12	16	17	17	18	17	17	17	14
Multilateral agencies	11	14	16	21	23	26	31	35	37	..	30
Non-concessional	22	25	27	32	31	30	33	32	32	..	26
Export credits (OECD)	8	9	10	12	11	11	12	11	10	10	8
Multilateral agencies	6	6	7	8	8	7	7	6	6	..	5
Total short-term	5	6	7	8	7	8	10	9	10	9	8
Total external debt	59	69	80	97	101	105	114	118	122	127	100
of which:											
use of IMF credit	5	5	5	6	6	5	5	5	5	5	4
Debt service											
Total long-term	3.6	3.7	4.8	4.4	4.6	4.9	4.5	3.9	2.9	3.0	95
Concessional	0.8	1.0	1.5	1.5	1.7	1.7	1.5	1.3	1.2	..	39
OECD countries	0.3	0.3	0.4	0.4	0.5	0.5	0.5	0.4	0.4	0.4	13
Multilateral agencies	0.3	0.4	0.6	0.6	0.6	0.6	0.6	0.6	0.6	..	21
Non-concessional	2.7	2.8	3.3	2.9	2.9	3.2	3.1	2.6	1.7	..	56
Export credits (OECD)	1.0	1.1	1.3	1.2	1.2	1.2	1.3	0.8	0.6	0.7	20
Multilateral agencies	1.0	1.0	1.5	1.3	1.1	1.3	1.3	1.3	0.9	..	28
Total short-term	0.5	0.4	0.4	0.4	0.5	0.5	0.4	0.3	0.1	0.2	5
Total debt service	4.1	4.2	5.2	4.8	5.1	5.4	5.0	4.2	3.0	3.2	100
of which:											
use of IMF credit	0.8	0.8	1.3	1.0	0.8	1.1	0.8	0.6	0.4	0.3	12

Source:UNCTAD secretariat calculations, based on OECD data.

Note: Figures for total debt and total debt service cover both long- and short-term debt, as well as the use of IMF credit.

a   Preliminary estimates.

b   Percentage of total debt or debt service.

obligations would have to take into account not only scheduled payments for the current year, but also the liability to settle arrears, further adding to this burden.

Country debt burdens

If progress in dealing with LDCs' debt situation when analysed at aggregate level appears limited, the picture at individual country level is, in most cases, one of unmitigated strain and persistence of unsustainable debt burdens. Only a few countries in the LDC group (e.g. Bhutan, Botswana and some of the island LDCs) have relatively low levels of debt as measured in relation to the size of GDP, and have been able to maintain low debt-service ratios without recourse to the accumulation of arrears or reschedulings. In a number of cases, relatively low payments in 1992 correlated with mounting arrears. Other LDCs registered debt-service ratios in the range of 20 to 40 per cent and still were not able to acquit themselves of all their obligations. In all, 19 LDCs devoted close to or more than 20 per cent of their export receipts to the servicing of external debt in 1992. Three

Chart 5: External debt and debt service payments of LDCs, 1984-1993

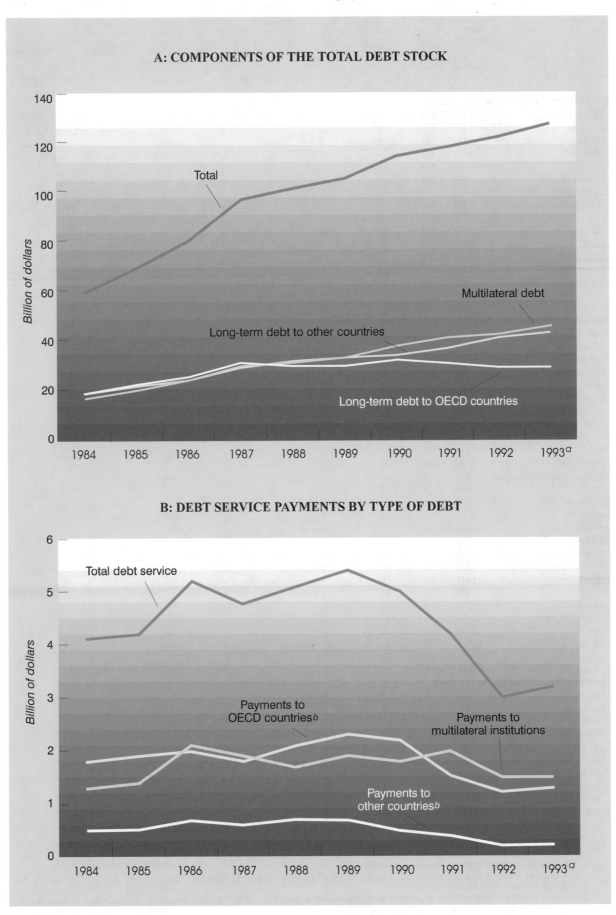

A: COMPONENTS OF THE TOTAL DEBT STOCK

Billion of dollars

Total

Multilateral debt

Long-term debt to other countries

Long-term debt to OECD countries

1984 1985 1986 1987 1988 1989 1990 1991 1992 1993ᵃ

B: DEBT SERVICE PAYMENTS BY TYPE OF DEBT

Billion of dollars

Total debt service

Payments to OECD countriesᵇ

Payments to multilateral institutions

Payments to other countriesᵇ

1984 1985 1986 1987 1988 1989 1990 1991 1992 1993ᵃ

Source: UNCTAD secretariat, based on OECD data.

a Preliminary estimates.

b Payments on long-term debt only.

Table 24: LDCs - Debt indicators and debt relief measures

Country/group [b]	Outstanding debt end-1992 ($ Million)	Ratio of total debt to GDP 1992 (%)	Ratio (to 1992 total exports) [a] of: Total debt service (%)	Multi-lateral debt service (%)	Increase in arrears in 1992 [c]	ODA debt cancellations in 1990-1993 [d]	Paris Club agreements under enhanced concessional terms	"Fifth dimension" support 1990-1994	SPA eligible (1994)	SAF/ ESAF support (1990-1994)
Debt to GDP ratio over 100% in 1992										
Afghanistan*	9517	110	4	1	..					
Burundi*	1150	105	38	23		x			x	x
Equatorial Guinea*	256	161	6	5	x	x	1992		x	x
Ethiopia*	8852	178	27	9	x	x	1992	x	x	x
Gambia**	427	123	11	5		x			x	x
Guinea-Bissau*	635	288	35	20	x	x			x	
Lao People' Democratic Repulic	1966	167	5	3		x				x
Liberia*	1720	131	9	0	x	x				
Madagascar*	3699	123	24	12	x	x		x	x	x
Mali*	2829	102	13	6	x	x	1992		x	x
Mauritania*	2032	171	17	13	x	x	1993	x	x	x
Mozambique*	4748	387	21	6	x	x	1993		x	x
Sao Tome and Principe*	178	414	33	22	x				x	x
Sierra Leone *	768	110	17	14		x	1992, 1994	x	x	x
Somalia*	2405	204	13	0	x	x				
Sudan*	10513	114	41	7	x	x				
United Republic of Tanzania*	5647	206	21	14		x	1992	x	x	x
Tuvalu	30	266	..	..	..					
Vanuatu	261	143	16	1		x				
Zaire*	9348	106	23	6	x	x				
Zambia*	5377	163	31	22	x	x	1992	x	x	
Subtotal	**72358**	**138**	**20**	**10**						
Debt to GDP ratio 50-100% in 1992										
Bangladesh**	13036	55	18	8		x		x		x
Benin	1419	65	7	4		x	1991, 1993		x	x
Cambodia*	1787	89	44	28		x				x
Central African Republic*	915	69	13	5	x	x	1994		x	
Chad	769	59	5	2	x	x			x	
Comoros**	207	79	8	6		x			x	x
Guinea**	2785	96	13	7		x	1992	x	x	x
Lesotho	690	95	5	2		x				x
Malawi**	1709	92	22	14		x		x	x	x
Maldives**	134	75	4	1		x			x	
Nepal**	1970	66	10	4		x				x
Niger*	1691	72	24	5	x	x	1994		x	x
Rwanda*	907	58	24	11		x			x	x
Samoa	118	80	10	6						
Solomon Islands	186	89	17	2						
Togo**	1388	89	14	6		x	1992	x	x	x
Uganda*	2761	85	44	36		x	1992	x	x	x
Yemen**	9092	89	13	7	x	x				
Subtotal	**41564**	**71**	**15**	**7**						
Debt to GDP ratio below 50% in 1992										
Bhutan	83	33	7	1						
Botswana	603	16	4	3		x				
Burkina Faso	1248	42	11	6		x	1993		x	x
Cape Verde	157	46	13	8	x	x				
Djibouti	221	49	6	2		x				
Haiti	767	24	2	0	x	x				
Kiribati	16	47	4	4						
Myanmar*	5168	14	7	7	x	x				
Subtotal	**8263**	**17**	**9**	**4**						
Total	**122185**	**76**	**16**	**8**						

Source: UNCTAD secretariat, based mainly on information from OECD and The World Bank.

a   Exports of goods and services (including non-factor services).

b   An asterisk indicates a country classified as severely indebted by The World Bank in *World Debt Tables, 1993-94*; and a double asterisk one that is classified as moderately indebted.

c   An "x" indicates a country where payments arrears as recorded in *World Debt Tables, 1993-94* increased in 1992, and arrears amounted to 5 per cent or over of total outstanding debt at end-1992.

d   As reported by donors in response to UNCTAD questionnaires on the implementation of the Programme of Action for LDCs for the 1990s.

LDCs (Cambodia, Sudan and Uganda) had debt-service ratios over 40 per cent.

At least two thirds of LDCs can be considered debt distressed. Of these, 24, or fully half of them, have debt-burden indicators above critical levels classifying them as severely indebted according to World Bank criteria, and another nine are classified as moderately indebted.[18] As shown in table 24, a large number of LDCs carry debt burdens which are much higher than the average debt-to-GDP ratio for the group as a whole. Of these LDCs, 21 had debt-to-GDP ratios over 100 per cent in 1992, while in several others corresponding ratios were approaching that level. These countries on average also had a somewhat higher debt-service ratio, and, not surprisingly, ran up arrears more frequently and more massively. They accounted for most of the accumulation of new arrears by LDCs in 1991 and 1992.

As indicated above, movement towards effective debt reduction for debt-distressed LDCs was not yet discernible during the period under review. The scale and extent of ODA debt cancellations, although important at the level of individual donor countries, was in the aggregate far from sufficient to remove ODA debts, let alone bring down levels of total indebtedness. While write-offs and rescheduling of debt service due provided some relief to LDCs which turned to the Paris Club (see table 24 and below), measures to reduce the stock of debt were still under discussion in that forum, and only a few commercial debt buy-backs had been implemented. As a consequence, external indebtedness of the large majority of LDCs continued to grow until 1992, and payment obligations remained at a level far exceeding their debt-servicing capacity. While the debt-to-GDP ratio declined in 21 LDCs over the period 1990-1992, it increased in another 25 of these countries, in some of them markedly. Two LDCs, the Gambia and Malawi, are regarded as having exited from Paris Club reschedulings, but it may be noted that both still have debt-burden indicators close to critical levels according to the World Bank classification. They continue to have debt-to-GDP ratios above the LDC average, and Malawi recorded a debt-service ratio over 20 per cent in 1992.

In absolute terms, the largest LDC debtors continue to be Bangladesh and Sudan, each with over $10 billion of external debt in 1992, followed by Afghanistan, Ethiopia, Myanmar, the United Republic of Tanzania, Yemen, Zaire and Zambia, all having external debt outstanding in the range of $5-10 billion. Together, these nine countries account for close to two thirds of

LDCs' total external debt; except for Bangladesh and Yemen, they all have debt-burden indicators classifying them as severely indebted. However, some of the smaller LDCs also have dramatically high debt burdens, e.g. Guinea-Bissau and Sao Tome and Principe with debt-to-GDP ratios close to 3:1 for the former, and over 4:1 for the latter. Eliminating LDCs' debt overhang will require effective debt-reduction programmes for all these countries.

Measures with respect to official bilateral debt

ODA debt to OECD countries

Throughout the period 1990-1992, bilateral concessional debt from all donors accounted for around 35 per cent of LDCs' total outstanding debt. The share of aid loans from OECD countries in bilateral concessional debt has decreased somewhat, but in absolute terms there has been little net reduction in LDCs' ODA debt to this donor group. Such debt still amounted to an estimated $17 billion at end-1993, the same level as the previous year. Debt-service payments on this debt amounted to over one tenth of total debt service acquitted by LDCs in 1992 and 1993. The five largest creditors in this group are France, Germany, Italy, Japan and the United States. Japan alone accounts for almost half of LDCs' outstanding ODA debt to the OECD countries.

The Programme of Action in 1990 noted that many countries had responded to Trade and Development Board resolution (S-IX) adopted in 1978 by cancelling or providing equivalent relief for ODA debt, while others had not yet implemented such measures. Since then, additional steps to cancel LDCs' ODA debt have been taken by the OECD countries. Notably, three of the five major DAC donors concerned (France, Italy and United States) initiated such programmes in the late 1980s or early 1990s, while Germany (as well as other donors holding smaller amounts of ODA claims on LDCs) continued similar programmes adopted earlier.[19] On the contrary, outright cancellation was not provided for by Japan, which has seen the fulfilment of repayment obligations as an essential part of an aid process built on the self-help concept, and has extended ODA debt relief mainly in the form of offsetting cash grants for debt service payments.

New debt relief measures were announced in early 1994 by France in support of countries in the CFA zone following their decision in January to devalue the CFA franc. Aid debts of the poorest countries in the zone would be written off in their totality, implying some additional relief for LDCs, and certain debt-service payments in arrears waived in order to permit new financing flows.[20]

Most LDCs have benefited from ODA debt cancellations by OECD countries, but there has been no clear across-the-board movement towards net reduction of the stock of such debt. Significantly lower levels of ODA debt to the OECD countries in 1992 than in 1990 were registered in relatively few cases. Three countries, Bangladesh, Myanmar and Zaire, account for half of LDCs' outstanding ODA debt to these donors. In 1990-1993, LDCs still paid some $400 million each year in ODA debt service to OECD countries, only about $100 million less annually than in the preceding three-year period.

A number of reasons can be given for the relatively slow progress so far in effectively reducing LDCs' stock of ODA debt to the OECD countries. The effects of the additional debt-cancellation programmes undertaken since the turn of the decade are not yet fully reflected in outstanding debt figures, as some programmes are still ongoing, and in some cases debt service is written off only as it is falling due, with remaining debt being kept on the books. At the same time, and although most OECD/DAC donors are now providing aid to LDCs on a grant-only basis, loan financing still continued under some aid programmes, adding to the debt stock. Other explanatory factors, apart from the relative importance of claims by Japan and the special features of that country's debt-relief policy, are the selectivity of some debt-relief programmes (with cancellations conditional on performance under economic reform programmes) and procedural delays, for instance when new countries become classified as LDCs and eligible for ODA debt forgiveness.

Nevertheless, as the principle of providing ODA to LDCs mainly in the form of grants has now been both generally adopted and largely implemented by donor countries, there seems to be little reason to maintain bilateral ODA claims on these countries, and to continue to collect debt-service payments on past aid loans. More determined efforts should be made to implement ODA debt-cancellation programmes expeditiously, and to eliminate this part of the LDCs' debt overhang. A possible way forward could be to include bilateral ODA debt in debt-stock reduction to be undertaken in the Paris Club, and to address this issue in consultative and aid group and round-table meetings for LDCs that do not opt for debt reorganization in that forum.

Other official debts to OECD countries

With respect to non-concessional official credits from the OECD countries (mainly official and officially guaranteed export credits), the Programme of Action pointed out that although the value of this debt is relatively low, it accounts for a significant part of LDCs' debt-service payments. This picture of the relative weight of OECD export credits in LDCs' debt-servicing is still valid, with related payments accounting for an estimated one fifth of total debt-service payments in 1992 and 1993.

However, this is one area where some progress has been made since the adoption of the Programme of Action. With relatively little new financing in this form and partial write-off of debt service offered under Paris Club reschedulings, LDCs' stock of outstanding non-concessional official debt to the OECD countries decreased from $12 billion in 1990 to an estimated $10 billion in 1993. Meanwhile, debt-service payments actually made on this account almost halved during this period, and their relative share in total debt service paid also declined somewhat.

A particularly important policy development was the introduction of enhanced concessional terms for the poorest countries in the Paris Club at the end of 1991. The new terms have provided for a higher degree of relief than previously on current maturities under the debt-service forgiveness options (see below), and also overall enhanced concessionality, as most of the creditor countries concerned have since associated themselves with these highly concessional options in the relevant agreements. From the introduction of the enhanced concessional treatment until mid-1994, 15 LDCs - all of them in Africa - undertook debt reorganization on these terms in the Paris Club, involving some $3.7 billion in all. Of the nine LDCs in the CFA zone, two (Niger and the Central African Republic) did so in the first half of 1994, after the devaluation of the CFA franc. Five others (Benin, Burkina Faso, Equatorial Guinea, Mali and Togo) had already obtained debt relief on enhanced concessional terms in the Paris Club (see also table 24).[21]

Meanwhile, discussions continued in the Paris Club on the need for deeper debt reduction, as well as on the modalities for possible future debt-stock operations. Relief has so far been provided on arrears and/or debt service falling due during limited consolidation periods, with eligible debt further circumscribed by variously timed cut-off dates. The options under the enhanced concessional treatment offered since end-1991 have provided for a reduction by 50 per cent of the net present value of debt-service payments on eligible debt through partial cancellation, interest rate reduction, or a combination of interest-rate reductions and interest-payment capitalization.[22] Under an important new provision in the agreements concluded under the enhanced concessional terms, the creditors have agreed, in principle, to consider the matter of the debtor country's stock of debt after a three- to four-year period, subject to successful implementation of previous agreements and of adjustment programmes. The first case eligible for such consideration was expected to come before the Paris Club at the beginning of 1995 at the earliest.

The Group of Seven, at its summit meeting in Naples in July 1994, encouraged the Paris Club to pursue its efforts to improve the debt treatment of the poorest and most indebted countries, taking a clear stand in favour of "where appropriate, ... a reduction in the stock of debt and an increase in the concessionality for those countries facing special difficulties."[23] Proposals discussed have ranged from two-thirds debt forgiveness as under the "Trinidad terms"[24] to up to 80 per cent reduction of the stock of debt. Agreement was finally reached in the Paris Club in December 1994 on the possibility of increasing the percentage of debt forgiveness offered under the enhanced concessional treatment to up to 67 per cent for the poorest and most indebted countries, and on an additional "exit" option providing for a reduction of the same magnitude of the stock of debt (likely to be implemented only for a small number of countries with a sufficient track record of adjustment; the expectation being that having completed their exit programme, they would no longer return to the Paris Club).

LDCs could in principle become primary beneficiaries of these new terms. Agreement on these was reached as this report was being finalized, and assessment will have to await the implementation in practice of the new terms, in particular as regards the eligibility of countries and the exit option. Some issues still require attention. Conditionality is one: first and foremost the performance criteria which debtor countries will have to fulfil to become eligible for debt-stock reduction.[25] Further, assessment undertaken of the impact of Paris Club debt reorganization under various terms indicates that, while in some cases, LDCs' debt-servicing obligations would be significantly reduced, e.g. under concessionality corresponding to the Trinidad terms, for other countries overall debt burdens would still remain too high.[26] The

economic and debt situation of some LDCs is such that complete cancellation of their official bilateral debt is warranted, and to meet the requirements of these neediest countries, it would be important to provide for full forgiveness of such debt. Furthermore, for the most indebted countries, and where debt owed to Paris Club creditors is a relatively small proportion of a country's total debt (for instance, because of the relative importance of debt to creditors outside this grouping), it is critical to seek to complement Paris Club operations by simultaneous action on other types of debt. This is also a question of burden-sharing among creditor countries, as discussed below.

Moreover, there is the issue of those LDCs that have opted for consistently honouring their debt-servicing obligations despite sometimes very difficult economic circumstances. Some LDCs have thus not, as yet, sought debt relief from the Paris Club and may not wish to exercise this option in future, although they would no doubt be eligible for concessional treatment were they to do so. Consideration needs to be given to the measures that could be taken to offer them equivalent support. This again is a question of fair treatment of debtors. Some donor countries that have special arrangements for debt-relief funding within their aid budgets have already been able to offer supplementary measures for this purpose.

Official debts to non-OECD countries

Over the recent past, LDCs' debts to non-OECD countries have increased both in absolute terms and as a share of LDCs' total stock of bilateral debt. Most of this debt is assumed to be official. According to preliminary estimates, it amounted to $43 billion in 1993 ($41 billion in 1992), as compared with $27 billion of corresponding long-term debt to OECD countries. However, debt-service payments to non-OECD countries represent only a small share of their total debt service, an estimated $0.2 billion annually in 1992 and 1993, while corresponding debt service to OECD countries amounted to some $1 billion annually. Payments have declined steadily since the late 1980s (see also chart 5).

Of LDCs' total debt to non-OECD countries in 1992, some 65 per cent, or $26 billion, is estimated to have been contracted on concessional terms. A major part of the total debt is owed to the former CMEA countries, notably the former Soviet Union, claims now assumed by the Russian Federation. They are estimated to have amounted to $30 billion at the end of 1992, while OPEC countries held some $7 billion and other countries close to $4 billion. Together, these claims by non-OECD countries represented about one third of LDCs' total external debt at end-1992. Some LDCs owe a much higher share of their debt, or even most of it, to non-OECD countries. Examples are Afghanistan, Cambodia, Ethiopia, the Lao People's Democratic Republic, Mozambique and Yemen.

The low (and declining) amount of debt-service payments by LDCs to non-OECD countries indicates that part of this debt is simply not being serviced. This seems particularly to be the case of loans contracted with the former Soviet Union.[27] However, non-OECD countries have also taken various measures to provide debt relief to LDCs. Such arrangements are already required under Paris Club rescheduling operations. All Paris Club agreements contain clauses under which the debtor country agrees to seek terms comparable with those obtained in the rescheduling from other creditors. The provisions for debt relief from other official bilateral creditors are set out in a specific clause, which requires the debtor not to extend more favourable treatment to non-participating creditor countries than that accorded to Paris Club creditors. In subsequent bilateral agreements concluded in parallel with Paris Club agreements, non-participating official bilateral creditors have adopted a variety of approaches, some of them involving substantial concessions. OPEC countries and China, as well as some other creditors, are among those that have negotiated rescheduling agreements with LDCs and extended other types of official debt relief to them in this context.[28]

Specific measures include the cancellation of some $300 million in official credits owed by low-income countries in sub-Saharan Africa, announced by Saudi Arabia in 1991, from which six LDCs are reported to have benefited. More recently, Saudi Arabia and Kuwait have concluded individual reschedulings with some other LDCs, such as Burkina Faso, Mali and Mauritania. China for its part has, in recent years, agreed to reschedulings on highly concessional terms for a number of debtor countries, including conversion of payments into local currency. For example, China has agreed to a moratorium on debt-service payments from Mali, has repeatedly rescheduled loans to Benin interest free, and has provided interest-free reschedulings for other countries.[29]

There seems to have been less progress in dealing with debts owed to the former CMEA countries due, *inter alia*, to the uncertainties resulting from the transition process in these countries, affecting in particular LDCs with heavy liabilities to the former Soviet Union. The Russian Federation has now reportedly begun discussions with most of the countries concerned and has concluded a number of agreements, although discussions are still at a preliminary stage in many cases. They often involve complex issues of data verification and reconciliation, as well as of the valuation of claims, contributing to difficulties and delays in finalizing agreements. However, in some cases involving a number of LDCs (e.g. Afghanistan, Lao People's Democratic Republic and Mali), the Russian Federation has agreed to continue rescheduling agreements providing for reduction or deferral of scheduled payments which were originally negotiated between the countries concerned and the former Soviet Union. Some agreements have implied substantial debt relief, as in the case of Mali, where the Russian Federation accepted a complete moratorium on debt-service payments for 1992 and very limited payments in local currency to cover obligations falling due in 1993. Negotiations are reportedly under way with other countries having substantial debts to the countries of the former Soviet Union, such as Benin, Ethiopia and Mozambique.[30]

Comparability of treatment is an important principle from both creditors' and debtors' points of view. Creditors who do not participate in Paris Club reschedulings should not benefit unfairly from relief offered by participating creditors. As regards the debtors, little overall progress would be made if resources released under Paris Club debt reorganization and other debt relief programmes are claimed by payment obligations to other creditors. The necessary assistance should be given to LDCs to help them negotiate debt-relief agreements with non-OECD countries in parallel with Paris Club and other programmes, and conclude such agreements expeditiously. In some cases, obligations due to official bilateral creditors that do not participate in Paris Club reschedulings may be small, but in other cases such debts are very substantial. In particular, liabilities to the former Soviet Union are looming large in LDCs' debt burden. This is the case especially for some individual LDCs, as noted above. Consideration might be given to setting up tripartite debt-reduction programmes for such countries, bringing together the debtor LDC, the concerned creditor country and third parties (current main donors and relevant international financial institutions) to seek to settle this problem.

Private commercial debt

Borrowings from financial markets currently play a marginal role in LDCs' external financing. Recorded outstanding long-term commercial bank debt owed by LDCs to OECD countries fell by some $1 billion from end-1990 to end-1992, representing less than 2 per cent of total long-term debt in the latter year. Corresponding debt-service payments have also fallen significantly, although they continue to represent a proportionally more important part of total debt service paid, some 7 per cent over the period 1991-1992.

A variety of mechanisms has been developed to alleviate low-income countries' commercial debt-servicing obligations, including the Debt Reduction Facility (DRF) set up in 1989 by the World Bank. This facility was initially funded with a transfer of $100 million from the International Bank for Reconstruction and Development's (IBRD) net income, and received a $100 million replenishment in September 1993.[31] Until mid-1994, however, debt buy-back operations under this facility had been completed for only five countries, of which three were LDCs (Mozambique, Niger and Uganda).

Negotiating debt buy-backs even for very poor countries, the value of whose debt on secondary markets would tend to be very low (average discount for the first operations under the DRF was 85 per cent), has proved to be a lengthy process. The DRF was originally mandated to help eligible countries reduce their long-term commercial bank debt, but has since been expanded to cover short-term suppliers' and trade credits in arrears for some time, and to provide technical assistance grants to these operations. This appears to have given some impetus to the process, and the number of DRF buy-backs under realization has increased. Operations for two more LDCs, Sao Tome and Principe and Zambia, were already completed in August and September 1994, respectively. Five others (for Ethiopia, Guinea, Mauritania, Sierra Leone and the United Republic of Tanzania) were being prepared and are expected to be completed in 1995.[32]

Bilateral contributions from a number of donors have helped to bring the first DRF operations to a successful conclusion. In seeking to solve LDCs' private commercial debt-overhang, a primary requirement is to cater to the needs of all countries that have expressed interest in this facility. The necessary resources need to be secured, through replenishments of the DRF as required, and donor countries must also stand ready to further contribute the requisite supplementary funds.

While a good deal of LDCs' outstanding commercial bank debt may ultimately be eliminated through DRF operations, not all LDCs are likely to have access to this facility in the near future, if only because of the conditionalities involved: not all of them have the economic programmes required. The Programme of Action recommended greater use, not only of the DRF, but also of other similar mechanisms (debt buy-back and conversion schemes) being useful tools in managing the debt burden, and which may bring additional benefits when coupled with other objectives, such as reconstruction, environment and assistance for the poor and for children.

There is a variety of such debt-for-development schemes, often involving NGOs, building on the idea of first buying back debt at a discount in the secondary market and then exchanging the debt with the debtor country for local currency to be used to finance development projects in various areas, including, for instance, environmental protection (debt-for-nature). So far, the number and scale of such swap transactions in LDCs seem to have been fairly limited. In Sudan, commercial banks donated their claims to UNICEF and the funds provided have been subsequently used for various development programmes (involving water, sanitation, health education and UNICEF programmes in rural areas). Similar programmes have been implemented in Madagascar and Zambia.[33] More recently, a debt-for-development option was included in the DRF buy-back for Zambia, with a total of 13 NGOs participating.

Scope remains for increased use of such mechanisms and more cooperation among LDCs, creditors, donor countries and NGOs in this area. This may be one means, for example, of helping needy populations in strife-torn countries, which are not likely to be prime candidates for DRF operations, and would ultimately also facilitate their task of reconstruction and economic rehabilitation.

Other debt-conversion programmes

Debt-conversion programmes need not necessarily be restricted to commercial bank debts. For instance, Paris Club agreements under the enhanced concessional terms have contained a provision for a certain amount of debt-for-nature, debt-for-aid, debt-for-equity or other local currency swaps which each participating creditor country may undertake in a voluntary manner. One of the instruments set up under Switzerland's debt reduction facility (and currently being implemented) is based on this type of approach. The facility has thus been used for buying back outstanding bilateral commercial debts guaranteed by the Swiss export risk-guarantee agency (and in some cases non-guaranteed debts also), from a total of 15 countries of which 6 were LDCs. Subsequently, the debts were cancelled, and the beneficiary country would pay in a certain amount of local currency counterpart funds that would be used for various development projects in collaboration with NGOs.

The former CMEA countries have again shown some interest in debt-for-equity conversions. A first swap of this kind (to equity) involving claims of the former Soviet Union was signed with the United Republic of Tanzania in early 1993.[34]

The use of debt-conversion schemes to mobilize domestic resources which could be used for investment in the small-scale sector was suggested at the UNCTAD Standing Committee on Poverty Alleviation at its session in July 1994. In the Committee's contribution to the preparations of the World Summit for Social Development, debt conversion was proposed as a practical and innovative approach for donors to assist developing countries to develop their export potential under conditions of high external indebtedness. Under such schemes, a certain proportion of counterpart funds generated could be utilized in support of small-scale enterprises and smallholders engaged in production for export.

In all cases, debt buy-back and conversion programmes require a well-prepared project portfolio suitable for these types of operation, as well as adequate private-sector development and privatization programmes to facilitate conversions to equity. As experience has shown, not only direct buy-backs but also swap operations are fairly complex and time-consuming to prepare and implement.

Multilateral debt - a growing problem?

Perspectives on multilateral debt

The share of multilateral debt in LDCs' total debt increased from 29 per cent in 1984 to around 35 per cent in 1992 and 1993. The corresponding share in total debt service has increased even more over the past decade, from just below 30 per cent to almost 50 per cent in 1992 and 1993. Outstanding debt to multilateral lending institutions alone amounted to $43 billion in 1992,

corresponding to 27 per cent of LDCs' aggregate GDP that year. In volume terms, debt-service payments to multilateral lending institutions peaked at a level of over $2 billion in 1986 (when total debt service paid by LDCs reached a record level of over $5 billion), but have since come down to a level of around $1.5 billion, claiming an estimated 8 per cent of their total export earnings in 1992. Again, trends in actual debt service do not necessarily follow payment obligations; a number of LDCs have not been able to acquit themselves fully of their obligations to the multilateral institutions although they retain preferred creditor status, and some LDCs were in protracted arrears to these institutions.

The continuing growth in LDCs' multilateral debt reflects the increasingly important role these institutions have assumed in LDCs' external financing, but have obligations increased so that they overtax LDCs' debt-servicing capacity? The Programme of Action acknowledged that the non-concessional part of multilateral debt in particular caused serious difficulties for many countries, and called on all institutions concerned to give serious attention to measures to alleviate the burden of the debt LDCs owe to them. More recently, the UNCTAD Trade and Development Board, at its review of progress in the implementation of the Programme of Action in 1994, noted with particular concern the increasing share of multilateral obligations in the overall debt stock and debt-servicing of LDCs. At that occasion, LDCs and some donors called for improvement and continuation of the scope and coverage of existing debt-relief schemes and mechanisms, including those relating to debt-service obligations to multilateral institutions.

There has been a notable shift towards softer terms in multilateral lending to LDCs over the past decade. For instance, most World Bank lending to these countries is now on IDA terms, while, in the case of IMF, use of SAF and ESAF has in the main replaced other financing facilities. As a consequence, while two thirds of LDCs' outstanding multilateral debt stock in 1984 was due to concessional lending, this share had increased to 87 per cent by 1992. As past non-concessional loans are being repaid, LDCs' stock of outstanding loans on such terms has been decreasing, albeit fairly slowly, since end-1987 (it fell below the $6 billion mark in 1992). However, non-concessional multilateral debt-service payments remained well above $1 billion annually during most of the same period. They fell below that level only in 1992, still representing well over one half of multilateral debt-service payments and over one quarter of total debt service paid by LDCs in that year.

The non-concessional debt burden of LDCs has, to some extent, been alleviated through the supplementary IDA adjustment credit programme of the World Bank, the so-called "fifth dimension", the main initiative taken so far for providing relief on multilateral debt.[35] So far, 11 LDCs have benefited from this scheme. In the World Bank's fiscal year 1994, LDCs obtained $34 million in such credits covering interest payments on IBRD loans contracted in the past (see also table 24). A few donor countries have made additional contributions under this scheme to help countries meet debt-service obligations on these loans. In relation to LDCs' total debt-service obligations on non-concessional multilateral account, however, the relief provided through the fifth dimension remains on a relatively modest scale.

The increased concessionality of multilateral lending constitutes a significant positive development in LDCs' indebtedness to multilateral institutions, but in spite of this a perception of an increasingly heavy multilateral debt burden can be explained. As noted above, the relative weight of multilateral obligations has risen to represent a major part of debt service, around one half of the total payments currently made. Moreover, these obligations are, according to the generally accepted principle, non-negotiable, i.e. not eligible for reschedulings or similar mechanisms of debt relief, while (apart from the fifth dimension, and some bilateral donor support provided to a limited number of countries) little help is available in meeting such payments; at the same time, difficulties and delays in servicing multilateral debt can have very serious consequences and risk strangling inflows of new finance. In this context, in LDCs in financial distress and experiencing little export growth, servicing multilateral debt can be felt as particularly cumbersome.

In assessing LDCs' multilateral debt burden, it is also important to take account of and examine individual country situations. In the aggregate, the "multilateral debt-service ratio" (multilateral debt-service payments actually made in relation to export earnings) has been contained below 10 per cent since 1988. In individual countries, such obligations have claimed a much higher share of resources. For instance, multilateral debt service paid by Uganda in 1992 amounted to a level corresponding to as much as 36 per cent of the country's export earnings in that year. Another set of countries that face special problems in this regard are LDCs in arrears to the international financial institutions, in particular those with long overdue obligations to the Bretton Woods institutions. In the following paragraphs, the situation of LDCs in arrears will be referred to separately; then an attempt will be made to identify other LDCs facing heavy multilateral debt-servicing obligations, which may require special support measures.

Multilateral arrears

The large majority of LDCs have so far maintained a satisfactory payment record with the multilateral lending institutions, in particular with the World Bank and the IMF (a somewhat larger number have run up arrears with other institutions, such as the African Development Bank.) Several LDCs have, over the recent past, taken steps to clear their arrears to the Bretton Woods institutions. Two of them, Sierra Leone and Zambia, have concluded rights accumulation programmes (RAPs) under the IMF arrears strategy. Under this approach, a member country having protracted arrears at the end of 1989 could earn rights towards future disbursements up to the equivalent of arrears outstanding at the outset of the programme. Such accumulation of rights is contingent upon sustained performance during the multi-year programme. There is also a similar arrangement at the World Bank. Sierra Leone successfully completed its RAP programme with the IMF in February 1994 and subsequently concluded new financing arrangements under SAF and ESAF. The programme in Zambia is scheduled to run through March 1995, whereafter (i.e. following successful completion and clearance of its arrears to the IMF), it would again become eligible for financial support from the IMF under a successor arrangement. Meanwhile, in October 1993, a third LDC, Cambodia, cleared its arrears to the IMF with the help of grants provided by a support group and has since also been able to draw again on IMF resources.

Five other LDCs (Haiti, Liberia, Somalia, Sudan and Zaire) still had overdue financial obligations to the IMF and/or the World Bank as of mid-1994; the problems of these countries transcend the debt issue. However, it must be assumed that sooner or later the external support needs of these countries will encompass assistance in restoring relations with creditor countries and institutions, whether through RAP-type programmes or even stronger debt-relief measures. They would stand to benefit from improvements which could be brought to bear on the current strategy for dealing with multilateral arrears.[36] Already, agreement among donor nations to assist Haiti to clear its arrears to the international financial institutions was announced in October 1994.[37]

The questions of dealing with payment arrears to the African Development Bank and the lending practices of that institution, again have a bearing on the debt-servicing problems of a number of African LDCs. These questions came to the forefront at the annual meeting of the Bank in 1994 and the negotiations for a replenishment of the African Development Fund (ADF). Contrary to most other multilateral institutions with major lending programmes with the LDCs, the African Development Bank group has continued to extend new loans on non-concessional terms to these countries, besides lending on soft terms. Here also, fifth-dimension type arrangements and extending concessional loans only to the poorest borrowers (ADF-only approach) have been suggested as solutions. However, these issues have been complicated by resource constraints and by the fact that an ADF-only approach would considerably limit the Bank's ability to operate in many of its borrowing member countries.[38]

Prospective multilateral debt-servicing capacity

As noted above, the burden implied in multilateral debt-servicing obligations varies among the LDCs. In 1992, the corresponding debt-service ratio was still contained below 10 per cent of export earnings in most of these countries. However, 12 LDCs had multilateral debt-service ratios higher than 10 per cent, in some cases considerably higher, six countries registering ratios of 20 per cent or more (see table 24: ratios calculated on the basis of actual as opposed to scheduled payments).

In future years, as multilateral debt-service obligations increase and unless export earnings grow at a rate to cover them sufficiently, a larger number of LDCs may confront overly heavy debt-servicing burdens on this account. Available information on LDCs' future multilateral debt-service obligations and illustrations of resulting debt-service ratios under two different export growth scenarios for the 1990s are given in table 25. Part A of that table summarizes available projections of multilateral debt-servicing obligations up to the year 2000 for LDCs as a group, and the resulting multilateral debt-service ratio under assumptions of zero export growth and 5 per cent export growth, respectively. They exclude the settlement of obligations which are currently overdue during the projection period,[39] as well as obligations arising out of new loan commitments. They thus represent minimum projections; action taken to

settle arrears and new lending would tend to raise the figures. This would be particularly true for repayments by those countries with large arrears, and for possible new IMF arrangements which might, in particular, affect the payment schedule towards the end of the decade. On the other hand, in view of the low interest rates and long grace periods of most other new multilateral lending to LDCs, the bulk of repayments of new lending contracted from 1993-1994 onward should fall due only after the year 2000 and not overly affect payment schedules up to that year. With these reservations, the projections in table 25(A) give some indication of the scale of claims of multilateral debt service on LDCs' resources during the rest of the decade.

The projections show that, for the LDCs as a group, multilateral debt service is scheduled to increase steadily, albeit not dramatically, over most of the remainder of the decade. Part of the increase comes from current IMF arrangements, which have shorter grace and repayment periods than the IDA or similar grant-like terms characteristic for most other current multilateral borrowings of LDCs. The shift in the debt profile which has taken place away from non-concessional to increasing concessional lending again may explain the levelling-off in the growth of non-IMF multilateral debt-servicing obligations during the second half of the decade. However, the projections also indicate that relatively robust export growth (contrary to what the LDCs as a group have experienced over the recent past) would be required in order to contain the aggregate multilateral debt-service ratio below 10 per cent during the remainder of the decade.

When examining these projections at the country level, important variations in degrees of multilateral indebtedness emerge. In some countries, levels of multilateral debt and ensuing debt-servicing obligations are still relatively low in relation to export-earning capacity, and, barring major external or other economic shocks, they should be able to contain the multilateral debt-service ratio below 10 per cent throughout the 1990s. In others, sustained export growth will be necessary to achieve the same result, and unless exports grow fairly strongly, these countries will be confronted with a situation in which multilateral debt service will claim an increasing part of external receipts. In yet other LDCs, multilateral indebtedness already seems to have reached critical levels, with scheduled debt-service obligations on this account alone currently corresponding to up to one third to one

Table 25: Debt service obligations of LDCs to multilateral institutions, 1993-2000

A. Projected debt service 1993-2000 for LDCs as a group[a]

	1993	1994	1995	1996	1997	1998	1999	2000
Debt service obligations to institutions other than IMF, $ billion	1.5	1.6	1.7	1.8	1.8	1.8	1.8	1.8
Debt service obligations to IMF, $ billion	0.3	0.3	0.4	0.5	0.5	0.5	0.5	0.4
Total debt service obligations to multilateral institutions, $ million	1.8	2.0	2.1	2.2	2.3	2.3	2.3	2.2
Multilateral debt service ratio,[b] under zero-export growth scenario (per cent)	10	10	11	11	12	12	12	12
Multilateral debt service ratio,[b] under assumption of 5 per cent annual growth in exports (per cent)	9	9	9	9	9	9	8	8

B. Debt service projections for individual LDCs 1993-1995

1993-1995 average annual debt service obligations on multilateral debt[a] above 20 per cent of 1992 exports: Burundi, Guinea-Bissau, Rwanda, Sao Tome and Principe, Somalia, Sudan, Uganda

1993-1995 average annual debt service obligations on multilateral debt[a] between 10 and 20 per cent of 1992 exports: Burkina Faso, Cape Verde, Central African Republic, Comoros, Ethiopia, Liberia, Madagascar, Malawi, Mauritania, Mozambique, Myanmar, Niger, United Republic of Tanzania, Zaire, Zambia

Source: Estimates based on The World Bank, *World Debt Tables, 1993-1994*, and on data from IMF.
  a   Excluding overdue obligations.
  b   Ratio to total projected exports of scheduled multilateral debt service payments, excluding settlement of arrears.

half of export earnings in the most extreme cases.

Part B of table 25 lists the countries in which average annual multilateral debt service obligations alone in 1993-1995 correspond to over 20 per cent of 1992 export earnings and may serve to identify the countries where multilateral indebtedness is a cause of particular concern, and where the prospective capacity to service multilateral debt is especially sensitive to assumptions about economic stability and export developments. The situation of some of these countries carrying the relatively most heavy multilateral debt burden would not necessarily change, even if exports pick up during the current decade. With payment obligations projected to rise, the corresponding debt-service ratio would, in some cases, fall only marginally, or even increase over the next few years.

Part B of table 25 also shows that under an assumption of zero export growth (a hypothesis which unfortunately may not be unreasonable for some of these countries), the number of LDCs with multilateral debt-service ratios over 10 per cent in 1993-1995 would increase to 22, not far from one half the number of LDCs. In seven countries, this ratio would surpass the benchmark of 20 per cent of export earnings.[40] Most of the LDCs that have been in arrears to multilateral institutions, other than to the IMF and the World Bank, are among those countries with the relatively most heavy multilateral debt-servicing burdens. However, others listed here have stayed current on their payments. Most of the LDCs have clearly struggled to do so both with regard to the Bretton Woods and other multilateral institutions, and there is no reason to assume that they would change their policy of fulfilling their obligations, in spite of the heavy cost involved.

Need for special support measures

Just as debt-servicing capacity in general is determined by export earnings capacity, LDCs' ability to meet their multilateral debt-service obligations over the rest of the decade will critically depend on export opportunities and developments. As indicated above, unless their economic fortunes change, an increasing number of countries may find their multilateral debt-service obligations growing heavier and contributing to future financial and payment difficulties. And even in the case of positive export development, there are two groups of countries that are likely to need special support measures over the coming years to manage an overhang of multilateral debt. These are: (a) countries in arrears to the international financial institutions, in particular those with large arrears to the Bretton Woods institutions, discussed above (and where one can draw on the experience of support groups and of RAP-type mechanisms); and (b) a number of other countries in which the obligations they have contracted seem inordinately high in relation to debt-servicing capacity and prospects for export growth; in these, issues of limits to exposure of the lending institutions and how to ensure continued multilateral support to these countries also arise. It would be important to find early solutions which can be applied also in the latter type of situation.

Among possible solutions, consideration might be given to enlarging the fifth dimension to supply further assistance to needy countries in meeting payments due and possibly to provide a framework for measures to address multilateral debt problems in general. Benefits of the existing supplementary IDA adjustment credit programme could be substantially enhanced for LDCs by extending this scheme to include payments not only of interest, but also of principal, and by enlarging country coverage. Agreement on similar mechanisms in other multilateral lending institutions holding non-concessional claims on LDCs, notably within the African Development Bank, would also be important. In this context, outright refinancing of loans on concessional terms would also be a way to reduce debt-servicing obligations on non-concessional account. Increased bilateral support, with more donor countries contributing supplementary funds, would be essential to underpin an enlarged fifth-dimension scheme. Thought also needs to be given to the scope for debt-reduction measures to bring overly heavy multilateral debt-servicing obligations down to sustainable levels. In some of the LDCs concerned, the amounts involved would be relatively small in absolute terms.

Concrete proposals in this respect have been made by the United Kingdom. This initiative, presented at the meeting of Commonwealth Finance Ministers in Valetta, Malta in September 1994, recognizes that for some countries debt relief on bilateral official debt may not be enough to escape from an unsustainable debt burden. The United Kingdom Chancellor of the Exchequer in Valetta called on all the international financial institutions to consider what more they could do to help their poorest and most indebted members. Specifically, he proposed that the IMF should convert a small part of its gold reserves into income-earning assets; the income earned could then be used to provide loans on easier terms to those of the IMF's poorest, most indebted members which have shown a sustained commitment to economic reform and which have significant debts to the IMF. This would improve their ability to cope with repayments. The underlying investments could form part of the IMF's reserves, ensuring that financial soundness is not compromised.

Removing LDCs' debt overhang: conclusions

Debt-relief measures taken so far have not been sufficient to remove LDCs' debt overhang. For most of these countries, external debt-servicing obligations continue to seriously drain resources, compromising the successful implementation of ongoing reform programmes and stabilization efforts. Further measures including, in many cases, a substantial reduction of their outstanding debt stock, are needed to help them redress their economies and assure their long-term external viability and development prospects. Agreement on a comprehensive strategy of debt reduction for LDCs would be a major contribution towards improving their chances of economic progress in the second half of the decade. Such a strategy needs to be complemented by providing additional new resources on the softest possible terms to support LDCs' adjustment and development programmes, in line with the aid targets and commitments set out in the Programme of Action.

Action aimed at reducing the non-concessional components of LDCs' outstanding debt -- export credits and commercial bank

**Box 18: Debt and development: sharing of experiences -
Ministerial Meeting of Non-Aligned Countries**

The tenth Summit of Heads of State and Government of the Non-Aligned Movement (NAM) held in Jakarta, Indonesia, in September 1992, reviewed, *inter alia*, the external debt situation of non-aligned and other developing countries. Recognizing the generally unsatisfactory experience of these countries in achieving effective settlements of their debt problem, the Summit called on its members to continue their mutual consultations on this topic. In the way of follow-up, Indonesia, as chair of the NAM, convened in Jakarta in August 1994 a Ministerial Meeting of Non-Aligned Countries on Debt and Development: Sharing of Experiences. Apart from the host country, it was attended by invited Ministers and officials from 24 countries - all LDCs. Discussion was able to draw on the Report of the Non-Aligned Movement Ad Hoc Advisory Group of Experts on Debt,[1] which was submitted to the meeting.

At the meeting in Jakarta in August 1994, various aspects of the current debt problem were discussed and a number of major conclusions drawn:

The debt situation today continues to be severe in many countries, and remains a veritable impediment to economic growth and development. As countries are obliged to give priority to servicing their external debt, Governments have been forced to reduce essential public investments, particularly on physical and social infrastructure. Despite repeated attempts at debt rescheduling, and some debt relief, it is clear that the remaining debt stock of poor developing countries remains so high that the possibility of it being settled in full is virtually nil.

Debt reduction vs. rescheduling. Substantial debt reduction, as opposed to repeated debt rescheduling, was endorsed as the most appropriate approach for the resolution of the debt crisis. The following general principles for debt reduction were endorsed:

- a once-and-for-all arrangement for settling all outstanding debt;

- the application of debt reduction to all categories of debt, including multilateral debt; and

- the application of these principles, as well as an adequate degree of debt reduction for all countries, although, within such an overall framework, there will necessarily be a case-by-case approach in dealing with the debt of individual countries.

The need to address multilateral debt. Debt-reduction efforts, if they are to result in the easing of the debt burden of the debt-distressed countries, must also include multilateral debt. Debt owed to multilateral financial institutions now constitutes the bulk of outstanding debt for many countries, and the servicing of such debt accounts for a large share of debt-service payments. Hence, unless measures are taken to reduce multilateral debt and debt service, it will be impossible to provide effective debt-reduction measures for many poor countries.

Debt owed to the former Soviet Union. Several developing countries owe substantial amounts of such debt. It was agreed that debts incurred to the former Soviet Union for development purposes should be treated in the same manner as other debts. For some poor debt-distressed countries, however, as a high proportion of the debt owed to the former Soviet Union was incurred for military purchases during the Cold War era, there is a need for a special and separate consideration of such debts.

Debt relief, economic reform and new resources. While substantial debt reduction is a necessary condition to allow countries to begin to devote their resources to development, it alone will not result in economic growth and development. Countries will need to adopt sound economic policies to restore growth and external viability. In particular, they should seek to restore macroeconomic stability through fiscal and monetary discipline. Equally important, the international community will need to increase the supply of concessional funds and help create a more favourable international economic environment to enable these countries to achieve high rates of economic growth, without relapsing into a new debt crisis.

South-South Cooperation. The need for greater cooperation on different aspects of the debt problem was recognized. The Jakarta meeting called for various measures in this field, including keeping the debt situation under regular review and continuing the exchange of views and experiences; engaging creditor countries in the appropriate international forums to begin discussions that could lead to the adoption of a common set of principles for future debt negotiations; and strengthening technical cooperation among developing countries on debt management and debt-negotiation techniques, as well as bilateral cooperative arrangements on debt and development issues.[2]

---

1   *The Continuing Debt Crisis of the Developing Countries.* Report of the Non-Aligned Movement Ad Hoc Advisory Group of Experts on Debt (August 1994).
2   *The Ministerial Meeting of Non-Aligned Countries on Debt and Development: Sharing of Experiences,* 13-15 August 1994, Jakarta, Indonesia. Report of the Chairman of the Meeting, 15 August 1994.

loans, as well as non-concessional multilateral debt -- would be particularly effective in rapidly reducing their debt-servicing burden. The fact that LDCs now receive mainly concessional finance also provides a strong argument for clearing the overhang of non-concessional obligations contracted in the past. According to similar reasoning, the principle of bilateral ODA debt forgiveness for these countries has already been widely accepted.

Eliminating most of LDCs' obligations on non-concessional account would free their financial resources and economic management capacities to deal with their concessional debts, in particular their multilateral obligations. This would also be in line with and support the external-financing strategies adopted by many LDCs as part of their structural adjustment programmes; a standard element in these is a policy of not contracting any new loans on non-concessional terms. Under such a programme, supported by further bilateral ODA debt forgiveness, and with reasonable export growth, one might assume that most LDCs would be able to service remaining (concessional) multilateral debt, building up their borrowing capacities and relations with relevant creditor institutions offering soft-term financing. Even so, additional action on multilateral debt may be needed in some cases to bring such debt down to sustainable levels.

The following would be essential elements in a debt-reduction strategy for LDCs. Debt-relief programmes for individual countries would need to be tailored case-by-case, in accordance with each country's circumstances and specific debt profile:

- continued financing on grant or grant-like terms, with adequate replenishment of the soft windows of the international financial institutions to assure continued substantial net transfers from them to LDCs;

- measures to implement ODA debt-cancellation programmes expeditiously and across the board with a view to complete elimination of LDCs' remaining ODA debts; this would require setting up debt-cancellation programmes similar to those of other donors by all major creditors (including non-OECD creditors) still holding such claims;

- deepest possible debt relief and generous debt-stock reduction in the Paris Club, with full forgiveness of all official bilateral debts for the most heavily indebted countries;

- equivalent debt-relief measures by other official creditors, and provision of the necessary technical support to enable LDCs to conduct and complete negotiations with these creditors as promptly as possible;

- setting up special debt-reduction programmes for countries that are heavily indebted to non-Paris Club creditors, including possible tripartite arrangements involving the debtor country, creditor country/creditors and concerned third parties (current main donors and relevant international financial institutions);

- use of DRF to extinguish LDCs' commercial bank debts, supplemented as necessary with other debt buy-back and debt-conversion schemes;

- consideration of the extension of DRF or setting up a DRF-like mechanism to cover other types of debt, e.g. under tripartite debt-reduction programmes suggested above;

- setting up support groups for countries in protracted arrears to the Bretton Woods institutions and offering grant assistance or improved RAP-type programmes to help them settle their overdue obligations;

- an enlarged fifth dimension combining supplemental credits, refinancing arrangements and bilateral donor support with a double mission: (a) to help LDCs meet current debt-service payments on their remaining non-concessional multilateral debt; and (b) to undertake debt-stock operations for countries where overall multilateral obligations have reached levels that are clearly unsustainable in relation to the debtor country's economic and financial capacities;

- provision of the necessary technical assistance for capacity-building in the formulation of external financing and borrowing strategies and in debt management, including capacity for debt negotiations and reorganization.

A strategy for debt reduction will also have to address the question of resources. Debt-relief mechanisms set up so far have drawn on bilateral funds, as well as on funding arrangements within multilateral institutions. An effective debt-reduction programme would require increased bilateral donor support, as well as further mobilization of resources for this purpose within creditor institutions. As regards bilateral funding arrangements, special debt-relief facilities or specific budget lines for the provision of such relief set up by some donor countries have proved a useful tool in addressing debt problems, and other bilateral donors may also wish to consider similar schemes. In view of the current squeeze on aid budgets, recourse to new sources of funds, such as SDR allocations and IMF gold sales (e.g. as proposed by the United Kingdom), should also be considered to ensure both adequate levels and additionality of funding. In this context, ways could be explored to utilize resources that will eventually become available through new SDR allocations for the purpose of providing debt relief and debt reduction to LDCs, for instance through trust-fund arrangements.

Another issue that requires attention is that of coordination of debt relief and mechanisms for debt-reduction programmes at the country level. While the Paris Club provides a forum for dealing with specific requests for debt relief, creditor participation is mainly limited to OECD countries and deals with official bilateral debts only; moreover, for various reasons, not all LDCs with debt problems warranting attention can turn to this forum or may wish to exercise this option. UNCTAD has long argued for the integration of the treatment of debt relief and overall financing issues and a closer coordination of Paris Club proceedings with consultative and aid groups and the round-table process.[41] Moreover, there is a need to couple debt reorganization in that forum with active debt-reduction programmes in other areas, e.g. in the most heavily indebted countries and/or where debt owed to non-Paris Club creditors is important. Such programmes should not only aim to deal with already overdue obligations. An equally important aim should be to prevent the emergence or persistence of debt-servicing difficulties. Here, arrangements to address individual LDCs' debt problems in a more forward-looking and comprehensive manner could be to: (1) introduce a specific agenda item on debt in consultative and aid groups and in round-table meetings; (2) set up subgroups under these mechanisms to deal with the debt issue; or (3) organize formal or informal support groups among donors for countries where no other type of consultative mechanism is available. Relevant multilateral institutions could take the lead in setting up such groups for debt-distressed LDCs.

Over the longer term, LDCs' ability to service debt will depend on progress in domestic resource mobilization and in enhancing export revenue. Insufficient export growth in itself goes a long way to explain the debt-servicing problems that these countries are currently confronting. Some LDCs facing the heaviest debt burdens are countries where export receipts grew little if at all, or fell significantly over the past decade. Support for their trade expansion and diversification efforts and expanded export opportunities are needed to solve their debt problems on a lasting basis and to enable LDCs to, over time, grow out of their current dependence on aid.

NOTES

1   Official development financing flows, as measured by the OECD/DAC, consist of bilateral ODA, concessional and non-concessional resources from multilateral sources, and other bilateral official flows made available for reasons unrelated to trade.

2   OECD, *Development Co-operation, 1994 Report*, Statistical Annex, table 42 (Paris, 1995).

3   *The Least Developed Countries, 1993-1994 Report*, Part One, chap. I, sect.E, and annex table 22 in that report.

4   UNCTAD, *World Investment Report, 1994: Transnational Corporations, Employment and the Workplace*, chap.II, sect.B, pp.60-65.

5   OECD, *op.cit.*, chap.IV.

6   Since the adoption of the Programme of Action, UNCTAD has annually sent out a questionnaire to donor countries on measures taken for the implementation of the Programme. Of the 21 countries members of DAC, 18 have responded to the questionnaire and provided valuable information about their aid programmes in LDCs.

7   *The Least Developed Countries, 1993-1994 Report*, Part One, chap.III, sect.B; and *The Least Developed Countries, 1992 Report*, chap.IV, sect.A.

8   In particular, available information on the outcomes of recent consultative and aid group meetings give little indication of significant upwards shifts in aid levels. Year-to-year comparisons of amounts committed are in general

not feasible for round-table countries, as these meetings tend to be held on a less regular basis.

9 *The Least Developed Countries, 1993-1994 Report*, Part One, chap.III.

10 Press communiqué issued after the meeting of the Development Committee of the Boards of Governors of the World Bank and IMF, Madrid, 3 October 1994, para. 5.

11 *The Least Developed Countries, 1993-1994 Report*, Part One, chap.III. In addition to the implications of donors' aid policy conditionalities, this chapter deals with issues in aid coordination and enhancing aid effectiveness.

12 *The World Bank Annual Report, 1994.*

13 *The Least Developed Countries, 1992 Report*, chap.IV.

14 Elliot J. Berg (Coordinator), *Rethinking Technical Cooperation: Reforms for Capacity Building in Africa*, UNDP and Development Alternatives Inc., New York 1993. New approaches to technical cooperation were further explored at a joint DAC/UNDP/World Bank high-level seminar in June 1994.

15 Cf. statement by the DAC chairman to the meeting of the Development Committee of the IMF/World Bank, October 1994 (OECD press release SG/NR(94)56).

16 Cf. *The Least Developed Countries, 1992 Report*, chap.IV, sect.A.

17 *The Least Developed Countries, 1993-1994 Report*, Part One, chap.I, sect.E.

18 See table 24 of this chapter and World Bank, *World Debt Tables 1993-94*, Vol.1, Appendix 1. The World Bank classification is based on the present value of scheduled debt service in relation to GNP and exports.

19 For details of OECD countries' ODA debt-cancellation programmes, see previous issues of UNCTAD's LDC Reports.

20 The latter measure concerns payments arrears to the French development financing agency, Caisse française de développement. Of the 14 countries in the CFA zone, 9 are LDCs. They had already had, in principle, their outstanding aid debts forgiven by France (*The Least Developed Countries, 1990 Report*, chap.II, sect.A, pp.37-38). The additional relief extended by France as part of the support package in connection with the devaluation of the CFA franc concerns repayment obligations on subsequent drawings on remaining aid loans, which are now also to be cancelled. ODA debts owed to OECD countries by LDCs in the CFA zone still amounted to one fifth of their outstanding long-term debt at the end of 1992, accounting for 15 per cent of their total external debt service in that year.

21 Official non-concessional debts owed by the LDCs in the CFA zone to OECD countries at the end of 1992 amounted to less than 10 per cent of their long-term debt, but accounted for as much as one quarter of their total external debt service in that year.

22 A further option retained from the original Toronto terms provides for longer repayment periods at market rates (with no reduction of payment obligations.) See further, *The Least Developed Countries, 1992 Report*, chap.IV, p.97, note 22.

23 Excerpt published in *IMF Survey*, 25 July 1994.

24 Initiative launched by the United Kingdom at a meeting of Commonwealth Finance Ministers in Trinidad and Tobago in 1990. See further, e.g. UNCTAD, *Trade and Development Report, 1991*, Part One, chap.II, sect.B.

25 *Trade and Development Report, 1993*, Part Three, chap.II, sect.B.

26 *Ibid.*; also see *Trade and Development Report, 1992*, Part Two, chap.I, sect.H; and *The Least Developed Countries, 1992 Report*, appendix to chap.IV.

27 See also annex table 26.

28 IMF, *Official Financing for Developing Countries*, Washington, D.C., April 1994, pp.29-31 and table A11.

29 *Ibid.* The stock of outstanding debt owed by LDCs to OPEC and other countries, i.e. excluding debt to OECD and the former CMEA countries, remained broadly stable over the period 1990-1992.

30 *Ibid.,,* pp.31-32.

31 The facility makes support available on a grant basis for buy-backs of commercial bank debt undertaken by severely indebted IDA-only countries that have adjustment programmes and have drawn up comprehensive programmes to deal with their debt problems.

32 *CFS Link* (Cofinancing and Financial Advisory Services, The World Bank), July 1994, and information from The World Bank.

33 Another UNICEF debt-swap programme involving health, nutrition, education, social mobilization and area-based programmes was implemented in Madagascar in 1992, funds in this case having been acquired at half the face value of the debt. Debt-for-nature swaps involving the World Wildlife Fund and Conservation International have been reported for Madagascar and Zambia. See The World Bank, *World Debt Tables, 1993-94*, vol.1, Appendix 3, pp.116-117.

34 The World Bank, *op. cit,.* p.114.

35 This programme, established in 1988 and financed from a 10 per cent share of IDA reflows and from IDA investment income earmarked for this purpose, provides supplementary resources to help meet interest payments on IBRD debt previously contracted by countries which are now IDA-only borrowers, are current in their debt-service payments to both IBRD and IDA, and have in place IDA-supported adjustment operations.

[36] See further, *Trade and Development Report, 1993*, Part Three, chap.III. The IMF rights approach remains available for three of the five countries mentioned, i.e. Liberia, Somalia and Sudan.

[37] The arrears were paid in December 1994.

[38] Cf. Percy S. Mistry, *Multilateral Debt: An Emerging Crisis?*, Forum on Debt and Development (FONDAD), The Hague, February 1994. A few donors have already helped LDCs to settle arrears to the African Development Bank.

[39] Including debt-service obligations to the IMF of Zambia, which is currently implementing a rights accumulation programme.

[40] Countries where the 1993-1995 average annual multilateral debt-service obligations, including IMF obligations but excluding settlement of IMF and other arrears, correspond to over 10 and 20 per cent, respectively, of exports of goods and services in 1992.

[41] See, in particular, *Trade and Development Report, 1993*, Part Three, chap.II; and *The Least Developed Countries, 1993-1994 Report*, Part One, chap.I. sect.E.

VI. International Support Measures and National Actions in Selected Areas of External Trade

A. Implications of the Final Act of the Uruguay Round for LDCs

Introduction

The implications of the Final Act of the Uruguay Round of Multilateral Trade Negotiations for LDCs have been discussed in a number of UNCTAD documents.[1] This section seeks to revisit the likely consequences on LDCs of agreements in the areas of market access, agriculture, textiles and clothing, trade-related aspects of intellectual property rights (TRIPs), trade-related investment measures (TRIMs), multilateral trade rules, and services. The issue of policy measures to promote LDC participation in international trade will be taken up in the concluding subsection.

It should be noted that LDCs had to accept the overall package of the Uruguay Round in its entirety as a single undertaking. This involved assumption of obligations on their part some of which had hardly been acceptable to industrialized countries even a few years ago. These include, *inter alia*, the following.[2]

- increased scope of tariff bindings and establishment of a tariff schedule on goods as a requirement for becoming an original member of the World Trade Organization (WTO);

- accepting tighter disciplines in the application of balance-of-payment measures, which entails giving preference to price-based measures rather than to quantitative restrictions;

- accepting the general obligations in the General Agreement on Trade in Services (GATS) including the establishment of schedule on initial commitments on services as a condition for obtaining original membership in the WTO;

- accepting the same level of obligations as all other countries in respect of the Agreement on TRIPs, extending the scope of protection to new areas of intellectual

property never covered before by their national intellectual property regimes;

- accepting multilateral disciplines in the use of investment measures inconsistent with GATT Articles III and XI, including notification of such measures;

- increased transparency in their trade policies, particularly through the Trade Policy Review Mechanism.

To alleviate the concerns of LDCs with regard to the overall package, a political commitment was made in the Ministerial decision adopted at Marrakesh entitled "Measures in favour of Least Developed Countries". It affirms, *inter alia*, that:

- as long as LDCs comply with the general rules, they will be required only to undertake commitments and concessions consistent with their individual development, financial and trade needs, or their administrative and institutional capabilities; and

- the rules set out in the various agreements, as well as the transitional provisions, should be applied in a flexible and supportive manner for LDCs. To this effect, sympathetic consideration shall be given to specific concerns raised by LDCs in the Councils and Committees of WTO.

For LDCs, however, the nature of dispensation accorded to them raises a number of concerns. For example, the adoption of common rules and disciplines and the extension of multilateral trading rules to new subjects, as well as reciprocity-based negotiations that imply that most favoured nation (MFN) tariffs will be reduced, will spur other countries to strengthen their competitive capacities for success and survival in the international market-place. As a result, investments in these countries in infrastructure, technology and human resources will receive greater priority so that they can adjust to the new competitive pressures. The competitive gap between LDCs and the rest of the world may widen more if LDCs remain outside the mainstream of the world trading environment. Consequently, while longer transition periods and other contingency measures are necessary for LDCs to cope with the consequences of the Final Act, it is in their long-term interest that the dispensations accorded do not distract them from strengthening their competitive capabilities as rapidly as possible. Necessary national actions and international support measures should be in place to expedite this process.

The analysis in this section is essentially qualitative. Data are not yet available for a reliable assessment to be made of the quantitative implications and consequences of the Uruguay Round agreements for developing countries, nor for LDCs. The preliminary quantitative assessments made by researchers and the GATT secretariat are tentative and based on a number of speculations that depend on when and how the various agreements will be implemented. In addition, the full import of the various complex agreements are yet to be adequately understood.

Implications for LDCs of agreements in selected areas

Market access (industrial products, excluding petroleum)

In the case of industrial products, excluding petroleum, tariff reductions in developed countries will average 40 per cent and will reduce the pre-Uruguay Round average tariff from 6.3 per cent to 3.8 per cent (table 26). Of the different product groups, above-average tariff cuts will be made in 7 groups, which account for over two thirds of the developed countries' total imports; while below-average tariff reductions will be made in 4 product groups. Below-average tariff cuts will be made in three product groups of export interest to developing countries and LDCs, namely, textiles and clothing (a reduction of 22 per cent); leather, rubber, footwear, and travel goods (18 per cent); and fish and fish products (26 per cent). On the other hand, there will be above-average tariff cuts in three product groups of export interest to some LDCs, namely: metals (62 per cent); mineral products, precious stones and metals (52 per cent); and wood, pulp, paper and furniture (69 per cent).

Table 26: Tariff reductions by developed countries in the Uruguay Round according to industrial product group [a]

(Percentage)

	Average tariff		
Product group	*Pre-Round*	*Post-Round*	*Percentage reduction*
All industrial products	**6.3**	**3.8**	**40**
Textiles and clothing	15.5	12.1	22
Metals	3.7	1.4	62
Mineral products, precious stones and metals	2.3	1.1	52
Electric machinery	6.6	3.5	47
Leather, rubber, footwear and travel goods	8.9	7.3	18
Wood, pulp, paper and furniture	3.5	1.1	69
Fish and fish products	6.1	4.5	26
Non-electric machinery	4.8	1.9	60
Chemicals and photographic supplies	6.7	3.7	45
Transport equipment	7.5	5.8	23
Manufactured articles, *n.e.s.*	5.5	2.4	56

Source: GATT, The results of the Uruguay Round of Multilateral Trade Negotiations, November 1994.

    a   Excluding petroleum products.

Note: The value of import statistics used to calculate tariff reductions, in the three related tables, ranges from 1988 to 1992 (1988 for most of the developed countries). The import data is drawn from GATT Secretariat's Integrated Data Base (IDB). It accounts for approximately 98 and 90 per cent of the merchandise trade of GATT contracting parties, and total world trade respectively. See source for further details.

The proportion of goods at zero MFN tariff entering the markets of developed countries will increase from 20 to 43 per cent, two-fold rise due mainly to a substantial increase in zero tariff treatment for the following groups: mineral products, precious stones, and metals; electric and non-electric machinery; wood, pulp, paper and furniture; and manufactured articles not specified elsewhere. Because of this, the average tariff cuts in these product groups are substantial.

In terms of exports of industrial products from developing countries and LDCs to developed countries, tariff cuts will average 37 per cent for developing countries, excluding LDCs, and 25 per cent for LDCs. But if two product groups, namely, textiles and clothing and fish and fish products are excluded, the average tariff cuts will rise sharply to 50 per cent for developing countries and 61 per cent for LDCs (table 27).

Two issues of major concern to developing countries and LDCs discussed in the Uruguay Round were tariff "peaks" (tariffs exceeding 15 per cent) and tariff "escalation". The share of imports by industrial countries subject to tariff peaks will decline from 7 to 5 per cent, but significant clusters of peaks will remain for textiles and clothing (28 per cent); leather, rub-

ber, footwear and travel goods (11 per cent); and transport equipment (7 per cent).

Tariff escalation has been a cause for concern because it seeks to impose higher tariffs as the degree of processing rises and thereby discourages the export of products with a higher value-added content. Products of actual or potential export interest to LDCs, which are especially affected by tariff escalation, are tropical beverages and spices, fish, vegetables, fruits, yarn and fabrics, natural rubber, wood, natural fibres, minerals and metals. It is estimated that tariff escalation will, in general, be reduced, as duties in different stages of production are harmonized. Data for selected product groups indicate that tariff escalation will be substantially reduced for paper and pulp, jute, tobacco and wood products, but may remain the same for many other products.

LDCs and erosion of preferences

An issue of serious concern to LDCs, especially those in Africa, is the erosion of their margin of preferences and thereby the loss of their competitiveness in major export markets because of the reduction in MFN tariffs at the Uruguay Round. Most of the trade of the African countries enjoyed duty-free access or tariffs at 0 to 5 per cent in their major export markets, especially the European Union (EU), under the

Table 27: Tariff reductions by developed countries on industrial products [a]
imported from selected groups of countries
(Percentage)

Import from	Import value ($ billion)	Trade-weighted tariff average		
		Pre-Round	Post-Round	Percentage reduction
All industrial products				
Developed countries	736.9	6.3	3.8	40
Developing countries (other than LDCs)	165.8	6.8	4.3	37
LDCs	3.9	6.8	5.1	25
Industrial products (excluding textiles and clothing, fish and fish products)				
Developed countries	652.1	5.4	2.9	46
Developing countries (other than LDCs)	123.7	4.8	2.4	50
LDCs	2.1	1.8	0.7	61

Source: As for table 26.

a   Excluding petroleum products.

generalized system of preferences (GSP) or Lomé Convention arrangements.

Erosion of preferences is discussed in section B. There is a strong case for improving the existing schemes of preferences with a view to offsetting the loss of preferential margins likely to be experienced by LDCs in the wake of the adoption of the Final Act. At the same time, it will be in the interest of LDCs to press for reduction and binding of MFN tariffs and to eliminate overt and covert non-tariff barriers to their export trade which, through their trade-creation effects, can go a long way to mitigate the erosion of concessions.

Agriculture

Agriculture was put on the agenda of the Uruguay Round largely by the pressure and persistence of the 14-member Cairns group, 10 of whom (that is, those other than Australia, Canada, Hungary and New Zealand) are developing countries in Asia and Latin America. Removal of the restrictions and distortions in world agricultural markets was their foremost objective at the Round. Net food-importing countries, most of whom are LDCs, voiced their concern about the likely increase in world prices of agricultural commodities and with their inability to bear the cost of higher import bills. This concern was recognized in the Ministerial decision adopted at Marrakesh entitled "Measures concerning the possible negative effects of the Reform Programme on least-developed and net food-importing developing countries".

While LDCs are also required to tariffy and bind their tariffs, they are exempt from obligations to reduce domestic subsidies. However, the real implication for LDCs lies not in this exemption from obligations that the agricultural agreement entails for them, but in the possibility that their food import bill may rise sharply and affect their capacity to devote their resources to other areas of their economic development. To a lesser extent, the erosion of tariff preferences on certain agricultural items in the export basket of LDCs, such as coffee and cocoa beans, could affect their export earnings.

While the objective of agricultural trade liberalization is that the world prices of agricultural commodities should be allowed to rise to distortion-free levels, it is difficult to forecast the nature and extent of the rise in prices of food imports. Assuming, however, that world food prices will rise in the medium to long term, the Ministerial decision has recommended certain measures to assist LDCs to cope with the problem. As was noted in chapter II, net food imports of LDCs steadily increased over the last quarter century and were three times higher during 1989-1993 than during the 1970s. Their increasing dependence on imported food underscores the urgency with which the Ministerial decision should be implemented. In particular, it is important that the donor countries and international agencies (The World Bank and IMF in particular) provide adequate financial and technical assistance to LDCs so that they can meet their import bills and improve their agricultural productivity and infrastructure.

Finally, the agricultural agreement requires developed countries to reduce both the existing tariffs on agricultural products and the tariffs resulting from conversion of non-tariff border measures by an average of 36 per cent over a six-year period, with a minimum reduction of 15 per cent on individual items. For developing countries, the respective percentages are 24 and 10 per cent, with no reduction obligations for LDCs, although they also are required to tariffy. Commitments made by developed countries for tariff reductions on agricultural product groups are shown in table 28. Tropical products will have an above-average tariff reduction of 43 per cent. Thus, both in tropical and natural resource-based products, the MFN tariff reductions are tangible, which is an advantage for developing countries as a whole, although LDCs will have to balance it against the erosion of their tariff preferences.

Textiles and clothing

This item was put on the agenda of the Uruguay Round by the developing countries. The phasing out of the highly discriminatory Multi-Fibre Arrangement (MFA) and the integration of the textiles and clothing sector into GATT rules and disciplines are regarded as major gains for developing countries. In fact, in the "package approach" adopted at the Uruguay Round, where gains accruing in one sector were traded off against obligations accepted in another, the phasing out of MFA by industrialized countries encouraged the developing countries to accept the obligations in the new areas of the Uruguay Round, such as TRIPs, investments and services.

The textile sector is important to a number of LDCs like Bangladesh, Haiti and Nepal, while cotton yarn and cotton fabrics figure to a minor extent in the export basket of several African LDCs. Although phasing out the MFA might help some of these countries, they still must cope with the challenge that, in a quota-free world, they will face severe competition from

Table 28: Tariff reductions by developed countries on agricultural product groups

Product group	value of imports ($ billion)	Percentage reduction in tariffs
All agricultural products	**84.2**	**37**
Coffee, tea, cocoa, sugar, maté	9.1	35
Sugar	1.7	30
Spices and cereal preparations	2.8	35
Fruits and vegetables	14.6	36
Oilseeds, fats and oils	12.6	40
Animals and products	9.6	32
Beverages and spirits	6.6	38
Dairy products	1.3	26
Flowers, plants, vegetable materials	1.9	48
Tobacco	3.1	36
Grains	5.3	39
Other agricultural products	15.6	48
Tropical products	**24.0**	**43**
Tropical beverages	8.7	46
Tropical nuts and fruits	4.3	37
Certain oilseeds, oils	3.4	41
Roots, rice, tobacco	4.6	40
Spices, flowers and plants	3.0	52

Source: As for table 26.

some other developing countries (e.g. China, India, Indonesia, Pakistan, Sri Lanka and Vietnam). Although the agreement on textiles and clothing contains some special provisions for favouring small suppliers and new entrants, there is no substantial dispensation for LDCs.

It is, therefore, imperative that LDCs use the transition period to upgrade the efficiency and competitiveness of their textile and clothing industry. Modernization and technological advances, improved quality and design, better marketing, diversification towards higher value items, and active support for the industry, including, in particular, the observance of the importing countries' environmental requirements, are areas that will require the priority attention of Governments, donors and the industry itself. Encouragement of foreign investment, especially relocation of investments by other countries seeking lower cost-production bases, will also require pro-action.

TRIPs

The TRIPs agreement does not provide for any special treatment for LDCs in the observ-ance of the basic norms and standards for the protection and enforcement of intellectual property rights (IPRs). LDCs, however, have been given an 11-year transition period (as compared with 5 years for other developing countries) from the date of establishment of the WTO to abide by the provisions of the TRIPs agreement.

The real issue then for LDCs is not about the immediate impact of the agreement, but what their approach should be towards protecting IPRs. They have the option to avail themselves of the 11-year transition period and may request even more time in specific areas. But it is a moot point whether their long-term development objectives would be served by these transition periods alone. It may be in the interest of LDCs, with financial and technical assistance from the international community, to begin establishing a legal, institutional and enforcement framework for adapting to internationally accepted norms and standards for the protection and enforcement of IPRs, while taking advantage of the transition periods to improve their productive and technological base. Such a strategy could be actively used to: (a) encourage the building up of domestic technological capacities wherever feasible; and (b) attract foreign investment and technology through subsidiaries, joint ventures and licensing arrangements. The agreement specifically calls on the developed countries to provide incentives to enterprises and institutions in their territories for the purpose of promoting and encouraging technology transfer so that LDCs will be able to create a sound and viable technological base.

As with other developing countries, another concern for LDCs in the wake of the TRIPs agreement is the possible increase in the cost of imported goods covered by IPRs in other countries, as, for example, for pharmaceuticals and agrochemicals. The cost to import technology would also increase. Domestic administrative capacities to obtain equivalent non-patented or off-patent products and technologies from competitive sources will need to be strengthened.

TRIMs

As in the case of TRIPs, no special treatment was made for LDCs in the substantive provisions of the TRIMs agreement, although they have been accorded a longer transition period (seven years) to eliminate any TRIMs that may be inconsistent with the provisions of the agreement. TRIMs is a thin agreement of the Uruguay Round to the effect that no member country shall apply any TRIM that is inconsistent with the provisions of Article III (national treatment) or Article XI (quantitative restrictions) of GATT 1994. In essence, the TRIMs contemplated are those that obligate foreign-owned enterprises to compulsorily use domestic products or to limit their use of imported products in relation to the value of volume of their local production or exports. The agreement prohibits the application of such "performance requirements" in a discriminatory manner to foreign-owned enterprises.

There is hardly any requirement in the TRIMs agreement that is not in keeping with the current foreign investment regime of developing countries, including LDCs. Since the beginning of the Uruguay Round, the foreign investment policies of these countries have undergone so much liberalization that the TRIMs agreement by itself does not pose serious policy problems for them. The TRIMs agreement does not apply to quantitative restrictions employed by developing countries under Article XVIII of GATT.

Services

GATS imposes a contractual obligation on members to give priority to LDCs when taking

specific capacity-building measures to increase the participation of developing countries in world trade in services. However, it is still only a framework agreement because the schedules of initial commitments have yet to be negotiated and settled. While "MFN" and "transparency" requirements will apply to the entire universe of service activities, "national treatment" and "market access" will depend on the specific negotiated commitments incorporated in the schedule of a member country. Thus, the balance of benefits and concessions rests upon the negotiation of the schedules between developed and developing countries.

The merit of the services agreement from the standpoint of the developing countries, including LDCs, is that they now have an opportunity to negotiate under a multilateral agreement the cross-border movement of natural persons in return for their giving market access in the services sector of interest to developed countries. They would, in any event, need the involvement of foreign enterprises in banking, insurance, telecommunications and similar capital and technology-intensive service sectors. Unilateral liberalization in these sectors is already taking place in many of these countries. It would be in their interest to use such a liberalization process to negotiate specific and tangible commitments from developed countries for the movement of skilled and professional people.

The two Marrakesh Ministerial decisions, "Movement of Natural Persons" and "Professional Services", are intended to enhance the opportunities for developing countries in the services trade. Active participation in the negotiations carried out by the Negotiating Group on the Movement of Natural Persons is essential to secure higher levels of commitments from the developed countries. Similarly, it is important for LDCs to participate in the work programme of the Working Party on Professional Services to ensure that qualification requirements and procedures, technical standards and licensing requirements in the field of professional services are not disguised barriers to their trade interests.

Article IV of GATS aims to increase developing countries' participation in services trade and should also receive the attention of developing countries and LDCs. There are a number of recommendations under this Article relating to access to technology, distribution channels and information networks, and establishment of contact points in developed countries. The Article also recommends liberalization of market access in sectors and modes of supply of export interest to developing countries. There is a specific recommendation that 'special priority' shall be given to LDCs in the implementation of the recommendations and that the 'serious difficulty' that LDCs have in accepting specific commitments should be noted. These are no doubt "best endeavour" clauses, but it is necessary to monitor their implementation.

Multilateral trade rules

An important achievement of the Uruguay Round is the strengthening of the multilateral trading rules. This is particularly true in the areas of dispute settlements, safeguards, anti-dumping, subsidies, balance-of-payment provisions, customs valuation, rules of origin, etc. A rule-based multilateral trading system, with a strong mechanism to settle disputes, is to the advantage of developing countries, even if it contains some provisions inconsistent with the level of their development.

The understanding on balance-of-payment provisions does not take away the cover available to developing countries under Article XVIII B, but emphasizes the use of "price based measures" rather than quantitative restrictions to address the problem. It also emphasizes transparency in balance-of-payment measures.

The subsidy code allows LDCs and developing countries with a per capita GNP of less than $1,000 to grant subsidies contingent on export performance (e.g. exempting export income from corporate taxation). It also allows developing countries five years and LDCs eight years to phase out any export subsidy granted by them based on preferential use of domestic over imported goods. (It is not clear whether developing countries or LDCs use such subsidies in any significant manner). The subsidies code also requires termination of a countervailing duty investigation against LDCs and developing countries with per capita income below $1,000 if the level of subsidy enjoyed by the product in question is less than 3 per cent of its value. The real issue, however, is not so much the attractiveness of such special provisions. Subsidization is a costly route for developing countries to follow, especially LDCs, and it can hardly provide an enduring basis for their export efficiency. The anti-dumping code strengthens the rules and procedures for initiating and conducting anti-dumping investigations and levying anti-dumping duties or terminating such investigations. Although there is no dispensation for developing countries or LDCs in the code (except for certain threshold levels for margin of dumping and volume of dumped imports, and a "best endeavour" clause for

recognizing the special situation of developing countries), strengthening the code should alleviate the concerns that such investigations could be used to adversely affect their promising exports.

The safeguards agreement, although not as significant to LDCs as it is to advanced developing countries, is an important outcome of the Uruguay Round. Its key features, namely, a stricter definition of the criteria for determining "serious injury", non-discriminatory application of a safeguard measure, prohibition of "grey area" measures, and multilateral surveillance of the measures adopted, would bring order into the system and mitigate the possibility of safeguard measures being used as non-tariff barriers. The two new areas added to the Uruguay Round, namely, agriculture and textiles and clothing, will have their own safeguards regimes that allow for the possibility of lax and discriminatory application of the measures by importing countries.

International support measures for LDCs

LDCs face twin challenges in translating the results of the Uruguay Round into their greater participation in international trade and their integration into the process of globalization. On the one hand, they need to develop and strengthen institutional and human capacities to formulate and manage legislation implementing the complex set of agreements of the Round. On the other hand, they need to minimize difficulties and maximize the opportunities arising from these agreements. In facing this dual challenge, LDCs will require substantial external support, which should have two main objectives: first, to assist LDCs in offsetting the adverse consequences in the short run; and secondly, to ensure that they can take full advantage of the special measures accorded to them in the various agreements, and in the process enhance their participation in international trade. This will, in turn, warrant action on three broad fronts:

- operationalize the Ministerial decisions in favour of LDCs and the net food-importing countries;

- set up compensatory (or "safety net") measures, to enable LDCs to overcome unfavourable consequences; and

- provide adequate financial and technical assistance, debt relief, improved market access and other trade- and investment-related support to enhance their supply capacity of tradeable goods and services.

While further work is necessary to elaborate specific policies and measures in the above areas, the following observations are warranted. First, it is important that the international community implement the two main Ministerial decisions in favour of LDCs and net food-importing developing countries to mitigate the possible adverse effects of the erosion of tariff preferences and the rise in the cost of food imports. The Ministerial decision in favour of LDCs recommends that MFN concessions and non-tariff measures on products of export interest to LDCs be implemented autonomously, in advance and without staging. It also recommends that the rules and disciplines of the Uruguay Round agreements be applied in a flexible and supportive manner for LDCs. This can be done, for example, if importing countries refrain from applying anti-dumping, countervailing duty or safeguard measures against LDC exports. Technical assistance in establishing policy, legal and institutional framework in tune with the emerging international trading system, training officials responsible for formulation and implementation of trade policies, and provision of data and information on trade policies of value to LDCs are other areas where action can assist LDCs.

The erosion of preferential margins of LDC products in major markets, the implications for export earnings, the possible rise in food prices arising from the implementation of the Agreement on Agriculture, and the resulting pressure on LDCs' balance of payments, make a strong case for instituting compensatory measures. While further analysis is required to elaborate the nature and contents of such safety nets, the main elements are the following: greater market access, improved financial transfers, debt relief, and food aid.

A limitation inherent in the outcome of the Uruguay Round and the multilateral trading rules is that they can at best exempt LDCs from certain obligations or allow them longer transition periods. The eventual challenge for LDCs posed by the Uruguay Round is competition in the international market-place. The problems confronting LDCs to meet such competition are of a long-term structural nature and their resolution lies beyond the ambit of the multilateral trading system and WTO.

These problems have been extensively documented in UNCTAD's annual reports on LDCs: a narrow and fragile economic and export base; dependence on a few primary commodity exports; volatile prices for commodity exports; and continuously declining terms of trade, lack of infrastructure, weak technological capacity, substantial debt-servicing burden and inadequate financial assistance from the international community. Unless these fundamental problems are dealt with, the prospects for LDCs to benefit from liberalized access to world markets will be poor. Supply-side constraints are at the root of LDCs' weak participation in international trade. Reduction of tariffs, grants for special tariff concessions, elimination of non-tariff restrictions and exemptions from obligations or reciprocal concessions will provide relief, but unless the supply-side constraints are removed, there can hardly be an enduring and effective participation of LDCs in international trade. The commitment and support of the international community to solve these problems and assist LDCs to diversify their production and export structure, as well as to move into higher value-added processing and production is even more crucial in the long run than granting preferences and concessions. Improving the efficiency of the trading process is an area where national and international actions in favour of LDCs can be very useful (box 19). Adequate technical and financial assistance to enhance agricultural productivity and infrastructure of LDCs is as important as food aid or financing commercial imports of foodstuffs. In addition, LDCs can benefit from improvements in market access in their favour by neighbouring countries and at the subregional or regional levels.

Box 19: LDCs and trade efficiency

Product development and diversification, transfer of technology and greater market access are of vital importance for growth and development in LDCs. Equally important for enterprises in these countries - particularly the small and medium-sized ones - is to avoid exclusion from international markets because of lack of human skills, infrastructural facilities and financial resources commensurate with the challenges posed by the globalization of international trade and the increased use of modern information technologies. Access to adequate telecommunications, transport and financial services; availability of up-to-date and easily accessible business information; simpler national administrative procedures and the use of best business practices are essential ingredients for a more efficient trading process. Such micro-economic issues are addressed within UNCTAD's Trade Efficiency Programme, where practical solutions are sought to allow for increased participation in international trade, more particularly by actors who otherwise would run the risk of being further marginalized by the current structural changes in trade patterns and the foreseeable development of electronic commerce.

The Trade Efficiency Programme

Trade Efficiency was included in the UNCTAD programme of work at the eighth session of the Conference (Cartagena de Indias, Colombia, February 1992). Six work areas have been defined by the Ad Hoc Working Group established by the Conference: official controls (including customs), business information, transport, telecommunications, banking and insurance and business practices. Recommendations and guidelines covering these sectors and addressed to Governments, commercial parties and relevant organizations, have been developed by the Ad Hoc Working Group[1] in cooperation with international organizations such as the Customs Co-Cooperation Council (now the World Customs Organization), the International Trade Centre UNCTAD/GATT, the UN/ECE Working Party on Facilitation of International Trade Procedures. Recommendations and Guidelines based on that work were adopted, together with a Ministerial Declaration, by the United Nations International Symposium on Trade Efficiency (Columbus, Ohio, 17-21 October 1994). Two essential components of the Programme are the Trade Point Global Network (officially launched at Columbus) and the customs computerized programme, ASYCUDA (Automated System for Customs Data).

The Trade Point Global Network

Trade Points bring together participants in foreign trade, such as customs, freight-forwarders, banks and insurance companies, either physically under the same roof, or by connecting them electronically. At a Trade Point, traders are advised on international trade procedures and can make use of the services provided to complete their foreign trade transactions on the spot at an affordable cost. Through Trade Points, traders (particularly small and medium-sized companies that cannot afford their own export departments) can gain access to international trade.

When the first Trade Point was inaugurated in Cartagena, Colombia during UNCTAD VIII, it was decided that 16 pilot Trade Points would be set up prior to the Symposium. However, with the growing number of requests, that decision was waived and there are now 50 Trade Points at different stages of development, including in LDCs. These are: Bangladesh, Cape Verde, Guinea-Bissau, Laos, Mauritania, Mozambique, Nepal, Sao Tome and Principe, Sierra Leone and Zambia.

The Trade Points are connected with one another and with other international networks in a worldwide electronic network, viz., the Global Trade Point Network.

ASYCUDA

ASYCUDA is an UNCTAD project which aims at introducing institutional reform within the Customs Revenue Administrations. ASYCUDA potentially provides the most cost-effective solution for countries wishing to modernize their customs administrations and data-collection services. Customs computerization using ASYCUDA has been adopted by 68 countries and regions around the world including 27 LDCs.[2] It has produced impressive results in reducing customs clearance times from several days to a couple of hours, in increasing customs revenue (even in cases where the duty rates were lowered), and in providing up-to-date and reliable foreign trade statistics.

---

[1] See in particular United Nations International Symposium on Trade Efficiency: Recommendations and Guidelines for Trade Efficiency (TD/SYMP.TE/2) and Compendium of Trade Facilitation Recommendations (UNCTAD/SYMP.TE/3).

[2] Bangladesh, Benin, Burkina Faso, Burundi, Cape Verde, Central African Republic, Chad, Comoros, Equatorial Guinea, Gambia, Guinea, Guinea-Bissau, Haiti, Madagascar, Maldives, Mali, Mauritania, Mozambique, Myanmar, Niger, Rwanda, Sao Tome and Principe, Sudan, Togo, Uganda, United Republic of Tanzania and Zaire.

B. THE GENERALIZED SYSTEM OF PREFERENCES AND LDCs

Introduction

The need for special and more favourable treatment for LDCs in GSP had already been stressed in the early 1960s, and in 1968 UNCTAD II recommended its establishment.[3] That need has since been reaffirmed by numerous resolutions and decisions adopted in different international forums, including UNCTAD, GATT and the First and Second United Nations Conferences on LDCs. Almost all preference-giving countries are adopting special commercial policy measures for LDCs within their respective GSP schemes. At present, GSP is one of the most important and comprehensive systems to accord LDCs preferential access to markets. In 1993, the markets of the countries providing LDCs with GSP treatment absorbed nearly three quarters of their exports,[4] of which about 60 per cent were dutiable (with preference-giving country members of OECD accounting for 72 per cent, of which 60 per cent were dutiable imports).[5]

In so far as the LDCs are concerned, the usefulness of each scheme and of GSP as a whole depends on:

- whether more favourable treatment is accorded to LDCs than to other beneficiaries;

- the extent to which the schemes are being used by LDC exporters; and

- improvements in the schemes, particularly for LDCs, bearing in mind that there will be an erosion of GSP preferences as a result of the implementation of the agreements of the Final Act of the Uruguay Round.

Beneficiaries

Preference-giving countries have drawn up their own lists of LDCs as beneficiaries according to the list of LDCs as defined by the United Nations General Assembly. Since the introduction of GSP schemes, there has been a trend towards increasing the number of LDCs as beneficiaries, and by end-1994, most preference-giving countries had included all LDCs in their lists.[6]

Nevertheless, in principle, an LDC, like any other preference-receiving country, can be excluded from these lists for various reasons. The United States GSP scheme, for example, has related exclusion to such considerations as workers' rights and failure to compensate for nationalization. The countries thus excluded are the Central African Republic, Liberia, Mauritania, Myanmar and Sudan on the grounds that "recognized workers' rights" were being violated, and Afghanistan, Ethiopia and the Lao People's Democratic Republic for failure to compensate for nationalization.[7]

Product coverage

Only a part of dutiable imports from LDCs has been eligible for preferential treatment under GSP schemes. Between 1976 and 1992, dutiable imports from LDCs under the OECD schemes rose six-fold - from $522 million to $3,043 million, while the covered imports rose by more than seven-fold - from $256 million to $1,876 million. As a result, the product coverage ratio[8] under the GSP schemes of OECD countries for LDCs increased from 48.9 per cent in 1976 to 61.7 per cent in 1992.

Coverage of LDC products under GSP schemes can be analysed in terms of the following:

- comparison of coverage of products among LDCs under various GSP schemes;

- comparison of coverage of products from LDC beneficiaries with coverage of products from other beneficiaries under the same GSP schemes;

- share of GSP-covered imports from LDCs under schemes of individual preference-giving countries, as a percentage of the total of OECD GSP schemes.

There are three types of coverage regarding the first two points. First, the widest coverage for LDCs has been granted by New Zealand, Norway and Sweden, as well as by some Eastern European countries (e.g. Bulgaria, Hungary and the Russian Federation). These countries have accorded coverage for all dutiable products (chapters 1 to 97 of the Harmonized Systems, HS) imported from LDCs, whereas for other preference-receiving countries (non-LDCs), they have granted coverage for selected dutiable products only.

Second, the EU, Finland and Switzerland have provided extended coverage for LDCs.

Under the EU scheme, LDCs can enjoy a broader product coverage for their agricultural products than non-LDCs. For LDCs, this coverage includes all products listed in HS chapter 03 (fish and aquatic invertebrates), 05 (products of animal origin), 06 (live trees, other plants, cut flowers and ornamental foliage), 09 (coffee, tea, mate and spices), 13 (lacs, gums, resins and other vegetable saps and extracts), 14 (vegetable plaiting materials, etc.), 18 (cocoa and cocoa preparations), 19 (preparations of cereals, flour, starch or milk pastry cooks' products), 20 (preparations of vegetables, fruits, nuts or other parts of plants) and 24 (tobacco and unmanufactured tobacco substitutes).[9] The Finnish scheme covered five additional HS headings for LDCs' agricultural products, including some dried leguminous vegetables, roasted and non-roasted coffee and coffee extracts and 113 additional HS headings for a large number of various LDC industrial products, including textiles, clothing and footwear.[10] The Swiss scheme has a broader coverage for LDC agricultural products than for those of non-LDCs, for example, soya beans, oil seeds and oleaginous fruits, fresh and preserved pineapples, pineapple juice and jam, cocoa powder and unsweetened and parboiled rice.[11]

Table 29: OECD GSP-covered imports from LDCs as a percentage of MFN dutiable imports[a]

Preference-giving country	Least-developed beneficiaries			Memo item: all beneficiaries		
	1976	*1981*	*1992*	*1976*	*1981*	*1992*
Australia	91.0	98.4	98.0	46.6	67.6	96.9
Austria	95.7	91.1	96.1	88.9	85.4	92.3
Canada	66.7	88.5	22.9	53.0	54.4	58.5
European Union[b]	42.4	89.7	98.2	60.7	77.9	68.5
Finland	84.6	100.0	52.4	20.2	40.8	33.0
Japan	22.8	18.2	73.5	52.9	64.3	34.7
New Zealand	86.4	98.4	100.0	93.3	89.9	99.8
Norway	100.0	100.0	100.0	46.6	43.3	61.9
Sweden	1.3	18.5	100.0	20.1	48.1	55.2
Switzerland	41.2	49.7	96.0	44.8	42.9	71.0
United States	66.1	53.4	6.5	29.8	31.3	39.3
OECD Totals	48.9	67.3	61.7	45.8	51.6	51.6

Source: UNCTAD, Seventeenth general report on the implementation of the generalized system of preferences: Recent changes and policy issues, TD/B/SCP/6, tables 1 and 3 (1 March 1994).

a   As the list of LDC beneficiaries under each GSP scheme was sometimes subject to change, figures in this table for corresponding years are not comparative in absolute terms. The table, however, shows an order of magnitude of the preferential imports from LDC beneficiaries into the OECD preference-giving countries.

b   Effective LDC beneficiaries only are included. Under the EU scheme, 69 African, Caribbean and Pacific (Group of States) (ACP) developing countries, including 39 LDCs in the 1992 United Nations list, received beneficiary status according to the Lomé IV arrangement, Article 168: "products originating in the ACP States shall be imported into the Community free of customs duties and charges having equivalent effect". Thus, those LDCs enjoying such special treatment are only nominal beneficiaries of GSP of the EU, while effective beneficiaries include Afghanistan, Bangladesh, Bhutan, the Lao People's Democratic Republic, Maldives, Myanmar, Nepal and Yemen.

Table 30: GSP-covered imports from LDCs
by OECD preference-giving countries, as a percentage of OECD totals

Preference-giving country	*Least-developed beneficiaries*			*Memo item: all beneficiaries*		
	1976	*1981*	*1992*	*1976*	*1981*	*1992*
Australia	2.0	3.8	0.5	1.7	3.4	3.2
Austria	2.6	1.1	5.9	4.2	3.6	2.9
Canada	0.4	0.5	0.5	2.4	2.1	2.5
European Union	38.5	51.1	62.1	45.8	42.2	47.6
Finland	0.4	2.4	0.6	0.1	0.2	0.3
Japan	2.8	1.8	19.7	14.1	15.1	17.1
New Zealand	0.7	1.1	2.1	0.6	0.4	0.3
Norway	0.2	0.2	0.9	0.2	0.2	0.4
Sweden	0.1	0.1	1.0	0.8	0.7	0.7
Switzerland	6.5	5.1	3.1	2.7	2.1	2.0
United States	45.7	32.8	3.6	27.4	29.8	22.8
OECD Totals	100.0	100.0	100.0	100.0	100.0	100.0

Source: As for table 29.

Third, Canada, Japan and the United States have provided equal product coverage for all preference-receiving countries, whether or not they are LDCs. The exclusion of textiles, clothing, carpets, footwear and leather goods, etc., has substantially reduced the coverage of industrial products, especially by the United States. Product coverage under the Japanese scheme has become more relevant to LDCs' export pattern, compared with other preference-receiving countries, than the coverage of Canada and the United States These three types are reflected in the product coverage ratio for LDCs and other beneficiaries (table 29).

As regards the GSP-covered imports from LDCs by OECD member countries under their different GSP schemes as a percentage of their totals, the most important are those of the EU (62 per cent) and of Japan (20 per cent) (table 30). In 1992, they covered more than four fifths of imports from LDCs under OECD schemes.

Extent of tariff cuts

With the exception of the United States, which provides duty-free treatment under its GSP scheme, all preference-giving countries granting special treatment to LDCs have provided important tariffs advantages for them as compared with other beneficiaries.[12] The largest cuts have been made by Bulgaria, Hungary, Norway, the Russian Federation and Sweden. They have granted duty-free status for all products originating in LDCs, whether or not they are covered by their GSPs. Canada, the Czech Republic, the EU, Japan, Poland, the Slovak Republic and the United States allow duty-free entry for all products originating in LDCs, but they must be covered by these countries' GSP. Austria has a duty-free entry for agricultural products from most LDCs, but a few of their products have been subject to reduced duties. It has also accorded duty-free entry to the industrial products originating in LDCs and covered by its scheme, with the exception of sensitive items within HS chapters 50-62 and 65 for which 50 to 75 per cent tariff cuts from MFN rates have been applied. Finland has duty-free status for all LDC agricultural products, with the exception of the items under 11 HS headings which are liable to duty, and also has a duty-free entry for all industrial products excepting items within 14 HS headings which are liable to half the duty. New Zealand has accorded duty-free treatment for all LDC products with a few exceptions for some industrial goods such as apparel and footwear. Switzerland has granted duty-free entry for all products originating in LDCs covered by its scheme, with the exception of a few agricultural products.

Utilization of GSP schemes

Extent of utilization

Only a part of the GSP-covered imports from LDC beneficiaries has received preferential treatment under GSP schemes. Between 1976 and 1992, preferential imports from LDCs under the GSP schemes of OECD preference-giving countries rose by seven-fold, from $140 million to $979 million, while the covered imports rose by more than seven-fold from $256 million to $1,876 million. As a result, the utilization ratio[13] in the OECD preference-giving countries' schemes, taken together, decreased slightly from 54.8 per cent in 1976 to 52.2 per cent in 1992.

The preferential imports under GSP schemes can be analysed in terms of the following:

* comparison of the real preferential imports under various schemes;

* comparison of the preferential imports for LDC products with those for other beneficiaries under the same schemes;

* share of preferential imports under individual schemes in all preferential imports of all GSP schemes taken together.

For preference-giving countries, the size of the utilization ratio is determined by applying non-tariff restrictions and rules of origin. For LDC beneficiaries, it is determined by the familiarity and capacity to deal with one or another scheme.

Almost all preference-giving countries' schemes have no provisions for quantitative limitations on preferential imports from LDCs, except for a limited number of agricultural and textile products in the EU scheme. The EU has applied quantitative limitations, in the form of globally reduced levies amounts, for 28 agricultural products (at an 8-digit level). They were added to the EU scheme at the beginning of 1990. Quantitative limitations may also be applied by the EU as well as by other OECD countries' GSP schemes to LDC textile products if they are agreed within the framework of the MFA.[14]

Notwithstanding LDCs' limited use of GSP schemes, they can, nevertheless, receive indirect benefits to access their products to the EU market because of stricter and expanded quantitative limitations in EU schemes for products from non-LDC preference-receiving countries. LDCs can also receive indirect benefits in the

Table 31: Share of GSP-preferential imports from LDCs as a percentage of GSP covered imports under OECD GSP schemes[a,b]

Preference-giving country	Least-developed beneficiaries				Memo item: all beneficiaries			
	1976	*1981*	*1991*	*1992*	*1976*	*1981*	*1991*	*1992*
Australia	100.0	98.9	100.0	100.0	100.0	100.0	100.0	100.0
Austria	11.9	17.6	3.9	5.1	12.6	12.4	37.3	39.0
Canada	20.0	34.8	69.3	68.8	73.0	73.0	66.9	68.0
European Union	47.9	62.9	53.2	51.7	35.9	37.6	47.4	48.0
Finland	63.6	88.5	88.9	9.1	71.1	81.8	58.5	49.9
Japan	45.8	57.0	32.9	62.1	53.1	61.4	47.5	46.1
New Zealand	100.0	100.0	99.3	98.5	100.0	100.0	89.6	86.4
Norway	20.0	37.5	12.1	60.5	50.5	52.1	64.0	69.0
Sweden	33.3	60.0	26.3	26.3	76.6	68.9	66.4	63.1
Switzerland	29.3	42.0	61.6	58.8	40.5	38.1	40.1	43.1
United States	65.0	31.2	59.5	53.3	48.4	49.8	50.8	46.9
OECD Totals	54.8	51.2	49.6	52.2	43.7	47.4	50.5	49.5

Source: As for table 29.

a   The ratio of preferential imports (or imports which actually received preferential treatment) to covered imports.

b   Conditional estimate. The European Union utilization ratio for effective beneficiary suppliers only.

markets of Japan, New Zealand and the United States, where the products originating from other than LDCs' are subject to limitations (quantitative restrictions for about half of all the industrial products in Japan, country and product graduation system in New Zealand, and competitive need limitations under the United States scheme). A similar kind of "comparative opportunity" for LDC products are possible under the schemes in which limitations on preferential imports can be established in the light of the level of development and the financial and commercial situation of the preference-giving countries, for example the Swiss scheme.[15]

Within the LDC group, not many countries have been able to use GSP schemes. For example, in 1991 under the GSP schemes of Finland, Norway, Japan, Sweden, Switzerland and the United States, there were respectively 7, 12, 13, 23, and 29 least-developed beneficiaries. In 1991-1993, Bangladesh alone supplied more than 80 per cent of LDCs' preferential imports to Sweden. Four LDCs (Burundi, Ethiopia, Malawi and United Republic of Tanzania) together supplied Finland with about 80 per cent of preferential imports from LDC beneficiaries as a whole. Nine beneficiaries accounted for 75 per cent of the total preferential imports from LDCs into the United States. Similar situations prevail in the schemes of Japan, Norway and Switzerland.

Comparison of the preferential imports of LDC products with the preferential imports of other beneficiaries under various schemes shows that in effect the utilization ratio of the schemes for other beneficiaries grew more or less steadily, while the utilization ratio of the schemes for LDCs fluctuated and showed a downward trend between 1976 and 1992 (table 31). The phenomenon can be partly explained by the fact that in other beneficiaries there were more developed export sectors as well as human and institutional facilities to deal with GSP schemes than there were in LDCs.

The relative importance of preferential imports from LDCs by OECD member countries under their different GSP schemes as a percentage of their totals is reflected in table 32. The table shows, *inter alia*, that the most important schemes for the least developed beneficiaries in 1981 were the schemes of the EU (62.8 per cent) and the United States (20 per cent) and in 1992 those of the EU (61.2 per cent) and Japan (23.4 per cent).

Rules of origin

Except for Canada and the EU, no other GSP scheme has accorded special treatment to LDCs in the rules of origin. The Canadian rules of origin implement a full and global cumulation and allow LDCs a higher percentage of the

Table 32: GSP-preferential imports from LDCs
by OECD preference-giving countries, as a percentage of OECD totals

Preference-giving country	Least-developed beneficiaries				Memo item: all beneficiaries			
	1976	*1981*	*1991*	*1992*	*1976*	*1981*	*1991*	*1992*
Australia	3.6	7.4	0.9	1.1	4.0	7.4	6.7	6.4
Austria	0.6	0.4	0.5	0.6	1.2	0.9	2.5	2.3
Canada	0.1	0.3	0.8	0.7	4.0	3.2	4.2	3.5
European Union	33.6	62.8	57.0	61.2	37.7	33.5	40.6	46.1
Finland	0.5	0.4	1.0	0.1	0.1	0.4	0.4	0.3
Japan	2.3	2.0	25.3	23.4	17.2	19.6	18.8	15.9
New Zealand	1.4	2.2	4.5	4.0	1.3	0.9	0.6	0.5
Norway	0.1	0.1	1.2	1.0	0.2	0.2	0.7	0.6
Sweden	0.1	0.1	0.5	0.5	1.4	1.0	1.6	1.0
Switzerland	3.5	4.1	3.0	3.5	2.4	1.7	2.4	1.8
United States	54.2	20.0	5.2	3.6	30.4	31.2	21.4	21.6
OECD Totals	100.0	100.0	100.0	100.0	100.0	100.0	100.0	100.0

Source: As for table 29.

foreign component in the product cost of the imported goods (up to 60 per cent, as compared with non-LDC beneficiaries of up to 40 per cent).[16] Under the EU scheme, there is a case-by-case system of temporary derogations from the normal rules. The rules of origin are the most complex part of the GSP schemes for prefer-ence-receiving countries, including LDCs. These rules differ from one GSP scheme to another in terms of their criteria of origin, consignment conditions and documentary evidence required. This diversity prevents a clear understanding and hence the proper application of the schemes by the countries listed as beneficiaries, espe-cially LDCs.

Some of the major users of GSP schemes within the LDC group (e.g. Bangladesh, Lao People's Democratic Republic, Lesotho, Nepal and Zambia) reported that they could not ben-efit from these schemes to the desired extent because of unfavourable rules of origin, par-ticularly for garments and textile products. They argued in favour of full and global cumulation instead of a regional cumulation from which they cannot benefit. They consider that under the schemes of the EU, European Free Trade Association (EFTA) preference-giving countries and Japan, agricultural and mineral products mostly can meet rules of origin requirements since the rules are strict for other products. In addition, wider product coverage (including all ready-made garments and textile products), to-gether with more substantial tariff reductions, are also required to give a more competitive edge to their manufactured products.

Human resources and institutional constraints

In LDCs, a greater application of the schemes is complicated by the lack of skills and inad-equate institutional capacities. Not all LDCs have a national focal point responsible for using GSP schemes, nor do all chambers of commerce or export promotion centres in these countries know how to deal with procedures of the rules of origin. There are still some trade authorities in LDCs responsible for GSP which do not yet have working contacts with GSP administra-tions in the preference-giving countries. Many LDCs have not yet notified preference-giving countries of the names of their certifying au-thorities, a procedure which is a prerequisite for the utilization of some GSP schemes. For in-stance, eight least-developed beneficiaries from the Japanese GSP scheme and 25 least-devel-oped beneficiaries from the Swedish GSP scheme have not yet notified these preference-giving countries of the names of their certifying au-thorities.[17]

The LDCs are divided into four groups ac-cording to their capacity to deal with different GSP schemes. The first group, including Bang-ladesh, the Lao People's Democratic Republic, Lesotho, Myanmar, Nepal, Samoa and Zambia, are countries where the officials and exporters are more familiar with the GSP schemes than other LDCs. Dissemination of information and publications, as well as seminars, can help offi-cials and exporters to make further use of the GSP schemes. However, these measures can have an impact only if the real problems of these countries (e.g. the rules of origin, quantitative restrictions, etc.) are resolved.

The second group, includes, *inter alia*, the Central African Republic, Kiribati, Malawi, Mozambique, Solomon Islands and the United Republic of Tanzania. While officials and ex-porters have some experience with GSP schemes, the real problem lies in their undiversified ex-port structure. In addition to the measures recommended for the first group of countries, there is a strong case for diversifying the exports as well as for strengthening their GSP focal points.

The third group of LDCs, which have just started to use GSP includes Benin, Burkina Faso, Guinea, Mali, Niger, Sudan and Zaire. With the technical assistance of UNCTAD, their Govern-ments have set up GSP focal points. The fourth group includes, for example, Chad, Sao Tome and Principe and Sierra Leone, which have not yet up GSP focal points. For these two groups, whose exporters have little knowledge of GSP schemes and their procedures, it is imperative to focus on expanding their supply capacity for tradeable goods in order to obtain better ben-efits from GSP schemes and to initiate compe-tent technical assistance programmes to de-velop and strengthen human and institutional capacities in the areas of GSP.

GSP and the Uruguay Round Agreements

As indicated in section A, the adoption of the Final Act of the Uruguay Round marks a shift from a trading environment, in which prefer-ences were a paramount factor in the competi-tiveness of LDCs' exporters, to one in which the MFN principle prevails. As a result, LDC ex-porters will need to compete, more than before, on the basis of economic factors, such as pro-ductivity and quality of production, rather than on the basis of special treatment. It is evident that LDCs will have more difficulties in adapt-ing to new market access conditions, which stems from the erosion of existing preferential margins under GSP schemes, particularly in the area of tropical products and natural resource-based products, where their exports are heavily concentrated. On a trade-weighted basis, the average overall loss is 50 to 60 per cent in GSP margins for the two groups of products sectors, respectively, in the three major markets of the EU, Japan and the United States.

A priority task of the international community will be to assist LDCs in coping with the loss of preferential margins of their products through improvements in GSP schemes. For example, at the twenty-first session of the Special Committee on Preferences, there was a general consensus on the need to take measures in regard to comprehensive product coverage, duty- and quota-free treatment and relaxed rules of origin requirements in favour of least developed countries, taking into account their special circumstances.[18] Such improvement in the GSP schemes will help LDCs to compensate for the erosion of preferences. Technical assistance will be required to maximize the utilization of the GSP schemes by LDCs as well as to identify the areas for compensation.

Two areas for improvements in the GSP schemes deserve priority considerations: provision of comprehensive product coverage and liberal application of rules of origin. For example, ready-made garments could be introduced in all GSP schemes, particularly for LDCs. Moreover, there should be no negative lists for these countries. OECD preference-giving countries should consider full duty-free access to products of export interest to LDCs. As regards the rules of origin, the percentage criterion should be reduced to 25 per cent. Full global regional cumulation should be granted to LDC exports by the GSP schemes and their trade prospects should not be circumscribed by new issues such as the environment and labour standards. Preference-giving countries should explore the possibility of applying the GSP concept to services including movement of persons, in the context of assisting LDCs.

C. THE IMPACT OF DEVALUATION ON LDCs IN THE FRANC ZONE:

INITIAL ASSESSMENT

On 12 January 1994, the Franc zone member countries decided to devalue the CFA franc by 50 per cent - from CFA francs 50 for 1 French franc (F) to CFA francs 100 for F1; the Comorian franc was devalued by 33 per cent - from CF 50 for F1 to CF 75 for F1. This ended a period of unchanged parity between CFA francs and the French franc, which began in 1948, as well as that between the Comorian franc and the French franc which has been in vogue since 1988. Although it is too early to judge the impact of the devaluation on the Franc zone economies, this section presents an initial assessment.

The Franc zone mechanism

The Franc zone comprises the French Republic, Monaco and the 14 African countries whose currencies are linked with the French franc at a fixed rate of exchange. The member states of the zone agreed to hold their reserves mainly in French francs and to exchange them on the Paris market. The 14 developing states of the zone consist of the Comoros and two groups of countries. One group includes the seven members of the Union économique et monétaire ouest-africaine (UEMOA, West African Economic and Monetary Union):[19] Benin, Burkina Faso, Côte d'Ivoire, Mali, Niger, Senegal and Togo. This group also formed a common central bank the Banque Centrale des Etats de l'Ouest (BCEAO). The other group includes the six members of the Communauté économique et monétaire en Afrique centrale (CEMAC, Economic and Monetary Community in Central Africa):[20] Cameroon, the Central African Republic, Chad, the Congo, Equatorial Guinea and Gabon. The common central bank formed by this group is the Banque des Etats de l'Afrique Centrale (BEAC). Each of these groups maintained separate currencies, although they are commonly referred to as the CFA franc. Both the central banks as well as the central bank of Comoros kept an operation account with the French treasury, where 65 per cent of their foreign exchange holdings was deposited.

Traditionally, there have been three ways to control monetary growth in the zone:[21]

- Credit provided by the central banks to the Governments of each of the African Franc zone member countries cannot exceed 20 per cent of the preceding year's fiscal revenue. However, monetary growth has been controlled by encouraging financial discipline and discouraging inflation.

- Interest is charged on overdrafts and paid on credit balances in the central banks' operation accounts.

- When the balance in a central bank's operation accounts falls below an agreed level, credit expansion must be restricted.

Rationale for the devaluation

Currency devaluation is one of the major tools used in SAPs. As regards the African Franc zone countries, the system of fixed parity prevented the individual countries from devaluing their currencies. The CFA franc mechanism served to maintain relative price stability in the African zone countries for over two decades. As of 1985, however, their economic and financial situation began to deteriorate. For example, between 1985 and 1992, the annual average per capita real GDP at market prices decreased by -3 per cent for UMOA members

and by -4 per cent for UDEAC members, while the annual average growth rates of exports were negative (-2 and -1 per cent respectively) during 1990-1992.

From mid-1980 to the early 1990s, the economies of the 14 Franc zone members and their 17 neighbours with variable exchange-rate regimes were buffeted by the same external forces, such as deteriorated terms of trade, reduced availability of external bank credit and increased interest rates on outstanding debts. During 1986-1991, the terms of trade of the African Franc zone countries deteriorated by at least 30 per cent (due mainly to the fall in world market prices for their major exports, such as cocoa, coffee and petroleum), whereas the terms of trade of the other 17 countries deteriorated by only 20 per cent.[22] However, the main reason for the crisis was the diminished competitiveness of the zone members' exports due to, *inter alia*, the depreciation of the dollar; the appreciation

Table 33: Overvaluation, GDP, money supply, terms of trade and per capita real GDP growth rates of Franc zone countries

	Overvaluation rate (01.01.1994)	GDP in 1992 (% of total[a])	Money supply in 1992 (% of total[a])	Terms of trade 1980 = 100 (21.12.1992)	Per capita real GDP average growth rate (1985-1992)
LDCs					
Benin	..	4.1	5.2	88	-1.5
Burkina Faso	28	6.2	5.3	103	0.9
Central African Republic	25	2.8	1.7	78	-2.4
Chad	18	2.9	2.0	116	1.3
Comoros	..	0.5	0.5	..	-2.3
Equatorial Guinea	13	0.3	0.1	..	-0.3
Mali	29	5.4	4.7	112	-1.9
Niger	22	5.5	3.6	93	-1.5
Togo	31	3.6	4.0	60	-1.5
Other countries					
Cameroon	68	19.9	23.0	53	-6.7
Congo	38	6.2	5.4	68	-3.0
Côte d'Ivoire	54	19.6	24.9	62	-5.7
Gabon	31	10.7	8.2	69	-2.1
Senegal	41	12.3	11.4	101	0.3
Total	..	100	100	..	..

Source: UNCTAD secretariat calculations, based on estimates of The World Bank and the African Franc zone central banks.

a   Total of African Franc zone countries.

of the French franc; and a lack of policy response to these developments from zone members. In sum, the guaranteed convertibility of the CFA franc against the French franc led to the former's overvaluation *vis-à-vis* other hard currencies which, in turn, contributed to the deterioration of competitiveness of the industrial and agricultural products of the zone countries.

At the same time, the markets of the zone countries became very attractive to other neighbouring developing countries that had no hard currencies. The CFA francs had become the real currencies of exchange between the zone countries and their non-zone neighbours. There were probably more CFA francs in some of the latter countries than in the smaller Sahelian Franc zone states. As a result of all these factors, it became necessary for the zone countries to discontinue the unlimited convertibility of the CFA franc *vis-à-vis* the French franc. Each member country of the zone was affected differently by the overvaluation and by the deterioration of the terms of trade. As indicated in table 33, LDC members of the zone contributed less to the overall worsening of the economic situation than other members of the zone. Moreover, the overvaluation itself in LDCs was lower and the terms of trade better than in the other zone countries. This notwithstanding, the LDC members agreed to the devaluation.

Accompanying national and international measures to the devaluation

The main actors in implementing these measures are the LDC Governments of the zone, their central banks and the bilateral and multilateral donors.

Central Banks

To avoid inflation, stimulate savings and attract capital again, the central banks increased their interest rates and returned to monetary programming. BCEAO also tried to solve the problems caused by freezing transfers.

LDC Governments of the zone

Measures were introduced by LDC Governments to broaden the tax base, reduce tax evasion and improve tax collection. Tax exemptions on certain goods and public utilities were eliminated. The multiple tax-rate system was replaced by a single-rate system in some LDCs (e.g. Burkina Faso and Niger). As a result of these measures, the ratio of budgetary revenue to GDP is expected to rise in certain countries (e.g. from 1994 to 1996 by 6 per cent in Mali, and by 2.2 per cent in Niger). Customs tariff measures were introduced soon after the devaluation. On the one hand, the percentages of cumulative taxes and duties on essential goods and intermediate products were reduced (e.g. by 50 per cent in Niger and 40 per cent in Burkina Faso). On the other hand, ad hoc exemptions were eliminated in all LDCs concerned.

To limit inflation, LDCs of the zone tried to improve budgetary allocations for operations and maintenance while containing the wage bill and reducing non-essential expenditures. For example, in 1994 the nominal increase of the civil service wage bill was limited to an 8 per cent increase in Burkina Faso, 10 per cent in Mali and 14 per cent in Niger, as compared with 1993. Efforts were also made to limit price increases of imported goods and to mitigate the inflationary impact of imports on domestic prices by encouraging consumers to purchase cheaper substitutes and locally made products, and to lower import duties.[23]

The main objective of the credit policy in 1994 was to limit growth in net credit to the Governments (0.5 per cent in Mali, 2.5 per cent in Burkina Faso and 10.7 per cent in Niger), while allowing reasonable credit expansion to the rest of the economy (9 per cent in Burkina Faso, 11.5 per cent in Mali and 30 per cent in Niger). Increase in money supply was limited to 20.5 per cent in Burkina Faso, 36.8 per cent in Mali and 15 per cent in Niger.[24]

The Governments have not introduced price controls except for some essential products and public utilities. In Mali and Niger, for example, price control on almost all goods and services was abolished by the end of March 1994. The Government of Burkina Faso adhered to a six-month freeze on the retail prices of several essential genetic drugs, rice, petroleum products, utility rates and school supplies.

To stem possible social discontent, the reasons for the new exchange policies were explained to the most vulnerable segments of the population, including fixed-income earning groups, and they were assured that a substantial part of the export earning increases would be passed on to them.

Regional integration

Following devaluation, the Governments of some of the zone LDCs sought to strengthen the institutional mechanisms for harmonization of macroeconomic, fiscal and sectoral policies. In 1994, the seven UMOA members signed a treaty changing UMOA to the Union économique et monétaire Ouest-africaine (UEMOA); and the six countries of UDEAC signed a treaty to create

Table 34: Multilateral ODA commitment and debt rescheduling for Franc zone countries, 1994-1996
($ million)

		IMF		World Bank	Paris Club
	Form of assessment	Commitments		Adjustment credit for 1994	Estimated amounts of debts rescheduled in 1994
		1994	1994-1996		
LDCs					
Benin	ESAF	18.1	54.4	15	-
Burkina Faso	ESAF	17.1	48.6	45	-
Central African Republic	Stand-by	16.5	48.4	18	31
Chad	Stand-by	16.5	48.6	5	-
Comoros	ESAF	1.4	6.5	..	-
Equatorial Guinea	ESAF	3.7	11.0	..	-
Mali	ESAF	29.5	88.4	47	-
Niger	Stand-by	18.6	57.2	30	160
Togo	ESAF	21.7	65.2	19	-
Other countries					
Cameroon	Stand-by	54.0	162.1	176	1340
Congo	Stand-by	23.2	69.5	100	-
Côte d'Ivoire	ESAF	119.1	333.5	335	1800
Gabon	Stand-by	60.1	120.8	30	1200
Senegal	Stand-by	47.6	142.7	25	223

Source: UNCTAD secretariat calculations, based on World Bank data, IMF Survey and on Paris Club Agreed Minutes.

Table 35: ODA to Franc zone countries from France, IMF and the World Bank in 1994
(per capita in dollars)

	France	IMF; World Bank	Total
LDCs			
Benin	1.3	8.3	9.6
Burkina Faso	2.4	7.4	9.8
Central African Republic	2.9	13.7	16.6
Chad	1.3	7.7	9.0
Comoros	..	2.0	..
Equatorial Guinea	..	16.1	..
Mali	3.1	9.9	13.0
Niger	0.9	8.0	8.9
Togo	2.5	..	..
Other countries			
Cameroon	6.1	21.6	27.7
Congo	30.3	56.1	86.4
Côte d'Ivoire	17.5	48.5	66.0
Gabon	22.6	73.2	95.8
Senegal	5.9	11.9	17.8

Source: *Jeune Afrique économie*, No. 187, 2 January 1995, pp.66-67 (Paris).

Box 20: Devaluation and improvement in productive capacity -the case of the manufacturing sector of Franc zone LDCs

In theory, opportunities created by devaluation include potential increased demand for locally manufactured goods which, given their low capacity utilization in recent years, can be met without any major new investments in plants and equipment. For example, the devaluation offered Governments an opportunity to restore some of the eroded purchasing power in rural areas by passing on to the farmers increases in domestic currency prices for cash crops. Consequently, purchasing power has shifted from those with a taste for sophisticated imports to rural dwellers who seek more basic manufactured goods that can be produced locally or, where the national market is too small, at a subregional level.

In practice, however, a sustained recovery in the manufacturing sector depends not only on a shift in the pattern of demand but also on an expansion in the size of the demand itself, which depends on economic recovery and improvements in the enabling environment, an issue on which Governments must take the lead, in consultation with the private sector. However, in the aftermath of the devaluation, the LDCs concerned and donors focused on the consumer. Price freezes were introduced on basic essentials in an attempt to stem social discontent and to contain inflation. But these freezes created distortions, for example, for manufacturers of soap and table oil produced from palm oil, whose prices are dictated by world markets even when these products are locally produced. Consequently, the manufacturers found themselves paying twice in local currency for their main input while the price of their end-product was frozen. Moreover, prices of imported inputs increased in the wake of the devaluation, with implications for production costs. Donor funding tended to be directed towards alleviating social hardships, such as providing subsidies for imports of basic goods or medicines, or, on a large scale, to the resumption of structural adjustment lending and deficit financing for Governments rather than towards the productive sectors.

Manufacturers from LDC Franc zone member countries were able to air their views at two subregional meetings on the impact of the devaluation on the manufacturing sector, organized by the United Nations Industrial Development Organization (UNIDO) in Bamako, Mali in June 1994 and in Brazzaville, Congo in December 1994. They noted that it was an "illusion" to assume that the manufacturing sector could realize its full competitive potential without the support of an enabling environment. They concluded that countries concerned must ensure the functioning of the legal system, political stability and security of goods and persons, labour codes that reflect the needs of a market economy, settlement of internal public debt arrears, including the back salaries of civil servants, and improved communications infrastructure and professional and entrepreneurial training. The establishment of an environment conducive to a healthy and growing manufacturing sector is also a *sine qua non* for attracting new investment to the region.

---

the Communauté économique et monétaire en Afrique central (CEMAC).

Bilateral and multilateral donors

Bilateral and multilateral donors also committed themselves to the devaluation's accompanying support measures. To cushion the impact of the parity change, France agreed to write off the LDC zone aid debt of F6.6 billion, the major beneficiaries of which were Benin, Burkina Faso, Mali and Niger. France also cancelled arrears to the Caisse Française de Développement (CFD) that permitted LDCs to receive subsidies.

The IMF and the World Bank have also established assistance programmes at the Governments' request. The IMF will provide $1.5 billion to the zone countries over the next three years, initially in the form of stand-by credits and subsequently drawings on the ESAF. Table 34 shows the multilateral ODA flows and commitments as well as debt relief to the zone countries following devaluation.

Agreements with IMF should help to revive economic growth by creating favourable conditions for investment and private initiative and to soften the impact of higher prices for some critical imports. However, aid is still inadequate and LDCs were not the major recipients of aid provided to the Franc zone countries. This disparity in aid is shown in table 35.

Preliminary assessment of the impact of devaluation

The Summit on the Devaluation in the Franc Zone (Libreville, Gabon, 27 June 1994), the Colloquium on the New CFA Franc Parity (Bordeaux, France, 27 June 1994) and the Semestral Meeting of the Ministers of Finance of the Franc Zone (Brazzaville, Congo, 15 September 1994) positively assessed the first stage of the devaluation and its accompanying measures in the French Franc zone countries as a whole. Estimates for LDCs are less optimistic.

Devaluation has created some opportunities for production and exports in a number of areas in zone LDCs: cotton, coffee, textiles, stock-breeding products, etc.. For example, in agriculture, the parity adjustment has improved competitiveness for cotton (20 per cent of exports from Benin, 50 per cent from Burkina Faso, 40 per cent from Mali, 20 per cent from Chad and Togo, and 10 per cent from the Central African Republic and Niger). After the parity change, the zone countries' production costs were 1.5 to 4 times lower compared with the main cotton-exporting countries.[25] Realignment of the exchange rate also provides an opportunity to export cowpeas and onions. Rice farming has benefited from the parity change with increases in the already high import costs.[26] Stockbreeders from Chad and Mali (both with total exports of live animals of about 50 per cent), as well as from Burkina Faso and Niger (both with a share of more than 10 per cent of exports) were among the first beneficiaries of the devaluation.[27] LDC meat producers can compete more in West Africa with imports from the EU and South America. After the parity adjustment, official exports of meat from Mali and Chad, as well as from Burkina Faso and Niger, to Nigeria, Côte d'Ivoire, Benin and Togo may become economically competitive with the EU or with imports of South America's chilled meat. The parity change could also improve the profitability of mining companies, including the uranium companies in Niger and processing and manufacturing industries (on implications for manufacturing, see box 20) that have an important share of local labour and other inputs in their production

cost. The fall of 10 to 25 per cent in tariffs for some French-based tour operators in Benin, Burkina Faso, Mali and Niger could help to develop tourism.

The devaluation is also like to curtail the unrecorded cross-border trade between the zone LDCs and their closest neighbours. While data on such trade are lacking, its scale is believed to be considerable. Consequently, the implications for overall trade transactions between zone countries and their neighbours could be sizeable.

Devaluation has, however, raised a number of concerns. First, inflation, of which cumulative rates for the first eight to nine months after devaluation were higher than initially projected for all of 1994 in six LDCs (table 36), thus eroding the nominal devaluation entirely for four countries. Second, devaluation is likely to reduce customs revenues which, in turn, may affect fiscal stabilization programmes (e.g. by more than 30 per cent in Mali and by about 50 per cent in the Central African Republic). Thirdly, they were lower than projected investments, which are explained partly by the absence or insufficiency of appropriate accompanying measures, especially in the manufacturing sector. Finally, living standards in urban areas have fallen, access to health care has declined and resources for schools are distributed more thinly.[28]

Table 36: Inflation in Franc zone LDCs

	Cumulative inflation rate from 11 January 1994 for the first 9 months of 1994	IMF initially projected inflation rate for 1994
Benin	52.0	32.7
Burkina Faso	29.0	31.2
Central African Republic	36.6[a]	36.0
Chad	56.8[a]	42.3
Comoros	20.0	35.5
Equatorial Guinea	42.7[a]	35.0
Mali	21.0	30.0
Niger	48.0	36.7
Togo	54.0	41.0

Source: Information from national statistical services. See also: Rigobert Roger Andely "La politique de crédit de la BEAC dans la période après dévaluation et son incidence sur le redemarrage du secteur manufacturier", p.11. Paper submitted to UNDP/UNIDO workshop on the Impact of the Devaluation of the CFA Franc on the Manufacturing Sector of countries of the CEMAC (Brazzaville, Congo: 30 November - 3 December 1994).

a   Eight months only.

Box 21: Progress in Mali during the first half of 1994

The recent round-table conference for Mali (September 1994) noted with satisfaction the country's impressive economic performance, on several fronts, in the first six months following the devaluation. The target for total Government revenue was exceeded by CFA francs 7 billion (i.e. CFA francs 65 billion instead of 58 billion), despite the fact that customs revenue was 32 per cent below target due to a greater than expected decline in the value of imports and a change in their composition exacerbated by continued customs fraud and weak customs administration. Public expenditures were kept below projected limits of CFA francs 29 billion (i.e. CFA francs 100 billion instead of 129 billion). The wage bill was CFA francs 20.5 billion compared with the projected CFA francs 22 billion. The overall fiscal deficit was CFA francs 40.9 billion compared with a target of CFA francs 77.2 billion, or 4 per cent of GDP as compared with the target of 7.4 per cent.

Inflation was more moderate than expected (table 36). As of 1 July 1994, the prices of all goods had risen to a level that adequately reflected increased costs arising from the parity change and the lower impact of the tax and tariff cuts. Prices of essential generic drugs, provided by the public sector, did not increase because of subsidies to health services from key donors. Increases in key utilities stayed within 10 to 20 per cent, and petroleum product prices increased between 10 and 30 per cent. All other prices remained market determined.

Some progress was made in implementing structural reforms, mostly in the agricultural sector (e.g. a revised "contract-plan" with producers and the cotton company, CMDT). There were some positive signs in the export-oriented sectors (cotton, livestock, fruits and vegetables). For example, the financial viability of the cotton sector was restored. Recorded livestock exports to Côte d'Ivoire increased in the first half of 1994 to over 175 per cent compared with the first half of 1993, as did exports of potatoes and onions to neighbouring countries. These changes have allowed increased returns to farmers and stockbreeders and boosted rural incomes.

The moderate inflation since the parity change, on the one hand, and programmes financed under social safety nets, together with a successful labour-intensive public works programme, on the other hand, contributed to the social peace needed in order for the devaluation and its follow-up measures to succeed.

At the country level, while Burkina Faso and Mali appear to be doing well, it is too early to determine how much and how soon countries like Benin, Niger and Togo will benefit from the devaluation. Equatorial Guinea and the Comoros, which have limited economic potential, are unlikely to benefit much unless aided by enhanced external support. Other countries (e.g. the Central African Republic and Chad) have been unable to abide by the agreements with IMF on the adjustment of the exchange-rate accompanying measures, which led to IMF terminating its financial support. For these countries, the outlook is at best uncertain.

In their meeting in Brazzaville in September 1994, the finance ministers of Franc zone countries decided that the zone countries had to adhere to structural adjustment programmes and to pursue the devaluation follow-up measures, *inter alia*: increase their budget revenues and make their budget expenditures more rational; resolve accumulated domestic and external payment arrears; encourage private economic operators to invest in production; accelerate subregional integration within the zone's framework; increase the international community's support of the zone's LDCs' devaluation accompanying measures; and strengthen and mobilize the national administrations responsi-

ble for LDC economies. The latter is crucial for domestic efforts and international support measures to succeed now, and for when the positive impact of the devaluation is diminished.

Conclusions

By using the devaluation accompanying measures, the zone LDCs and their bilateral and multilateral supporters have tried to maximize the devaluation's positive effects and minimize its negative effects. As noted above, it is too early to assess the effectiveness of these measures. However, a number of general observations can be made.

In the immediate term, the main participants implementing the devaluation accompanying measures recognized the need to strengthen preconditions, to improve the competitiveness of the zone LDCs' exports and their import substitutes, to increase Government revenues, to halt the flight of capital and to ensure that devaluation's positive effects are not eroded by inflation.

Due to temporary price control on basic goods and services and the Governments' explanations of the new exchange regulations, devaluation was accepted by the urban population who had fixed incomes and so socio-political stability was not seriously threatened.

Beyond the immediate term, the realignment process is expected to stimulate the repatriation of private capital and to ensure an improvement of public finances that would allow increased public savings for investment and increased spending in the health and education sectors. The change in parity and accompanying measures should help to increase the Governments' receipts from import duties because of the enlarged duty base and by the prospect of unrecorded trade being conducted through official channels. Reduction of tax exemptions and extension of VAT coverage to public utilities could increase the Governments' revenues. Estimates indicate that in 1995 revenue should

exceed expenditure in some LDCs (e.g. Mali) and come close to it in some others (e.g. Benin, Burkina Faso).

In the end, however, the positive results expected from the devaluation and its accompanying measures, particularly in raising the economic and external competitiveness of the concerned LDCs and increasing their growth performance, would be critically influenced by the efficiency of national measures as well as the adequacy, terms and timeliness of external support measures.

NOTES

[1] An interim assessment based on the Draft Final Act of December 1991 was made in *The Least Developed Countries, 1992 Report* (TD/B/39(2)/10), chap.V. Following the adoption of the Final Act, an initial assessment of its implications for the developing countries and LDCs was provided in the *Trade and Development Report, 1994*, and its *Supporting Papers* (UNCTAD/TDR/14 and Supplement).

[2] *Trade and Development Report, 1994* (Supplement), p.24.

[3] GSP was first implemented in 1971. It provides for granting preferential tariffs by the developed countries, on a non-reciprocal basis, on imports of selected products from developing countries. Currently, 16 autonomous GSP schemes are applied by Australia, Austria, Bulgaria, Canada, Czech Republic, European Union, Finland, Hungary, Japan, New Zealand, Norway, Poland, Russian Federation, Slovak Republic, Sweden, Switzerland and the United States.

[4] 96 per cent of these three quarters related to the OECD countries.

[5] Estimate based on UNCTAD data.

[6] There are some exceptions in the cases of Bulgaria (Vanuatu), the Czech Republic and the Slovak Republic (Kiribati and Tuvalu), Japan (Comoros, Djibouti, Zaire and Zambia), Poland (Liberia) and the United States (Afghanistan, Central African Republic, Ethiopia, Lao People's Democratic Republic, Liberia, Mauritania, Myanmar and Sudan).

[7] Seventeenth General Report on the implementation of the Generalized System of Preferences: recent changes and policy issues (UNCTAD/TD/B/SCP/6), 1 March 1994, p.25.

[8] The product coverage ratio is a quantitative indication of the extent to which products from preference-receiving countries to preference-giving countries are eligible for preferential treatment.

[9] Official Journal of the European Communities, 31 December 1990: No. L 370/86, Council Regulation (EEC) No.3833/90; and No.L 370/121, Council Regulation (EEC) No.3834/90. Council Regulation (EEC) Nos.3833/90 and 3834/90. Handbook on Major Trade Laws of the European Economic Community: Generalized System of Preferences (UNCTAD/TAP/276/Rev.2), p.35; Generalized System of Preferences: digest of schemes (UNCTAD/TAP/136/Rev.7), p.17, p.18 and p.22.

[10] TD/B/GSP/Finland/17, Annex II; Generalized System of Preferences, UNCTAD, *op.cit.*, p.22.

[11] *Ibid.*, p.41; UNCTAD/ITP/21, p.13.

[12] "The role of GSP in improving LDCs' access to markets: some recent developments". Note by the UNCTAD secretariat (TD/B/39(2)/CRP.7), 19 March 1993, pp.3-6.

[13] The utilization ratio is a quantitative indication of the extent to which beneficiaries use GSP schemes of preference-giving countries. It is equal to preferential imports under a GSP scheme of a preference-giving country divided by imports covered by this country.

[14] Generalized System of Preferences, UNCTAD, *op.cit.*, p.18.

[15] UNCTAD Handbook, Japan GSP 1994/95; UNCTAD/TAP/277/Rev.1; Generalized System of Preferences, UNCTAD/TAP/136/Rev.7; UNCTAD/TAP/278. In sum, more than 20 per cent of GSP-covered imports of non-LDC beneficiaries are covered by one or more NTMs. Quantitative restrictions covered about one eighth

of GSP-covered imports (Don P. Clark and S. Zarilli, "non-Tariff Measures and Industrial Nation Imports of GSP-covered Products", in *Southern Economic Journal*, vol.59, No.2 1992, p.287).

16   Generalized system of preferences: Scheme of Canada (UNCTAD/TD/B/GSP/Canada/19), 27 January 1995, p.13.

17   As for Japan, these eight LDCs are: Bhutan, Central African Republic, Chad, Guinea, Guinea-Bissau, Sierra Leone, Vanuatu and Yemen (Mission Permanente du Japon, Genève, AO/IC/D.396, 1 December 1992). In the case of Sweden, these 25 LDCs were: Benin, Bhutan, Cambodia, Central African Republic, Comoros, Djibouti, Equatorial Guinea, Gambia, Guinea, Kiribati Lao People's Democratic Republic, Madagascar, Mali, Mauritania, Niger, Rwanda, Samoa, Sao Tome and Principe, Sierra Leone, Somalia, Togo, Tuvalu, Uganda, Vanuatu and Yemen (Swedish Delegation, Geneva, 17 November 1992).

18   Report of the Special Committee on Preferences on its twenty-first session (UNCTAD TD/B/41(1)/2), Geneva, 1994. Annex III, p.38, para.7 (Chairman's summary).

19   Formerly Union monétaire ouest-africaine (UMOA, West African Monetary Union).

20   Established by a treaty signed in March 1994 by countries belonging to Union douanière et économique de l'Afrique centrale.

21   "The Franc Zone", in *Africa, South of the Sahara, 1995*, (London, Europa Publications Ltd., 1994), pp.107-108; and *IMF Survey*, 24 January 1994, p.18.

22   The African Franc zone countries had a number of economic difficulties long before the second half of the 1980s. Compared with their neighbours in the zone, wages were too high as was the share of non-productive investment. Cheaper industrial and agricultural products from the neighbouring countries without hard currencies (especially Ghana, Nigeria and Zaire) were being purchased in vast quantities in the markets of the zone countries, hampering the zone's economic development. However, during the first half of the 1980s, the zone's economic performance was relatively satisfactory, partly because of more or less satisfactory terms of trade, but also because of the fact that their REER depreciated as the dollar appreciated *vis-à-vis* the French franc.

23   It should be pointed out that "production of a large number of wage goods.....is...limited by structural, natural and institutional factors. Hence, a shortage of imports of these goods would contribute to inflation. Further shortages of capital and intermediate goods contribute to inflation through their negative impact on the production process, that is, on the utilization of existing capacity and its expansion". Mehdi Shafaeddin, Import Shortages and the Inflationary Impact of Devaluation in Developing Countries, UNCTAD, Reprint series No.75, 1993, p.22.

24   UNCTAD secretariat calculations, based on World Bank data.

25   *Marchés Tropicaux*, No.503, 11 March 1994.

26   In Niger, for example, domestically produced rice became 1.5 times cheaper than imported rice (*Jeune Afrique*, No. 1753/1754, 11-24 August 1994, p.51).

27   *Africa International*, July-August 1994, pp.12-25.

28   *The Financial Times*, 24 February 1995.

Annex

BASIC DATA ON THE LEAST DEVELOPED COUNTRIES

Annexe

DONNÉES DE BASE RELATIVES AUX PAYS LES MOINS AVANCÉS

Les Pays les moins avancés. Rapport 1995 - Annexe

A-iii

Les Pays les moins avancés. Rapport 1995 - Annexe

A-v

EXPLANATORY NOTES

A. Definition of country groupings

Least developed countries

The United Nations has designated 47 countries as least developed : Afghanistan, Bangladesh, Benin, Bhutan, Botswana, Burkina Faso, Burundi, Cambodia, Cape Verde, Central African Republic, Chad, Comoros, Djibouti, Equatorial Guinea, Ethiopia, Gambia, Guinea, Guinea-Bissau, Haiti, Kiribati, Lao People's Democratic Republic, Lesotho, Liberia, Madagascar, Malawi, Maldives, Mali, Mauritania, Mozambique, Myanmar, Nepal, Niger, Rwanda, Samoa, Sao Tome and Principe, Sierra Leone, Solomon Islands, Somalia, Sudan, Togo, Tuvalu, Uganda, United Republic of Tanzania, Vanuatu, Yemen, Zaire and Zambia. Except where otherwise indicated, the totals for least developed countries refer to these 47 countries.

Major economic areas

The classification of countries and territories according to main economic areas used in this document has been adopted for purposes of statistical convenience only and follows that in the UNCTAD *Handbook of International Trade and Development Statistics 1993*[1]. Countries and territories are classified according to main economic areas as follows :

Developed market-economy countries : United States, Canada, EEC (Belgium, Denmark, France, Germany[2], Greece, Ireland, Italy, Luxembourg, Netherlands, Portugal, Spain, United Kingdom), EFTA (Austria, Finland, Iceland, Norway, Sweden, Switzerland), Faeroe Islands, Gibraltar, Israel, Japan, Australia, New Zealand, South Africa.

Countries in Eastern Europe : Albania, Bulgaria, Czechoslovakia, Germany (former Democratic Republic of), Hungary, Poland, and the former USSR.

Developing countries and territories : All other countries , territories and areas in Africa, Asia (except China, Democratic People's Republic of Korea, Mongolia, Viet Nam), America, Europe, and Oceania not specified above.

Other country groupings

DAC member countries : The countries members of the OECD Development Assistance Committee are Australia, Austria, Belgium, Canada, Denmark, Finland, France, Germany[2], Ireland, Italy, Japan, Luxembourg, Netherlands, New Zealand, Norway, Portugal, Spain, Sweden, Switzerland, United Kingdom and United States.

OPEC member countries : The countries members of the Organization of the Petroleum Exporting Countries are Algeria, Ecuador, Gabon, Indonesia, Iran (Islamic Republic of), Iraq, Kuwait, Libyan Arab Jamahiriya, Nigeria, Qatar, Saudi Arabia, United Arab Emirates and Venezuela.

B. Terms, definitions and sources used

The estimates of *population* are for mid-year and are primarily based on data from the Population Division of the Department of International Economic and Social Affairs of the United Nations Secretariat.

National accounts data are mainly based on information from the United Nations Statistical Office, the United Nations Economic Commission for Africa, the World Bank and national sources.

The estimates relating to *agricultural production*,

food and *nutrition*, are derived mainly from information provided by FAO.

Trade data are estimates by the UNCTAD secretariat mainly derived from the UNCTAD *Handbook of International Trade and Development Statistics 1993*. Unless otherwise indicated, trade data refer to merchandise trade. Exports are valued f.o.b. and imports c.i.f.

The figures concerning *aid flows* are mainly based

---

1   United Nations Publication, Sales No. E/F.94.II.D.24.

2   Data refer to the former Federal Republic of Germany only.

on information provided by the OECD secretariat. Following the DAC definitions[3], *concessional assistance* refers to flows which qualify as official development assistance (ODA), i.e., grants or loans undertaken by the official sector, with promotion of economic development and welfare as main objectives, and at concessional financial terms (if a loan, at least 25 per cent grant element). *Non-concessional flows* include grants from private agencies (private aid) and transactions at commercial terms : export credits, bilateral portfolio investment (including bank lending) by residents or institutions in donor countries; direct investment (including reinvested earnings); and purchases of securities of international organizations active in development. Figures for *commitments* reflect a firm obligation to furnish assistance specified as to volume, purpose, financial terms and conditions, while figures for *disbursements* represent the actual provision of funds. Unless otherwise specified, disbursement figures are shown net, i.e., less capital repayments on earlier loans. Grants, loans and credits for military purposes and loans and credits with a maturity of less than one year are excluded from aid flows.

Table 18 presents data for individual DAC member countries on the estimated amount of official development assistance provided to LDCs expressed as a percentage of the GNP of each donor. So as to give a clear picture of the total flow, an attempt has been made to estimate the share of multilateral flows to LDCs which is provided by each donor. In order to do so, the share of each agency's disbursements to LDCs, expressed as a percentage of its total disbursements to developing countries, was applied to the donor's contributions to the agency in question; the sum for all agencies thus calculated was then added to the donor's bilateral ODA and expressed as a percentage of its GNP.

Debt data are based on information provided by the OECD secretariat, except for tables 26 and 27 which are derived from the World Bank Debtor Reporting System.

With regard to other economic and social indicators, data on *area* are from the United Nations, *Demographic Yearbook 1992*[4].

The estimates relating to *urban population* are not strictly comparable from country to country because of differences in definitions and coverage. They have been mainly derived from the UNFPA, *The State of World Population 1994*.

The *labour force participation rate* refers to economically active population as a percentage of total population of sex(es) specified of all ages, as shown in ILO, *Economically active population 1950-2025*.

Crude birth rates and *crude death rates* indicate respectively the number of births and deaths per thousand of population. Together with *life expectancy at birth* and *infant mortality rates*, they have been derived mainly from the United Nations, *World Population Prospects : The 1994 revision*; UNICEF, *The State of the World's Children 1994*; UNDP, *Human Development Report 1994*; and ESCAP, *Statistical Yearbook for Asia and the Pacific 1992*[5].

Life expectancy at birth indicates the average number of years the newly born children would live, if subject to the same mortality conditions in the year(s) to which the life expectancy refers, while the *infant mortality rate* is the number of infants who die before reaching one

year of age per thousand live births in the reference year.

Under the heading *health at birth, low birth weight* directly reflects the nutritional status of mothers and indirectly, mediated through the status of women, that of the population in general. The figures are drawn from UNICEF, *The State of the World's Children 1994* and UNDP, *Human Development Report 1994*.

The *percentage of women attended during childbirth by trained personnel* is a good indicator of the availability of medical services. It reflects the geographical distribution of the facilities and hence their accessibility, and indeed whether the hospitals had the equipment and supplies to dispense effective medical care. This also indicates to some extent the status of women. Data are drawn from UNDP and UNICEF sources mentioned in the previous paragraph.

The *percentage of children immunized against DPT* (3 doses) refers to the vaccination coverage of children under one year of age for the target diseases of the Expanded Programme of Immunization (diphtheria, tetanus, whooping-cough, measles, poliomyelitis and tuberculosis). Data are drawn from WHO, *Expanded Program on Immunization 1994* and UNICEF, *The State of the World's Children 1994*.

The estimates of *average daily calorie intake per capita* were calculated by dividing the calorie equivalent of the food supplies in an economy by population. Food supplies are defined as domestic production, imports less exports, and changes in stocks; they exclude animal feed, seeds for use in agriculture, and food lost in processing and distribution. The data in this table are weighted by population and are taken from FAO, *Production Yearbook 1992* and *The State of Food and Agriculture 1992*.

The *percentages of population with access to safe water or adequate sanitation* are estimates by WHO[6] and UNICEF, *The State of the World's Children 1994*. The percentage with access to safe water refers to the share of people with "reasonable" access to treated surface waters or untreated but uncontaminated water, such as that from protected boreholes, springs and sanitary wells, as a percentage of their respective populations. In an urban area a public fountain or standpost located not more than 200 metres from a house is considered as being within "reasonable" access to that house; in rural areas, "reasonable" access would imply that the housewife or members of the household do not spend a disproportionate part of the day in fetching the family's water needs.

The *percentage of population with access to adequate sanitation* relates to the share of urban population served by connexions to public sewers or by systems (pit privies, pour-flush latrines, septic tanks, communal toilets, etc.) and the share of rural population with adequate disposal such as pit privies, pour-flush latrines, etc.

Data relating to *education and literacy* are mainly derived from various publications of UNESCO : *Compendium of Statistics on Illiteracy - 1990 Edition; Statistical Yearbook 1993* and *Trends and Projections of Enrolment by Level of Education and by Age, 1960-2025 (as assessed in 1993)*. The *adult literacy rate* is the percentage of people aged 15 and over who can read and write. The data on *school enrolment ratios* refer to estimates of total, male, and female enrolment of students

---

3   See, OECD *Development Co-operation, 1983 Review*, (Paris, 1983) , p.176.

4   United Nations Publication, Sales No. E/F.94.XIII.1.

5   United Nations Publication, Sales No. E/F.93.II.F.1.

6   WHO, *The International Drinking Water Supply and Sanitation Decade: End of Decade Review* (as at December 1990).

of all ages in primary/secondary school, expressed as percentages of the respective population of primary/secondary school age.

Data on *post offices open to the public per 100,000 inhabitants* are derived from Universal Postal Union, *Statistique des services postaux 1992*.

Data on *telephones per 1,000 inhabitants* are based on ITU, *Statistical Yearbook 1992*.

Data on *radio receivers per 1,000 inhabitants* are based on data from UNESCO, *Statistical Yearbook 1993*. The ratio uses the number of receivers in use and/or licences issued, depending on the method of estimation used in each reporting country.

Data on *circulation of daily newspapers per 1,000 inhabitants* refer to circulation of "daily general interest newspapers" and are derived from UNESCO, *Statistical Yearbook 1993*.

As regards transport indicators, special problems of comparability arise in the case of *roads,* where the definition may vary widely from country to country. The main sources used are IRU, *World Transport Data 1990,* IRF, *World Road Statistics* (various issues), ESCAP, *Statistical Yearbook for Asia and the Pacific 1992* and national sources.

The figures for *railways* cover domestic and international traffic on all railway lines within each country shown, except railways entirely within an urban unit and plantation, industrial mining, funicular and cable railways.

The figures relating to passenger-kilometres include all passengers except military, government and railway personnel when carried without revenue. Those relating to ton-kilometres are freight net ton-kilometres and include both fast and ordinary goods services but exclude service traffic, mail, baggage and non-revenue governmental stores. The data are mainly derived from *The Railway Directory and Yearbook 1987* and IRU, *World Transport Data 1990*.

The figures relating to *civil aviation* cover both domestic and international scheduled services operated by airlines registered in each country. Scheduled services include supplementary services occasioned by overflow traffic on regularly scheduled trips and preparatory flights for new scheduled services. Freight means all goods, except mail and excess baggage, carried for remuneration. The data are derived from *ICAO Digest of Statistics - Airport Traffic 1992*.

Data on *energy consumption per capita* refer, on the one hand, to forms of primary energy, including hard coal, lignite, peat and oil shale, crude petroleum and natural gas liquids, natural gas, and primary electricity (nuclear, geothermal, and hydroelectric power) - often called "commercial energy" - and, on the other hand, to the use of fuelwood, charcoal and bagasse. All data are converted into coal equivalent and are based on information from United Nations, *Energy Statistics Yearbook 1991*[7] and *Statistical Yearbook 1985/1986*[8].

The data on *installed electricity capacity* are derived from United Nations, *Energy Statistics Yearbook 1991*.

C. Calculation of annual average growth rates

In general, they are defined as the coefficient b in the exponential trend function $y' = ae^{bt}$, where t stands for time. This method takes all observations in a period into account. Therefore, the resulting growth rates reflect trends that are not unduly influenced by exceptional values. For aggregation purposes, available trend data are assumed to be valid for missing years in the case of countries with incomplete time series data for 1980-1993.

D. Other notes

"Dollars" ($) refer to United States dollars, unless otherwise stated.

Details and percentages in tables do not necessarily add up to totals, because of rounding.

The following symbols have been used :

A dash (-) indicates that the amount is nil or

negligible.

Two dots (..) indicate that the data are not available or are not separately reported.

A dot (.) indicates that the item is not applicable.

Use of a hyphen (-) between dates representing years, e.g. 1970-1980, signifies the full period involved, including the initial and final years.

---

7   United Nations Publication, Sales No. E/F.93.XVII.5.

8   United Nations Publication, Sales No. E/F.86.XVII.7.

E. Abbreviations used

ACBF	African Capacity Building Foundation
AfDB	African Development Bank
AfDF	African Development Fund
AFESD	Arab Fund for Economic and Social Development
AFTAAC	Arab Fund for Technical Assistance to African and Arab Countries
AsDB	Asian Development Bank
BADEA	Arab Bank for Economic Development in Africa
BDEAC	Banque de Développement des Etats de l'Afrique Centrale
BOAD	West African Development Bank
CCCE	Caisse centrale de coopération économique (France)
CIDA	Canadian International Development Agency
CMEA	Council for Mutual Economic Assistance
CRS	Creditor Reporting System (OECD)
DAC	Development Assistance Committee (of OECD)
DANIDA	Danish International Development Agency
DCD	Development Cooperation Department (Italy)
DRS	Debtor Reporting System (World Bank)
ECA	United Nations Economic Commission for Africa
EDF	European Development Fund
EEC	European Economic Community
EIB	European Investment Bank
ESAF	IMF Enhanced Structural Adjustment Facility
FAC	Fonds d'aide et de coopération (France)
FAO	Food and Agriculture Organization of the United Nations

GTZ	German Technical Assistance Corporation
KFAED	Kuwait Fund for Arab Economic Development
KfW	Kreditanstalt für Wiederaufbau
IBRD	International Bank for Reconstruction and Development (World Bank)
ICAO	International Civil Aviation Organization
IDA	International Development Association
IDB	Inter-American Development Bank
IFAD	International Fund for Agricultural Development
IFC	International Finance Corporation
IMF	International Monetary Fund
LDCs	Least Developed Countries
mill.	Millions
OAPEC	Organization of Arab Petroleum Exporting Countries
ODA	Official development assistance
OECD	Organization for Economic Co-operation and Development
OECF	Overseas Economic Co-operation Fund
OPEC	Organization of the Petroleum Exporting Countries
SAAFA	Special Arab Aid Fund for Africa
SAF	IMF Structural Adjustment Facility
SDC	Swiss Development Corporation
SFD	Saudi Fund for Development
SITC	Standard International Trade Classification (Revision 1, unless otherwise indicated)
SNPA	Substantial New Programme of Action for the 1980s for the Least Developed Countries
UN	United Nations
UNDP	United Nations Development Programme
UNFPA	United Nations Population Fund
UNHCR	Office of the United Nations High Commissioner for Refugees
UNICEF	United Nations Children's Fund
UNTA	United Nations Technical Assistance
USAID	United States Agency for International Development
WFP	World Food Programme

NOTES EXPLICATIVES

A. Définition des groupements de pays

Pays en développement les moins avancés

Les Nations Unies a designé 47 pays en tant que pays les moins avancés : Afghanistan, Bangladesh, Bénin, Bhoutan, Botswana, Burkina Faso, Burundi, Cambodge, Cap-Vert, Comores, Djibouti, Ethiopie, Gambie, Guinée, Guinée-Bissau, Guinée équatoriale, Haïti, Iles Salomon, Kiribati, Lesotho, Libéria, Madagascar, Malawi, Maldives, Mali, la Mauritanie, Mozambique, Myanmar, Népal, Niger, Ouganda, République centrafricaine, République démocratique populaire lao, République-Unie de Tanzanie, Rwanda, Samoa, Sao Tomé-et-Principe, Sierra Leone, Somalie, Soudan, Tchad, Togo, Tuvalu, Vanuatu, Yémen, Zaïre et Zambie. Les totaux concernant l'ensemble des pays les moins avancés se rapportent à ces 47 pays.

Grandes zones économiques

Le classement des pays et territoires par grandes zones économiques, utilisé dans ce document, n'a été adopté qu'aux fins de présentation des statistiques et il suit celui qui est utilisé dans le *Manuel de statistiques du commerce international et du développement 1993* [9]. Les pays et territoires sont classés en grandes zones économiques, constituées comme suit :

Les pays développés à économie de marché : Etats-Unis d'Amérique, Canada, Communauté économique européenne (Allemagne[10] , Belgique, Danemark, Espagne, France, Grèce, Irlande, Italie,

Luxembourg, Pays-Bas, Portugal, Royaume-Uni), AELE (Autriche, Finlande, Islande, Norvège, Suède, Suisse), Gibraltar, îles Féroé, Israël, Japon, Australie, Nouvelle-Zélande, Afrique du Sud.

Pays d'Europe orientale : Albanie, Allemagne (ancienne République démocratique d'), Bulgarie, Hongrie, Pologne, Roumanie, Tchécoslovaquie, ancienne URSS.

Les pays et territoires en développement : tous les autres pays, terrritoires et zones d'Afrique, d'Asie (à l'exclusion de la Chine, la Mongolie, la République populaire démocratique de Corée, et le Viet Nam), d'Amérique, d'Europe et d'Océanie non mentionnés ci-dessus.

Autres groupements de pays

Les pays membres du Comité d'aide au développement (CAD) sont les suivants : Allemagne[10], Australie, Autriche, Belgique, Canada, Danemark, Espagne, Etats-Unis, Finlande, France, Irlande, Italie, Japon, Luxembourg, Norvège, Nouvelle-Zélande, Pays-Bas, Portugal, Royaume-Uni, Suède et Suisse.

Les pays membres de l'Organisation des pays exportateurs de pétrole (OPEP) sont les suivants : Algérie, Arabie saoudite, Emirats arabes unis, Equateur, Gabon, Indonésie, Iraq, Iran, République islamique d', Koweit, Jamahiriya arabe libyenne, Nigéria, Qatar et Venezuela.

B. Définitions, terminologie et sources utilisées

Les estimations de la *population* sont des estimations de milieu d'année fondées essentiellement sur des données fournies par la Division de la population du Département des affaires économiques et sociales internationales de l'ONU.

Les données se rapportant aux *comptes nationaux* ont été établies principalement d'après des informations provenant du Bureau de statistique des Nations Unies, de la Commission économique pour l'Afrique et de la Banque

mondiale, ainsi que de sources nationales.

Les estimations concernant la *production agricole, l'alimentation et la nutrition,* sont surtout tirées d'informations communiquées par la FAO.

Les données se rapportant au *commerce* sont des estimations du secrétariat de la CNUCED tirées en grande partie *du Manuel de statistiques du commerce international et du développement 1993.* Sauf indication contraire, les

---

9 Publication des Nations Unies, no. de vente E/F.94.II.D.24.

10 Les données se rapportant à l'ancienne République fédérale d'Allemagne seulement.

données du commerce se rapportent au commerce de marchandises. Les exportations sont données en valeur f.o.b. et les importations en valeur c.a.f.

Les chiffres se rapportant aux *apports d'aide* sont principalement fondés sur des informations communiquées par le secrétariat de l'OCDE. Suivant les définitions du CAD[11], *l'aide concessionnelle* désigne les apports qui sont considérés comme une "aide publique au développement" (APD), c'est-à-dire les dons ou les prêts accordés par le secteur public, dans le but essentiel d'améliorer le développement économique et le niveau de vie, et assortis de conditions financières libérales (dans le cas des prêts, 25 pour cent au moins d'élément de don).

- Les apports *non-concessionnels* comprennent les dons des organismes privés (aide privée) et les transactions assorties de conditions commerciales: crédits à l'exportation, investissements bilatéraux de portefeuille (prêts bancaires compris) effectués par des résidents ou des institutions des pays donneurs; investissements directs (bénéfices réinvestis compris) et achats de titres d'organisations internationales s'occupant du développement. Les données concernant les *engagements* se rapportent au moment où le donneur prend l'engagement ferme de fournir une aide déterminée quant à son volume, sa destination, ses conditions financières et ses modalités, tandis que les données concernant les *versements* correspondent à la fourniture effective des fonds. Sauf indication contraire, les chiffres des versements sont indiqués "nets", c'est-à-dire déduction faite des remboursements effectués au titre de prêts antérieurs. Les dons, les prêts et les crédits de caractère militaire, ainsi que les prêts et les crédits dont la durée de remboursement est inférieure à un an, sont exclus.

Le tableau 18 présente des estimations, pour les divers pays membres du CAD, sur le montant de l'aide publique au développement qui a été fourni aux PMA, exprimé en pourcentage du PNB de chaque donneur. Afin de donner un aperçu précis des apports totaux, on a essayé d'estimer la part des apports multilatéraux qui a été fournie par chaque donneur aux PMA. A cette fin, on a appliqué aux contributions du pays donneur à chacune des institutions multilatérales, la part respective des versements nets de chacune de ces institutions aux PMA exprimée en pourcentage des versements nets correspondant à l'ensemble des pays en développement. La somme ainsi obtenue pour l'ensemble des institutions est ajoutée à l'aide bilatérale du pays donneur et exprimée en pourcentage de son PNB.

Les données concernant la *dette* sont fondées sur des renseignements communiqués par le secrétariat de l'OCDE, à l'exception des tableaux 26 et 27 qui sont tirés du système de déclaration des débiteurs de la Banque mondiale.

En ce qui concerne les autres indicateurs économiques et sociaux, les données relatives aux *superficies* sont tirées de l'*Annuaire démographique 1992* des Nations Unies[12].

Les estimations concernant la *population urbaine* ne sont pas toujours comparables d'un pays à l'autre en raison des différences qui existent dans les définitions et la couverture. Elles sont principalement tirées de *Etat de la Population Mondiale 1994* de FNUAP.

Le *taux d'activité* est le rapport (en pourcentage) entre la population active et la population du ou des sexes indiqués, tous âges confondus. Les chiffres sont tirés de la

Population active 1950-2025 du BIT.

Les *taux bruts de natalité et de mortalité* indiquent respectivement le nombre de naissances vivantes et de décès pour mille habitants. Ces taux, ainsi que *l'espérance de vie à la naissance* et les *taux de mortalité infantile*, sont principalement tirés d'informations fournies par *World Population Prospects : The 1994 revision* des Nations Unies, FISE, *La situation des enfants dans le monde 1994*; *Rapport mondial sur Le Développement Humain 1994* de PNUD et *L'Annuaire statistique pour l'Asie et le Pacifique 1992* de CESAP[13].

L'espérance de vie à la naissance indique le nombre moyen d'années que vivrait un nouveau-né pour autant que les conditions de mortalité ne changent pas, alors que le *taux de mortalité infantile* exprime le nombre de décès d'enfants de moins d'un an pour mille naissances vivantes survenus pendant l'année de référence.

Sous la rubrique *santé à la naissance,* le *poids insuffisant à la naissance* reflète directement le statut nutritionnel des mères et indirectement, compte tenu du statut de la femme, celui de la population en général. Les chiffres sont tirés de *La situation des enfants dans le monde 1994* de la FISE, et du *Rapport mondial sur Le Développement Humain 1994* de PNUD.

Le *pourcentage de femmes ayant reçu des soins prodigués par du personnel qualifié pendant l'accouchement* constitue un indicateur de la disponibilité des services médicaux. Il reflète la distribution géographique de l'équipement et par conséquent leur accessibilité et dans quelle mesure les hôpitaux disposent du matériel et des fournitures qu'il faut pour offrir des soins médicaux efficaces. Il reflète aussi dans une certaine mesure le statut de la femme. Les données sont tirées des sources de la FISE et de PNUD mentionnés dans le paragraph précédent.

Le *pourcentage d'enfants vaccinés DTC (3 doses)* se rapporte à la couverture vaccinale des enfants de moins d'un an pour les maladies cibles du programme élargi de vaccination (diphtérie, tétanos, coqueluche, rougeole, poliomyélite et tuberculose). Les données sont tirées de l'OMS, *Expanded Program on Immunization 1994.* et de la FISE, *La situation des enfants dans le monde 1994.*

On a calculé les *disponibilités alimentaires* en divisant l'équivalent en calorie de l'offre de denrées alimentaires disponible dans un pays par sa population totale. Cette offre comprend la production intérieure, les importations diminuées des exportations et les variations de stocks; elle ne recouvre ni l'alimentation du bétail, ni les semences utilisées dans l'agriculture, ni les pertes en cours de traitement et de distribution. Les chiffres présentés sur ce tableau sont pondérés par la population. Les données sont tirées de l'*Annuaire de la production 1992* et de *La situation mondiale de l'alimentation et de l'agriculture 1992* de la FAO.

Les *pourcentages de la population disposant d'eau saine ou de mesures suffisantes d'hygiène du milieu* sont des estimations de l'OMS[14] et de la FISE, *La situation des enfants dans le monde 1994.* Le *pourcentage de la population disposant d'eau saine* indique la part en pourcentage de personnes jouissant d'un accès "raisonnable" aux eaux superficielles traitées ou à une eau non traitée mais non contaminée, provenant par exemple de forages, de sources et de puits protégés, par rapport à la population en question. Dans une zone urbaine, une fontaine publique ou une borne-fontaine située dans un

---

11 Voir OCDE, *Coopération pour le développement, examen 1983* (Paris 1983), p. 200.

12 Publication des Nations Unies, no. de vente E/F.94.XIII.1.

13 Publication des Nations Unies, no. de vente E/F.93.II.F.1.

14 OMS, *The International Drinking Water Supply and Sanitation Decade : End of Decade Review* (as at December 1990).

rayon de 200 mètres est considérée comme étant d'accès "raisonnable". Dans les zones rurales, pour que l'accès soit "raisonnable" il faut que la ménagère ou toute autre personne faisant partie du ménage ne passe pas une trop grande partie de la journée à se procurer l'eau nécessaire à la famille.

Le pourcentage de la population disposant de mesures suffisantes d'hygiène du milieu comprend la part de la population urbaine jouissant de raccordements aux égouts publics ou de systèmes ménagers (cabinets à fosse, latrines à entrainement par eau, fosses septiques, toilettes communales, etc.) et la part de la population rurale jouissant de moyens suffisants d'évacuation (cabinets à fosses, latrines à entrainement par eau, etc.).

Les données concernant *l'enseignement et l'alphabétisme* sont principalement tirées des diverses publications de l'UNESCO : *Compendium des statistiques relatives à l'analphabétisme - Edition 1990, l'Annuaire statistique 1993 et Trends and Projections of Enrolment by level of Education and by Age, 1960-2025 (as assessed in 1993)*. Le *taux d'alphabétisation des adultes* est le pourcentage de la population âgée de 15 ans ou plus, sachant lire et écrire. Les données concernant les *taux d'inscription scolaire* sont des estimations du nombre total de garçons et du nombre de filles inscrits à l'école primaire et secondaire, de tous âges, exprimées en pourcentage de la population totale, masculine et féminine en âge de fréquenter l'école primaire ou secondaire.

Les données concernant les *bureaux de poste ouverts au public* sont tirés de la *Statistique des services postaux 1992* de l'Union Postale Universelle.

Les données sur les *téléphones pour mille habitants* se basent sur l'*Annuaire statistique 1992* de l'UIT.

Les données sur les *postes récepteurs de radio pour mille habitants* sont établies d'après des données de l'*Annuaire statistique 1993* de l'UNESCO. Le rapport est calculé à partir du nombre de postes récepteurs en service et/ou de licenses délivrées selon la méthode d'estimation employée dans chaque pays qui fournit des données.

Les données sur la *circulation des journaux quotidiens pour mille habitants* se rapportent à "la circulation des journaux quotidiens d'information générale" et sont établies d'après des données de l'*Annuaire statistique 1993* de l'UNESCO.

En ce qui concerne les indicateurs de transports,

des problèmes spéciaux de comparabilité se posent dans le cas des *routes* dont la définition peut varier largement de pays à pays. Les principales sources utilisées sont IRU, *Statistiques mondiales de Transport 1990*, IRF, *Statistiques Routières Mondiales* (diverses parutions), *Annuaire statistique pour l'Asie et le Pacifique 1992* de CESAP et sources nationales.

Les données concernant les *chemins de fer* se rapportent au trafic intérieur et international de toutes les lignes du pays indiqué; en sont exclues, les lignes entièrement urbaines ou desservant une plantation, une entreprise industrielle ou minière, les téléfériques et les funiculaires. Les passagers (voyageurs-kilomètres) comprennent tous les voyageurs à l'exception des voyageurs transportés gratuitement (militaires, fonctionnaires et le personnel des chemins de fer). Le frêt se rapporte aux tonnes-kilomètres nettes en petite et grande vitesse à l'exception des transports pour les besoins du service, le courrier, les bagages et les transports gratuits du matériel du gouvernement. Les données sont tirées principalement de *The Railway Directory and Yearbook 1987* et IRU, *Statistiques mondiales de Transport 1990*.

Les données concernant *l'aviation civile* se rapportent aux services réguliers, intérieurs ou internationaux, des compagnies de transport aérien enregistrées dans chaque pays. Les services réguliers comprennent aussi les vols supplémentaires nécessités par un surcroît d'activité des services réguliers et les vols préparatoires en vue de nouveaux services réguliers. Par frêt, on entend toutes les marchandises transportées contre paiement, mais non le courrier et les excédents de bagages. Les données sont tirées du *Recueil de statistiques - Trafic d'aéroport 1992*, OACI.

Les données concernant la *consommation d'énergie par habitant* se rapportent, d'une part, aux formes d'énergie primaire (houille, lignite, tourbe et schiste bitumineux, pétrole brut et liquides extraits du gaz naturel, et électricité primaire (nucléaire, géothermique et hydraulique) - souvent appelées "énergie commerciale" - et, d'autre part, à l'utilisation de bois de chauffage, de charbon de bois et de bagasse. Toutes les données sont converties en équivalent charbon et ont été établies d'après l'*Annuaire des statistiques de l'énergie 1991*[15] et l'*Annuaire statistique 1985/86*[16] des Nations Unies.

Les données sur la *puissance électrique installée* sont tirées de l'*Annuaire des statistiques de l'énergie 1991* des Nations Unies.

C. Calcul des taux moyens de croissance annuelle

En général, ces taux sont définis par le coefficient b de la fonction expotentielle de tendance $y' = ae^{bt}$, où t représente le temps. Cette méthode permet de prendre en compte toutes les observations concernant une période donnée. Les taux de croissance obtenus traduisent ainsi des tendances qui ne sont pas faussées par des valeurs ex-

ceptionnelles. Aux fins d'aggrégation, il a été considéré que les données tendancielles disponibles couvraient les années manquantes dans le cas des pays pour lesquels les séries chronologiques pour la période 1980-1993 étaient incomplètes.

---

15 Publication des Nations Unies, no. de vente E/F.93.XVII.5.

16 Publication des Nations Unies, no. de vente E/F.86.XVII.7.

D. Autres notes

Sauf indication contraire, le terme "dollar" s'entend du dollar des Etats-Unis d'Amérique.

Les chiffres étant arrondis, les totaux indiqués ne correspondent pas toujours à la somme des composantes et des pourcentages portés dans les tableaux.

Les symboles suivants ont été utilisés :

Un tiret (-) signifie que le montant est nul ou négligeable.

Deux points (..) signifient que les données ne sont pas disponibles ou ne sont pas montrées séparément.

Un point (.) signifie que la rubrique est sans objet.

Le trait d'union (-) entre deux millésimes, par exemple (1970-1980), indique qu'il s'agit de la période tout entière (y compris la première et la dernière année mentionnée).

E. Abréviations utilisées

ACDI	Agence canadienne de développement international
AID	Association internationale de développement
APD	Aide publique au développement
ATNU	Assistance technique des Nations Unies
BADEA	Banque arabe pour le développement économique de l'Afrique
BAfD	Banque africaine de développement
BAsD	Banque asiatique de développement
BDEAC	Banque de Développement des Etats de l'Afrique Centrale
BEI	Banque européenne d'investissement
BID	Banque interaméricaine de développement
BIRD	Banque internationale pour la reconstruction et le développement (Banque mondiale)
BOAD	Banque ouest-africaine de développement
CAD	Comité d'aide au développement (de l'OCDE)
CAEM	Conseil d'assistance économique mutuelle
CCCE	Caisse centrale de coopération économique (France)
CEA	Nations Unies, Commission économique pour l'Afrique
CEE	Communauté économique européenne
CTCI	Classification type pour le commerce international (révision 1, sauf indication contraire)
DANIDA	Agence danoise de développement international
DCD	Development Cooperation Department (Italie)
FAATPAA	Fonds arabe de l'assistance technique aux pays africains et arabes
FAC	Fonds d'aide et de coopération (France)
FADES	Fonds arabe de développement économique et social
FAfD	Fonds africain de développement
FAO	Organisation des Nations Unies pour l'alimentation et l'agriculture
FAS	Facilité d'ajustement structurel du FMI
FASR	Facilité d'ajustement structurel renforcée du FMI

FED	Fonds européen de développement
FIDA	Fonds international pour le développement agricole
FMI	Fonds monétaire international
FNUAP	Fonds des Nations Unies pour la population
FRCA	Fondation pour le renforcement des capacités en Afrique
FSAAA	Fonds spécial d'aide arabe à l'Afrique
GTZ	Office allemand de la coopération technique
KFAED	Fonds koweïtien pour le développement économique arabe
KfW	Kreditanstalt für Wiederaufbau
mill.	millions
NPSA	Nouveau Programme d'Action pour les années 80 en faveur des pays les moins avancés
OACI	Organisation de l'aviation civile internationale
OCDE	Organisation de coopération et de développement économiques
OECF	Fonds de coopération économique d'outre-mer
ONU	Organisation des Nations Unies
OPAEP	Organisation des pays arabes exportateurs de pétrole
OPEP	Organisation des pays exportateurs de pétrole
PAM	Programme alimentaire mondial
PMA	Les pays les moins avancés
PNUD	Programme des Nations Unies pour le développement
SFD	Fonds saoudien pour le développement
SFI	Société financière internationale
SNPC	"Système de notification des pays créanciers" de l'OCDE
SNPD	"Système de notification des pays débiteurs" de la Banque mondiale
SSD	Société suisse de développement
UNHCR	Haut Commissariat des Nations Unies pour les réfugiés
UNICEF	Fonds des Nations Unies pour l'enfance
USAID	Agence des Etats-Unis pour le développement international

Tables

Tableaux

1. Per capita GDP and population : levels and growth

1. PIB par habitant et population : niveaux et croissance

Country	Per capita GDP in 1993 dollars PIB par habitant en dollars de 1993				Annual average growth rates of per capita real GDP (%) Taux d'accroissement annuels moyens du PIB réel par habitant (%)		Population			Pays
	Actual Réel		Projected 2000 Projection 2000				Level Niveau (mill.)	Annual average growth rates (%) Taux d'accroissement annuels moyens		
	1980	1993	A [a]	B [b]	1970-1980	1980-1993	1993	1970-1980	1980-1993	
Afghanistan [c]	765	522 [d]	425	556	0.8 [e]	-1.7 [e][f]	17.7	1.8	0.4	Afghanistan [c]
Bangladesh [g]	162	215	250	296	-0.5	2.2	115.2	2.9	2.0	Bangladesh [g]
Benin	442	425	416	554	-0.3	-0.3	5.1	2.5	3.0	Bénin
Bhutan [h]	79	139	188	193	..	4.6 [i]	1.6	2.0	2.1	Bhoutan [h]
Botswana [g]	1358	2862	4275	3748	10.5	5.9	1.4	3.6	3.4	Botswana [g]
Burkina Faso	256	288	307	386	2.2	0.9	9.8	2.3	2.6	Burkina Faso
Burundi	141	163	176	215	2.9	1.1	6.0	1.6	3.0	Burundi
Cambodia	..	199	..	266	..	..	9.7	-0.9	3.2	Cambodge
Cape Verde	576	878	1102	1164	2.1	3.3	0.4	0.7	1.9	Cap-Vert
Central African Rep.	464	391	357	531	0.0	-1.3	3.2	2.3	2.4	Rép. centrafricaine
Chad	134	199	246	263	-2.9	3.1	6.0	2.1	2.2	Tchad
Comoros	484	408	372	511	-4.2	-1.3	0.6	3.4	3.6	Comores
Djibouti	1740	834 [i]	561	1157	-3.4	-6.1 [f]	0.6	6.6	5.7	Djibouti
Equatorial Guinea	509	413	369	556	..	-1.6	0.4	-3.5	4.2	Guinée équatoriale
Ethiopia [k]	83	68	61	89	0.0	-1.5	51.9	2.4	2.8	Ethiopie [k]
Gambia [g]	396	366	351	474	2.2	-0.6	1.0	3.3	3.9	Gambie [g]
Guinea	682	491	411	641	3.0	-2.5	6.3	1.3	2.7	Guinée
Guinea-Bissau	183	231	262	320	-2.0	1.8	1.0	4.5	1.9	Guinée-Bissau
Haiti [l]	699	464 [m]	372	645	2.0	-2.9 [i]	6.9	1.7	2.0	Haïti [l]
Kiribati	551	447 [m]	399	627	-1.7	-1.5 [i]	0.1	1.7	2.2	Kiribati
Lao People's Dem. Rep.	226	289	330	381	-1.7	1.9	4.6	1.6	2.9	Rép. Dém. populaire lao
Lesotho [h]	301	380	431	507	7.1	1.8	1.9	2.3	2.9	Lesotho [h]
Liberia	771	479 [d]	371	614	-0.8	-3.9 [n]	2.8	3.1	3.2	Libéria
Madagascar	333	243	205	313	-2.2	-2.4	13.9	2.8	3.3	Madagascar
Malawi	238	193	172	268	2.7	-1.6	10.5	3.2	4.4	Malawi
Maldives	297	770 [m]	1286	991	10.9 [o]	7.6	0.2	3.2	3.2	Maldives
Mali	263	263	263	341	2.6	0.0	10.1	2.2	3.1	Mali
Mauritania	490	447	426	601	-1.2	-0.7	2.2	2.4	2.6	Mauritanie
Mozambique	93	93	93	119	-4.9	0.0	15.1	2.6	1.5	Mozambique
Myanmar [h]	1060	906	833	1259	2.3	-1.2	44.6	2.2	2.2	Myanmar [h]
Nepal [p]	115	154	181	207	0.0	2.3	20.8	2.6	2.6	Népal [p]
Niger	430	260	198	330	-2.3	-3.8	8.6	3.0	3.3	Niger
Rwanda	260	211 [m]	188	283	1.4	-1.6	7.6	3.3	3.0	Rwanda
Samoa	887	899 [m]	905	1289	..	0.3 [i]	0.2	0.9	0.3	Samoa
Sao Tome and Principe	275	313	336	437	3.1	1.0	0.1	2.6	2.3	Sao Tomé-et-Principe
Sierra Leone [g]	196	170	157	231	-0.7	-1.1	4.3	2.0	2.2	Sierra Leone [g]
Solomon Islands	502	692	823	886	2.4	2.6 [i]	0.4	3.5	3.5	Iles Salomon
Somalia	142	133 [d]	128	177	1.3	-0.6 [q]	9.0	3.5	2.2	Somalie
Sudan [g]	438	355 [m]	317	473	2.1	-1.8 [i]	26.6	3.1	2.8	Soudan [g]
Togo	441	326	277	422	1.4	-2.3	3.9	2.5	3.1	Togo
Tuvalu	..	1236 [r]	..	1786	..	..	0.0	4.0	1.3	Tuvalu
Uganda	162	202	227	263	-5.2	1.7	19.9	2.9	3.3	Ouganda
United Rep. of Tanzania	100	101 [m]	102	133	0.0	0.0 [i]	28.0	3.1	3.2	Rép.-Unie de Tanzanie
Vanuatu	1104	1163 [m]	1196	1566	..	0.4 [i]	0.2	3.0	2.5	Vanuatu
Yemen	..	956	..	1188	..	..	13.2	2.7	3.5	Yémen
Zaire	342	221 [i]	175	286	-3.2	-2.8 [i]	41.2	2.9	3.3	Zaïre
Zambia	501	356	296	475	-1.7	-2.6	8.9	3.2	3.5	Zambie
All LDCs	328	307	296	406	-0.4	-0.5	554.2	2.6	2.7	Ensemble des PMA
All developing countries	1037	1135	1192	1576	3.1	0.7	3001.4	2.4	2.3	Ensemble des pays en développement
Developed market economy countries	16696	21598	24810	.	2.2	2.0	858.5	0.9	0.7	Pays développés à économie de marché
Countries in Eastern Europe	1667	2156 [m]	2477	.	4.6	2.0 [q]	390.6	0.9	0.7	Pays d'Europe orientale

Source: UNCTAD secretariat calculations based on data from the United Nations Statistical Office, the World Bank, the Asian Development Bank and other international and national sources.

a At 1980-1993 growth rate.
b Based on the target rate of 7.0 per cent for total GDP growth as called for by the International Development Strategy for the Fourth United Nations Development Decade.
c Years beginning 21 March. *d* 1989. *e* Net material product.
f 1980-1991. *g* Years ending 30 June.
h Years beginning 1 April. *i* 1980-1992. *j* 1991.
k Years ending 7 July. *l* Years ending 30 September.
m 1992. *n* 1980-1989. *o* 1974-1980.
p Years ending 15 July. *q* 1980-1990. *r* 1990.

Source: Chiffres calculés par le secrétariat de la CNUCED d'après des données du Bureau de statistique des Nations Unies, de la Banque mondiale, de la Banque asiatique de développement et d'autres sources internationales et nationales.

a D'après le taux d'accroissement 1980-1993.
b D'après l'objectif de croissance du PIB total de 7,0 pour cent prévu dans la Stratégie Internationale du développement pour la quatrième décennie de développement des Nations Unies.
c Années commençant le 21 Mars. *d* 1989. *e* Produit matériel net.
f 1980-1991. *g* Années finissant le 30 juin.
h Années commençant le 1er avril. *i* 1980-1992. *j* 1991.
k Années finissant le 7 juillet. *l* Années finissant le 30 septembre.
m 1992. *n* 1980-1989. *o* 1974-1980.
p Années finissant le 15 juillet. *q* 1980-1990. *r* 1990.

2. Real GDP, total and per capita : annual average growth rates

In per cent

Country	Total real product / Produit réel total						
	1970-1980	1980-1993	1988-1989	1989-1990	1990-1991	1991-1992	1992-1993
Afghanistan a b	2.6	-2.2 i	-2.5	-3.4	-4.0	..	..
Bangladesh c	2.3	4.2	2.5	6.6	3.4	4.2	4.4
Benin	2.2	2.7	-2.4	3.4	4.8	4.2	3.3
Bhutan d	..	6.9 i	2.6	3.6	3.0	3.0	..
Botswana c	14.5	9.5	12.9	5.9	8.9	2.7	3.0
Burkina Faso	4.5	3.5	3.1	-0.2	6.3	0.6	0.4
Burundi	4.5	4.1	1.6	3.6	5.2	2.7	-1.2
Cambodia	..	..	3.5	1.2	7.6	7.0	4.1
Cape Verde	2.8	5.2	6.4	1.9	2.5	3.4	4.0
Central African Rep.	2.2	1.1	2.7	0.7	-1.6	-2.3	-2.5
Chad	-0.9	5.4	5.2	0.7	6.8	0.3	-2.9
Comoros	-0.9	2.2	-1.6	0.8	2.1	1.6	1.2
Djibouti	3.0	-0.3 i	0.3	1.2	1.6	..	..
Equatorial Guinea	..	2.5	-1.3	3.3	-1.0	13.7	7.3
Ethiopia e	2.4	1.3	1.6	-1.6	-0.6	-7.5	7.7
Gambia c	5.6	3.3	5.6	0.7	5.5	1.4	1.5
Guinea	4.3	0.2	3.2	4.3	2.5	3.2	4.5
Guinea-Bissau	2.4	3.8	5.1	3.0	2.8	2.8	2.9
Haiti f	3.7	-1.0 i	-0.6	-2.9	-3.0	-5.0	..
Kiribati	..	0.6 i	-3.0	-4.5	2.4	1.5	..
Lao People's Dem. Rep.	-0.1	4.8	13.4	6.7	4.0	7.0	5.9
Lesotho d	9.5	4.7	12.1	4.1	2.0	2.8	6.2
Liberia	2.2	-0.8 k	2.5	..	..	..	..
Madagascar	0.6	0.9	4.1	3.2	-6.7	1.1	1.9
Malawi	6.0	2.8	5.2	4.6	6.4	-8.0	8.8
Maldives	14.7 h	11.1	9.3	16.2	7.6	6.3	6.2
Mali	4.9	3.0	12.3	0.7	-1.8	3.1	7.7
Mauritania	1.2	1.8	4.2	-2.1	2.8	1.8	5.0
Mozambique	-2.4	1.5	6.5	1.0	4.9	-0.8	19.1
Myanmar d	4.6	0.9	3.7	2.8	-1.0	10.9	5.8
Nepal g	2.7	5.0	4.5	7.9	4.6	2.1	2.9
Niger	0.6	-0.6	-3.5	5.2	2.5	-6.5	1.4
Rwanda	4.7	1.3	1.6	0.6	-2.2	2.5	3.2
Samoa	..	0.6 i	3.7	-4.4	-0.4	-3.3	..
Sao Tome and Principe	5.7	3.3	1.5	-3.1	51.2	4.5	12.2
Sierra Leone c	1.3	1.1	2.7	4.9	2.6	-4.5	0.7
Solomon Islands	5.9	6.2 i	8.1	1.8	3.2	8.2	..
Somalia	4.8	2.0 l	-0.1	-1.6	..	..	..
Sudan c	5.3	0.9 i	7.4	-1.5	0.7	11.3	..
Togo	4.0	0.7	4.0	0.2	-0.9	-9.4	-12.7
Tuvalu	..	..	-1.9	7.5	11.4	8.9	8.7
Uganda	-2.4	5.1	7.1	4.1	3.6	3.0	6.4
United Rep.of Tanzania	3.0	3.3 i	3.9	5.7	3.9	3.8	..
Vanuatu	..	2.9 i	4.5	5.2	2.0	1.0	..
Yemen	..	..	..	-3.7	-3.9	..	..
Zaire	-0.3	0.4 i	-2.0	-2.3	-7.2	-10.6	..
Zambia	1.4	0.8	-0.9	0.5	-0.6	-2.7	6.8
All LDCs	2.2	2.1	2.7	2.1	0.6	1.0	3.3
All developing countries	5.6	3.1	3.6	3.3	3.1	4.0	3.6
Developed market economy countries	3.1	2.7	3.2	2.1	0.5	1.7	1.4
Countries in Eastern Europe	5.4	2.7 l	2.1	-5.9	..	..	..

Source: UNCTAD secretariat calculations based on data from the United Nations Statistical Office,
the World Bank, the Asian Development Bank and other international and national sources.

a	Years beginning 21 March.	g	Years ending 15 July.
b	Net material product.	h	1974-1980.
c	Years ending 30 June.	i	1980-1991.
d	Years beginning 1 April.	j	1980-1992.
e	Years ending 7 July.	k	1980-1989.
f	Years ending 30 September.	l	1980-1990.

2. Produit intérieur brut réel, total et par habitant : taux d'accroissement annuels moyens

En pourcentage

Per capita real product / Produit réel par habitant							Pays
1970-1980	*1980-1993*	*1988-1989*	*1989-1990*	*1990-1991*	*1991-1992*	*1992-1993*	
0.8	-1.7 i	-4.2	-6.4	-8.2	..	..	Afghanistan a b
-0.5	2.2	0.6	4.6	1.3	2.0	2.1	Bangladesh c
-0.3	-0.3	-5.3	0.3	1.6	1.0	0.1	Bénin
..	4.6 i	0.4	1.7	1.5	1.9	..	Bhoutan d
10.5	5.9	9.2	2.5	5.5	-0.5	-0.1	Botswana c
2.2	0.9	0.4	-2.9	3.4	-2.2	-2.4	Burkina Faso
2.9	1.1	-1.4	0.5	2.1	-0.4	-4.1	Burundi
..	..	0.4	-1.9	4.3	3.8	1.0	Cambodge
2.1	3.3	4.2	-0.4	-0.1	0.5	1.2	Cap-Vert
..	-1.3	0.2	-1.7	-4.0	-4.7	-4.9	Rép. centrafricaine
-2.9	3.1	3.1	-1.6	4.2	-2.3	-5.5	Tchad
-4.2	-1.3	-5.2	-2.7	-1.7	-2.0	-2.5	Comores
-3.4	-6.1 i	-4.6	-2.9	-1.6	..	..	Djibouti
..	-1.6	-3.0	1.3	-3.2	11.0	4.5	Guinée équatoriale
..	-1.5	-1.3	-4.4	-3.5	-10.2	4.5	Ethiopie e
2.2	-0.6	1.0	-3.6	1.1	-2.5	-2.4	Gambie c
3.0	-2.5	0.1	1.2	-0.6	0.1	1.4	Guinée
-2.0	1.8	2.9	0.8	0.7	0.6	0.7	Guinée-Bissau
2.0	-2.9 i	-2.6	-4.9	-4.9	-6.9	..	Haïti f
-1.7	-1.5 i	-5.4	-6.8	0.0	-1.0	..	Kiribati
-1.7	1.9	9.8	3.4	0.8	3.8	2.7	Rép. dém. pop. lao
7.1	1.8	9.2	1.3	-0.7	0.1	3.3	Lesotho d
-0.8	-3.9 k	-0.7	..	..	..	..	Libéria
-2.2	-2.4	0.6	-0.2	-9.7	-2.1	-1.3	Madagascar
2.7	-1.6	-0.1	-0.2	2.0	-11.5	5.2	Malawi
10.9 h	7.6	5.7	12.3	2.8	2.8	2.8	Maldives
2.6	..	9.0	-2.4	-4.9	-0.1	4.3	Mali
-1.2	-0.7	1.6	-4.5	0.3	-0.7	2.3	Mauritanie
-4.9	..	5.6	-0.3	3.1	-2.9	16.2	Mozambique
2.3	-1.2	1.5	0.6	-3.1	8.5	3.6	Myanmar d
..	2.3	1.9	5.2	1.9	-0.6	0.3	Népal g
-2.3	-3.8	-6.5	1.9	-0.8	-9.6	-2.0	Niger
1.4	-1.6	-1.2	-2.1	-4.8	-0.1	0.6	Rwanda
..	0.3 i	3.1	-4.4	-1.6	-3.8	..	Samoa
3.1	1.0	-1.1	-5.6	48.7	2.0	9.6	Sao Tomé-et-Principe
-0.7	-1.1	0.5	2.5	0.2	-6.8	-1.7	Sierra Leone c
2.4	2.6 i	4.3	-1.4	-0.2	4.4	..	Iles Salomon
1.3	-0.6 l	-1.8	-3.0	..	..	..	Somalie
2.1	-1.8 i	4.5	-4.1	-2.0	8.4	..	Soudan c
1.4	-2.3	0.8	-2.9	-4.0	-12.2	-15.4	Togo
..	..	-3.5	5.9	9.7	7.2	7.1	Tuvalu
-5.2	1.7	3.3	0.5	..	-0.5	2.7	Ouganda
..	0.0 j.	0.6	2.4	0.8	0.7	..	Rép.-Unie de Tanzanie
..	0.4 i	1.7	3.1	-0.7	-1.6	..	Vanuatu
..	..	..	-7.6	-8.4	..	..	Yémen
-3.2	-2.8 i	-5.2	-5.5	-10.2	-13.4	..	Zaïre
-1.7	-2.6	-4.2	-2.7	-3.7	-5.6	3.7	Zambie
-0.4	**-0.5**	**0.0**	**-0.6**	**-2.1**	**-1.8**	**0.4**	**Ensemble des PMA**
							Ensemble des pays
3.1	**0.7**	**1.3**	**1.0**	**0.8**	**1.8**	**1.4**	**en développement**
							Pays développés
2.2	**2.0**	**2.5**	**1.2**	**-0.3**	**0.9**	**0.7**	**à économie de marché**
							Pays d'Europe
4.6	**2.0 l**	**1.5**	**-6.2**	**..**	**..**	**..**	**orientale**

Source: Chiffres calculés par le secrétariat de la CNUCED d'après des données
du Bureau de statistique des Nations Unies, de la Banque mondiale,
de la Banque asiatique de développement et d'autres sources internationales et nationals.

a	Années commençant le 21 mars.	*g*	Années finissant le 15 juillet.
b	Produit matériel net.	*h*	1974-1980.
c	Années finissant le 30 juin.	*i*	1980-1991.
d	Années commençant le 1er avril.	*j*	1980-1992.
e	Années finissant le 7 juillet.	*k*	1980-1989.
f	Années finissant le 30 septembre.	*l*	1980-1990.

3. Agricultural production, total and per capita : annual average growth rates

	Percentage share of agriculture in: Total labour force		GDP		Annual average growth rates (%) Taux d'accroissement annuels moyens (%)						
	Part en pourcentage de l'agriculture dans : *La main d'oeuvre totale*		*le PIB*		*Total agricultural production* *Production agricole totale*						
Country	1980	1993	1980	1993	1970-1980	1980-1993	1988-1989	1989-1990	1990-1991	1991-1992	1992-1993
Afghanistan	61	53	..	..	2.3	-2.4	-2.2	1.0	2.0	-4.7	1.1
Bangladesh	75	67	50	33	2.3	2.0	8.9	1.0	1.7	-0.9	1.7
Benin	70	59	35	37 ᵃ	2.8	5.4	4.3	5.3	7.4	1.4	-3.5
Bhutan	93	90	57	42	2.4	0.1	1.8	5.7	2.2	2.9	2.2
Botswana	70	61	13	5	-0.4	0.2	-3.8	4.2	3.1	-16.3	-2.1
Burkina Faso	87	84	39	44 ᵇ	1.0	5.7	0.6	-4.9	21.3	3.2	-1.4
Burundi	93	91	62	54	1.5	2.6	-6.3	7.9	2.6	1.9	-0.5
Cambodia	75	69	45 ᶜ	53	-6.8	4.9	1.2	0.2	-1.2	0.6	6.7
Cape Verde	52	41	14	13 ᵃ	5.3	6.0	-5.8	-8.8	-10.4	0.0	4.4
Central African Rep.	72	59	40	50	2.3	1.8	0.1	-0.6	0.9	2.8	1.4
Chad	83	72	54	44	1.7	3.0	-3.4	-1.6	11.9	1.3	-1.3
Comoros	83	78	34	39	1.4	2.6	1.8	1.5	16.6	-11.4	2.5
Djibouti	..	..	2	3 ᵇ	..	..	..	..	..	..	..
Equatorial Guinea	66	52	41	47	..	..	..	..	..	..	..
Ethiopia	80	73	51	48	1.6	1.3	2.8	3.2	0.4	2.3	-1.1
Gambia	84	80	30	28 ᵈ	-2.1	0.6	7.1	-14.4	11.0	-10.1	3.2
Guinea	81	72	48	25	1.3	2.3	6.1	5.0	4.2	-9.5	11.4
Guinea-Bissau	82	77	44	44	3.2	2.2	2.8	5.6	1.8	-1.3	1.5
Haiti	70	62	..	..	1.2	-1.3	0.7	-5.3	-5.8	-17.7	-2.4
Kiribati	..	..	21	25 ᵃ	..	..	..	..	..	..	..
Lao People's Dem.Rep.	76	70	54 ᵉ	60 ᵃ	2.0	2.8	14.6	7.0	-9.5	9.7	0.8
Lesotho	86	77	24	10	0.7	0.1	-2.1	8.5	-22.4	-11.2	11.0
Liberia	74	68	36	38 ᶠ	2.6	-3.1	1.2	-34.8	-7.5	3.5	-10.5
Madagascar	81	75	30	34	1.6	1.7	3.1	2.1	-0.9	2.4	2.5
Malawi	83	72	37	38	4.1	0.9	-2.3	-1.1	8.9	-18.0	29.0
Maldives	..	..	35	31 ᵍ	2.5	1.7	4.4	1.9	-0.2	0.4	0.3
Mali	86	79	58	42	3.0	2.7	1.2	-2.9	9.1	-1.3	3.7
Mauritania	69	63	30	27	0.8	1.6	4.8	-3.2	3.8	-9.6	1.1
Mozambique	84	81	37	33	-0.6	-0.3	0.9	3.0	-6.4	-16.9	11.0
Myanmar	53	45	47	61	2.6	1.2	-10.6	1.7	1.1	6.4	8.1
Nepal	93	91	62	49	1.5	4.0	2.6	3.9	-0.5	-4.2	2.9
Niger	91	86	43	39	4.3	2.4	-5.9	2.0	17.7	-0.3	1.4
Rwanda	93	91	46	41 ᵃ	4.4	0.7	5.4	-1.8	6.3	-2.8	-6.0
Samoa	..	..	46	40 ᵃ	1.8	-1.5	7.0	-8.0	-5.0	-3.6	0.7
Sao Tome and Principe	..	..	..	..	-3.4	-1.3	-7.0	-8.5	-0.9	-4.9	6.1
Sierra Leone	70	60	33	38 ᵈ	1.6	1.4	2.8	0.0	-7.5	1.2	0.0
Solomon Islands	..	..	55 ʰ	44 ᶜ	5.6	2.3	10.7	4.1	1.4	3.3	-2.8
Somalia	76	68	68	65 ᵇ	3.0	-3.8	-1.3	-14.3	-33.2	-35.4	46.1
Sudan	71	57	34	34 ᵃ	2.4	1.2	-20.3	-8.0	31.3	15.8	-4.0
Togo	73	69	27	49	1.0	3.8	7.4	3.1	0.0	1.0	6.3
Tuvalu	..	..	18 ᵍ	21 ᵇ	..	..	..	..	..	..	..
Uganda	86	79	72	56	-1.0	3.2	8.2	3.8	2.3	0.4	8.4
Un. Rep. of Tanzania	86	79	44	61 ᵃ	3.9	1.8	6.1	2.4	-1.9	-3.4	2.9
Vanuatu	..	..	19	20 ᵇ	4.4	1.5	-8.0	29.1	-12.2	9.6	1.2
Yemen	62	54	26 ᵉ	21	2.5	1.9	0.3	0.4	-6.3	11.5	0.9
Zaire	72	64	25	44 ᵈ	1.8	2.3	2.0	1.1	2.6	1.2	0.2
Zambia	73	68	14	29	4.0	3.1	1.9	-10.4	4.7	-13.5	33.2
All LDCs	76	69	39	42	1.8	1.6	1.8	0.0	1.8	0.2	4.1
All developing countries	60	53	18	17 ᵈ	2.7	2.7	2.6	1.7	2.3	1.5	1.2

Source: UNCTAD secretariat calculations, based on data from FAO, the Economic Commission for Africa, the World Bank and other international and national sources.

a	1992.	*b*	1990.
c	1987.	*d*	1991.
e	1985.	*f*	1989.
g	1986.	*h*	1984.

3. Production agricole totale et par habitant : taux d'accroissement annuels moyens

Annual average growth rates (%)							
Taux d'accroissement annuels moyens (%)							
Per capita agricultural production							
Production agricole par habitant							
1970-1980	*1980-1993*	*1988-1989*	*1989-1990*	*1990-1991*	*1991-1992*	*1992-1993*	*Pays*
0.5	-2.8	-3.9	-2.1	-2.5	-9.8	-5.0	Afghanistan
-0.5	0.0	7.0	-0.9	-0.4	-3.0	-0.5	Bangladesh
0.3	2.4	1.2	2.1	4.1	-1.7	-6.5	Bénin
0.4	-2.0	-0.4	3.8	0.8	1.8	1.3	Bhoutan
-3.9	-3.1	-7.0	0.8	0.0	-18.9	-5.0	Botswana
-1.2	3.0	-2.1	-7.5	18.0	0.4	-4.2	Burkina Faso
-0.1	-0.4	-9.0	4.8	-0.5	-1.2	-3.4	Burundi
-5.9	1.6	-1.8	-2.8	-4.2	-2.4	3.5	Cambodge
4.5	4.1	-7.8	-11.0	-12.8	-2.8	1.5	Cap-Vert
0.0	-0.6	-2.3	-3.0	-1.6	0.3	-1.2	Rép. centrafricaine
-0.4	0.8	-5.4	-3.8	9.2	-1.4	-4.0	Tchad
-2.0	-1.0	-1.9	-2.1	12.3	-14.6	-1.2	Comores
..	..	..	..	..	..	..	Djibouti
..	..	..	..	..	..	..	Guinée équatoriale
-0.8	-1.5	-0.2	0.2	-2.5	-0.7	-4.1	Ethiopie
-5.2	-3.2	2.5	-18.0	6.4	-13.6	-0.8	Gambie
0.0	-0.4	3.0	1.9	1.1	-12.2	8.0	Guinée
-1.3	0.2	0.8	3.4	-0.2	-3.5	-0.6	Guinée-Bissau
-0.5	-3.2	-1.4	-7.3	-7.7	-19.4	-4.4	Haïti
..	..	..	..	..	..	..	Kiribati
0.4	0.0	11.0	3.7	-12.3	6.4	-2.2	Rép. dém. pop. lao
-1.5	-2.7	-4.6	5.6	-24.5	-13.6	8.1	Lesotho
-0.4	-6.1	-1.9	-36.9	-10.5	0.0	-13.4	Libéria
-1.2	-1.5	-0.3	-1.3	-4.1	-0.9	-0.7	Madagascar
0.9	-3.4	-7.3	-5.7	4.3	-21.1	24.6	Malawi
-0.7	-1.5	1.0	-1.5	-4.7	-2.8	-2.8	Maldives
0.7	-0.4	-1.8	-5.8	5.7	-4.4	0.5	Mali
-1.6	-0.9	2.2	-5.6	1.2	-11.9	-1.4	Mauritanie
-3.1	-1.8	0.0	1.7	-7.9	-18.6	8.3	Mozambique
0.4	-0.9	-12.6	-0.5	-1.1	4.2	5.8	Myanmar
-1.1	1.4	0.0	1.3	-3.0	-6.7	0.2	Népal
1.3	-0.9	-8.8	-1.2	13.9	-3.6	-2.0	Niger
1.1	-2.2	2.5	-4.5	3.5	-5.3	-8.4	Rwanda
0.8	-1.8	6.4	-8.0	-6.1	-4.2	-0.5	Samoa
-5.9	-3.5	-9.4	-10.8	-2.6	-7.2	3.6	Sao Tomé-et-Principe
-0.3	-0.8	0.5	-2.4	-9.6	-1.2	-2.3	Sierra Leone
2.1	-1.1	6.7	0.8	-1.9	-0.3	-5.8	Iles Salomon
-0.5	-5.9	-2.9	-15.6	-33.9	-36.0	44.7	Somalie
-0.6	-1.5	-22.5	-10.4	27.8	12.8	-6.5	Soudan
-1.5	0.6	4.1	0.0	-3.0	-2.2	2.9	Togo
..	..	..	..	..	..	..	Tuvalu
-3.8	-0.1	4.4	0.2	-1.2	-3.0	4.7	Ouganda
0.8	-1.4	2.7	-0.8	-4.9	-6.2	-0.1	Rép.-Unie de Tanzanie
1.4	-0.9	-10.5	26.5	-14.5	6.8	-1.3	Vanuatu
-0.2	-1.6	-3.2	-3.6	-10.7	5.8	-4.3	Yémen
-1.0	-1.0	-1.4	-2.2	-0.7	-2.0	-2.9	Zaïre
0.8	-0.4	-1.5	-13.3	1.5	-16.2	29.3	Zambie
-0.7	**-0.9**	**-0.8**	**-2.5**	**-0.9**	**-2.6**	**1.1**	**Ensemble des PMA**
0.3	**0.3**	**0.3**	**-0.5**	**0.0**	**-0.8**	**-0.9**	**Ensemble des pays en développement**

Source: Chiffres calculés par le secrétariat de la CNUCED,
d'après des données de la FAO, de la Commission économique pour l'Afrique,
de la Banque mondiale, et d'autres sources internationales et nationales.

a 1992. *b* 1990.
c 1987. *d* 1991.
e 1985. *f* 1989.
g 1986. *h* 1984.

4. Food production, total and per capita : annual average growth rates

In per cent

Country	Total food production / Production alimentaire totale						
	1970- 1980	1980- 1993	1988- 1989	1989- 1990	1990- 1991	1991- 1992	1992- 1993
Afghanistan	2.3	-2.5	-1.9	1.2	0.6	-4.9	1.2
Bangladesh	2.4	2.1	9.5	0.7	1.7	-0.8	1.5
Benin	3.1	5.1	4.9	4.1	6.4	2.0	-3.3
Bhutan	2.4	0.1	1.8	5.7	2.3	2.9	2.2
Botswana	-0.4	0.2	-3.8	4.2	3.0	-16.3	-2.1
Burkina Faso	0.9	5.6	0.4	-6.1	22.9	3.3	-1.3
Burundi	1.4	2.7	-6.0	8.9	2.1	3.0	1.4
Cambodia	-6.8	4.6	1.6	-1.2	-0.9	0.0	7.0
Cape Verde	5.4	6.1	-6.0	-8.6	-10.3	0.0	4.4
Central African Rep.	2.5	1.9	0.7	-0.2	2.1	2.2	2.6
Chad	1.8	2.9	-4.4	-2.0	11.9	3.6	-0.1
Comoros	1.4	2.6	1.8	1.5	16.6	-11.4	2.5
Djibouti	..	..	..	..	..	..	..
Equatorial Guinea	..	..	..	..	..	..	..
Ethiopia	1.6	1.3	2.8	3.2	0.2	2.3	-1.4
Gambia	-2.2	0.2	6.7	-15.9	10.8	-12.7	2.7
Guinea	1.3	2.1	4.7	4.8	4.5	-9.9	12.2
Guinea-Bissau	3.2	2.2	2.9	5.6	1.9	-1.3	1.5
Haiti	1.3	-1.3	0.9	-5.4	-6.3	-17.8	-2.6
Kiribati	..	..	..	..	..	..	..
Lao People's Dem. Rep.	2.0	2.8	15.5	6.8	-10.0	10.0	0.5
Lesotho	1.4	0.1	-4.1	9.6	-24.2	-11.9	12.3
Liberia	3.4	-1.1	2.1	-26.2	-0.5	-1.2	-3.4
Madagascar	1.6	1.8	2.7	2.6	-0.8	2.5	2.6
Malawi	3.7	0.2	-4.6	-2.8	8.8	-20.8	34.5
Maldives	2.5	1.7	4.4	1.9	-0.2	0.4	0.3
Mali	2.6	2.3	-0.3	-3.2	8.6	-1.4	2.7
Mauritania	0.8	1.6	4.8	-3.2	3.8	-9.6	1.1
Mozambique	0.0	-0.2	1.2	3.0	-6.3	-16.0	11.3
Myanmar	2.6	1.3	-11.0	2.3	1.0	6.2	8.0
Nepal	1.5	4.1	2.5	3.9	-0.6	-4.0	2.8
Niger	4.3	2.4	-5.9	2.1	17.7	-0.3	1.4
Rwanda	4.2	0.5	8.9	-2.3	5.2	-0.9	-6.6
Samoa	1.8	-1.6	7.1	-8.1	-5.6	-3.5	0.7
Sao Tome and Principe	-3.4	-1.3	-7.0	-8.5	-0.9	-4.9	6.2
Sierra Leone	1.6	1.0	2.9	-0.2	-8.2	1.7	0.4
Solomon Islands	5.6	2.3	10.7	4.1	1.5	3.3	-2.8
Somalia	3.0	-3.8	-1.2	-14.4	-33.2	-35.4	46.1
Sudan	3.3	1.6	-22.0	-6.0	32.8	16.8	-3.1
Togo	1.0	3.3	8.0	3.1	-2.8	1.0	7.1
Tuvalu	..	..	..	..	..	..	..
Uganda	-0.6	3.2	8.1	4.2	2.1	0.7	7.8
United Rep.of Tanzania	4.6	1.8	6.5	2.7	-3.1	-3.2	3.2
Vanuatu	4.5	1.5	-8.1	29.2	-12.5	9.8	1.2
Yemen	2.6	1.9	0.5	0.0	-6.7	11.9	0.8
Zaire	1.9	2.3	1.9	1.0	2.8	1.3	0.3
Zambia	4.1	3.0	2.2	-9.8	3.5	-12.1	31.0
All LDCs	**2.0**	**1.6**	**1.7**	**0.2**	**1.6**	**0.4**	**4.1**
All developing countries	2.9	2.8	2.6	1.7	2.1	1.9	1.2

Source: UNCTAD secretariat calculations based on data from FAO.

4. Production alimentaire totale et par habitant : taux d'accroissement annuels moyens

En pourcentage

Per capita food production / Production alimentaire par habitant							*Pays*
1970-1980	*1980-1993*	*1988-1989*	*1989-1990*	*1990-1991*	*1991-1992*	*1992-1993*	
0.5	-2.8	-3.5	-2.0	-3.8	-10.0	-4.9	Afghanistan
-0.4	0.0	7.5	-1.3	-0.3	-2.9	-0.7	Bangladesh
0.6	2.0	1.8	1.0	3.2	-1.2	-6.3	Bénin
0.4	-2.0	-0.4	3.8	0.8	1.8	1.3	Bhoutan
-3.9	-3.1	-7.0	0.9	-0.2	-18.9	-5.0	Botswana
-1.4	2.9	-2.3	-8.6	19.5	0.5	-4.1	Burkina Faso
-0.2	-0.2	-8.8	5.7	-1.0	0.0	-1.6	Burundi
-6.0	1.4	-1.4	-4.2	-3.9	-3.1	3.8	Cambodge
4.6	4.1	-8.0	-10.8	-12.6	-2.8	1.5	Cap-Vert
0.2	-0.5	-1.7	-2.7	-0.4	-0.3	0.0	Rép. centrafricaine
-0.2	0.7	-6.3	-4.2	9.1	0.9	-2.9	Tchad
-1.9	-1.0	-1.9	-2.1	12.3	-14.6	-1.2	Comores
							Djibouti
..	..	..	..	..	..	..	Guinée équatoriale
-0.8	-1.4	-0.1	0.2	-2.7	-0.7	-4.3	Ethiopie
-5.3	-3.5	2.1	-19.5	6.2	-16.1	-1.3	Gambie
0.0	-0.6	1.6	1.7	1.4	-12.6	8.8	Guinée
-1.2	0.3	0.8	3.4	-0.2	-3.5	-0.6	Guinée-Bissau
-0.4	-3.2	-1.2	-7.3	-8.2	-19.4	-4.6	Haïti
..	..	..	..	..	..	..	Kiribati
0.4	0.0	11.9	3.5	-12.7	6.7	-2.4	Rép. dém. pop. lao
-0.9	-2.7	-6.5	6.7	-26.2	-14.2	9.3	Lesotho
0.3	-4.2	-1.1	-28.5	-3.7	-4.5	-6.5	Libéria
-1.2	-1.5	-0.7	-0.8	-4.0	-0.8	-0.6	Madagascar
0.4	-4.1	-9.5	-7.3	4.3	-23.8	30.0	Malawi
-0.7	-1.5	1.0	-1.5	-4.7	-2.8	-2.8	Maldives
0.4	-0.8	-3.3	-6.2	5.2	-4.5	-0.6	Mali
-1.6	-0.9	2.2	-5.6	1.2	-11.9	-1.4	Mauritanie
-2.6	-1.6	0.3	1.7	-7.9	-17.7	8.6	Mozambique
0.4	-0.8	-12.9	0.2	-1.2	4.0	5.8	Myanmar
-1.0	1.5	0.0	1.3	-3.1	-6.5	0.2	Népal
1.3	-0.9	-8.8	-1.1	13.9	-3.6	-2.0	Niger
0.9	-2.4	5.9	-5.0	2.5	-3.4	-8.9	Rwanda
0.9	-1.9	6.4	-8.1	-6.7	-4.0	-0.5	Samoa
-5.8	-3.5	-9.5	-10.8	-2.5	-7.2	3.7	Sao Tomé-et-Principe
-0.4	-1.1	0.6	-2.4	-10.3	-0.7	-2.0	Sierra Leone
2.1	-1.1	6.8	0.8	-1.9	-0.3	-5.8	Iles Salomon
-0.5	-5.9	-2.9	-15.6	-34.0	-36.0	44.6	Somalie
0.3	-1.2	-24.1	-8.5	29.3	13.7	-5.6	Soudan
-1.5	0.2	4.7	0.0	-5.8	-2.2	3.8	Togo
..	..	..	..	..	..	..	Tuvalu
-3.4	0.0	4.3	0.6	-1.5	-2.8	4.2	Ouganda
1.5	-1.4	3.2	-0.5	-6.0	-6.1	0.2	Rép.-Unie de Tanzanie
1.5	-0.9	-10.6	26.6	-14.8	7.0	-1.3	Vanuatu
0.0	-1.6	-3.0	-4.1	-11.1	6.1	-4.4	Yémen
-1.0	-1.0	-1.4	-2.3	-0.5	-1.9	-2.8	Zaïre
0.9	-0.5	-1.2	-12.7	0.3	-14.8	27.1	Zambie
-0.5	**-0.9**	**-0.9**	**-2.4**	**-1.2**	**-2.4**	**1.2**	**Ensemble des PMA**
0.5	0.4	0.3	-0.5	-0.1	-0.3	-0.9	**Ensemble des pays en développement**

Source: Chiffres calculés par le secrétariat de la CNUCED d'après des données de la FAO.

5. The manufacturing sector : annual average growth rates and shares in GDP

5. Le secteur manufacturier : taux d'accroissement annuels moyens et parts dans le PIB

Country	Share in GDP Part dans le PIB		Annual average growth rates [a] Taux d'accroissement annuels moyens [a] (In per cent / En pourcentage)							Pays
	1980	1993	1970-1980	1980-1993	1988-1989	1989-1990	1990-1991	1991-1992	1992-1993	
Afghanistan	..	..	..	..	..	..	..	..	..	Afghanistan
Bangladesh	11	9	5.1	3.4	2.8	7.2	2.4	7.3	8.0	Bangladesh
Benin	8	8	3.7	5.0 b	1.2	8.9	2.0	..	..	Bénin
Bhutan	3	9 d	0.0	13.2 c	16.2	16.5	13.5	15.0	..	Bhoutan
Botswana	4	5	22.9	8.8	5.4	4.8	6.6	6.4	5.0	Botswana
Burkina Faso	13	13 e	4.1	3.1	8.0	8.0	3.2	6.8	1.0	Burkina Faso
Burundi	7	11	3.8	5.2	-2.1	9.6	4.2	5.6	-3.1	Burundi
Cambodia	10 f	5	0.0	5.9 g	13.9	-4.3	6.8	3.2	7.9	Cambodge
Cape Verde	..	..	..	..	..	..	..	..	..	Cap-Vert
Central African Rep.	..	..	..	..	..	..	..	..	..	Rép. centrafricaine
Chad	17 h	16	0.0	2.6 i	30.3	7.9	-18.0	-6.6	-3.0	Tchad
Comoros	4	4	-4.9	4.5	1.3	5.2	1.8	5.6	3.6	Comores
Djibouti	5	5 e	6.3	1.5 j	0.0	..	..	..	..	Djibouti
Equatorial Guinea	5	11	..	-10.9 k	2.4	-1.7	10.2	6.2	10.0	Guinée équatoriale
Ethiopia	11	8 d	2.5	0.7	1.9	-3.8	-18.7	-10.0	21.9	Ethiopie
Gambia	7	7 l	..	..	..	..	..	..	..	Gambie
Guinea	3	5	1.6	-1.1	5.0	9.4	3.2	3.8	5.0	Guinée
Guinea-Bissau	12 m	11 n	..	2.2 o	1.2	..	..	..	..	Guinée-Bissau
Haiti	..	..	8.5	-2.1 j	1.6	..	..	..	..	Haïti
Kiribati	2	2 d	..	-0.9 p	2.5	-2.3	-1.2	0.1	..	Kiribati
Lao People's Dem.Rep.	10 q	13 d	..	12.4 r	39.5	15.5	29.7	9.4	7.7	Rép. Dém. pop. lao
Lesotho	7	16	18.0	12.2	13.9	-3.9	9.2	15.1	5.0	Lesotho
Liberia	8	8 n	7.0	-2.9 j	-8.2	..	..	..	..	Libéria
Madagascar	..	..	..	..	..	..	..	..	..	Madagascar
Malawi	12	13	8.0	3.9	8.5	11.3	3.0	3.0	-1.0	Malawi
Maldives	4	5 m	..	11.3	10.5	15.4	10.0	8.7	9.5	Maldives
Mali	4	9	..	..	..	..	..	..	..	Mali
Mauritania	13 q	12	..	-0.6 k	-2.9	-8.4	6.2	11.1	6.2	Mauritanie
Mozambique	..	..	..	..	..	..	..	..	..	Mozambique
Myanmar	10	8	4.2	0.2	11.3	0.1	-4.1	13.7	7.3	Myanmar
Nepal	4	8	..	..	..	..	..	..	..	Népal
Niger	4	7	..	..	..	..	..	..	..	Niger
Rwanda	15	16 d	4.9	1.6 c	0.4	-4.0	-2.2	3.2	..	Rwanda
Samoa	6	11 d	..	..	..	..	..	..	..	Samoa
Sao Tome and Principe	..	..	..	..	..	..	..	..	..	Sao Tomé-et-Principe
Sierra Leone	6	5 l	-2.1	-4.6 c	-10.0	5.0	-20.7	-2.0	..	Sierra Leone
Solomon Islands	4 s	3 f	..	3.6 t	2.3	0.0	1.1	..	..	Iles Salomon
Somalia	5	5 e	-0.3	-1.7 j	-20.0	..	..	..	..	Somalie
Sudan	7	9 d	3.9	3.6 t	0.7	5.0	6.5	..	..	Soudan
Togo	8	7	0.5	1.2	16.7	13.7	5.5	-9.8	-40.8	Togo
Tuvalu	2 m	5 e	..	7.9 u	-2.1	8.1	14.7	8.3	5.8	Tuvalu
Uganda	4	5	..	5.7 v	10.8	1.6	12.7	3.6	3.7	Ouganda
United Rep.of Tanzania	11	5 d	13.3	0.5 c	7.7	-2.5	12.0	1.9	..	Rép.-Unie de Tanzanie
Vanuatu	4	6 e	..	14.9 w	13.2	12.5	..	..	..	Vanuatu
Yemen	12 q	11	..	..	..	-12.2	-0.5	..	..	Yémen
Zaire	14	8 l	56.1	0.0 t	-4.1	-14.6	-21.5	..	..	Zaïre
Zambia	18	26	2.4	4.4	-0.5	7.8	0.0	5.6	5.8	Zambie
All LDCs	**10**	**9**	**7.7**	**1.6**	**1.0**	**-0.5**	**-4.0**	**3.7**	**4.1**	**Ensemble des PMA**

Source: UNCTAD secretariat calculations based on data from the United Nations Statistical Office, the World Bank, the Asian Development Bank and other international and national sources.

Source: Chiffres calculés par le secrétariat de la CNUCED d'après des données du Bureau de statistique des Nations Unies, de la Banque mondiale, de la Banque asiatique de développement et d'autres sources internationales et nationales.

a At constant prices.		b 1980-1991.	
c 1980-1992.	d 1992.	e 1990.	
f 1987.	g 1987-1992.	h 1983.	
i 1983-1992.	j 1980-1989.	k 1985-1992.	
l 1991.	m 1986.	n 1989.	
o 1986-1989.	p 1982-1992.	q 1985.	
r 1984-1992.	s 1984.	t 1980-1991.	
u 1988-1992.	v 1983-1992.	w 1983-1990.	

a Aux prix constants.		b 1980-1991.	
c 1980-1992.	d 1992.	e 1990.	
f 1987.	g 1987-1992.	h 1983.	
i 1983-1992.	j 1980-1989.	k 1985-1992.	
l 1991.	m 1986.	n 1989.	
o 1986-1989.	p 1982-1992.	q 1985.	
r 1984-1992.	s 1984.	t 1980-1991.	
u 1988-1992.	v 1983-1992.	w 1983-1990.	

6. Investment [a] : annual average growth rates and shares in GDP

6. Investissement [a] : taux d'accroissement annuels moyens et parts dans le PIB

Country	Share in GDP Part dans le PIB		Annual average growth rates [b] Taux d'accroissement annuels moyens [b] (In per cent / En pourcentage)							Pays
	Average 1980-1989	1990-1993	1970-1980	1980-1993	1988-1989	1989-1990	1990-1991	1991-1992	1992-1993	
Afghanistan	..	..	..	..	..	..	..	..	..	Afghanistan
Bangladesh	13	12	4.8	1.6	3.6	2.6	-9.1	8.7	8.8	Bangladesh
Benin	15	14	11.4	-3.0	-18.0	18.1	-0.7	15.1	13.2	Bénin
Bhutan	37	35 c	..	7.6 d	..	..	..	..	..	Bhoutan
Botswana	27	36	6.9	6.6 e	112.9	..	..	..	..	Botswana
Burkina Faso	20	21	4.4	7.9	3.9	-11.7	35.3	-12.5	3.5	Burkina Faso
Burundi	17	14	16.3	3.1	12.5	1.5	2.6	8.2	5.3	Burundi
Cambodia	10 f	11	..	5.0 g	26.8	-23.5	22.0	11.3	4.0	Cambodge
Cape Verde	45	33 c	14.4	-0.4 h	-5.6	5.4	0.0	21.1	..	Cap-Vert
Central African Rep.	11	11	-9.7	0.6	-8.3	9.4	-3.6	-7.1	-30.5	Rép. centrafricaine
Chad	7 i	9	..	12.7 i	15.6	11.2	-9.1	-1.7	2.2	Tchad
Comoros	27	18	-1.0	-5.2	-15.5	4.6	-30.3	40.7	-22.6	Comores
Djibouti	21	17 k	-1.4	-5.3 l	18.0	-10.2	..	..	..	Djibouti
Equatorial Guinea	17	29	..	..	..	..	..	..	..	Guinée équatoriale
Ethiopia	13	12	..	..	..	..	..	..	..	Ethiopie
Gambia	19	20 c	31.4	1.4 m	23.3	-4.2	2.4	..	..	Gambie
Guinea	15	17	-0.9	-0.7	-0.2	18.0	-7.4	8.2	7.5	Guinée
Guinea-Bissau	29	25	-1.7	5.8	33.3	-27.2	100.4	26.7	-41.0	Guinée-Bissau
Haiti	14	11 k	13.7	-4.0 h	-1.0	1.8	-8.0	-22.3	..	Haïti
Kiribati	55	67 c	..	..	..	..	..	..	..	Kiribati
Lao People's Dem.Rep.	9 n	13 o	..	-1.1 m	11.2	2.5	10.7	..	..	Rép. Dém. pop. lao
Lesotho	47	72	23.4	9.4	48.8	23.7	1.2	7.3	7.3	Lesotho
Liberia	13	..	5.2	-16.7 p	..	..	..	..	..	Libéria
Madagascar	11	12	0.4	2.5	4.8	28.0	-56.6	45.4	9.9	Madagascar
Malawi	19	18	4.2	-2.2	14.2	6.5	39.0	-17.9	-17.7	Malawi
Maldives	44	64 k	..	18.0 m	24.8	13.9	49.6	..	..	Maldives
Mali	19	22	3.3	6.9	5.9	13.5	-0.2	11.1	2.0	Mali
Mauritania	30	21	8.3	-2.7	-30.8	5.8	-7.7	27.7	15.3	Mauritanie
Mozambique	20	39	-7.1	3.3	7.3	8.5	2.5	-9.6	10.0	Mozambique
Myanmar	15	14	8.0	-1.0	-0.7	29.1	15.9	2.5	-5.5	Myanmar
Nepal	20	21	..	..	..	..	..	..	..	Népal
Niger	17	7	7.6	-7.7	-16.7	5.3	-28.8	-47.7	35.4	Niger
Rwanda	15	14 c	10.4	2.5	-5.7	-18.9	-27.4	21.2	-8.2	Rwanda
Samoa	30	39 c	-32.2	-4.6 q	..	..	..	..	..	Samoa
Sao Tome and Principe	31	56	15.8	13.9	-11.4	-31.2	288.9	19.0	31.8	Sao Tomé-et-Principe
Sierra Leone	13	12	-1.2	-1.9	62.7	-6.6	-11.0	39.8	-20.8	Sierra Leone
Solomon Islands	31	29 o	..	..	..	..	..	..	..	Iles Salomon
Somalia	29	16 k	18.1	-2.6 e	21.7	..	..	..	..	Somalie
Sudan	14	13 o	8.2	-0.7 h	1.6	-4.8	-10.0	16.9	..	Soudan
Togo	26	21	11.9	-0.4	0.0	12.9	-10.3	-11.9	-54.3	Togo
Tuvalu	54 f	35 k	..	..	..	..	..	..	..	Tuvalu
Uganda	9	15	..	8.6 i	1.8	5.0	-1.0	-4.1	22.9	Ouganda
United Rep.of Tanzania	21	42 c	12.8	5.6 h	-2.9	-5.9	35.5	-11.2	..	Rép.-Unie de Tanzanie
Vanuatu	31 r	44 k	..	6.1 s	19.2	13.4	..	..	..	Vanuatu
Yemen	18 t	20	..	..	..	-13.9	-21.8	..	..	Yémen
Zaire	11	6 r	4.2	-14.9 m	10.4	-97.2	..	..	..	Zaïre
Zambia	16	14	-10.9	0.7	-6.9	48.8	53.3	-21.4	15.3	Zambie
All LDCs	**16**	**16**	**3.6**	**1.1**	**8.1**	**-2.6**	**4.9**	**0.3**	**2.4**	**Ensemble des PMA**

Source: UNCTAD secretariat calculations based on data from the United Nations Statistical Office, the World Bank, the Asian Development Bank and other international and national sources.

a Gross fixed capital formation *plus* change in stocks.
b Real investment.   *c* Average 1990-1992.
d 1980-1988.   *e* 1980-1989.
f Average 1988-1989.   *g* 1987-1992.
h 1980-1992.
i Average 1982-1989.   *j* 1983-1992.
k 1990.   *l* 1980-1990.
m 1980-1991.   *n* Average 1980-1989.
o Average 1990-1991.   *p* 1980-1986.
q 1980-1985.   *r* Average 1983-1989.
s 1983-1990.   *t* Average 1985-1989.

Source: Chiffres calculés par le secrétariat de la CNUCED d'après des données du Bureau de statistique des Nations Unies, de la Banque mondiale, de la Banque asiatique de développement et d'autres sources internationales et nationales.

a Formation brute de capital fixe *plus* variation des stocks.
b Investissements réels.   *c* Moyenne 1990-1992.
d 1980-1988.   *e* 1980-1989.
f Moyenne 1988-1989.   *g* 1987-1992.
h 1980-1992.
i Moyenne 1982-1989.   *j* 1983-1992.
k 1990.   *l* 1980-1990.
m 1980-1991.   *n* Moyenne 1980-1989.
o Moyenne 1990-1991.   *p* 1980-1986.
q 1980-1985.   *r* Moyenne 1983-1989.
s 1983-1990.   *t* Moyenne 1985-1989.

7. Export value and purchasing power of exports : annual average growth rates

Country	Total ($ million) Totales (millions de dollars)	As % of GDP En % du PIB	Per capita ($) Par habitant (dollars)	1970- 1980	1980- 1993	1988- 1989	1989- 1990	1990- 1991	1991- 1992	1992- 1993
Afghanistan	180	2	10	21.2	-12.2	-40.3	-0.4	-40.4	42.9	-10.0
Bangladesh	2420	10	21	6.3	10.8	5.4	18.2	1.9	27.5	11.2
Benin	50	2	10	1.8	5.0	36.6	3.1	10.0	4.5	-56.5
Bhutan	..	..	..	..	..	..	..	..	..	..
Botswana	2160	54	1542	34.4	16.4	26.8	-3.2	40.7	-7.6	-7.6
Burkina Faso	125	4	13	18.4	6.3	-33.1	58.9	-30.5	38.1	-13.8
Burundi	65	7	11	17.2	-0.2	-41.4	-3.8	21.3	-17.6	-13.3
Cambodia	4	..	..	-7.2	-1.9	0.0	0.0	0.0	0.0	0.0
Cape Verde	4	1	11	4.0	3.8	133.3	-14.3	0.0	-16.7	-20.0
Central African Rep.	110	9	35	13.4	0.5	103.0	-62.7	86.0	33.3	-11.3
Chad	150	13	25	14.0	8.2	-2.5	25.2	0.0	-9.3	-14.8
Comoros	22	9	36	13.0	2.7	-14.3	0.0	33.3	0.0	-8.3
Djibouti	18	4	32	-2.6	4.8	8.7	0.0	-32.0	17.6	-10.0
Equatorial Guinea	32	20	84	-4.4	8.5	-16.3	-9.8	-2.7	-2.8	-8.6
Ethiopia	160	5	3	13.3	-6.4	7.4	-35.0	-35.7	-10.6	-5.3
Gambia	72	19	69	11.9	4.5	-56.5	51.9	4.9	86.0	-10.0
Guinea	400	13	63	28.5	0.9	16.4	12.6	-37.4	4.8	-9.1
Guinea-Bissau	6	3	6	16.3	-1.5	-12.5	35.7	5.3	-70.0	0.0
Haiti	109	3	16	19.6	-3.9	-19.6	9.7	-34.8	3.9	1.9
Kiribati	5	14	64	13.1	-3.8	0.0	-20.0	-25.0	66.7	0.0
Lao People's Dem.Rep.	75	6	16	19.1	9.4	-32.1	18.2	1.5	21.2	-6.2
Lesotho	100	14	51	26.0	7.6	3.1	-9.1	11.7	62.7	-8.3
Liberia	310	23	109	10.8	-3.9	16.2	-28.3	3.0	2.9	-11.4
Madagascar	265	8	19	12.3	-1.6	15.0	-1.9	-1.0	-12.7	-0.7
Malawi	300	15	29	16.4	3.2	-6.0	56.6	13.2	-20.5	-20.2
Maldives	43	23	180	7.7	15.8	12.5	15.6	3.8	-25.9	7.5
Mali	300	11	30	21.1	7.2	8.8	24.7	4.7	-7.1	-8.8
Mauritania	455	47	211	1.2	6.3	23.4	7.3	-6.2	2.3	1.1
Mozambique	125	9	8	2.4	-4.3	1.9	20.0	28.6	-14.2	-10.1
Myanmar	540	1	12	14.3	-0.6	26.5	54.8	29.2	26.9	1.3
Nepal	330	10	16	9.8	10.7	-17.2	31.4	24.9	43.3	-11.8
Niger	250	11	29	33.8	-3.5	-15.6	16.0	10.2	-9.3	-11.7
Rwanda	60	4	8	21.1	-2.7	19.8	9.1	-29.5	-26.9	-11.8
Samoa	6	4	36	13.3	-7.0	-13.3	-30.8	-22.2	-14.3	0.0
Sao Tome and Principe	5	13	39	12.4	-8.0	-50.0	-20.0	25.0	0.0	0.0
Sierra Leone	110	15	26	6.4	-0.4	29.0	3.6	1.4	2.8	-26.2
Solomon Islands	90	37	254	24.3	1.7	-7.4	-6.7	20.0	-10.7	20.0
Somalia	50	4	6	15.0	-6.1	-3.5	-2.4	0.0	0.0	-37.5
Sudan	380	4	14	7.0	-1.9	32.0	-18.2	-1.8	-25.9	-5.0
Togo	290	23	75	21.1	2.6	1.2	9.4	-5.6	27.3	-9.9
Tuvalu	..	..	..	..	..	..	..	..	..	..
Uganda	160	4	8	4.6	-6.5	-8.8	-39.2	32.2	-28.9	11.9
Un. Rep. of Tanzania	220	8	8	7.5	-3.7	38.7	11.3	-13.3	21.4	-49.7
Vanuatu	28	15	174	14.3	-3.2	10.0	-13.6	5.3	20.0	16.7
Yemen	680	5	52	17.4	-0.8	16.6	-10.3	-4.4	0.0	4.6
Zaire	480	5	12	6.2	-3.6	12.7	-21.0	-10.2	-53.0	15.4
Zambia	1260	40	141	3.5	1.0	14.3	-33.3	-13.8	50.7	7.9
All LDCs	**13004**	**8**	**24**	**10.1**	**1.8**	**9.6**	**-3.3**	**1.9**	**2.5**	**-3.8**
All developing countries	**885161**	**30**	**295**	**25.9**	**4.4**	**13.4**	**13.5**	**4.6**	**6.8**	**6.6**

Source: UNCTAD secretariat estimates mainly based on UNCTAD *Handbook of International Trade and Development Statistics 1993*, and table 10.

7. Valeur et pouvoir d'achat des exportations : taux d'accroissement annuels moyens

Purchasing power of exports							
Pouvoir d'achat des exportations							
Annual average growth rates (%)							
Taux d'accroissement annuels moyens (%)							
1970- 1980	*1980- 1993*	*1988- 1989*	*1989- 1990*	*1990- 1991*	*1991- 1992*	*1992- 1993*	*Pays*
7.9	-14.1	-42.4	-7.0	-40.1	39.9	-8.4	Afghanistan
-6.1	8.5	1.8	11.1	3.3	25.4	14.2	Bangladesh
-10.2	2.7	32.8	-4.0	11.3	2.4	-55.7	Bénin
..	..	..	..	..	..	..	Bhoutan
18.5	14.1	22.6	-10.1	42.6	-9.7	-5.4	Botswana
5.2	4.1	-35.4	47.9	-29.6	35.4	-12.1	Burkina Faso
3.4	-2.1	-43.3	-10.7	23.0	-19.5	-11.3	Burundi
-18.2	-3.9	-3.3	-7.1	1.4	-2.3	2.3	Cambodge
-8.3	1.8	125.7	-20.4	1.4	-18.6	-18.1	Cap-Vert
1.0	-2.2	97.7	-64.8	84.8	30.4	-10.1	Rép. centrafricaine
1.4	5.8	-5.8	16.3	0.5	-11.3	-13.2	Tchad
-0.3	0.7	-17.1	-7.1	35.2	-2.3	-6.2	Comores
-14.1	2.7	5.1	-7.1	-31.1	14.9	-7.9	Djibouti
-15.7	6.3	-19.1	-16.2	-1.4	-5.0	-6.4	Guinée équatoriale
-0.9	-7.8	3.6	-40.6	-33.9	-12.5	-2.6	Ethiopie
-1.4	2.3	-57.9	42.8	6.0	82.8	-8.5	Gambie
13.3	-1.1	12.6	4.6	-36.6	2.3	-7.0	Guinée
2.5	-3.5	-15.4	26.1	6.7	-70.7	2.3	Guinée-Bissau
5.5	-5.8	-22.2	1.9	-33.9	1.5	4.3	Haïti
-0.3	-5.7	-3.3	-25.7	-24.0	62.8	2.3	Kiribati
5.1	7.3	-34.3	9.8	2.9	18.4	-4.1	Rép. dém. pop. lao
11.1	5.5	-0.2	-15.6	13.2	58.9	-6.1	Lesotho
-2.9	-4.8	10.7	-34.2	6.6	1.3	-8.9	Libéria
-2.0	-3.7	12.1	-9.5	0.6	-14.8	1.7	Madagascar
3.2	0.9	-8.5	44.4	14.5	-22.4	-18.5	Malawi
-5.1	13.5	8.8	7.3	5.3	-27.6	10.0	Maldives
7.2	5.0	5.0	15.5	5.9	-9.0	-7.1	Mali
-10.3	4.2	18.9	0.9	-4.8	0.7	3.0	Mauritanie
-10.4	-5.9	-1.5	10.0	31.8	-16.0	-7.7	Mozambique
0.8	-3.3	24.9	44.2	29.5	23.6	3.2	Myanmar
-3.1	8.6	-19.9	22.1	26.6	40.0	-9.7	Népal
18.7	-5.0	-19.4	6.4	13.2	-11.0	-9.3	Niger
7.5	-4.9	15.9	2.3	-29.0	-28.3	-9.7	Rwanda
0.0	-8.8	-16.2	-35.7	-21.2	-16.3	2.3	Samoa
-0.9	-9.8	-51.6	-25.7	26.7	-2.3	2.3	Sao Tomé-et-Principe
-6.2	-2.1	24.5	-3.5	3.2	0.9	-24.7	Sierra Leone
9.6	-0.3	-10.4	-13.3	21.6	-12.8	22.8	Iles Salomon
1.4	-8.3	-6.5	-7.3	0.5	-1.7	-36.3	Somalie
-5.9	-3.7	27.2	-23.5	-0.2	-27.2	-3.2	Soudan
6.7	1.2	-2.8	0.6	-3.1	24.9	-7.7	Togo
..	..	..	..	..	..	..	Tuvalu
-7.5	-9.2	-10.1	-43.3	31.4	-30.8	13.5	Ouganda
-5.5	-5.3	33.8	2.2	-11.0	19.0	-48.3	Rép.-Unie de Tanzanie
0.8	-5.1	6.4	-19.8	6.7	17.2	19.4	Vanuatu
3.5	-2.8	12.8	-16.7	-3.1	-2.3	7.1	Yémen
-6.7	-5.8	9.7	-25.9	-9.5	-54.0	17.4	Zaïre
-8.3	-0.9	11.0	-38.5	-12.7	47.2	10.2	Zambie
-2.9	**-0.2**	**6.0**	**-10.2**	**3.2**	**0.1**	**-1.5**	**Ensemble des PMA**
							Ensemble des pays
10.1	**2.6**	**9.7**	**4.9**	**6.8**	**4.3**	**10.0**	**en développement**

Source: Estimations du secrétariat de la CNUCED principalement d'après le
Manuel de statistiques du commerce international et du développement 1993,
de la CNUCED et le tableau 10.

8. Import value and volume : annual average growth rates

| Country | Imports in 1993 / Importations en 1993 | | | Import value / Valeur des importations | | | | | | |
| | Total ($ million) / Totales (millions de dollars) | As % of GDP / En % du PIB | Per capita ($) / Par habitant (dollars) | Annual average growth rates (%) / Taux d'accroisement annuels moyens (%) | | | | | | |
				1970-1980	1980-1993	1988-1989	1989-1990	1990-1991	1991-1992	1992-1993
Afghanistan	740	8	42	19.4	-1.6	-8.7	13.9	-56.1	70.3	5.7
Bangladesh	4000	16	35	16.4	7.2	21.3	-3.1	0.4	19.6	2.9
Benin	630	29	124	19.5	-0.4	-36.5	35.3	12.5	14.3	75.0
Bhutan	..	..	..	..	..	..	..	..	..	..
Botswana	1800	45	1285	28.2	11.6	25.4	31.1	36.9	-9.6	-26.0
Burkina Faso	655	23	67	21.8	5.9	-34.2	67.7	4.8	13.4	2.0
Burundi	220	22	37	22.4	2.5	-8.7	25.5	8.5	-10.2	-4.3
Cambodia	30	2	3	-6.1	-9.7	0.0	0.0	0.0	0.0	0.0
Cape Verde	177	54	478	11.8	8.1	5.7	21.4	8.1	22.4	-1.7
Central African Rep.	170	14	54	8.9	4.9	6.4	-32.0	42.2	13.8	3.0
Chad	320	27	53	7.5	10.3	-6.7	10.2	14.7	1.0	6.7
Comoros	56	23	92	11.8	4.2	-18.2	25.0	20.0	1.9	1.8
Djibouti	220	47	395	9.4	2.8	-2.5	9.7	-0.5	0.5	2.3
Equatorial Guinea	70	45	185	-6.8	9.0	-9.8	9.1	16.7	0.0	0.0
Ethiopia	715	20	14	15.7	-0.8	-12.2	12.9	-56.1	49.8	1.1
Gambia	247	65	237	25.5	6.4	19.3	20.5	14.4	12.6	-1.2
Guinea	620	20	98	18.7	7.5	4.0	12.2	-18.5	5.3	3.3
Guinea-Bissau	100	42	97	5.8	4.5	-1.4	-1.4	-1.5	25.4	19.0
Haiti	410	13	59	22.3	-1.2	-15.4	1.4	26.8	7.0	2.5
Kiribati	15	43	193	14.4	3.2	4.5	17.4	-3.7	-38.5	-6.3
Lao People's Dem.Rep.	260	20	56	2.4	7.5	4.9	15.3	7.1	16.2	6.6
Lesotho	690	93	355	30.8	4.3	6.1	13.5	19.3	16.2	-26.0
Liberia	360	26	127	15.6	-5.0	18.7	-31.9	4.5	4.3	50.0
Madagascar	540	16	39	13.7	-0.2	-6.0	67.0	-23.8	3.9	19.5
Malawi	650	32	62	17.1	6.5	24.2	12.8	23.0	-0.9	-7.0
Maldives	180	98	755	25.3	15.7	16.7	22.9	17.1	25.2	-4.8
Mali	580	22	57	23.2	3.2	-2.5	-13.6	3.5	6.7	21.6
Mauritania	700	73	324	18.2	8.4	-7.5	187.8	-6.1	11.7	4.5
Mozambique	890	63	59	6.1	1.8	13.0	8.7	2.4	-11.2	11.5
Myanmar	630	2	14	8.8	3.5	-21.7	36.6	136.0	6.0	-3.5
Nepal	800	25	38	18.6	7.1	-14.6	18.1	10.8	4.2	1.0
Niger	420	19	49	27.5	-2.0	-6.2	7.2	-8.7	-6.8	26.9
Rwanda	275	17	36	26.4	1.3	-9.8	-12.6	5.2	-5.9	-4.5
Samoa	105	70	629	18.5	5.9	1.3	-2.6	28.0	17.7	-7.1
Sao Tome and Principe	18	45	142	10.5	1.4	28.6	-27.8	38.5	0.0	0.0
Sierra Leone	145	20	34	12.0	-5.6	15.9	-9.9	-1.2	-19.1	10.7
Solomon Islands	95	39	268	19.3	4.0	-2.6	-19.3	0.0	8.7	-5.0
Somalia	170	14	19	21.0	-6.2	2.3	20.3	0.0	-6.3	13.3
Sudan	1030	11	39	19.2	-2.8	14.2	-33.9	62.5	-25.4	6.2
Togo	390	31	100	26.9	1.3	-3.1	23.1	-23.6	-5.9	-6.7
Tuvalu	..	..	..	..	..	..	..	..	..	..
Uganda	510	13	26	2.9	1.6	-28.3	-24.9	-32.8	161.9	-1.2
Un. Rep. of Tanzania	1050	37	37	14.2	0.5	24.0	2.3	14.6	28.4	-30.1
Vanuatu	78	42	484	17.1	2.5	-1.4	37.1	-13.5	-2.4	-3.7
Yemen	3200	25	242	32.5	-1.5	3.1	2.1	-8.3	9.1	33.3
Zaire	550	6	13	0.9	-0.1	10.1	5.7	-2.8	-53.1	34.5
Zambia	1000	31	112	5.6	-0.6	-7.2	59.6	-35.6	8.6	14.9
All LDCs	26511	16	49	15.0	2.3	3.2	9.9	0.5	6.1	2.9
All developing countries	947016	32	316	23.8	5.8	11.3	14.8	10.7	12.4	5.0

Source: UNCTAD secretariat estimates mainly based on UNCTAD *Handbook of International Trade and Development Statistics 1993*, and table 10.

Les Pays les moins avancés. Rapport 1995 - Annexe

A-15

8. Valeur et volume des importations : taux d'accroissement annuels moyens

Import volume *Volume des importations*							
Annual average growth rates (%) *Taux d'accroissement annuels moyens (%)*							
1970- *1980*	*1980-* *1993*	*1988-* *1989*	*1989-* *1990*	*1990-* *1991*	*1991-* *1992*	*1992-* *1993*	*Pays*
6.3	-3.7	-12.0	6.4	-55.9	66.8	7.6	Afghanistan
2.8	5.0	17.1	-8.9	1.8	17.5	5.6	Bangladesh
5.4	-2.5	-38.3	26.0	13.8	11.9	78.2	Bénin
..	..	..	..	..	..	..	Bhoutan
13.1	9.4	21.3	21.8	38.7	-11.7	-24.3	Botswana
8.2	3.7	-36.4	56.1	6.1	11.2	4.0	Burkina Faso
8.0	0.5	-11.7	16.6	10.0	-12.2	-2.1	Burundi
-17.2	-11.5	-3.3	-7.1	1.4	-2.3	2.3	Cambodge
-1.4	5.9	2.2	12.8	9.6	19.6	0.6	Cap-Vert
-3.0	2.1	3.6	-35.9	41.3	11.3	4.4	Rép. centrafricaine
-4.4	7.8	-9.9	2.4	15.3	-1.2	8.6	Tchad
-1.4	2.1	-20.9	16.1	21.6	-0.5	4.2	Comores
-3.5	0.8	-5.7	1.9	0.9	-1.9	4.7	Djibouti
-17.8	6.9	-12.8	1.3	18.3	-2.3	2.3	Guinée équatoriale
1.2	-2.2	-15.3	3.2	-54.9	46.7	4.1	Ethiopie
10.5	4.1	15.4	13.3	15.6	10.6	0.4	Gambie
4.7	5.4	0.6	4.2	-17.3	2.8	5.7	Guinée
-6.7	2.5	-4.7	-8.5	-0.1	22.5	21.8	Guinée-Bissau
7.9	-3.1	-18.2	-5.8	28.5	4.5	4.9	Haïti
0.9	1.2	1.1	9.1	-2.4	-39.9	-4.1	Kiribati
-9.7	5.4	1.5	7.1	8.6	13.5	9.0	Rép. dém. pop. lao
15.3	2.2	2.6	5.4	20.9	13.5	-24.3	Lesotho
1.3	-5.9	13.2	-37.6	8.2	2.7	54.4	Libéria
-0.8	-2.3	-8.4	54.1	-22.6	1.5	22.4	Madagascar
3.8	4.1	20.9	4.0	24.5	-3.2	-5.0	Malawi
10.5	13.5	12.9	14.1	18.6	22.3	-2.5	Maldives
9.0	1.1	-6.0	-20.0	4.6	4.5	23.8	Mali
4.7	6.2	-10.9	170.6	-4.7	9.9	6.4	Mauritanie
-7.2	0.1	9.2	-0.4	4.9	-13.1	14.5	Mozambique
-4.1	0.6	-22.7	27.3	136.4	3.2	-1.7	Myanmar
4.6	5.0	-17.4	9.7	12.3	1.8	3.4	Népal
13.2	-3.5	-10.5	-1.7	-6.3	-8.5	30.3	Niger
12.2	-1.0	-12.7	-18.0	6.0	-7.7	-2.3	Rwanda
4.5	3.8	-2.0	-9.5	29.7	15.0	-4.9	Samoa
-2.5	-0.6	24.4	-32.9	40.3	-2.3	2.3	Sao Tomé-et-Principe
-1.3	-7.2	11.9	-16.1	0.5	-20.6	12.9	Sierra Leone
5.2	1.9	-5.7	-25.0	1.4	6.2	-2.8	Iles Salomon
6.7	-8.5	-0.8	14.3	0.5	-7.8	15.5	Somalie
4.9	-4.6	10.0	-38.2	65.2	-26.6	8.2	Soudan
11.8	-0.1	-6.9	13.2	-21.5	-7.6	-4.3	Togo
..	..	..	..	..	..	..	Tuvalu
-9.1	-1.4	-29.4	-29.9	-33.2	154.8	0.2	Ouganda
0.4	-1.1	19.7	-6.0	17.5	25.8	-28.3	Rép.-Unie de Tanzanie
3.2	0.5	-4.6	27.4	-12.4	-4.7	-1.5	Vanuatu
16.8	-3.4	-0.3	-5.1	-7.1	6.6	36.5	Yémen
-11.3	-2.4	7.1	-1.0	-2.0	-54.0	36.8	Zaïre
-6.4	-2.6	-9.8	47.1	-34.7	6.1	17.4	Zambie
1.4	**0.3**	**-0.2**	**2.1**	**1.8**	**3.6**	**5.3**	**Ensemble des PMA**
8.3	**3.9**	**7.7**	**6.1**	**13.0**	**9.9**	**8.3**	**Ensemble des pays en développement**

Source: Estimations du secrétariat de la CNUCED principalement d'après le
Manuel de statistiques du commerce international et du développement 1993,
de la CNUCED et le tableau 10.

9. Leading exports of all LDCs in 1990-1991

9. Principales exportations de l'ensemble des PMA en 1990-1991

SITC CTCI	Item	Value [a] ($ million) Valeur [a] Millions (dollars)	In per cent of total: En pourcentage du total:			Produit
			All LDCs Tous les PMA	All developing countries Tous les pays en développement	World Monde	Ensemble des produits
	All commodities	**10475.3**	**100.00**	**1.52**	**0.31**	**Ensemble des produits**
682	Copper	1115.7	10.65	15.48	4.98	Cuivre
263	Cotton	867.5	8.28	22.74	9.61	Coton
071	Coffee and coffee substitutes	663.9	6.34	9.80	7.72	Café et succédanés du café
287	Ores and concentrates of base metals, n.e.s.	577.5	5.51	8.30	3.84	Minerais de métaux communs, même enrichis, n.d.a.
667	Pearls, precious and semi-precious stones	446.6	4.26	8.22	1.69	Perles fines, pierres gemmes et similaires
333	Petroleum oils, crude and crude oils obtained from bituminous minerals	434.1	4.14	0.30	0.22	Huiles brutes de pétrole ou de minéraux bitumineux
036	Crustaceans and molluscs, fresh, chilled, frozen, salted, in brine or dried	401.4	3.83	6.12	3.37	Crustacés, mollusques et coquillages, frais, réfrigérés, congelés ou séchés
842	Men's outer garments, of textile fabrics	364.2	3.48	4.72	2.02	Vêtements de dessus pour hommes en matières textiles
121	Tobacco, unmanufactured	352.1	3.36	12.89	6.43	Tabacs bruts
281	Iron ore and concentrates	321.3	3.07	7.96	3.84	Minerai de fer et concentrés
247	Other wood in the rough or roughly squared	318.8	3.04	10.63	3.69	Autres bois bruts ou simplement équarris
524	Radio-active and associated materials	249.0	2.38	56.61	4.17	Matières radioactives et produits associés
001	Live animals chiefly for food	243.1	2.32	16.20	2.75	Animaux vivants destinés à l'alimentation humaine
057	Fruits and nuts (excluding oil nuts), fresh or dried	171.4	1.64	2.35	0.86	Fruits (sauf fruits oléagineux), frais ou secs
211	Hides and skins, (except fur skins), raw	168.7	1.61	35.55	3.32	Cuirs et peaux, (exclu pelleteries), bruts
292	Crude vegetable materials, n.e.s.	157.1	1.50	7.59	1.38	Matières brutes d'origine végétale, n.d.a.

Source: UNCTAD secretariat computations based on data from the United Nations Statistical Office.

a Annual average.

Source: Calculs du secrétariat de la CNUCED basés sur des données du Bureau de statistique des Nations Unies.

a Moyenne annuelle.

Les Pays les moins avancés. Rapport 1995 - Annexe

A-17

10. Unit value indices of imports
1980 = 100

10. Indices de valeur unitaire des importations
1980 = 100

Country	1981	1982	1983	1984	1985	1986	1987	1988	1989	1990	1991	1992	1993	Pays
Afghanistan	93	90	87	87	88	92	98	103	107	115	114	117	115	Afghanistan
Bangladesh	94	90	89	88	88	91	98	105	109	116	114	116	113	Bangladesh
Benin	95	92	89	87	87	92	99	105	108	116	115	117	115	Bénin
Burkina Faso	95	92	88	88	88	92	98	104	107	115	114	116	114	Burkina Faso
Central African Rep.	94	91	89	88	89	97	103	111	114	121	121	124	122	Rép. centrafricaine
Chad	95	92	89	89	90	94	101	106	109	118	117	120	118	Tchad
Ethiopia	99	96	92	90	90	89	97	100	104	114	111	113	110	Ethiopie
Gambia	93	89	86	85	85	90	97	103	107	113	112	114	112	Gambie
Liberia	98	94	90	88	87	84	91	94	99	108	104	106	103	Libéria
Madagascar	97	95	92	91	91	94	102	108	110	120	118	121	118	Madagascar
Malawi	96	94	91	90	91	95	102	107	110	119	118	121	118	Malawi
Mali	95	92	89	88	89	92	99	104	107	116	115	117	115	Mali
Mauritania	94	90	87	85	85	90	96	103	107	113	112	113	111	Mauritanie
Mozambique	98	96	92	90	90	90	98	102	105	115	112	114	111	Mozambique
Myanmar	96	94	92	90	91	99	107	114	116	124	124	127	125	Myanmar
Niger	97	94	90	89	89	89	96	99	104	113	110	112	109	Niger
Rwanda	94	91	89	89	89	93	100	107	110	118	117	119	116	Rwanda
Sierra Leone	95	91	88	86	85	88	95	100	104	112	110	112	110	Sierra Leone
Somalia	93	88	87	86	86	93	99	107	111	116	116	118	116	Somalie
Sudan	95	91	88	86	86	89	96	102	105	113	111	113	111	Soudan
Togo	97	93	89	88	87	87	94	98	102	111	108	110	108	Togo
Uganda	95	93	91	90	91	100	107	114	116	124	125	129	127	Ouganda
United Rep. of Tanzania	98	95	91	90	89	90	98	102	106	115	112	114	111	Rép.-Unie de Tanzanie
Zaire	94	91	89	87	87	93	100	107	110	117	116	119	116	Zaïre
Zambia	96	94	90	89	90	92	99	104	107	116	114	117	115	Zambie
All LDCs [a]	96	92	89	88	88	91	98	104	107	115	114	116	114	Ensemble des PMA [a]
All developing countries	96	93	90	89	89	90	97	102	106	114	112	115	111	Ensemble des pays en développement

Source: UNCTAD secretariat estimates.

a This index is derived from the indices for the individual countries shown above. It has been applied to obtain the data on import volume, export purchasing power and aid in constant prices shown in other tables of this annex, for those countries where a unit value index was not available.

Source: Estimations du secrétariat de la CNUCED.

a Cet indice est basé sur les indices pour les pays individuels qui figurent ci-dessus. On l'a utilisé pour obtenir les données concernant le volume des importations, le pouvoir d'achat des exportations, et l'aide en prix constants figurant dans d'autres tableaux de cet annexe dans les cas des PMA pour lesquels un indice de valeur unitaire n'était pas disponible.

11. Commodity structure of exports of LDCs by main category, 1991 (or latest year available)

11. Composition des exportations des PMA, par principales catégories de produits 1991 (ou année la plus récente disponible)

Main category of exports (in %)
Principales catégories de produits exportés (en %)

Country / Pays	All food items / Produits alimentaires (0+1+22+4)	Agricultural raw materials / Matières premières d'origine agricole (2-22-27-28)	Fuels / Combustibles (3)	Ores and metals / Minerais et métaux (27+28+68)	Manufactured goods / Produits manufacturés (5+6+7+8-68)	Unallocated / Non distribués (9)
Afghanistan	13.8	14.7	47.6	0.1	23.7	0.1
Bangladesh	13.5	9.0	0.8	-	76.5	0.2
Benin / Bénin	..	75.6	19.5	..	..	4.9
Bhutan / Bhoutan	13.3	9.8	28.4	18.5	21.3	8.6
Botswana	3.2	0.6	-	8.2	82.1	5.9
Burkina Faso	27.5	42.0	-	0.1	11.0	19.4
Burundi	90.2	2.6	-	0.1	2.5	4.5
Cambodia / Cambodge	35.4	14.9	-	-	49.7	-
Cape Verde / Cap-Vert	80.6	1.4	-	-	18.1	-
Central African Rep. / Rép. centrafricaine	17.3	27.6	-	5.2	48.2	1.7
Chad / Tchad	44.6	45.9	-	0.3	9.0	0.2
Comoros / Comores	63.9	-	-	-	30.1	6.0
Djibouti	..	..	..	..	..	..
Equatorial Guinea / Guinée équatoriale	31.9	60.1	..	-	4.2	3.8
Ethiopia / Ethiopie	59.9	13.9	1.9	-	24.0	0.3
Gambia / Gambie	62.3	0.5	-	-	37.2	-
Guinea / Guinée	5.2	1.7	-	78.7	14.1	0.3
Guinea-Bissau / Guinée-Bissau	92.3	7.0	..	..	-	0.7
Haiti / Haïti	13.2	1.3	-	0.2	83.2	2.2
Kiribati	79.9	19.8	-	-	-	0.3
Lao People's Dem.Rep. / Rép. dém. pop. lao	3.6	7.7	24.5	2.0	61.9	0.3
Lesotho	11.6	3.7	-	-	84.6	0.1
Liberia / Libéria	2.6	28.0	2.6	34.6	31.7	0.5
Madagascar	66.8	5.5	0.5	7.1	19.7	0.4
Malawi	90.5	3.1	-	-	5.0	1.4
Maldives	76.2	-	-	-	23.8	-
Mali	17.8	68.0	-	1.0	7.7	5.4
Mauritania / Mauritanie	47.2	-	2.0	49.5	0.2	1.1
Mozambique	63.0	2.5	1.2	13.0	19.1	1.2
Myanmar	53.4	28.9	1.5	5.1	10.9	0.2
Nepal / Népal	0.4	15.7	-	-	83.8	-
Niger	18.3	2.2	-	67.9	0.1	11.5
Rwanda	84.4	4.2	..	-	-	11.4
Samoa	87.3	-	-	-	-	12.7
Sao Tome and Principe / Sao Tomé-et-Principe	99.8	-	-	-	-	0.2
Sierra Leone	24.7	3.4	3.4	41.1	26.7	0.7
Solomon Islands / Iles Salomon	50.5	43.8	-	-	-	5.7
Somalia / Somalie	90.4	6.8	0.2	1.1	1.1	0.4
Sudan / Soudan	41.7	56.3	-	-	1.4	0.5
Togo	24.1	22.9	-	43.7	7.8	1.6
Tuvalu	..	23.4	-	-	76.6	-
Uganda / Ouganda	90.4	9.1	-	-	0.5	-
United Rep.of Tanzania / Rép.-Unie de Tanzanie	36.6	17.5	2.0	11.5	19.4	13.0
Vanuatu	79.7	8.6	3.0	-	3.0	5.5
Yemen / Yémen	6.6	3.2	88.8	0.4	0.6	0.4
Zaire / Zaïre	8.8	4.4	12.7	55.9	16.3	1.7
Zambia / Zambie	3.2	0.9	-	87.2	8.7	-
All LDCs / Ensemble des PMA	**24.9**	**12.9**	**7.7**	**18.4**	**33.4**	**2.7**
All developing countries / Ensemble des pays en développement	**11.2**	**2.9**	**24.8**	**3.8**	**56.0**	**1.3**

SITC / CTCI

Source: UNCTAD, *Handbook of International Trade and Development Statistics 1993*, and other international and national sources.

Source: CNUCED, *Manuel de statistiques du commerce international et du développement 1993*, et autres sources internationales et nationales.

12. Commodity structure of imports of LDCs by main category, 1991 (or latest year available)

12. Composition des importations des PMA, par principales catégories de produits 1991 (ou année la plus récente disponible)

	Main category of imports (in %) Principales catégories de produits importés (en %)						Selected commodity groups (in %) Quelques groupes de produits (en %)			
Country	All food items Produits alimentaires	Agricultural raw materials Matières premières d'origine agricole	Fuels Combustibles	Ores and metals Minerais et métaux	Manufactured goods Produits manufacturés	Un-allocated Non distribués	Cereals Céréales	Crude and manufactured fertilizers Engrais bruts et manufacturés	Transport equipment Matériel de transport	Pays
SITC	0+1+22+4	2-22-27-28	3	27+28+68	5+6+7+8-68	9	04	271+56	73	CTCI
Afghanistan	13.3 a	0.1 b	2.7	..	75.1 c	8.8	16.5	..	46.2 d	Afghanistan
Bangladesh	29.9	3.3	13.7	2.5	50.2	0.4	10.3	1.9	4.8	Bangladesh
Benin	27.3 a	3.7 b	15.3	..	52.4 c	1.3	..	..	5.8	Bénin
Bhutan	22.0	0.4	11.8	0.8	65.0	-	8.4	0.6	14.4	Bhoutan
Botswana	13.4	0.6	6.3	1.1	74.8	3.7	2.6	0.3	15.9	Botswana
Burkina Faso	21.6	1.5	11.2	1.1	64.5	0.1	7.8	3.0	10.6	Burkina Faso
Burundi	8.8	1.6	11.3	0.9	64.9	12.5	5.1	2.0	9.7	Burundi
Cambodia	..	..	..	..	..	..	..	..	..	Cambodge
Cape Verde	27.9 a	2.9 b	7.5	0.2	61.5	..	5.4	..	19.9	Cap-Vert
Central African Rep.	19.0 a	1.1 b	6.7	1.9	71.2	0.1	5.1	..	15.3	Rép. centrafricaine
Chad	(4.9)	..	10.4	..	(84.7)	-	(14.1)	..	..	Tchad
Comoros	28.6 a	23.8 b	9.0	..	38.5 c	3.1	8.1	..	6.7	Comores
Djibouti	28.0 a	10.6 b	9.1	0.4	48.8	2.5	2.3	-	..	Djibouti
Equatorial Guinea	12.7	0.8	7.7	4.1	72.2	-	2.3	-	46.3	Guinée équatoriale
Ethiopia	5.6	0.9	10.6	0.5	82.4	-	3.0	5.0	28.0	Ethiopie
Gambia	37.1 a	0.9 b	10.7	..	50.1 c	1.2	3.0	..	14.7 d	Gambie
Guinea	12.8	0.7	29.2	2.9	53.9	0.5	5.3	0.3	7.8	Guinée
Guinea-Bissau	(44.1)	..	12.2	..	36.5 d	7.2	..	..	27.8	Guinée-Bissau
Haiti	31.5 a	2.3 b	14.6	..	50.6 c	1.0	..	..	17.7 d	Haïti
Kiribati	37.1	1.4	10.9	0.5	49.5	0.6	12.5	..	8.1	Kiribati
Lao People's Dem.Rep.	(20.8)	(0.1)	(18.9)	(3.6)	(53.5)	(3.1)	(16.2)	(3.3)	(14.1)	Rép. dém. pop. lao
Lesotho	25.0 a	0.8 b	8.3	..	63.9 c	2.0	6.1	..	9.4	Lesotho
Liberia	19.2 a	0.6 b	20.3	..	59.1	0.8	10.3	..	30.2 d	Libéria
Madagascar	11.3	1.2	12.2	0.7	74.5	..	4.9	0.8	16.1	Madagascar
Malawi	10.7	0.9	10.8	1.6	75.2	0.8	6.7	10.2	9.9	Malawi
Maldives	24.5 a	1.3 b	12.1	2.6	59.5	..	4.5	(0.1)	6.0	Maldives
Mali	(16.0)	..	(12.9)	..	(60.5)	(10.5)	6.7	..	32.9 d	Mali
Mauritania	(36.3)	..	13.9	-	(49.8)	-	..	..	9.7	Mauritanie
Mozambique	26.7 a	18.1 b	10.9	..	44.3 c	-	..	..	32.5 d	Mozambique
Myanmar	1.2 a	0.3 b	0.9	..	97.0 c	0.5	..	..	63.4 d	Myanmar
Nepal	14.0 a	11.4 b	11.2	..	62.9 c	0.5	..	..	17.8 d	Népal
Niger	(32.2)	(4.0)	12.2	..	(38.9)	12.7	23.8	..	7.7	Niger
Rwanda	12.1	2.1	13.3	3.6	63.1	5.8	4.0	0.6	8.2	Rwanda
Samoa	26.1 a	0.7 b	16.9	..	54.1 c	2.2	..	..	23.5 d	Samoa
Sao Tome and Principe	(24.0)	..	16.0	..	(60.0)	-	..	..	..	Sao Tomé-et-Principe
Sierra Leone	38.2 a	2.2 b	10.4	..	49.2 c	3.8	..	..	18.9 d	Sierra Leone
Solomon Islands	21.1 a	14.7 b	7.6	..	52.8 c	(5.5)	..	..	15.8 d	Iles Salomon
Somalia	(28.3)	(6.3)	(26.2)	..	(33.7)	..	..	..	7.4	Somalie
Sudan	(11.8)	..	51.0	..	(37.2)	..	3.6	..	7.0	Soudan
Togo	23.1	1.3	9.8	1.3	63.7	0.8	4.8	1.1	10.2	Togo
Tuvalu	33.6 a	4.6 b	12.8	..	47.5 c	1.5	..	..	12.2 d	Tuvalu
Uganda	7.4 a	2.9 b	12.7	..	70.4 c	6.6	..	..	19.7	Ouganda
United Rep.of Tanzania	5.0 a	4.2 b	3.3	(1.6)	85.8	0.1	..	0.4	15.0	Rép.-Unie de Tanzanie
Vanuatu	21.8 a	0.8 b	9.0	..	58.7 c	9.7	..	..	27.2 d	Vanuatu
Yemen	31.6	2.5	16.3	2.0	47.6	..	11.7	(0.1)	5.7	Yémen
Zaire	20.7	1.8	7.6	2.1	67.3	0.7	7.3	0.7	8.8	Zaïre
Zambia	1.7 a	2.1 b	14.3	..	71.5 c	10.4	0.5	..	22.5	Zambie
All LDCs	19.6	2.8	13.5	1.1	61.0	2.0	6.2	0.9	14.4	**Ensemble des PMA**
All developing countries	8.7	2.7	9.0	2.6	74.3	2.7	..	..	..	**Ensemble des pays en développement**

Source: UNCTAD, *Handbook of International Trade and Development Statistics 1993*, and other international and national sources.
a SITC 0+1+4. *b* SITC 2. *c* SITC 5+6+7+8. *d* SITC 7.

Source: CNUCED, *Manuel de statistiques du commerce international et du développement 1993*, et autres sources internationales et nationales.
a CTCI 0+1+4. *b* CTCI 2. *c* CTCI 5+6+7+8. *d* CTCI 7.

13. Main markets for exports of LDCs : percentage shares in 1993 (or latest year available)

13. Principaux marchés aux exportations des PMA : parts en pourcentage en 1993 (ou année la plus récente disponible)

Country	Developed market economy countries — Pays développés à économie de marché					Countries in Eastern Europe — Pays d'Europe orientale	China — Chine	Developing countries — Pays en développement			Other and unallocated — Autres et non distribués	Pays
	Total	EEC / CEE	Japan / Japon	USA and Canada / Etats-Unis et Canada	Others / Autres			Total	OPEC / OPEP	Other / Autres		
Afghanistan	5.2	4.1	0.1	0.2	0.7	71.7	0.2	13.1	0.4	12.8	9.8	Afghanistan
Bangladesh	78.7	38.6	2.5	35.3	2.2	2.1	0.3	18.1	2.5	15.5	0.8	Bangladesh
Benin	53.8	31.0	0.7	10.3	11.7	-	-	46.2	2.8	43.4	-	Bénin
Bhutan	-	-	-	-	-	-	-	98.3	-	98.3	1.7	Bhoutan
Botswana	93.9	3.3	-	0.3	90.3	-	-	6.1	-	6.1	-	Botswana
Burkina Faso	13.8	12.6	0.9	0.4	0.4	69.9	-	16.1	0.2	15.9	0.2	Burkina Faso
Burundi	79.2	48.8	0.8	2.4	27.2	-	-	17.6	-	17.6	3.2	Burundi
Cambodia	29.4	19.9	5.7	3.8	-	-	-	66.6	0.6	66.0	3.9	Cambodge
Cape Verde	83.3	66.7	-	-	16.7	-	-	16.7	-	16.7	-	Cap-Vert
Central African Rep.	73.5	72.1	0.7	0.7	-	-	-	26.5	6.6	19.9	-	Rép. centrafricaine
Chad	78.4	74.3	4.1	-	-	-	-	20.3	-	20.3	1.4	Tchad
Comoros	40.7	24.1	-	16.7	-	-	-	59.3	-	59.3	-	Comores
Djibouti	4.5	4.5	-	-	-	-	-	95.5	-	95.5	-	Djibouti
Equatorial Guinea	100.0	66.7	22.2	11.1	-	-	-	-	-	-	-	Guinée équatoriale
Ethiopia	85.8	45.9	17.1	10.6	12.2	-	..	13.0	7.3	5.7	1.2	Ethiopie
Gambia	85.5	57.9	22.0	5.7	-	-	-	13.8	-	13.8	0.6	Gambie
Guinea	56.2	40.2	0.4	14.2	1.4	-	2.1	41.6	0.1	41.5	-	Guinée
Guinea-Bissau	58.8	52.9	2.9	-	2.9	0.1	2.9	38.2	-	38.2	-	Guinée-Bissau
Haiti	98.9	11.4	1.1	84.6	1.7	-	-	1.1	-	1.1	-	Haïti
Kiribati	82.8	19.8	49.4	13.0	0.6	-	..	17.2	-	17.2	-	Kiribati
Lao People's Dem.Rep.	49.3	31.6	8.1	6.6	2.9	0.7	2.2	47.8	..	47.8	-	Rép. dém. pop. lao
Lesotho	99.2	22.7	-	26.8	49.7	-	-	0.8	-	0.8	-	Lesotho
Liberia	77.1	71.1	-	0.5	5.5	-	0.8	22.1	1.5	20.6	-	Libéria
Madagascar	77.5	61.7	6.7	7.1	2.0	3.6	-	18.6	0.8	17.8	0.4	Madagascar
Malawi	82.3	35.1	13.7	17.4	16.0	2.9	-	14.9	-	14.9	-	Malawi
Maldives	63.6	25.8	1.5	34.8	1.5	-	1.5	34.8	-	34.8	-	Maldives
Mali	37.7	34.3	1.3	1.3	0.8	-	-	61.8	8.9	53.0	0.4	Mali
Mauritania	86.4	59.5	25.2	1.6	-	-	-	12.9	-	12.9	0.7	Mauritanie
Mozambique	58.5	40.1	8.3	6.5	3.7	1.8	2.8	33.6	3.7	30.0	3.2	Mozambique
Myanmar	22.4	6.6	7.8	6.1	1.8	-	18.1	59.0	2.2	56.9	0.5	Myanmar
Nepal	87.4	53.2	1.0	26.7	6.4	-	0.5	12.1	-	12.1	-	Népal
Niger	63.3	57.9	0.4	5.0	-	-	-	35.8	2.5	33.3	0.8	Niger
Rwanda	74.5	68.1	-	4.3	2.1	-	-	13.8	-	13.8	11.7	Rwanda
Samoa	83.3	-	-	16.7	66.7	-	-	16.7	-	16.7	-	Samoa
Sao Tome and Principe	87.5	75.0	-	12.5	-	-	-	12.5	-	12.5	-	Sao Tomé-et-Principe
Sierra Leone	76.2	51.5	0.4	22.5	1.8	-	-	1.8	-	1.8	22.0	Sierra Leone
Solomon Islands	80.9	13.0	63.4	2.3	2.3	-	-	19.1	-	19.1	-	Iles Salomon
Somalia	7.6	6.8	-	-	0.8	-	0.8	91.5	70.3	21.2	-	Somalie
Sudan	52.0	38.6	9.1	3.1	1.1	(0.6)	-	47.4	19.7	27.7	-	Soudan
Togo	38.1	18.8	-	13.7	5.6	3.0	0.5	58.4	7.1	51.3	-	Togo
Tuvalu	63.5	5.8	-	55.8	1.9	-	-	32.7	-	32.7	3.8	Tuvalu
Uganda	85.1	68.7	2.2	10.4	3.7	0.7	-	14.2	1.5	12.7	-	Ouganda
United Rep.of Tanzania	60.6	47.4	8.1	3.1	2.0	-	0.2	39.2	4.6	34.6	-	Rép.-Unie de Tanzanie
Vanuatu	87.0	34.8	26.1	17.4	8.7	-	-	13.0	-	13.0	-	Vanuatu
Yemen	70.9	43.2	14.3	6.1	7.2	0.1	6.4	21.0	1.7	19.3	1.6	Yémen
Zaire	92.2	60.7	5.3	22.8	3.5	-	0.3	7.5	0.2	7.3	-	Zaïre
Zambia	42.6	19.1	18.4	3.6	1.4	0.1	1.0	56.3	7.3	49.0	-	Zambie
All LDCs	**69.6**	**32.8**	**6.5**	**12.5**	**17.9**	**2.3**	**1.4**	**25.9**	**3.0**	**22.9**	**0.8**	**Ensemble des PMA**
All developing countries	**56.1**	**20.0**	**10.2**	**22.6**	**3.4**	**1.4**	**5.7**	**36.8**	**4.3**	**32.5**	**-**	**Ensemble des pays en développement**

Source: IMF, *Direction of Trade Statistics Yearbook 1994,* and other international and national sources.

Source: FMI, *Direction of Trade Statistics Yearbook 1994,* et autres sources internationales et nationales.

14. Main sources of imports of LDCs: percentage shares in 1993 (or latest year available)

14. Principales sources d'importation des PMA: parts en pourcentage en 1993 (ou année la plus récente disponible)

Country / Pays	Developed market economy countries / Pays développés à économie de marché					Countries in Eastern Europe / Pays d'Europe orientale	China / Chine	Developing countries / Pays en développement			Other and unallocated / Autres et non distribués
	Total	EEC / CEE	Japan / Japon	USA and Canada / Etats-Unis et Canada	Others / Autres	Autres	Chine	Total	OPEC / OPEP	Other / Autres	Autres et non distribués
Afghanistan	10.0	3.6	5.7	0.2	0.5	62.8	1.5	11.8	0.3	11.5	13.9
Bangladesh	35.5	12.2	12.5	5.4	5.4	1.4	5.1	41.8	5.3	36.5	16.2
Benin	50.9	42.5	2.6	3.0	2.8	-	6.8	41.6	0.6	41.0	0.7
Bhutan	33.8	27.3	6.0	0.1	0.3	-	-	61.5	-	61.5	4.7
Botswana	93.4	5.5	0.3	1.0	86.6	-	-	6.5	-	6.5	0.1
Burkina Faso	44.2	32.5	5.1	3.7	3.0	0.4	1.8	52.6	-	52.6	1.0
Burundi	55.5	42.3	6.8	1.4	5.0	0.5	2.7	37.7	10.9	26.8	3.6
Cambodia	41.5	5.5	11.7	10.8	13.5	-	4.6	28.7	-	28.7	25.2
Cape Verde	76.2	69.8	-	3.2	3.2	1.1	0.5	18.0	-	18.0	4.2
Central African Rep.	27.9	23.7	2.1	1.8	0.4	-	1.4	36.8	0.4	36.4	33.9
Chad	66.2	56.1	2.9	5.8	1.4	-	-	33.8	8.6	25.2	-
Comoros	82.2	78.9	2.2	-	1.1	1.1	-	16.7	1.1	15.6	-
Djibouti	53.9	43.0	6.1	3.6	1.2	-	2.9	39.8	10.9	28.9	3.4
Equatorial Guinea	57.7	51.8	1.2	4.7	-	-	1.2	38.8	-	38.8	2.4
Ethiopia	76.3	48.4	6.7	14.3	7.0	0.8	2.1	19.7	6.4	13.3	1.1
Gambia	49.1	41.2	3.7	2.9	1.3	1.1	20.2	26.8	0.3	26.5	2.9
Guinea	57.4	45.1	2.8	8.4	1.1	0.4	4.4	37.8	2.5	35.3	-
Guinea-Bissau	49.0	43.5	2.7	1.4	1.4	-	2.0	44.9	-	44.9	4.1
Haiti	73.2	15.8	4.2	51.6	1.7	-	0.2	26.6	1.0	25.6	-
Kiribati	70.3	1.5	18.4	3.6	46.8	..	5.2	24.1	-	24.1	0.4
Lao People's Dem.Rep.	23.7	4.4	12.1	1.8	5.3	0.6	12.1	63.3	..	63.3	0.3
Lesotho	90.8	4.6	-	0.6	85.6	-	-	9.2	-	9.2	-
Liberia	74.8	21.0	45.2	0.4	8.1	0.4	0.1	24.7	0.1	24.7	-
Madagascar	68.7	45.4	9.3	6.8	7.3	1.8	3.2	26.3	13.2	13.2	-
Malawi	77.5	18.9	5.0	3.5	50.1	-	0.4	22.2	-	22.2	-
Maldives	21.9	9.6	4.6	5.5	2.3	-	1.8	75.3	2.7	72.6	0.9
Mali	34.1	26.8	1.4	4.3	1.5	0.1	1.4	59.6	0.1	59.5	4.7
Mauritania	71.0	61.7	2.5	4.9	2.0	2.2	0.9	21.6	10.1	11.5	4.3
Mozambique	52.5	33.4	6.3	9.3	3.5	-	2.4	45.1	13.3	31.8	-
Myanmar	20.3	8.3	8.7	1.3	2.1	1.4	28.1	50.2	3.5	46.7	0.1
Nepal	37.5	10.5	13.8	1.7	11.6	0.4	6.8	55.3	2.0	53.3	-
Niger	44.5	37.2	2.0	3.4	2.0	-	3.2	25.5	1.2	24.3	26.8
Rwanda	60.6	46.1	9.2	3.5	1.8	-	1.1	29.9	1.1	28.9	8.4
Samoa	88.0	4.9	12.7	7.8	62.7	-	-	12.0	-	12.0	-
Sao Tome and Principe	92.5	77.5	-	7.5	7.5	-	-	7.5	-	7.5	-
Sierra Leone	65.0	45.9	4.9	9.8	4.5	0.4	6.5	26.0	4.1	22.0	2.0
Solomon Islands	62.8	4.1	10.7	2.5	45.5	-	0.8	36.4	-	36.4	-
Somalia	58.5	35.6	2.4	18.5	2.0	-	0.5	38.1	5.9	32.2	2.9
Sudan	43.7	31.4	4.3	5.4	2.5	3.1	2.9	50.3	24.6	25.7	-
Togo	32.6	26.4	1.2	2.5	2.5	0.2	21.1	46.0	1.9	44.0	0.2
Tuvalu	91.0	4.5	11.9	35.8	38.8	-	-	-	-	-	9.0
Uganda	58.8	38.6	8.4	7.4	4.5	-	1.8	39.4	2.9	36.5	-
United Rep.of Tanzania	56.1	36.6	9.4	3.3	6.8	0.1	2.9	40.9	13.6	27.3	-
Vanuatu	90.1	27.1	35.4	0.5	27.1	-	0.5	8.9	-	8.9	0.5
Yemen	45.2	23.2	5.1	12.7	4.2	2.5	2.9	39.8	7.4	32.5	9.7
Zaire	65.9	49.7	1.8	5.5	9.0	-	3.1	30.9	7.0	23.8	-
Zambia	65.7	27.1	5.6	7.8	25.3	-	0.7	33.6	15.9	17.7	-
All LDCs / Ensemble des PMA	**53.0**	**25.7**	**6.7**	**6.3**	**14.3**	**2.6**	**3.8**	**35.4**	**5.8**	**29.6**	**5.2**
All developing countries / Ensemble des pays en développement	**57.8**	**20.7**	**13.9**	**17.8**	**5.5**	**0.7**	**4.1**	**37.3**	**5.7**	**31.6**	**-**

Source: IMF, *Direction of Trade Statistics Yearbook 1994*, and other international and national sources.

Source: FMI, *Direction of Trade Statistics Yearbook 1994*, et autres sources internationales et nationales.

15. Composition of total financial flows to all LDCs in current and in constant dollars

Net disbursements

	Millions of current dollars / Millions de dollars courants										
	1983	1984	1985	1986	1987	1988	1989	1990	1991	1992	1993
Concessional loans & grants	9014	8777	10043	11905	13597	14377	14202	16132	16117	16419	14966
of which:											
DAC	6796	7325	8514	10143	12034	13222	13479	15320	15261	16273	14992
- Bilateral	4265	4436	5287	6508	7459	8599	7968	9262	8777	9060	8525
- Multilateral a	2531	2889	3227	3635	4574	4623	5510	6057	6484	7213	6467
- Grants	4834	5096	6236	7118	7804	9190	9399	11100	12081	12271	11896
- Loans	1961	2228	2278	3026	4230	4032	4079	4220	3180	4002	3096
- Technical assistance	1931	1874	2141	2518	2714	3095	3158	3309	3433	3672	3616
- Other b	4865	5450	6373	7625	9320	10127	10320	12010	11828	12601	11376
OPEC	1128	663	686	664	589	201	181	539	572	82	..
- Bilateral	951	567	613	585	522	177	164	526	574	75	..
- Multilateral c	177	97	73	79	67	24	17	14	-3	6	..
- Grants	397	414	430	385	448	135	92	481	503	58	..
- Loans	730	250	255	280	141	66	89	59	68	24	..
Non-concessional flows	35	704	288	-202	-223	602	75	1051	-337	283	..
of which:											
DAC	40	718	283	-183	-218	633	96	1038	-345	311	..
- Bilateral official	370	1156	446	461	465	449	104	589	147	162	..
- Multilateral a	128	94	267	90	77	52	3	58	-212	-32	..
- Export credits d	-423	-598	-386	-634	-561	-406	-142	-385	-282	-125	..
- Direct investment	90	-39	-84	-133	134	329	735	441	262	123	..
- Other e	-125	105	40	34	-332	209	-604	334	-260	183	..
Total financial flows	**9049**	**9481**	**10331**	**11703**	**13375**	**14979**	**14277**	**17182**	**15780**	**16702**	..

Source: UNCTAD secretariat calculations, mainly based on OECD/DAC data.

   a From multilateral agencies mainly financed by DAC member countries.

   b Grants (excluding technical assistance grants) and loans.

   c From multilateral agencies mainly financed by OPEC member countries.

   d Guaranteed private.

   e Bilateral financial flows originating in DAC countries and their capital markets in the form
     of bond lending and bank lending (either directly or through syndicated "Eurocurrency credits"). Excludes
     flows that could not be allocated by recipient country.

   f The deflator used is the unit value index of imports (see table 10).

15. Composition des courants financiers à l'ensemble des PMA en dollars courants et constants

Versements nets

					Millions of 1980 dollars f Millions de dollars de 1980 f						
1983	*1984*	*1985*	*1986*	*1987*	*1988*	*1989*	*1990*	*1991*	*1992*	*1993*	
10090	9950	11364	13058	13824	13880	13263	13995	14172	14103	13156	Prêts concessionnels et dons *dont:*
7607	8304	9634	11126	12235	12765	12587	13290	13420	13978	13179	CAD
4775	5028	5983	7138	7584	8302	7442	8035	7718	7782	7494	- Apports bilatéraux
2833	3275	3651	3987	4651	4463	5146	5255	5702	6196	5684	- Apports multilatéraux a
5412	5777	7057	7807	7934	8872	8778	9629	10623	10540	10457	- Dons
2196	2526	2578	3319	4300	3893	3809	3661	2797	3438	2722	- Prêts
2161	2125	2422	2762	2759	2988	2949	2871	3019	3154	3179	- Assistance technique
5446	6179	7212	8364	9475	9777	9638	10419	10401	10824	10000	- Autres b
1262	752	776	729	599	194	169	468	503	70	..	OPEP
1065	643	694	642	530	171	153	456	505	65	..	- Apports bilatéraux
198	110	82	87	68	23	16	12	-2	6	..	- Apports multilatéraux c
445	469	487	422	455	130	86	417	443	50	..	- Dons
818	283	289	307	144	64	83	51	60	20	..	- Prêts
40	798	326	-222	-226	581	70	911	-296	243	..	Courants financiers non concessionnels *dont:*
45	814	320	-200	-221	611	89	900	-304	267	..	CAD
414	1311	505	506	472	434	97	511	129	139	..	- Apports publics bilatéraux
144	107	302	98	78	50	3	51	-186	-27	..	- Apports multilatéraux a
-474	-677	-437	-696	-571	-392	-133	-334	-248	-107	..	- Crédits à l'exportation d
101	-45	-95	-146	136	318	686	383	231	105	..	- Investissements directs
-140	119	46	37	-338	202	-564	290	-229	157	..	- Autres e
10130	10748	11690	12836	13598	14461	13333	14906	13876	14346	..	Total des apports financiers

Source: Chiffres calculés par le secrétariat de la CNUCED d'après des données de l'OCDE/CAD.

a En provenance des institutions multilatérales essentiellement financées par les pays membres du CAD.

b Dons, non compris les dons d'assistance technique, et prêts.

c En provenance des institutions multilatérales essentiellement financées par les pays membres de l'OPEP.

d Privés garantis.

e Apports financiers bilatéraux provenant des pays membres du CAD ou passant par leurs marchés de capitaux, sous forme d'émissions d'obligations et de prêts bancaires (soit directement, soit comme crédits consortiaux en euromonnaies). Non compris les apports dont on ne pouvait pas alloués par pays bénéficiaires.

f Le déflateur utilisé est l'indice de valeur unitaire des importations (se rapporter au tableau 10).

16. **Distribution of financial flows to LDCs**
    and to all developing countries, by type of flow

In per cent

| | | | | | To least developed countries
 Aux pays les moins avancés | | | | | | |
	1983	1984	1985	1986	1987	1988	1989	1990	1991	1992	1993
Concessional loans & grants	99.6	92.6	97.2	101.7	101.7	96.0	99.5	93.9	102.1	98.3	..
of which:											
DAC	75.1	77.3	82.4	86.7	90.0	88.3	94.4	89.2	96.7	97.4	..
- Bilateral a	47.1	46.8	51.2	55.6	55.8	57.4	55.8	53.9	55.6	54.2	..
- Multilateral b	28.0	30.5	31.2	31.1	34.2	30.9	38.6	35.3	41.1	43.2	..
- Grants	53.4	53.8	60.4	60.8	58.4	61.4	65.8	64.6	76.6	73.5	..
- Loans	21.7	23.5	22.0	25.9	31.6	26.9	28.6	24.6	20.2	24.0	..
- Technical assistance	21.3	19.8	20.7	21.5	20.3	20.7	22.1	19.3	21.8	22.0	..
- Other c	53.8	57.5	61.7	65.2	69.7	67.6	72.3	69.9	75.0	75.4	..
OPEC	12.5	7.0	6.6	5.7	4.4	1.3	1.3	3.1	3.6	0.5	..
- Bilateral	10.5	6.0	5.9	5.0	3.9	1.2	1.2	3.1	3.6	0.5	..
- Multilateral d	2.0	1.0	0.7	0.7	0.5	0.2	0.1	-	-	-	..
- Grants	4.4	4.4	4.2	3.3	3.3	0.9	0.6	2.8	3.2	0.3	..
- Loans	8.1	2.6	2.5	2.4	1.1	0.4	0.6	0.3	0.4	0.1	..
Non-concessional flows	0.4	7.4	2.8	-1.7	-1.7	4.0	0.5	6.1	-2.1	1.7	..
of which:											
DAC	0.4	7.6	2.7	-1.6	-1.6	4.2	0.7	6.0	-2.2	1.9	..
- Bilateral official	4.1	12.2	4.3	3.9	3.5	3.0	0.7	3.4	0.9	1.0	..
- Multilateral a	1.4	1.0	2.6	0.8	0.6	0.3	-	0.3	-1.3	-0.2	..
- Export credits d	-4.7	-6.3	-3.7	-5.4	-4.2	-2.7	-1.0	-2.2	-1.8	-0.7	..
- Direct investment	1.0	-0.4	-0.8	-1.1	1.0	2.2	5.1	2.6	1.7	0.7	..
- Other e	-1.4	1.1	0.4	0.3	-2.5	1.4	-4.2	1.9	-1.6	1.1	..
Total financial flows	**100.0**	**100.0**	**100.0**	**100.0**	**100.0**	**100.0**	**100.0**	**100.0**	**100.0**	**100.0**	..

For sources and notes, see table 15.

16. Répartition des apports financiers aux PMA et à l'ensemble des pays en développement, par catégories d'apports

En pourcentage

				To all developing countries *A l'ensemble des pays en développement*							
1983	*1984*	*1985*	*1986*	*1987*	*1988*	*1989*	*1990*	*1991*	*1992*	*1993*	
42.8	38.5	72.6	54.9	67.7	63.1	55.2	72.9	65.3	54.3	..	Prêts concessionnels et dons *dont:*
33.6	31.1	61.0	45.4	58.8	56.9	51.5	64.2	61.5	53.3	..	CAD
23.4	21.9	43.3	33.4	43.7	42.1	37.2	47.2	44.4	37.7	..	- Apports bilatéraux
10.2	9.1	17.7	12.1	15.1	14.7	14.4	16.9	17.0	15.6	..	- Apports multilatéraux [a]
22.7	21.8	44.5	32.7	41.4	41.4	37.6	49.2	47.8	40.7	..	- Dons
10.9	9.2	16.5	12.8	17.4	15.5	14.0	15.0	13.7	12.6	..	- Prêts
10.8	9.6	18.4	13.8	18.0	17.8	15.2	18.7	17.1	16.5	..	- Assistance technique
22.8	21.5	42.5	31.7	40.9	39.1	36.4	45.4	44.4	36.8	..	- Autres [b]
6.1	4.9	7.1	5.9	4.9	2.9	1.8	7.7	2.7	0.9	..	OPEP
5.7	4.7	6.8	5.7	4.8	2.8	1.7	7.6	2.5	0.6	..	- Apports bilatéraux
0.5	0.2	0.3	0.2	0.1		0.2		0.2	0.3	..	- Apports multilatéraux [c]
4.1	4.3	6.2	5.3	4.9	3.0	1.8	7.7	2.9	0.7	..	- Dons
2.0	0.6	0.9	0.7		-0.1			-0.2	0.1	..	- Prêts
57.2	61.5	27.4	45.1	32.3	36.9	44.8	27.1	34.7	45.7	..	Courants financiers non concessionnels *dont:*
57.2	61.3	26.6	45.3	32.4	37.0	44.7	27.1	34.7	45.6	..	CAD
5.0	6.6	8.3	3.7	7.9	8.4	5.4	9.5	7.2	7.2	..	- Apports publics bilatéraux
10.4	10.2	16.7	11.3	10.8	8.7	8.1	13.0	6.9	3.0	..	- Apports multilatéraux [a]
7.0	4.9	3.7	-2.8	-5.4	-5.6	4.9	-2.4	-0.5	-1.2	..	- Crédits à l'exportation [d]
13.3	13.8	13.5	15.4	28.7	30.5	30.4	32.6	24.2	25.4	..	- Investissements directs
21.5	25.9	-15.6	17.7	-9.7	-5.0	-4.0	-25.6	-3.1	11.2	..	- Autres [e]
100.0	100.0	100.0	100.0	100.0	100.0	100.0	100.0	100.0	100.0	..	**Total des apports financiers**

Pour les sources et les notes, se reporter au tableau 15.

17. Share of LDCs in financial flows to all developing countries, by type of flow
In per cent

17. Part des PMA dans les apports financiers à l'ensemble des pays en développement, par catégories d'apports
En pourcentage

	1983	1984	1985	1986	1987	1988	1989	1990	1991	1992	1993	
Concessional loans & grants	31.2	29.3	32.5	32.4	33.0	32.8	31.8	29.4	27.7	29.9	30.4	Prêts concessionnels et dons
												dont:
DAC	29.9	30.2	32.8	33.3	33.6	33.5	32.4	31.7	27.9	30.2	30.5	CAD
- Bilateral	27.0	25.9	28.7	29.1	28.0	29.4	26.5	26.0	22.2	23.8	24.7	- Apports bilatéraux
- Multilateral a	36.7	40.5	42.8	44.9	49.8	45.2	47.5	47.5	42.7	45.7	44.0	- Apports multilatéraux a
- Grants	31.5	29.9	32.9	32.5	31.0	31.9	31.0	30.0	28.4	29.8	30.1	- Dons
- Loans	26.6	30.9	32.4	35.4	39.9	37.5	36.1	37.5	26.2	31.5	31.8	- Prêts
- Tech. ass.	26.3	25.2	27.3	27.3	24.8	25.1	25.8	23.5	22.6	22.0	21.7	- Assistance technique
- Other b	31.6	32.5	35.2	35.9	37.5	37.3	35.1	35.1	29.9	33.9	34.9	- Autres b
OPEC	27.2	17.4	22.7	16.7	19.6	10.1	12.3	9.3	23.8	9.2	..	OPEP
- Bilateral	24.8	15.4	21.2	15.3	17.8	9.2	12.3	9.2	25.4	12.1	..	- Apports bilatéraux
- Multilateral c	56.5	65.6	56.6	55.2	91.6	39.5	12.1	18.3	-	2.4	..	- Apports multilatéraux c
- Grants	14.3	12.3	16.3	10.9	14.9	6.5	6.2	8.3	19.6	7.7	..	- Dons
- Loans	53.0	53.3	68.3	63.3	-	-	-	-	-	18.0	..	- Prêts
Non-concessional flows	-	1.5	2.5	-	-	2.3	0.2	5.1	-	0.6	..	Courants financiers non-concessionnels
of which:												*dont:*
DAC	0.1	1.5	2.5	-	-	2.5	0.3	5.1	-	0.7	..	CAD
- Bilateral official	11.0	22.5	12.5	18.5	9.7	7.7	2.4	8.2	2.3	2.2	..	- Apports publics bilatéraux
- Multilateral a	1.8	1.2	3.8	1.2	1.2	0.9	-	0.6	-	-	..	- Apports multilatéraux a
- Export credits d	-	-	-	33.6	17.2	10.4	-	21.3	64.6	10.7	..	- Crédits à l'exportation d
- Direct investment	1.0	-	-	-	0.8	1.6	3.0	1.8	1.2	0.5	..	- Investissements directs
- Other e	-	0.5	-	0.3	5.6	-	18.6	-	9.5	1.6	..	- Autres e
Total financial flows	**13.4**	**12.2**	**24.3**	**17.5**	**22.0**	**21.6**	**17.7**	**22.8**	**17.7**	**16.5**	**..**	**Total des apports financiers**

Note: No percentage is shown when either the net flow to all LDCs or the net flow to all developing countries in a particular year is negative. For other notes and sources, see table 15.

Note: Aucune donnée n'est indiquée dans les cas où dans une année quelconque, les versements nets, soit aux PMA soit aux pays en développement dans leur ensemble, sont négatifs. Pour les autres notes et sources, se reporter au tableau 15.

18. Net ODA a from individual DAC member countries to LDCs as a group

18. Apports nets au titre de l'APD a de chaque pays membre du CAD à l'ensemble des PMA

Donor country c / Pays donateur c	% of GNP / En % du PNB								Millions of dollars / Millions de dollars							
	41 LDCs b				All LDCs				41 LDCs b				All LDCs			
	1987	1988	1989	1990	1990	1991	1992	1993	1987	1988	1989	1990	1990	1991	1992	1993
Norway / Norvège	0.38	0.42	0.40	0.44	0.52	0.52	0.53	0.44	310	371	354	458	538	545	585	439
Denmark / Danemark	0.32	0.36	0.40	0.34	0.37	0.35	0.36	0.37	319	374	397	426	465	437	492	474
Sweden / Suède	0.29	0.32	0.29	0.31	0.35	0.35	0.32	0.33	451	576	531	691	764	818	754	588
Netherlands / Pays-Bas	0.31	0.31	0.28	0.26	0.29	0.22	0.25	0.22	665	702	625	714	796	638	812	678
Portugal / Portugal	..	..	..	..	0.16	0.22	0.26	0.19	..	..	..	..	94	153	220	164
France / France	0.14	0.14	0.15	0.14	0.18	0.16	0.15	0.15	1260	1329	1472	1655	2124	1902	2031	1847
Finland / Finlande	0.18	0.23	0.22	0.21	0.24	0.26	0.23	0.12	154	236	244	275	320	304	228	91
Luxembourg / Luxembourg	..	..	..	..	0.06	0.10	0.09	0.12	..	..	..	..	8	13	12	16
Switzerland / Suisse	0.10	0.11	0.11	0.11	0.13	0.11	0.13	0.11	180	203	202	263	305	261	330	258
Canada / Canada	0.14	0.14	0.08	0.11	0.13	0.12	0.13	0.10	548	643	635	624	712	695	718	557
Germany d / Allemagne d	0.11	0.11	0.11	0.09	0.11	0.10	0.09	0.10	1200	1326	1330	1373	1692	1723	1783	1892
Belgium / Belgique	0.14	0.10	0.14	0.12	0.18	0.12	0.13	0.09	196	145	210	242	357	247	294	182
Ireland / Irlande	0.07	0.07	0.06	0.05	0.06	0.06	0.06	0.08	18	20	18	17	21	21	26	33
Italy / Italie	0.16	0.16	0.15	0.10	0.12	0.06	0.09	0.08	1189	1337	1283	1091	1324	670	1030	742
United Kingdom / Royaume-Uni	0.09	0.10	0.10	0.08	0.09	0.09	0.10	0.08	620	848	864	751	836	915	1020	774
Total DAC / Total CAD	**0.09**	**0.09**	**0.08**	**0.08**	**0.09**	**0.08**	**0.08**	**0.07**	**10310**	**12376**	**11042**	**12243**	**14650**	**13077**	**15018**	**13372**
Australia / Australie	0.05	0.11	0.08	0.06	0.06	0.08	0.07	0.07	93	253	231	157	172	222	208	183
Austria / Autriche	0.04	0.06	0.05	0.06	0.07	0.06	0.06	0.06	16	71	61	94	106	94	113	110
Japan / Japon	0.07	0.07	0.06	0.05	0.06	0.05	0.05	0.05	1584	1940	1610	1454	1639	1619	1748	1956
New Zealand / Nouvelle-Zélande	0.06	0.03	0.03	0.03	0.04	0.04	0.05	0.05	19	12	11	14	18	17	19	19
Spain / Espagne	..	..	..	..	0.04	0.03	0.03	0.03	..	..	..	..	180	159	152	131
United States / Etats-Unis	0.03	0.04	0.02	0.04	0.04	0.03	0.04	0.03	1487	1990	964	1945	2179	1624	2444	2239

Source: UNCTAD secretariat calculations, based on information from the OECD DAC secretariat.

a Including imputed flows through multilateral channels.

b Excluding Cambodia, Liberia, Madagascar, Solomon Islands, Zaire and Zambia, which were not included in the list at the time of the Second United Nations Conference on the Least Developed Countries.

c Ranked in descending order of the ODA/GNP ratio in 1993.

d Data refer only to the former Federal Republic of Germany.

Source: Chiffres calculés par le secrétariat de la CNUCED d'après des renseignements du secrétariat de l'OCDE/CAD.

a Y compris le montant imputé de l'APD fournie aux PMA à travers les voies multilatérales.

b Non compris le Cambodge, le Libéria, Madagascar, les îles Salomon, le Zaïre et la Zambie, qui ne figuraient pas dans la liste lors de la deuxième Conférence des Nations Unies sur les pays les moins avancés.

c Classés par ordre décroissant du rapport APD/PNB en 1993.

d Les données se rapportent seulement à l'ancienne République fédérale d'Allemagne.

19. Bilateral ODA from DAC member countries and total financial
    flows from multilateral agencies ª to all LDCs

$ million

	Net disbursements Versements nets										
	1983	1984	1985	1986	1987	1988	1989	1990	1991	1992	1993
A. Bilateral donors											
Australia	80.4	93.3	58.7	63.3	82.4	86.5	134.5	105.8	98.0	108.7	97.9
Austria	7.6	10.7	10.4	9.2	18.4	36.1	32.3	60.1	51.0	70.5	61.1
Belgium	147.8	134.9	173.9	229.1	229.7	229.7	172.4	259.4	167.7	209.5	182.1
Canada	260.3	284.3	318.9	251.4	375.9	393.5	347.4	361.4	382.2	390.3	251.6
Denmark	113.8	94.4	126.7	165.0	203.2	258.3	270.9	299.5	307.0	305.5	315.8
Finland	49.2	53.4	60.3	94.5	124.6	192.0	196.4	193.5	196.0	141.1	58.0
France	504.1	627.5	642.8	786.3	958.3	1072.4	1201.2	1617.8	1493.6	1401.3	1305.9
Germany ᵇ	618.9	514.0	581.0	709.4	855.1	928.5	926.5	1089.3	1148.9	1151.7	1127.2
Ireland	8.2	8.0	10.4	12.8	14.4	14.0	11.3	13.9	14.3	18.2	24.2
Italy	207.3	322.1	388.1	840.2	1000.8	1211.4	768.4	885.6	485.2	576.2	477.3
Japan	450.3	426.6	551.5	923.5	1097.0	1365.2	1195.3	985.8	998.8	947.4	1197.9
Luxembourg	-	-	-	-	-	-	-	5.6	11.3	8.9	12.4
Netherlands	241.4	291.1	246.7	388.2	457.6	502.9	446.9	560.4	415.4	547.9	477.8
New Zealand	6.2	7.1	7.0	8.3	15.9	11.2	10.1	13.4	12.5	15.3	15.0
Norway	158.7	136.0	165.6	249.6	239.8	289.4	267.3	369.0	380.5	419.3	312.0
Portugal	-	-	-	-	-	-	65.4	93.4	144.2	214.4	150.9
Spain	-	-	-	-	13.4	14.9	44.1	81.3	70.8	66.3	53.4
Sweden	217.0	178.0	189.4	335.5	306.7	431.2	382.7	517.0	603.8	507.0	429.0
Switzerland	81.4	81.5	82.6	127.2	134.6	164.8	162.8	215.4	218.4	225.5	194.4
United Kingdom	271.6	242.8	286.4	286.6	380.5	527.8	489.7	479.5	585.6	601.1	415.3
United States	841.0	930.0	1387.0	1028.0	951.0	869.0	843.0	1055.0	992.0	1134.0	1366.0
Total bilateral concessional	4265.1	4435.5	5287.4	6508.0	7459.4	8598.8	7968.5	9262.2	8777.2	9060.1	8525.2
B. Multilateral donors											
1. Concessional											
AfDF	135.1	95.2	173.5	218.8	302.4	291.4	440.1	528.7	544.5	542.5	573.0
AsDB	100.3	147.9	229.6	213.8	252.8	319.1	475.3	448.1	407.1	403.5	345.3
EEC(EDF)	488.5	578.3	544.5	626.9	686.7	974.3	1059.5	1099.1	1200.7	1760.9	1481.6 ᶜ
IBRD	2.6	0.5	0.4	- -	- -	- -	-	-	-	-	-
IDA	881.6	1075.8	1151.7	1562.6	1817.9	1599.0	1662.0	2026.0	1875.0	1981.4	1947.7
IDB	14.9	16.2	10.7	3.1	2.4	5.8	9.9	11.7	6.7	0.5	0.0
IFAD	56.0	62.3	108.3	124.0	159.8	55.9	65.8	119.1	43.8	7.6	40.1
IMF Trust fund	-18.3	-20.4	-103.1	- -	- -	- -	0.0	0.0	0.0	-	-
IMF(SAF/ESAF)	- -	- -	- -	-130.3	255.0	107.5	274.0	270.3	489.5	423.3	105.2
UN *of which:*	869.9	933.2	1111.1	1016.4	1097.5	1270.1	1523.5	1554.3	1917.1	2093.4	1973.8
UNDP	232.7	231.0	268.9	299.7	311.2	359.7	399.5	440.3	465.9	419.9	387.1
UNHCR	127.6	148.8	197.3	172.0	152.4	218.1	200.0	189.9	250.3	251.3	285.0
UNICEF	98.8	96.5	120.8	131.6	147.6	163.3	193.7	221.2	234.9	316.4	312.1
UNTA	49.9	38.8	60.5	48.6	65.6	45.8	65.3	57.0	74.5	55.6	91.1
WFP	271.1	323.8	358.0	255.2	309.3	358.4	406.2	480.4	769.3	926.9	775.2
Total	2530.5	2889.1	3226.6	3635.3	4574.4	4623.1	5510.0	6057.4	6484.3	7213.1	6466.8
2. Non-concessional											
AfDB	79.7	59.7	154.1	111.1	138.9	125.0	108.9	129.2	28.4	90.6	22.4
AsDB	-0.8	-0.9	-0.9	-0.9	-0.9	-0.4	-0.5	-0.5	-0.6	1.4	-0.6
EEC(EDF)	17.7	2.2	23.7	-11.8	-9.8	-19.0	-11.6	-3.9	0.1	7.3	-
IBRD	32.2	-5.0	69.9	-40.5	-56.0	-73.0	-83.0	-81.0	-229.0	-181.6	-114.1
IFC	-0.5	38.0	20.4	31.6	4.9	19.0	-11.0	14.7	-10.8	50.8	111.5
Total	128.4	94.0	267.2	89.6	77.2	51.6	2.7	58.5	-211.9	-31.6	19.0
Total concessional (A + B.1)	6795.6	7324.6	8514.0	10143.4	12033.9	13221.9	13478.5	15319.5	15261.5	16273.3	14992.0
GRAND TOTAL	6924.0	7418.6	8781.2	10233.0	12111.0	13273.5	13481.3	15378.0	15049.6	16241.7	15011.0

For sources and notes, see end of table.

19. APD bilatérale des pays membres du CAD et apports financiers totaux des institutions multilatérales ᵃ à l'ensemble des PMA

Millions de dollars

				Commitments *Engagements*							
1983	*1984*	*1985*	*1986*	*1987*	*1988*	*1989*	*1990*	*1991*	*1992*	*1993*	
											A. Donneurs bilatéraux
77.0	78.1	59.5	63.0	80.5	92.1	119.9	98.3	89.1	87.0	79.8	Australie
5.8	10.1	11.5	16.8	16.3	50.1	33.4	129.9	52.3	104.6	96.0	Autriche
94.3	90.9	81.0	211.7	220.2	266.8	173.3	259.4	259.4	259.4	..	Belgique
350.5	411.4	346.0	307.4	381.4	392.0	364.8	333.7	317.9	389.6	191.3	Canada
107.5	160.6	153.6	217.3	241.6	276.8	290.3	274.2	284.0	333.9	248.4	Danemark
36.5	80.6	127.5	122.3	126.2	185.6	289.6	124.9	265.3	77.6	69.2	Finlande
690.6	795.3	759.2	888.0	1038.4	1196.0	1280.5	1299.8	1180.0	1020.6	..	France
626.6	623.7	833.1	790.1	985.1	1026.3	1047.8	1242.0	1460.9	1299.1	..	Allemagne ᵇ
8.2	8.0	10.4	12.8	14.4	14.0	11.3	13.9	14.3	18.2	24.2	Irlande
390.5	351.4	474.6	1420.9	1621.6	1225.8	712.9	736.7	506.5	651.0	781.1	Italie
503.3	740.9	626.3	1027.7	1237.8	1580.2	1055.4	1044.5	1044.5	1281.9	..	Japon
-	-	-	-	-	-	-	-	-	10.3	..	Luxembourg
291.9	257.0	250.8	436.3	514.7	479.4	469.3	654.8	312.5	561.8	465.1	Pays-Bas
4.2	6.6	12.2	10.6	11.9	11.0	-	9.7	15.6	17.1	12.5	Nouvelle-Zélande
133.0	159.0	166.6	289.4	201.4	86.0	133.9	198.5	376.9	175.0	307.1	Norvège
-	-	-	-	-	-	-	-	36.8	62.8	86.0	Portugal
-	-	-	-	-	-	-	-	-	16.1	..	Espagne
206.0	208.5	206.8	335.5	286.4	397.9	382.3	317.7	354.3	364.2	244.0	Suède
91.3	64.1	129.7	124.3	162.6	228.9	216.7	209.6	223.4	206.5	165.2	Suisse
227.7	266.5	233.2	399.2	441.3	561.4	559.7	488.2	529.1	535.9	..	Royaume-Uni
947.2	1318.5	1324.0	1113.9	1028.3	1005.9	1195.1	1115.6	1799.8	1232.0	1444.3	Etats-Unis
4792.2	5631.3	5806.2	7787.4	8610.2	9076.3	8336.2	8551.3	9122.6	8704.6	..	Total des apports bilatéraux concessionnels
											B. Donneurs multilatéraux
											1. Apports concessionnels
275.9	305.3	345.2	476.8	625.5	607.4	840.3	765.0	852.5	848.1	663.8	FAfD
465.5	402.8	383.7	203.1	666.6	398.8	564.1	536.4	601.5	481.3	440.6	BAsD
600.1	629.9	570.7	695.0	1872.4	1783.7	1116.2	719.3	1561.6	2052.9	..	CEE(FED)
-	-	-	-	-	-	-	-	-	-	-	BIRD
1531.4	1533.9	1550.0	1862.3	2039.6	2202.0	2364.0	2859.0	2543.0	2469.1	1866.6	AID
17.4	-	24.7	56.0	-	-	-	56.0	12.4	0.3	..	BID
96.3	103.0	83.2	57.8	136.8	105.6	122.5	71.9	113.9	81.9	..	FIDA
-	-	-	-	-	-	-	-	-	-	-	Fonds fiduciaire du FMI
-	-	-	-	-	-	-	-	-	-	-	FMI(FAS/FASR)
869.9	933.2	1111.1	1016.4	1097.5	1270.1	1523.5	1554.3	1917.1	2093.4	..	ONU *dont:*
											PNUD
											UNHCR
											UNICEF
											ATNU
											PAM
3856.4	3908.1	4068.6	4367.4	6438.3	6367.7	6530.6	6561.8	7602.0	8026.9	..	Total
											2. Apports non concessionnels
											BAfD
											BAsD
											CEE(FED)
											BIRD
											SFI
											Total
8648.6	9539.4	9874.8	12154.8	15048.5	15443.9	14866.9	15113.1	16724.6	16731.5	..	*Total des apports concessionnels (A + B.1)*
											TOTAL GÉNÉRAL

Pour les sources et les notes, se reporter à la fin du tableau.

19.　Bilateral ODA from DAC member countries and total financial flows from multilateral agencies a to all LDCs *(concluded)*

19.　APD bilatérale des pays membres du CAD et apports financiers totaux des institutions multilatérales a à l'ensemble des PMA *(fin)*

A. Bilateral donors	Main recipients in 1993 d / Principaux bénéficiaires en 1993 d	A. Donneurs bilatéraux
Australia	Bangladesh, Cambodia/Cambodge, Lao People's Dem. Rep./Rép. dém. populaire lao, Vanuatu, Solomon Islands/Iles Salomon, Mozambique, Samoa, Nepal/Népal.	Australie
Austria	U.-R. of Tanzania/R.-U. de Tanzanie, Malawi, Uganda/Ouganda, Rwanda, Bhutan/Bhoutan, Mozambique, Nepal/Népal.	Autriche
Belgium	Burundi, Rwanda, Zaire/Zaïre, U.-R. of Tanzania/R.-U. de Tanzanie.	Belgique
Canada	Bangladesh, Mozambique, U.-R. of Tanzania/R.-U. de Tanzanie, Ethiopia/Ethiopie, Mali, Haiti/Haïti, Zambia/Zambie.	Canada
Denmark	U.-R. of Tanzania/R.-U. de Tanzanie, Uganda/Ouganda, Mozambique, Bangladesh, Burkina Faso, Ethiopia/Ethiopie, Nepal/Népal.	Danemark
Finland	U.-R. of Tanzania/R.-U. de Tanzanie, Zambia/Zambie, Mozambique, Nepal/Népal, Bangladesh.	Finlande
France	Madagascar, Burkina Faso, Mauritania/Mauritanie, Chad/Tchad, Central African Rep./Rép. centrafricaine, Niger, Guinea/Guinée, Mali.	France FIDA
Germany b	Mozambique, Zambia/Zambie, Bangladesh, U.-R. of Tanzania/R.-U. de Tanzanie.	Allemagne b
Ireland	U.-R. of Tanzania/R.-U. de Tanzanie, Zambia/Zambie, Lesotho, Sudan/Soudan, Somalia/Somalie.	Irlande
Italy	Somalia/Somalie, Mozambique, Sierra Leone, Zambia/Zambie, Djibouti, Cambodia/Cambodge.	Italie
Japan	Bangladesh, Nepal/Népal, Zambia/Zambie, U.-R. of Tanzania/R.-U. de Tanzanie, Myanmar, Cambodia/Cambodge.	Japon
Luxembourg	Cape Verde/Cap Vert, Burundi, Djibouti, Niger, Rwanda, Gambia/Gambie.	Luxembourg
Netherlands	U.-R. of Tanzania/R.-U. de Tanzanie, Bangladesh, Mozambique, Sudan/Soudan, Ethiopia/Ethiopie, Yemen/Yémen, Zambia/Zambie, Burkina Faso, Mali.	Pays-Bas
New Zealand	Samoa, Solomon Islands/Iles Salomon, Vanuatu, Kiribati, Tuvalu.	Nouvelle-Zélande
Norway	U.-R. of Tanzania/R.-U. de Tanzanie, Mozambique, Bangladesh, Zambia/Zambie.	Norvège
Portugal	Mozambique, Cape Verde/Cap Vert, Guinea-Bissau/Guinée-Bissau, Sao Tome and Principe/Sao Tomé-et-Principe.	Portugal
Spain	Mozambique, Equatorial Guinea/Guinée équatoriale, Mauritania/Mauritanie, Uganda/Ouganda, Niger.	Espagne
Sweden	U.-R. of Tanzania/R.-U. de Tanzanie, Mozambique, Ethiopia/Ethiopie, Zambia/Zambie, Bangladesh, Lesotho.	Suède
Switzerland	Rwanda, Mozambique, Madagascar, Bangladesh, Nepal/Népal, Niger, U.-R. of Tanzania/R.-U. de Tanzanie.	Suisse
United Kingdom	Bangladesh, Uganda/Ouganda, Mozambique, Zambia/Zambie, U.-R. of Tanzania/R.-U. de Tanzanie, Malawi.	Royaume-Uni
United States	Somalia/Somalie, Ethiopia/Ethiopie, Bangladesh.	Etats-Unis

B. Multilateral donors	Main recipients in 1993 d / Principaux bénéficiaires en 1993 d	B. Donneurs multilatéraux
1. Concessional		**1. Apports concessionnels**
AfDF	Ethiopia/Ethiopie, U.-R. of Tanzania/R.-U. de Tanzanie, Mozambique, Uganda/Ouganda, Malawi, Burkina Faso.	FAfD
AsDB	Bangladesh, Nepal/Népal, Lao People's Dem. Rep./Rép. dém. populaire lao.	BAsD
EEC(EDF)	Ethiopia/Ethiopie, Uganda/Ouganda, U.-R. of Tanzania/R.-U. de Tanzanie, Zambia/Zambie, Mozambique.	CEE(FED)
IDA	Bangladesh, Ethiopia/Ethiopie, Zambia/Zambie, Malawi, U.-R. of Tanzania/R.-U. de Tanzanie, Uganda/Ouganda, Guinea/Guinée.	AID
IDB	Haiti/Haïti.	BID
IFAD	Malawi, Bangladesh, Zambia/Zambie, Central African Rep./Rép. centrafricaine, Sudan/Soudan, Madagascar, Nepal/Népal, Rwanda, Zaire/Zaïre.	FIDA
IMF(SAF/ESAF)	Ethiopia/Ethiopie, Benin/Bénin, Mozambique, Mali, Burkina Faso, Lesotho, Lao People's Dem. Rep./Rép. dém. populaire lao, Mauritania/Mauritanie, Nepal/Népal.	FMI(FAS/FASR)
UN	Ethiopia/Ethiopie, Sudan/Soudan, Somalia/Somalie, Mozambique, Malawi, Bangladesh.	ONU
of which:		*dont:*
UNDP	Bangladesh, Cambodia/Cambodge, U.-R. of Tanzania/R.-U. de Tanzanie.	PNUD
UNHCR	Ethiopia/Ethiopie, Mozambique, Malawi, Somalia/Somalie, Cambodia/Cambodge, Bangladesh, Guinea/Guinée, Sudan/Soudan.	UNHCR
UNICEF	Sudan/Soudan, Somalia/Somalie, Bangladesh, Mozambique, Ethiopia/Ethiopie, Uganda/Ouganda.	UNICEF
UNTA	Bangladesh.	ATNU
WFP	Ethiopia/Ethiopie, Sudan/Soudan, Somalia/Somalie, Malawi, Liberia/Libéria, Mozambique, Rwanda, Afghanistan.	PAM
2. Non-concessional		**2. Apports non-concessionnels**
AfDB	Guinea/Guinée, Ethiopia/Ethiopie, Mauritania/Mauritanie, Sudan/Soudan.	BAfd
AsDB	Nepal/Népal.	BAsD
EEC(EDF) e	Guinea/Guinée, Mauritania/Mauritanie, Malawi.	CEE(FED) e
IBRD	Lesotho.	BIRD
IFC	Zambia/Zambie, Central African Rep./Rép. centrafricaine, Sierra Leone, Zaire/Zaïre.	SFI

Source:　UNCTAD secretariat, based on information from the OECD/DAC secretariat.

a Multilateral agencies mainly financed by DAC countries.
b Data refer only to the former Federal Republic of Germany.
c Provisional figures.
d Accounting each for 5 per cent or more of the total provided to all LDCs.
e Main recipients in 1992.

Source:　Secrétariat de la CNUCED, d'après des renseignements du secrétariat de l'OCDE/CAD.

a Institutions multilatérales essentiellement financées par les pays du CAD.
b Les données se rapportent seulement à l'ancienne République fédérale d'Allemagne.
c Chiffres provisoires.
d Recevant individuellement 5 pour cent ou davantage du total accordé à l'ensemble des PMA.
e Principaux bénéficiaires en 1992.

20. Grant element of ODA commitments [a]
from individual DAC member countries
to LDCs as a group

In per cent

20. Elément de libéralité des engagements de l'APD [a]
de chaque pays membre du CAD
en faveur de l'ensemble des PMA

En pourcentage

	1983	1984	1985	1986	1987	1988	1989	1990	1991	1992	1993 [c]	
Australia	100	100	100	100	100	100	100	100	100	100	100	Australie
Austria	99	91	100	97	100	97	96	92	95	90	100	Autriche
Belgium	96	97	97	97	100	100	100	100	100	99	..	Belgique
Canada	100	100	100	100	100	100	100	100	100	100	100	Canada
Denmark	98	100	98	99	100	100	100	100	100	100	100	Danemark
Finland	100	98	100	99	97	99	100	100	100	100	100	Finlande
France	76	74	74	76	77	75	80	87	98	99	86	France
Germany [b]	93	94	96	96	97	97	95	89	85	100	100	Allemagne [b]
Ireland	100	100	100	100	100	100	100	100	100	100	100	Irlande
Italy	82	83	97	96	79	87	88	82	96	97	100	Italie
Japan	84	79	84	82	83	88	90	90	94	95	76	Japon
Luxembourg	..	..	..	..	..	..	..	..	..	100	100	Luxembourg
Netherlands	99	99	98	100	99	100	100	100	100	100	100	Pays-Bas
New Zealand	100	100	100	100	100	100	-	100	100	100	100	Nouvelle-Zélande
Norway	100	100	100	99	99	100	99	99	99	98	100	Norvège
Portugal	..	..	..	..	..	..	..	..	100	93	..	Portugal
Spain	..	..	..	..	..	..	..	49	53	47	..	Espagne
Sweden	100	100	100	100	100	100	100	100	100	100	100	Suède
Switzerland	100	100	100	100	100	100	100	100	100	100	100	Suisse
United Kingdom	98	99	100	99	100	100	100	100	100	100	100	Royaume-Uni
United States	94	97	96	95	95	96	97	97	100	100	100	Etats-Unis
Total	**92**	**91**	**93**	**93**	**89**	**92**	**94**	**93**	**96**	**98**	**97**	**Total**

Source: OECD secretariat.

Note: The grant element, used as a standard measure of the concessionality of aid programmes, reflects the grant share of new commitments as well as the financial terms of loans (i.e. their interest rate, maturity and grace period).

a Excluding debt reorganization.

b Data refer only to the former Federal Republic of Germany.

c Preliminary estimates.

Source: Secrétariat de l'OCDE.

Note: L'élément de libéralité, pris comme étalon de la libéralité des programmes d'aide, rend compte de la proportion de dons dans les engagements nouveaux ainsi que des conditions financières des prêts (c'est-à-dire taux d'intérêt, échéance, et délai de grâce).

a Non compris la réorganisation de la dette.

b Les données se rapportent seulement à l'ancienne République fédérale d'Allemagne.

c Chiffres préliminaires.

**21. ODA to LDCs from DAC member countries and multilateral agencies
mainly financed by them : percentage distribution by donor
and shares allocated to LDCs in total ODA flows to all developing countries**

In per cent

	Percentage distribution by donor *Répartition en pourcentage par donneur*										
	1983	*1984*	*1985*	*1986*	*1987*	*1988*	*1989*	*1990*	*1991*	*1992*	*1993*
Bilateral donors											
Australia	1.2	1.3	0.7	0.6	0.7	0.7	1.0	0.7	0.6	0.7	0.7
Austria	0.1	0.1	0.1	-	0.2	0.3	0.2	0.4	0.3	0.4	0.4
Belgium	2.2	1.8	2.0	2.3	1.9	1.7	1.3	1.7	1.1	1.3	1.2
Canada	3.8	3.9	3.7	2.5	3.1	3.0	2.6	2.4	2.5	2.4	1.7
Denmark	1.7	1.3	1.5	1.6	1.7	2.0	2.0	2.0	2.0	1.9	2.1
Finland	0.7	0.7	0.7	0.9	1.0	1.5	1.5	1.3	1.3	0.9	0.4
France	7.4	8.6	7.6	7.8	8.0	8.1	8.9	10.6	9.8	8.6	8.7
Germany a	9.1	7.0	6.8	7.0	7.1	7.0	6.9	7.1	7.5	7.1	7.5
Ireland	0.1	0.1	0.1	0.1	0.1	0.1	-	-	-	0.1	0.2
Italy	3.0	4.4	4.6	8.3	8.3	9.2	5.7	5.8	3.2	3.5	3.2
Japan	6.6	5.8	6.5	9.1	9.1	10.3	8.9	6.4	6.5	5.8	8.0
Luxembourg	-	-	-	-	-	-	-	-	-	-	-
Netherlands	3.6	4.0	2.9	3.8	3.8	3.8	3.3	3.7	2.7	3.4	3.2
New Zealand	-	-	-	-	0.1	-	-	-	-	-	-
Norway	2.3	1.9	1.9	2.5	2.0	2.2	2.0	2.4	2.5	2.6	2.1
Portugal	-	-	-	-	-	-	0.5	0.6	0.9	1.3	1.0
Spain	-	-	-	-	0.1	0.1	0.3	0.5	0.5	0.4	0.4
Sweden	3.2	2.4	2.2	3.3	2.5	3.3	2.8	3.4	4.0	3.1	2.9
Switzerland	1.2	1.1	1.0	1.3	1.1	1.2	1.2	1.4	1.4	1.4	1.3
United Kingdom	4.0	3.3	3.4	2.8	3.2	4.0	3.6	3.1	3.8	3.7	2.8
United States	12.4	12.7	16.3	10.1	7.9	6.6	6.3	6.9	6.5	7.0	9.1
Total bilateral	62.8	60.6	62.1	64.2	62.0	65.0	59.1	60.5	57.5	55.7	56.9
Multilateral donors											
AfDF	2.0	1.3	2.0	2.2	2.5	2.2	3.3	3.5	3.6	3.3	3.8
AsDB	1.5	2.0	2.7	2.1	2.1	2.4	3.5	2.9	2.7	2.5	2.3
EEC/EDF	7.2	7.9	6.4	6.2	5.7	7.4	7.9	7.2	7.9	10.8	9.9
IBRD	-	-	-	-	-	-	-	-	-	-	-
IDA	13.0	14.7	13.5	15.4	15.1	12.1	12.3	13.2	12.3	12.2	13.0
IDB	0.2	0.2	0.1	-	-	-	-	-	-	-	-
IFAD	0.8	0.8	1.3	1.2	1.3	0.4	0.5	0.8	0.3	-	0.3
IMF Trust fund	-0.3	-0.3	-1.2	-	-	-	-	-	-	-	-
IMF SAF/ESAF	-	-	-	-1.3	2.1	0.8	2.0	1.8	3.2	2.6	0.7
UN	12.8	12.7	13.1	10.0	9.1	9.6	11.3	10.1	12.6	12.9	13.2
Total multilateral	37.2	39.4	37.9	35.8	38.0	35.0	40.9	39.5	42.5	44.3	43.1
Grand total	**100.0**	**100.0**	**100.0**	**100.0**	**100.0**	**100.0**	**100.0**	**100.0**	**100.0**	**100.0**	**100.0**

Source: UNCTAD secretariat, based on information from the OECD/DAC secretariat.

a Data refer only to the former Federal Republic of Germany.

**21. APD aux PMA en provenance des pays membres du CAD
et des institutions multilatérales essentiellement financées par ceux-ci :
répartition en pourcentage par donneur et parts allouées aux PMA
dans le total des apports d'APD aux pays en développement**

En pourcentage

				Share of LDCs in ODA flows to all developing countries							
				Parts des PMA dans le total des apports concessionnels aux pays en développement							
1983	*1984*	*1985*	*1986*	*1987*	*1988*	*1989*	*1990*	*1991*	*1992*	*1993*	
											Donneurs bilatéraux
15.2	15.6	11.3	12.7	15.8	14.4	19.8	14.7	14.4	15.7	15.3	Australie
6.2	8.0	6.1	6.7	11.8	25.0	21.9	31.6	15.7	18.3	15.8	Autriche
50.7	52.7	65.0	64.4	57.4	57.5	48.6	47.8	34.1	40.1	40.1	Belgique
30.9	27.6	32.5	24.3	30.7	25.5	22.5	22.3	22.1	23.9	16.7	Canada
49.3	43.1	57.8	48.1	46.6	56.3	53.0	43.8	45.3	41.4	42.8	Danemark
57.9	51.4	50.4	53.2	50.1	52.4	46.8	41.6	35.4	35.8	26.2	Finlande
22.8	26.3	27.0	25.6	24.1	26.8	28.0	29.4	26.6	22.9	21.8	France
32.1	29.9	31.8	28.2	29.0	30.8	31.1	26.4	28.9	24.0	27.2	Allemagne [a]
59.0	55.1	60.8	50.9	52.7	63.9	59.0	60.5	48.1	65.5	60.2	Irlande
47.5	52.5	50.7	57.9	56.6	52.8	37.4	43.7	25.7	27.9	28.3	Italie
21.7	21.0	25.4	27.6	24.0	23.8	20.1	16.3	12.2	13.6	18.2	Japon
-	-	-	-	-	-	-	38.8	44.7	45.4	41.5	Luxembourg
30.1	33.6	32.7	33.2	32.6	33.4	30.5	31.0	24.0	29.8	27.5	Pays-Bas
13.0	16.1	16.3	13.7	24.1	12.0	13.3	16.7	15.5	21.0	20.8	Nouvelle-Zélande
49.6	47.0	51.2	52.7	46.4	51.4	48.6	49.1	53.0	52.8	50.0	Norvège
-	-	-	-	-	-	80.9	85.7	87.0	88.5	80.1	Portugal
-	-	-	-	11.8	10.7	16.9	15.1	10.5	7.3	7.6	Espagne
45.6	38.5	35.6	47.4	35.9	45.0	31.9	40.2	43.7	30.7	35.5	Suède
37.5	37.6	36.6	39.6	35.3	38.2	39.5	39.9	31.1	33.9	32.8	Suisse
31.6	31.3	34.6	29.1	38.6	38.5	34.2	33.3	33.0	36.9	29.1	Royaume-Uni
19.7	17.8	22.5	18.3	15.9	15.6	14.9	15.0	12.2	19.2	24.7	Etats-Unis
27.0	26.0	28.7	29.1	28.0	29.4	26.5	26.0	22.2	23.8	24.7	Total bilatéraux
											Donneurs multilatéraux
85.6	85.5	82.6	80.5	81.0	83.1	89.4	87.7	86.8	80.0	83.9	FAfD
45.1	48.8	58.7	51.4	46.9	45.3	51.9	40.8	39.0	45.7	37.8	BAsD
43.9	47.4	41.4	43.3	41.6	40.2	44.9	44.0	35.4	45.3	45.3	CEE/FED
5.5	1.2	1.2	-	-	-	-	-	-	-	-	BIRD
38.9	45.6	48.4	51.4	58.0	53.0	60.2	59.5	50.5	49.5	54.8	AID
4.1	3.7	3.0	1.1	2.0	4.3	6.9	7.6	7.7	0.7	-	BID
39.7	38.9	43.3	47.0	48.0	61.5	59.6	52.3	42.2	475.0	42.3	FIDA
-	-	-	-	-	-	-	-	-	-	-	Fonds fiduciaire du FMI
-	-	-	-	-	-	34.0	65.9	47.8	57.7	44.7	FMI FAS/FASR
33.4	35.8	38.7	35.8	35.4	36.0	38.4	36.1	37.3	38.0	33.4	ONU
36.7	40.5	42.8	44.9	49.8	45.2	47.5	47.5	42.7	45.7	44.0	Total multilatéraux
29.9	30.2	32.8	33.3	33.6	33.5	32.4	31.7	27.9	30.2	30.5	Total général

Source: Secrétariat de la CNUCED d'après des renseignements du secrétariat de l'OCDE/CAD.

a Les données se rapportent seulement à l'ancienne République fédérale d'Allemagne.

22. Total financial flows and ODA from all sources

Net disbursements in $ million

Country	Total financial flows *Apports totaux de ressources financières*										
	1983	*1984*	*1985*	*1986*	*1987*	*1988*	*1989*	*1990*	*1991*	*1992*	*1993*
Afghanistan	396	228	214	289	257	261	261	165	590	204	..
Bangladesh	1158	1238	1113	1440	1780	1662	1808	2152	2027	1947	..
Benin	98	110	97	99	93	76	305	244	271	278	..
Bhutan	13	18	24	40	42	60	41	51	63	44	..
Botswana	130	182	161	157	219	102	149	155	216	170	..
Burkina Faso	195	186	189	280	287	299	290	351	424	438	..
Burundi	196	154	156	188	200	199	180	261	257	314	..
Cambodia	138	117	125	180	192	208	171	145	109	214	..
Cape Verde	69	70	76	115	89	88	90	112	95	128	..
Central African Rep.	101	134	116	140	188	207	192	260	210	155	..
Chad	94	113	182	161	205	263	258	318	279	260	..
Comoros	43	44	51	47	55	55	45	46	62	47	..
Djibouti	67	139	103	79	102	96	73	192	108	114	..
Equatorial Guinea	15	17	31	28	59	57	80	66	60	48	..
Ethiopia	482	576	909	837	738	1126	783	1059	1093	1174	..
Gambia	38	48	48	102	106	73	224	108	103	111	..
Guinea	60	76	108	162	247	281	339	274	396	417	..
Guinea-Bissau	67	67	64	75	110	134	125	138	102	127	..
Haiti	125	133	142	179	207	138	196	158	168	116	..
Kiribati	17	11	12	14	18	16	18	21	20	28	..
Lao People's Dem.Rep.	149	122	174	145	176	187	179	178	161	165	..
Lesotho	110	96	119	91	100	125	134	149	128	322	..
Liberia	-131	-252	-289	-240	-309	544	286	517	-61	441	..
Madagascar	186	309	223	322	381	317	376	432	470	343	..
Malawi	105	212	118	218	321	413	411	520	533	563	..
Maldives	9	5	8	17	24	25	59	38	44	41	..
Mali	220	332	391	366	359	440	457	484	463	442	..
Mauritania	225	181	233	255	233	178	211	228	212	223	..
Mozambique	255	243	398	506	670	910	733	1062	1037	1261	..
Myanmar	325	288	318	353	349	457	101	102	167	132	..
Nepal	198	200	244	335	379	465	503	430	448	497	..
Niger	210	134	300	299	433	326	284	384	314	397	..
Rwanda	164	162	199	215	262	254	232	288	366	351	..
Samoa	32	14	20	23	35	31	30	54	60	53	..
Sao Tome and Principe	13	12	13	19	20	41	45	55	50	58	..
Sierra Leone	66	73	66	98	96	118	108	76	137	150	..
Solomon Islands	31	25	22	30	70	65	50	58	38	47	..
Somalia	325	364	373	599	624	406	399	489	181	625	..
Sudan	1160	707	1123	840	779	944	755	739	876	501	..
Togo	108	114	91	128	102	215	165	259	201	215	..
Tuvalu	4	5	3	4	26	14	7	5	6	13	..
Uganda	156	165	223	204	373	407	494	631	620	697	..
United Rep.of Tanzania	641	597	536	627	967	984	859	1136	1113	1295	..
Vanuatu	35	45	39	-28	35	39	79	151	80	10	..
Yemen	629	492	456	396	526	312	297	447	273	259	..
Zaire	95	757	469	612	795	876	806	1409	457	274	..
Zambia	231	419	542	658	356	482	591	585	751	991	..
All LDCs	**9049**	**9481**	**10331**	**11703**	**13375**	**14979**	**14277**	**17182**	**15780**	**16702**	**..**
All developing countries	**67562**	**77928**	**42585**	**67024**	**60826**	**69495**	**80805**	**75298**	**89052**	**101091**	**..**
Memo items :											
In current dollars per capita :											
All LDCs	21.4	21.9	23.3	25.7	28.6	31.2	28.9	33.9	30.2	31.0	..
All developing countries	28.2	31.8	17.0	26.1	23.2	25.9	29.4	26.8	31.0	34.4	..
In constant 1980 dollars a *(million) :*											
All LDCs	10130	10748	11690	12836	13598	14461	13333	14906	13876	14346	..
All developing countries	74894	87846	48075	74157	62399	67932	76433	65854	79504	88181	..
In constant 1980 dollars a *per capita :*											
All LDCs	24.0	24.8	26.4	28.2	29.1	30.1	27.0	29.4	26.6	26.7	..
All developing countries	31.3	35.9	19.2	28.9	23.7	25.3	27.8	23.4	27.7	30.0	..

Source: UNCTAD secretariat estimates, mainly based on data from the OECD secretariat.
    a The deflator used is the unit value index of imports (see table 10).

22. Apports totaux de ressources financières et APD de toutes provenances

Versements nets en millions de dollars

					of which : ODA dont : APD							
1983	*1984*	*1985*	*1986*	*1987*	*1988*	*1989*	*1990*	*1991*	*1992*	*1993*	*Pays*
396	229	237	288	256	258	263	167	583	204	206	Afghanistan
1121	1203	1144	1459	1806	1661	1800	2103	1889	1835	1334	Bangladesh
93	78	95	141	138	166	287	270	269	269	280	Bénin
13	18	24	40	42	42	42	48	64	56	67	Bhoutan
104	103	99	104	156	151	160	148	136	115	110	Botswana
183	188	195	281	288	294	279	335	433	441	433	Burkina Faso
160	138	138	191	204	203	211	270	261	318	273	Burundi
138	119	125	179	192	208	184	145	106	207	313	Cambodge
65	69	75	112	89	90	91	113	108	124	117	Cap-Vert
94	133	109	136	182	206	189	253	177	177	181	Rép. centrafricaine
96	114	181	164	205	263	260	316	277	246	226	Tchad
41	43	48	47	54	53	45	46	65	48	51	Comores
66	111	81	115	105	93	75	195	108	114	124	Djibouti
13	15	20	32	56	48	58	65	63	62	55	Guinée équatoriale
464	517	840	790	725	1109	803	1072	1119	1181	1249	Ethiopie
42	53	50	103	105	93	100	100	103	111	90	Gambie
58	81	115	174	233	267	346	283	400	453	422	Guinée
65	61	59	74	114	104	118	133	119	118	101	Guinée-Bissau
133	133	150	181	213	142	197	172	182	102	127	Haïti
17	12	12	13	18	16	17	21	20	27	15	Kiribati
149	121	147	145	176	187	178	178	161	165	207	Rép. dém. pop. lao
108	101	94	87	107	111	137	143	126	145	138	Lesotho
122	135	95	98	78	65	59	112	158	119	120	Libéria
195	160	196	321	350	320	402	401	457	362	363	Madagascar
116	182	113	195	277	375	433	505	525	570	504	Malawi
11	6	9	16	19	28	29	22	35	39	31	Maldives
220	336	389	374	366	445	464	492	458	440	363	Mali
183	175	217	267	232	196	253	247	221	209	318	Mauritanie
229	300	368	568	768	993	888	1013	1107	1471	1172	Mozambique
323	279	355	398	366	436	201	158	179	115	92	Myanmar
201	197	234	297	353	436	501	429	453	435	366	Népal
176	160	316	313	381	381	310	398	379	370	335	Niger
154	165	195	208	252	252	229	293	363	353	392	Rwanda
27	20	19	23	35	31	31	48	57	54	52	Samoa
13	12	14	19	18	25	46	56	53	59	49	Sao Tomé-et-Principe
66	61	74	98	67	106	100	72	116	141	195	Sierra leone
28	19	21	30	57	58	49	45	35	45	65	Iles Salomon
346	352	356	509	590	437	427	494	186	653	873	Somalie
998	659	1135	949	902	949	773	827	881	547	475	Soudan
112	109	111	171	122	206	200	261	202	223	124	Togo
4	5	3	4	26	14	7	5	5	8	4	Tuvalu
141	163	183	193	301	397	497	631	636	712	706	Ouganda
662	554	485	676	914	1016	919	1181	1120	1346	976	Rép.-Unie de Tanzanie
27	24	22	24	51	39	40	52	55	41	33	Vanuatu
502	503	451	413	509	377	376	434	308	289	246	Yémen
305	303	303	427	674	554	731	895	476	268	188	Zaïre
235	260	341	456	426	476	396	482	883	1035	805	Zambie
9014	**8777**	**10043**	**11905**	**13597**	**14377**	**14202**	**16132**	**16117**	**16419**	**14966**	**Ensemble des PMA**
28904	**29967**	**30935**	**36782**	**41199**	**43844**	**44633**	**54857**	**58132**	**54919**	**49188**	**Ensemble des pays en développement**

Pour mémoire :

En dollars courants par habitant :

21.4	20.3	22.6	26.2	29.1	29.9	28.8	31.8	30.8	30.5	27.0	Ensemble des PMA
12.1	12.2	12.3	14.3	15.7	16.3	16.2	19.5	20.2	18.7	16.4	Ensemble des pays en développement

En dollars constants de 1980 a (millions):

10090	9950	11364	13058	13824	13880	13263	13995	14172	14103	13156	Ensemble des PMA
32041	33781	34923	40697	42264	42858	42218	47977	51899	47906	44262	Ensemble des pays en développement

En dollars constants de 1980 a par habitant :

23.9	23.0	25.6	28.7	29.6	28.9	26.9	27.6	27.1	26.2	23.7	Ensemble des PMA
13.4	13.8	13.9	15.8	16.1	15.9	15.4	17.1	18.1	16.3	14.7	Ensemble des pays en développement

Source: Estimations du secrétariat de la CNUCED principalement d'après des données du secrétariat de l'OCDE.
   a Le déflateur utilisé est l'indice de valeur unitaire des importations (se rapporter au tableau 10).

23. GDP growth and net external receipts of LDCs

LDCs classified according to population size [a]	GDP Annual growth — PIB croissance annuelle (%)	Net financial flows in $ per capita — Apports financiers nets en dollars par habitant — Total	ODA APD	% shares in total flows — Parts en % dans le total des apports — ODA APD	Other official flows — Autres apports publiques	Private flows — Apports privés	Ratios Rapports (%) — ODA/GDP APD/PIB	ODA/Domestic investment APD/Investissement intérieur	ODA/imports APD/importations
Large [b]									
Nepal	4.3	13.9	13.4	96.6	0.4	2.5	8.9	45.5	51.4
Uganda	5.1	12.3	10.9	88.7	12.8	-2.5	5.2	69.9	46.3
United Rep. of Tanzania	1.8	32.1	30.2	93.9	6.5	2.6	10.4	57.3	64.1
Mozambique	-6.7	28.0	23.5	84.1	3.8	12.1	15.6	94.0	49.0
Bangladesh	4.3	12.8	12.9	100.4	1.5	0.6	8.7	63.6	64.7
Malawi	3.6	23.6	20.9	88.4	6.6	5.2	12.1	68.6	48.2
Mali	2.2	39.3	39.3	99.8	0.7	0.4	23.3	133.5	85.4
Sudan	0.0	43.0	41.5	96.6	11.1	-3.1	9.4	66.9	72.6
Myanmar	3.5	9.6	9.3	96.5	0.0	3.3	5.2	29.7	108.0
Madagascar	0.9	31.6	23.1	73.2	21.7	6.4	7.2	78.3	56.9
Ethiopia	0.1	14.8	13.8	93.5	1.1	5.5	11.6	92.7	60.6
Afghanistan	2.0	18.9	19.1	101.2	-1.4	0.2	10.7	..	26.0
Zaire	2.4	16.3	11.5	70.3	43.4	-14.3	3.4	32.8	52.1
Yemen	..	59.6	55.2	92.7	0.7	7.2	8.5	38.6	17.3
Medium [c]									
Botswana	10.3	140.0	98.8	70.6	28.2	1.2	9.0	29.3	14.4
Lesotho	1.6	69.3	65.5	94.6	4.7	0.7	32.2	74.0	20.5
Lao People's Dem. Rep.	5.4	40.7	39.4	96.6	0.0	3.4	11.6	151.4	124.6
Cambodia	..	22.0	22.1	100.2	-	-0.2	9.0	..	296.0
Chad	8.9	22.9	23.3	102.0	-0.5	-1.9	17.4	306.5	62.7
Guinea-Bissau	2.2	79.8	76.4	95.7	3.7	0.6	33.8	126.4	121.0
Guinea	-4.2	21.9	21.2	97.0	1.3	1.8	6.6	45.8	28.6
Gambia	2.6	87.6	87.1	99.4	5.4	-4.8	24.2	127.5	58.7
Burundi	3.8	36.4	32.3	88.8	3.4	7.6	13.8	85.0	77.6
Bhutan	6.6	14.5	14.5	99.9	0.0	0.1	10.8	26.9	..
Burkina Faso	4.0	29.0	28.0	96.7	2.4	1.5	15.9	78.4	65.1
Benin	3.5	31.4	25.1	79.9	1.1	19.3	8.1	50.2	25.0
Liberia	-1.4	18.4	53.7	291.7	36.8	-228.5	10.3	87.1	30.4
Sierra Leone	-1.2	22.1	21.7	98.0	2.8	0.2	5.8	43.1	38.7
Mauritania	0.8	133.1	121.8	91.6	11.1	1.5	27.6	86.8	86.7
Niger	-3.5	42.5	37.6	88.5	9.0	3.5	13.2	91.9	61.8
Central African Republic	2.8	46.3	44.1	95.3	4.1	1.0	15.0	135.6	98.6
Zambia	-0.7	68.7	47.4	68.9	25.8	8.0	10.4	61.5	35.2
Rwanda	1.8	30.2	29.6	97.9	0.1	2.0	10.8	69.0	59.4
Togo	1.3	33.8	36.9	109.3	17.3	-26.6	12.6	49.2	32.5
Somalia	1.4	58.7	53.2	90.7	4.0	6.3	15.6	58.9	158.2
Haiti	-0.1	24.0	24.3	101.1	-0.7	-0.0	7.8	51.6	32.6
Small [d]									
Sao Tome and Principe	1.0	118.3	118.4	100.1	0.0	-0.1	31.5	92.0	89.6
Maldives	14.5	60.5	57.7	95.3	22.4	-4.9	14.8	44.5	21.5
Tuvalu	..	584.8	590.9	101.0	-	-1.0	117.0	..	-
Solomon Islands	6.7	108.3	102.2	94.4	4.4	1.3	18.3	63.1	39.9
Cape Verde	6.4	246.2	237.0	96.3	3.2	0.6	63.9	119.0	87.2
Vanuatu	4.5	198.0	200.9	101.5	-20.8	20.7	23.4	75.6	40.9
Equatorial Guinea	1.4	68.0	64.1	94.3	9.0	-3.3	23.2	158.5	57.2
Comoros	3.9	106.8	101.8	95.3	4.0	0.7	36.9	118.9	121.8
Djibouti	0.1	240.7	232.1	96.4	-0.1	3.7	25.2	102.4	42.1
Kiribati	0.9	245.3	225.5	91.9	8.6	-0.5	50.2	91.9	100.8
Samoa	2.0	142.6	145.2	101.8	-0.4	-1.3	23.6	78.7	44.8
ALL LDCs	2.1	24.5	22.7	92.6	7.6	1.0	9.6	63.8	49.3

Source: UNCTAD secretariat calculations based on data from the OECD secretariat, the World Bank, the Economic Commission for Africa, and other international and national sources.

 a Within each population group, the LDCs are ranked in descending order of their GDP growth in 1987-1992.

 b More than 10 million. *c* Between 1 and 10 million. *d* Less than 1 million.

23. Croissance du PIB et recettes extérieures nettes des PMA

GDP Annual growth / PIB croissance annuelle (%)	Net financial flows in $ per capita / Apports financiers nets en dollars par habitant — Total	ODA APD	% shares in total flows / Parts en % dans le total des apports — ODA / APD	Other official flows / Autres apports publiques	Private flows / Apports privés	Ratios Rapports (%) — ODA/GDP / APD/PIB	ODA/Domestic investment / APD/Investissement intérieur	ODA/imports / APD/importations	PMA classés d'après la taille de la population [a]
									Grands [b]
5.4	23.8	22.8	95.8	0.4	4.0	14.1	66.2	64.2	Népal
5.0	30.4	29.9	98.5	0.5	0.1	11.9	97.9	127.2	Ouganda
4.4	42.0	42.9	102.2	1.2	-3.4	35.7	97.7	101.5	Rép.-Unie de Tanzanie
4.1	66.7	73.4	110.0	-0.9	-9.1	88.2	250.1	132.1	Mozambique
4.0	17.7	17.2	97.5	0.1	2.4	8.8	70.5	58.7	Bangladesh
3.0	50.4	49.0	97.2	-0.9	3.7	26.8	141.5	84.1	Malawi
2.6	48.5	48.9	100.7	0.4	-1.1	19.5	88.6	97.1	Mali
2.3	31.5	33.5	106.2	-0.8	-5.4	4.2	30.0	77.8	Soudan
1.1	5.3	5.9	111.2	0.9	-12.1	1.1	8.3	65.2	Myanmar
0.8	31.2	30.9	98.8	5.3	-3.9	14.1	114.7	89.9	Madagascar
-1.0	21.3	21.4	100.6	0.2	-1.2	17.3	135.4	111.4	Ethiopie
-3.9	19.2	19.1	99.6	-	0.4	4.1	..	36.3	Afghanistan
-4.2	20.9	16.3	77.9	28.4	-6.6	7.0	70.7	79.0	Zaïre
..	31.5	34.1	108.4	-1.3	-7.1	5.1	26.4	16.7	Yémen
									Moyens [c]
9.1	134.1	114.9	85.7	6.3	8.0	5.1	17.0	8.1	Botswana
6.5	90.3	72.3	80.2	5.1	14.6	23.5	36.7	19.2	Lesotho
6.3	42.1	42.1	99.8	0.0	0.2	19.0	168.0	92.6	Rép. dém. pop. lao
5.2	19.9	19.9	100.2	0.7	-0.9	9.9	104.4	578.5	Cambodge
5.2	47.9	47.4	99.0	-0.1	1.1	23.4	266.8	91.7	Tchad
3.9	128.4	123.3	96.0	0.5	3.5	60.6	203.6	165.1	Guinée-Bissau
3.7	57.4	58.2	101.3	-2.2	0.9	12.2	74.6	56.0	Guinée
3.7	133.4	112.6	84.5	0.8	14.7	32.3	170.1	56.4	Gambie
3.5	43.3	45.0	104.0	-0.5	-3.4	21.8	122.8	111.0	Burundi
3.1	32.9	32.1	97.8	0.2	2.0	18.7	54.5	..	Bhoutan
3.0	39.2	38.9	99.1	0.5	0.4	14.1	67.2	69.2	Burkina Faso
2.5	46.2	51.1	110.5	12.4	-22.9	13.2	98.4	76.3	Bénin
2.4	93.1	38.8	41.7	-1.1	59.4	8.1	58.2	37.1	Libéria
2.1	28.8	25.4	87.9	4.5	7.6	12.2	106.1	64.5	Sierra Leone
1.6	108.1	114.3	105.8	-0.1	-5.7	21.9	97.7	52.1	Mauritanie
0.8	46.7	48.5	103.8	2.2	-6.1	16.0	148.4	103.9	Niger
0.4	69.8	68.2	97.8	0.7	1.5	16.4	135.4	130.7	Rép. centrafricaine
0.2	78.1	76.9	98.4	-1.3	2.9	18.4	134.9	70.1	Zambie
0.2	42.4	42.1	99.4	0.5	0.7	14.2	97.1	89.5	Rwanda
0.2	55.4	58.1	105.0	-2.7	-2.3	13.8	58.4	43.0	Togo
-0.7	52.9	54.1	102.3	0.7	-3.0	35.2	133.8	322.1	Somalie
-2.5	25.5	26.2	102.6	-0.3	-2.3	6.6	63.1	48.0	Haïti
									Petits [d]
10.4	382.8	364.5	95.2	0.5	4.3	87.0	233.8	270.1	Sao Tomé-et-Principe
10.1	183.0	135.2	73.9	13.4	12.7	22.4	35.6	23.0	Maldives
6.9	1345.5	1237.6	92.0	-	8.0	120.0	210.6	..	Tuvalu
4.7	173.5	153.1	88.2	5.4	6.4	23.3	76.9	48.6	Iles Salomon
3.9	296.5	302.3	102.0	-1.1	-0.9	40.2	120.2	78.6	Cap-Vert
3.1	444.7	313.7	70.5	2.6	26.8	30.3	88.3	59.0	Vanuatu
2.6	176.8	168.3	95.2	0.3	4.5	45.2	175.3	96.5	Guinée équatoriale
0.9	96.2	97.0	100.8	-2.3	1.5	23.1	116.8	108.8	Comores
0.9	228.0	229.3	100.6	-	-0.6	27.6	177.7	55.4	Djibouti
0.3	280.5	278.8	99.4	0.0	0.6	63.4	98.2	90.6	Kiribati
-1.1	270.0	261.8	97.0	-1.0	4.1	31.0	90.8	51.1	Samoa
1.8	**31.1**	**30.6**	**98.4**	**1.9**	**-0.4**	**10.5**	**69.4**	**65.9**	**Ensemble des PMA**

Source: Chiffres calculés par le secrétariat de la CNUCED d'après des données du secrétariat de l'OCDE, de la Banque mondiale, de la Commission économique pour l'Afrique, et d'autres sources internationales et nationales.

a Au sein de chaque groupe de population, les PMA sont répartis selon les taux de croissance de leur PIB pendant la période 1987-1992, en ordre décroissant.

b Plus de 10 millions. *c* Entre 1 et 10 millions. *d* Moins de 1 million.

24. ODA from DAC member countries and mutlilateral agencies mainly financed by them to individual LDCs

Country a	Average / Moyenne 1980-1986						
	Per capita ODA APD par habitant	Total ODA APD Totale	of which: Technical Assistance dont: Assistance Technique	Bilateral ODA APD Bilatérale	of which: Grants dont: Dons	Multilateral ODA APD Multilatérale	of which: Grants dont: Dons
	Dollars	$ mill. mill. de $	As % of total ODA En % de l'APD totale				
Bangladesh	12.1	1143.2	13.7	62.3	54.9	37.7	10.9
United Rep.of Tanzania	29.2	599.2	27.4	76.8	74.8	23.2	10.3
Mozambique	18.3	237.0	20.8	76.7	60.2	23.3	18.8
Ethiopia	9.5	371.7	20.2	51.4	49.0	48.6	35.4
Sudan	29.7	603.9	22.9	66.0	61.8	34.0	22.2
Zambia	44.3	283.4	28.0	77.1	53.5	22.9	9.4
Uganda	10.3	147.6	22.9	37.2	40.8	62.8	29.2
Zaire	11.9	355.3	36.8	70.5	49.1	29.5	12.8
Somalia	44.8	332.1	34.4	55.2	44.8	44.8	34.7
Malawi	21.1	143.8	26.4	46.5	43.9	53.5	15.8
Mali	33.3	248.8	26.3	65.2	50.8	34.8	20.7
Nepal	12.8	206.7	31.0	54.3	51.5	45.7	16.0
Madagascar	20.2	201.7	22.2	59.0	33.2	41.0	13.4
Niger	32.6	201.9	33.9	67.2	60.9	32.8	18.7
Burkina Faso	27.1	203.2	36.6	70.6	64.1	29.4	18.1
Guinea	20.4	97.1	20.5	46.6	28.5	53.4	22.5
Rwanda	28.2	160.7	35.2	63.7	59.7	36.3	19.6
Yemen	19.6	177.1	41.4	51.4	49.6	48.6	23.4
Chad	21.0	100.8	24.5	56.0	56.6	44.0	40.3
Burundi	29.3	131.6	34.9	55.0	47.9	45.0	20.0
Benin	23.4	88.4	32.5	52.2	46.5	47.8	21.6
Mauritania	67.9	113.9	30.6	66.2	57.3	33.8	24.5
Myanmar	8.7	314.9	13.0	71.1	25.3	28.9	7.4
Togo	35.0	99.9	31.3	55.2	57.1	44.8	18.0
Central African Rep.	43.4	107.7	32.6	65.8	56.0	34.2	17.9
Haiti	23.5	132.7	27.6	63.2	54.7	36.8	11.8
Botswana	95.5	96.3	43.6	77.6	78.1	22.4	20.0
Afghanistan	0.8	12.9	118.2	15.2	67.8	84.8	76.9
Lao People's Dem.Rep.	10.7	36.6	36.5	45.3	47.8	54.7	30.6
Lesotho	64.0	94.2	36.3	63.9	64.3	36.1	23.3
Guinea-Bissau	69.6	58.8	25.6	57.6	57.4	42.4	24.2
Sierra Leone	19.6	67.5	32.8	60.5	49.2	39.5	22.6
Cape Verde	214.4	64.5	26.9	70.7	69.7	29.3	22.6
Cambodia	10.8	76.2	58.7	20.4	20.5	79.6	79.6
Liberia	49.9	103.3	25.8	77.6	54.9	22.4	8.7
Gambia	75.7	53.2	33.6	54.6	53.0	45.4	28.2
Djibouti	164.6	56.9	55.9	78.7	78.9	21.3	16.9
Equatorial Guinea	50.5	13.7	36.6	41.6	41.6	58.4	41.0
Comoros	75.5	32.2	31.3	52.2	48.1	47.8	29.6
Solomon Islands	111.1	28.1	37.7	72.3	69.6	27.7	10.0
Bhutan	12.2	16.1	50.1	31.6	31.6	68.4	60.5
Sao Tome and Principe	92.6	9.4	25.2	37.0	37.0	63.0	49.3
Vanuatu	224.1	28.3	58.1	89.5	90.3	10.5	9.3
Samoa	142.3	22.8	36.5	64.1	63.9	35.9	19.7
Maldives	44.3	7.6	47.9	57.3	59.3	42.7	31.2
Kiribati	239.3	14.8	31.7	90.8	90.8	9.2	9.0
Tuvalu	596.9	4.8	32.7	90.0	90.0	10.0	9.7
All LDCs	18.2	7702.7	27.0	63.2	54.1	36.8	19.0
All developing countries	10.4	24798.8	30.6	70.6	53.5	29.4	15.4

Source: UNCTAD secretariat estimates mainly based on data from the OECD/DAC secretariat.

a Ranked in descending order of total ODA received in 1987-1993.

**24. APD reçue par chacun des PMA en provenance des pays membres du CAD
et des institutions multilatérales essentiellements financées par ceux-ci**

Per capita ODA	Total ODA	of which: Technical Assistance [c]	Bilateral ODA	of which: Grants	Multilateral ODA	of which: Grants	
APD par habitant	APD Totale	dont: Assistance Technique [c]	APD Bilatérale	dont: Dons	APD Multilatérale	dont: Dons	Pays [a]
Dollars	$ mill. mill. de $	As % of total ODA En % de l'APD totale					
16.2	1751.9	13.8	51.1	46.0	48.9	11.0	Bangladesh
41.3	1058.0	20.1	71.1	70.7	28.9	10.3	Rép.-Unie de Tanzanie
71.2	1018.6	13.1	72.8	60.4	27.2	16.1	Mozambique
20.5	972.2	20.5	45.8	44.2	54.2	38.2	Ethiopie
28.4	699.1	22.9	51.4	48.3	48.6	31.3	Soudan
78.6	640.7	20.4	73.0	72.3	27.0	10.7	Zambie
30.0	539.4	17.7	41.6	37.5	58.4	22.3	Ouganda
14.2	530.7	24.4	64.9	51.2	35.1	11.1	Zaïre
58.8	508.2	18.7	71.6	69.5	28.4	22.2	Somalie
48.9	455.6	23.3	41.6	38.3	58.4	32.3	Malawi
45.9	423.8	25.2	61.8	52.5	38.2	17.7	Mali
21.8	419.9	26.7	58.3	51.0	41.7	11.2	Népal
29.6	372.4	21.0	59.8	58.2	40.2	14.7	Madagascar
45.7	354.5	30.4	68.1	65.0	31.9	18.9	Niger
38.4	345.7	32.9	67.9	62.4	32.1	17.1	Burkina Faso
57.9	333.8	17.9	51.3	38.2	48.7	18.2	Guinée
42.6	297.9	29.2	58.2	55.1	41.8	24.3	Rwanda
23.3	267.6	36.9	66.7	51.4	33.3	17.4	Yémen
44.9	250.7	24.4	57.6	51.0	42.4	22.2	Tchad
43.8	241.5	24.6	49.4	44.0	50.6	23.9	Burundi
50.5	234.4	22.2	56.3	51.2	43.7	19.0	Bénin
111.4	223.4	22.5	57.7	50.1	42.3	20.0	Mauritanie
5.2	218.0	18.2	66.3	33.4	33.7	11.1	Myanmar
54.1	191.6	26.3	60.8	51.9	39.2	16.0	Togo
65.0	190.6	27.8	55.2	49.8	44.8	19.2	Rép. centrafricaine
25.1	162.8	35.3	72.2	75.2	27.8	16.3	Haïti
109.0	139.2	42.3	78.9	76.5	21.1	14.1	Botswana
9.0	138.6	54.0	64.2	68.2	35.8	36.9	Afghanistan
32.1	135.0	26.9	42.0	43.9	58.0	18.9	Rép. dém. pop. lao
72.5	130.1	34.0	55.8	52.0	44.2	23.8	Lesotho
113.3	109.4	31.3	55.6	53.3	44.4	18.4	Guinée-Bissau
26.7	106.8	27.3	60.5	49.7	39.5	25.3	Sierra leone
302.8	103.8	30.7	69.3	68.5	30.7	23.5	Cap-Vert
11.5	102.3	48.4	56.9	56.9	43.1	42.4	Cambodge
39.3	101.6	26.4	40.9	40.9	59.1	51.8	Libéria
109.3	101.0	25.6	52.8	51.0	47.2	20.8	Gambie
197.0	100.4	40.9	78.5	71.9	21.5	11.5	Djibouti
159.0	56.2	31.2	60.0	52.3	40.0	20.2	Guinée équatoriale
94.8	51.7	35.1	58.9	54.2	41.1	30.2	Comores
158.0	50.7	37.5	64.2	52.4	35.8	26.7	Iles Salomon
32.8	50.3	40.1	52.5	53.0	47.5	35.5	Bhoutan
369.5	43.9	22.0	48.4	42.9	51.6	20.6	Sao Tomé-et-Principe
292.0	43.7	47.7	75.8	72.4	24.2	16.4	Vanuatu
266.1	43.4	31.6	58.3	58.2	41.7	18.5	Samoa
132.5	28.5	31.8	59.2	59.2	40.8	21.2	Maldives
265.7	19.2	44.9	80.7	80.7	19.3	17.5	Kiribati
1117.2	9.9	29.0	92.2	92.2	7.8	7.8	Tuvalu
28.2	14368.6	22.9	59.3	53.9	40.7	19.4	**Ensemble des PMA**
16.4	46165.0	30.4	72.3	59.8	27.7	15.9	**Ensemble des pays développement**

Source: Estimations du secrétariat de la CNUCED principalement d'après des données du secrétariat de l'OCDE/CAD.

a Classés par ordre décroissant de l'APD totale reçue en 1987-1993.

25. External debt and debt service, by source of lending

| | External debt (at year end)
Dette extérieure (en fin d'année) | | | | | | | | | | |
| | Millions of dollars
En millions de dollars | | | | | | | | | % of total
En % de total | |
	1982	1985	1986	1987	1988	1989	1990	1991	1992	1982	1992
I. Long-term	48695	62955	72814	89861	93684	96930	103805	109187	112562	92.5	92.1
A. Concessional	27450	38187	45350	57548	62642	66744	70312	77251	80700	52.1	66.0
(a) OECD countries	6628	9727	12124	15914	16632	16618	17779	17429	17124	12.6	14.0
(b) Other countries	12013	14842	16764	20479	22779	24057	21534	25069	26532	22.8	21.7
(c) Multilateral agencies	8809	13617	16462	21154	23231	26069	31000	34753	37044	16.7	30.3
B. Non-concessional	21247	24765	27463	32312	31044	30189	33492	31938	31862	40.4	26.1
(a) OECD countries (i) official/	10691	12158	12620	14940	13842	13877	14424	13251	11709	20.3	9.6
officially guaranteed	7377	9244	10054	12217	10724	11147	11893	11285	10138	14.0	8.3
(ii) financial markets	3314	2913	2565	2723	3119	2730	2531	1966	1571	6.3	1.3
(b) Other countries	5492	6151	7605	9008	9511	9386	12262	12414	14392	10.4	11.8
(c) Multilateral agencies	5064	6456	7238	8363	7691	6926	6807	6273	5761	9.6	4.7
II. Short-term	3947	5730	6767	7539	7321	8055	10040	9208	9623	7.5	7.9
TOTAL	**52642**	**68676**	**79578**	**97398**	**101008**	**104991**	**113846**	**118393**	**122185**	**100.0**	**100.0**
of which :											
Use of IMF credit	4285	4938	5150	6002	5522	5033	5063	5158	5180	8.1	4.2

Source :   UNCTAD secretariat calculations, based on information from the OECD secretariat.

Note :   Figures for total debt and total debt service cover both long-term and short-term debt
as well as the use of IMF credit.

25. Dette extérieure et service de la dette, par catégorie de prêteur

Debt service *Service de la dette*											
Millions of dollars *En millions de dollars*									% of total *En % de total*		
1982	*1985*	*1986*	*1987*	*1988*	*1989*	*1990*	*1991*	*1992*	*1982*	*1992*	
2781	3743	4790	4351	4568	4890	4532	3851	2866	85.4	95.0	I. Dette à long terme
560	992	1519	1498	1693	1683	1454	1283	1186	17.2	39.3	A. Concessionnel
184	263	401	399	497	517	494	394	394	5.7	13.1	(a) Pays de l'OCDE
229	348	522	496	549	551	389	266	144	7.0	4.8	(b) Autres pays
147	381	596	603	647	615	571	623	648	4.5	21.5	(c) Institutions multilatérales
2221	2751	3270	2853	2876	3207	3078	2568	1680	68.2	55.7	B. Non-concessionnel
1297	1627	1624	1439	1631	1756	1718	1129	787	39.8	26.1	(a) Pays de l'OCDE
917	1122	1348	1190	1189	1152	1259	792	597	28.2	19.8	(i) Prêts de l'Etat et garantis par l'Etat
381	505	276	249	442	604	459	337	190	11.7	6.3	(ii) Marchés financiers
167	122	135	105	162	145	87	94	52	5.1	1.7	(b) Autres pays
757	1003	1511	1309	1082	1306	1273	1345	841	23.2	27.9	(c) Institutions multilatérales
476	432	392	431	537	495	420	307	184	14.6	6.1	II. Dette à court terme
3256	4174	5179	4776	5103	5380	4966	4157	3016	100.0	100.0	**TOTAL**
											dont :
538	*829*	*1281*	*1013*	*772*	*1052*	*842*	*562*	*361*	*16.5*	*12.0*	*Crédits du FMI*

Source :   Secrétariat de la CNUCED, d'après des renseignements du secrétariat de l'OCDE.

Note :   Les données concernant le total de la dette et le total du service de la dette comprennent la dette à long terme et à court terme ainsi que les crédits du FMI.

26. Bilateral concessional debt and debt service, by main creditor countries a and groups of countries
26. Dette au titre de l'APD bilatérale et service de cette dette, par principal pays créancier a et groupe de pays créanciers

| Creditor | Outstanding debt disbursed at year-end / Encours de la dette en fin d'année (montants versés) | | | | ODA debt service b / Service de la dette de l'APD b | | | | | Créancier |
| | $ billion / En milliards de $ | | % distribution / Répartition en % | | $ million / En millions de $ | | Average Moyenne | % distribution / Répartition en % | | |
	1982	1992	1982	1992	1982	1992	1993-1994	1982	1992	
DAC countries	6.71	18.81	44.2	53.2	168.2	370.5	981.1	46.8	71.7	Pays membres du CAD
of which:										*dont:*
Japan	2.20	8.05	14.5	22.8	47.2	206.8	456.3	13.1	40.0	Japon
United States	2.34	2.81	15.4	8.0	78.4	85.0	159.8	21.8	16.4	Etats-Unis
France	0.39	2.75	2.6	7.8	12.9	36.9	139.8	3.6	7.1	France
Germany	0.92	1.69	6.1	4.8	16.3	6.6	65.5	4.5	1.3	Allemagne
Italy	0.07	1.60	0.5	4.5	1.8	19.5	72.9	0.5	3.8	Italie
United Kingdom	0.09	0.43	0.6	1.2	5.0	3.4	12.2	1.4	0.7	Royaume-Uni
Denmark	0.17	0.22	1.1	0.6	0.1	0.4	8.3	0.0	0.1	Danemark
Austria	0.02	0.18	0.1	0.5	-	0.4	7.5	-	0.1	Autriche
Portugal	0.00	0.18	0.1	0.5	0.1	0.4	18.1	0.0	0.1	Portugal
Netherlands	0.12	0.18	0.8	0.5	3.1	4.1	9.6	0.9	0.8	Pays Bas
Switzerland	0.02	0.15	0.1	0.4	0.1	1.0	6.6	0.0	0.2	Suisse
Spain	0.05	0.15	0.4	0.4	0.3	0.6	9.0	0.1	0.1	Espagne
Belgium	0.07	0.14	0.5	0.4	0.0	2.1	4.7	0.0	0.4	Belgique
Norway	0.02	0.12	0.1	0.4	-	2.0	5.4	-	0.4	Norvège
Other developed countries	0.02	0.04	0.1	0.1	0.0	1.1	3.3	0.0	0.2	Autres pays développés
Countries in Eastern Europe	2.53	8.60	16.7	24.3	105.3	12.5	928.7	29.3	2.4	Pays d'Europe orientale
of which:										*dont:*
former USSR	2.15	8.10	14.2	22.9	85.2	8.5	876.0	23.7	1.6	ancien URSS
Czechoslovakia	0.22	0.34	1.4	1.0	9.8	2.8	40.2	2.7	0.5	Tchécoslovaquie
OPEC members	3.77	5.18	24.8	14.6	60.2	124.4	401.3	16.8	24.1	Pays membres de l'OPEP
of which:										*dont:*
Saudi Arabia	1.53	2.11	10.1	6.0	15.5	60.6	169.2	4.3	11.7	Arabie saoudite
Kuwait	0.77	1.18	5.1	3.3	20.9	39.3	91.1	5.8	7.6	Koweit
Libyan Arab Jamahiriya	0.31	0.47	2.0	1.3	4.7	1.0	35.8	1.3	0.2	Jamahiriya arabe libyenne
Iraq	0.55	0.42	3.6	1.2	11.8	-	21.3	3.3	-	Iraq
United Arab Emirates	0.40	0.40	2.6	1.1	6.7	21.9	36.4	1.9	4.2	Emirats arabes unis
Algeria	0.15	0.34	1.0	1.0	0.3	1.0	45.1	0.1	0.2	Algérie
Nigeria	0.00	0.22	0.0	0.6	-	-	0.0	-	-	Nigeria
Other developing countries	0.45	0.57	3.0	1.6	13.6	6.1	36.8	3.8	1.2	Autres pays en développement
China	1.71	1.47	11.3	4.1	12.2	1.8	92.2	3.4	0.4	Chine
Total bilateral concessional debt	**15.19**	**35.37**	**100.0**	**100.0**	**359.5**	**516.8**	**2480.7**	**100.0**	**100.0**	**Dette de l'APD bilatérale totale**

Source: The data in this table are derived from the World Bank Debtor Reporting System (DRS). They cover 43 LDCs only (Afghanistan, Cambodia, Kiribati and Tuvalu are not covered by the DRS). Hence they are not comparable with data shown in table 25.

a Countries with outstanding ODA loans to LDCs exceeding $100 million in 1992.

b Data for 1982 and 1992 refer to debt service paid whereas data for 1993-1994 refer to projected debt service payments falling due in that period, based upon debt outstanding (including undisbursed debt) as of end-1992.

Source: Les données du présent tableau sont tirées du système de déclaration des débiteurs de la Banque mondiale. Elles ne visent que 43 PMA (l'Afghanistan, le Cambodge, Kiribati, et Tuvalu n'étant pas couverts par le système de déclaration des débiteurs). Elles ne peuvent donc pas être comparées avec les données du tableau 25.

a Pays envers lesquels les PMA avaient une dette de l'APD dépassant 100 millions de dollars en 1992.

b Les données pour 1982 et 1992 concernent les sommes payées au titre du service de la dette, tandis que pour 1993-1994 il s'agit des paiements exigibles cette période là au titre du service de la dette d'après des projections fondées sur l'encours de la dette (y compris au titre de prêts non encore versés) à la fin de 1992.

Les Pays les moins avancés. Rapport 1995 - Annexe

A-43

27. Multilateral debt and debt service by main creditor agency a
27. Dette multilatérale et service de cette dette, par principale institution créancière a

	Outstanding debt disbursed at year-end / Encours de la dette en fin d'année (montants versés)				Debt service b / Service de la dette b				
	$ billion / En milliards de $		% of total / En % du total		$ million / En millions de $			% of total / En % du total	
	1982	1992	1982	1992	1982	1992	Average Moyenne 1993-1994	1982	1992
Concessional / Concessionnel	7.67	34.27	82.1	91.6	125.2	592.1	949.3	38.8	52.9
of which: / dont:									
IDA / AID	4.78	22.08	51.1	59.0	42.8	243.9	354.5	13.3	21.8
AsDB / BAsD	0.54	3.95	5.7	10.6	7.9	77.9	94.7	2.5	7.0
AfDF / FAfD	0.37	3.80	4.0	10.2	5.5	44.1	74.0	1.7	3.9
IFAD / FIDA	0.06	0.84	0.6	2.2	0.3	18.6	27.1	0.1	1.7
AFESD / FADES	0.42	0.61	4.4	1.6	21.8	50.9	102.9	6.8	4.6
OPEC Special Fund / Fonds spécial de l'OPEP	0.48	0.54	5.1	1.4	6.9	43.5	73.2	2.1	3.9
EDF / FED	0.12	0.47	1.3	1.3	1.5	12.0	26.9	0.4	1.1
EEC / CEE	0.12	0.43	1.3	1.2	0.4	5.2	17.3	0.1	0.5
EIB / BEI	0.06	0.40	0.6	1.1	2.4	19.8	36.0	0.7	1.8
Islamic Dev. Bank / Banque islamique de dév.	0.07	0.27	0.8	0.7	3.4	17.2	41.0	1.0	1.5
BADEA / BADEA	0.18	0.26	1.9	0.7	5.2	14.3	43.0	1.6	1.3
IDB / BID	0.08	0.16	0.9	0.4	1.1	0.4	7.9	0.3	0.0
IBRD / BIRD	0.22	0.14	2.4	0.4	22.7	32.8	24.1	7.0	2.9
Non-concessional / Non-concessionnel	1.68	3.14	17.9	8.4	197.6	526.8	627.6	61.2	47.1
of which: / dont:									
AfDB / BAfD	0.26	1.49	2.8	4.0	23.9	179.1	279.5	7.4	16.0
IBRD / BIRD	0.92	0.91	9.8	2.4	111.0	258.7	223.0	34.4	23.1
Arab Monetary Fund / Fonds monétaire arabe	0.15	0.17	1.6	0.5	10.0	14.8	11.1	3.1	1.3
EIB / BEI	0.10	0.11	1.0	0.3	8.9	16.5	21.7	2.8	1.5
Total multilateral debt c / Total de dette multilatérale c	**9.35**	**37.41**	**100.0**	**100.0**	**322.7**	**1118.9**	**1576.9**	**100.0**	**100.0**

Source: The data in this table are derived from the World Bank Debtor Reporting System (DRS). They cover 43 LDCs only (Afghanistan, Cambodia, Kiribati and Tuvalu are not covered by the DRS). Hence they are not comparable with data shown in table 25.

a Agencies with outstanding ODA loans to LDCs exceeding $100 million in 1992.

b Data for 1982 and 1992 refer to debt service paid whereas data for 1993-1994 refer to projected debt service payments falling due in that period, based upon debt outstanding (including undisbursed debt) as of end-1992.

c Excluding the use of IMF credit.

Source: Les données du présent tableau sont tirées du système de déclaration des débiteurs de la Banque mondiale. Elles ne visent que 43 PMA (l'Afghanistan, le Cambodge, Kiribati, et Tuvalu n'étant pas couverts par le système de déclaration des débiteurs). Elles ne peuvent donc pas être comparées avec les données du tableau 25.

a Institutions envers lesquelles les PMA avaient une dette de l'APD dépassant 100 millions de dollars en 1992.

b Les données pour 1982 et 1992 concernent les sommes payées au titre du service de la dette, tandis que pour 1993-1994 il s'agit des paiements exigibles cette période là au titre du service de la dette d'après des projections fondées sur l'encours de la dette (y compris au titre de prêts non encore versés) à la fin de 1992.

c Non compris les crédits du FMI.

28. Total external debt and debt service payments

$ million

Country	Debt (at year end) Dette (en fin d'année)										
	1982	1983	1984	1985	1986	1987	1988	1989	1990	1991	1992
Afghanistan	2020	2640	2060	2275	2753	4041	5154	5054	5086	8194	9517
Bangladesh	4941	5580	5800	6781	7943	10021	11006	10734	12088	12300	13036
Benin	628	728	628	774	946	1114	836	1177	1392	1413	1419
Bhutan	3	2	6	9	21	46	86	73	82	86	83
Botswana	341	360	341	449	566	699	679	566	579	632	603
Burkina Faso	380	424	428	545	668	818	834	905	1100	1151	1248
Burundi	270	331	364	472	577	792	819	888	1019	1075	1150
Cambodia	916	870	729	715	715	975	1149	1422	1548	1693	1787
Cape Verde	72	90	87	108	126	146	128	136	150	153	157
Central African Rep.	272	279	269	353	446	616	645	695	858	949	915
Chad	164	170	154	172	212	299	350	430	571	687	769
Comoros	80	86	105	135	164	201	194	201	210	204	207
Djibouti	47	64	140	237	224	273	257	217	212	217	221
Equatorial Guinea	119	115	71	111	149	173	171	178	223	231	256
Ethiopia	2641	3535	3405	4091	4859	6346	6905	6998	7440	8231	8852
Gambia	211	211	246	240	287	358	365	355	393	415	427
Guinea	1417	1245	1145	1355	1713	1991	2173	2363	2667	2707	2785
Guinea-Bissau	213	236	299	381	408	486	448	485	571	624	635
Haiti	590	702	673	732	717	857	864	862	870	783	767
Kiribati	8	9	10	11	11	18	13	15	15	15	16
Lao People's Dem.Rep.	1061	1137	1067	1142	1189	1408	1497	1484	1604	1821	1966
Lesotho	142	151	132	168	195	261	279	326	472	462	690
Liberia	936	1237	1287	1400	1591	1823	1739	1612	1756	1756	1720
Madagascar	1662	1949	1830	2139	2630	3235	3220	3600	3856	3835	3699
Malawi	938	964	912	1027	1136	1334	1348	1387	1568	1662	1709
Maldives	48	71	80	59	68	71	66	63	75	83	134
Mali	861	980	1125	1448	1712	2033	2129	2263	2620	2777	2829
Mauritania	1160	1380	1370	1469	1744	1916	1963	1938	2094	2050	2032
Mozambique	1588	1729	1837	2276	3660	4454	4105	4328	4577	4483	4748
Myanmar	2034	2288	2320	2976	3554	4445	4471	4368	4773	4976	5168
Nepal	354	455	475	608	752	1037	1256	1411	1687	1902	1970
Niger	882	964	1029	1238	1487	1646	1674	1676	1800	1646	1691
Rwanda	221	259	296	352	453	617	663	716	806	886	907
Samoa	63	70	72	74	75	80	78	77	93	114	118
Sao Tome and Principe	59	74	83	86	106	119	112	139	155	160	178
Sierra Leone	555	631	629	632	582	708	660	668	714	782	768
Solomon Islands	254	50	132	295	123	132	121	126	153	208	186
Somalia	1362	1772	1802	1883	1956	2283	2188	2283	2401	2487	2405
Sudan	6547	7038	7352	8346	8739	9926	9887	10492	11555	11213	10513
Togo	1066	942	908	971	1082	1294	1243	1307	1495	1392	1388
Tuvalu	0	0	0	0	0	0	0	0	1	0	30
Uganda	867	1053	1022	1156	1244	1657	1887	2129	2480	2574	2761
United Rep.of Tanzania	2723	3114	2906	3393	3732	4528	4291	4336	5183	5108	5647
Vanuatu	14	78	93	128	179	171	225	255	304	285	261
Yemen	3669	4354	4398	5148	6024	7476	8642	9249	8706	8496	9092
Zaire	4776	5594	4928	5795	7027	8730	8812	9489	10360	10013	9348
Zambia	3465	4052	3891	4521	5033	5745	5376	5515	5484	5462	5377
All LDCs	**52642**	**60060**	**58936**	**68676**	**79578**	**97398**	**101008**	**104991**	**113846**	**118393**	**122185**

Source: UNCTAD secretariat calculations, based on information from the OECD secretariat.

Note: Figures for total debt and total debt service cover both long-term and short-term debt as well as the use of IMF credit.

28. Encours de la dette extérieure totale et paiements totaux au titre du service de la dette

Millions de dollars

| | | | | | *Debt service*
Service de la dette | | | | | | |
1982	1983	1984	1985	1986	1987	1988	1989	1990	1991	1992	*Pays*
40	39	43	47	46	50	39	43	115	70	9	Afghanistan
232	241	348	396	463	522	520	556	624	539	477	Bangladesh
30	68	53	38	59	44	36	36	48	42	35	Bénin
2	0	0	0	0	1	3	8	5	9	7	Bhoutan
62	31	42	46	53	80	93	72	105	85	87	Botswana
27	27	27	33	36	35	47	56	36	56	39	Burkina Faso
18	27	26	26	35	45	43	43	45	45	42	Burundi
2	1	1	14	14	11	13	12	31	17	16	Cambodge
2	4	8	6	6	8	7	5	7	9	8	Cap-Vert
9	16	38	30	31	25	30	39	38	22	24	Rép. centrafricaine
3	2	13	15	7	7	9	14	15	12	14	Tchad
2	2	3	3	3	2	1	2	3	3	4	Comores
4	7	22	40	30	23	25	27	28	19	13	Djibouti
5	10	10	12	9	8	6	9	7	4	4	Guinée équatoriale
80	113	141	165	188	200	252	282	190	133	124	Ethiopie
17	15	15	13	33	29	26	24	34	33	25	Gambie
107	94	125	82	87	149	135	143	174	140	87	Guinée
4	5	9	17	11	14	13	14	8	12	7	Guinée-Bissau
27	41	41	45	51	55	52	46	34	24	5	Haïti
0	-	0	1	1	1	0	1	1	1	1	Kiribati
2	5	10	14	12	12	14	17	10	8	10	Rép. dém. pop. lao
14	27	25	22	15	16	26	26	31	34	35	Lesotho
119	162	121	87	80	77	68	52	69	65	48	Libéria
147	137	111	145	211	211	224	238	209	160	119	Madagascar
97	91	114	120	136	116	108	128	117	105	96	Malawi
2	7	26	12	12	7	7	7	6	7	8	Maldives
36	20	31	56	65	76	84	90	81	47	58	Mali
63	65	84	115	109	123	155	127	159	104	84	Mauritanie
186	191	150	184	156	98	123	122	117	122	77	Mozambique
215	264	248	275	326	317	270	274	105	92	29	Myanmar
20	26	26	24	31	34	56	76	77	66	67	Népal
172	134	121	124	150	172	182	159	131	154	80	Niger
10	13	24	27	20	24	27	35	32	32	25	Rwanda
4	4	6	7	7	7	8	8	6	5	5	Samoa
0	2	3	4	2	4	3	3	2	2	3	Sao Tomé-et-Principe
48	62	60	43	69	27	28	34	28	20	34	Sierra leone
3	15	7	16	13	8	8	10	12	26	18	Iles Salomon
32	47	73	56	87	55	49	68	35	17	14	Somalie
229	329	344	282	416	273	340	341	233	186	151	Soudan
61	74	113	78	110	100	155	134	123	90	66	Togo
-	-	-	0	0	0	0	0	0	0	0	Tuvalu
82	115	174	168	176	152	197	185	118	140	84	Ouganda
112	172	128	113	160	180	200	190	180	169	121	Rép.-Unie de Tanzanie
2	8	18	17	50	15	14	20	28	24	17	Vanuatu
121	179	249	285	314	431	520	502	174	181	123	Yémen
329	294	515	654	759	716	671	883	1089	357	228	Zaïre
477	368	346	218	531	215	215	220	246	669	388	Zambie
3256	**3555**	**4093**	**4174**	**5179**	**4776**	**5103**	**5380**	**4966**	**4157**	**3016**	**Ensemble des PMA**

Source: Secrétariat de la CNUCED, d'après des renseignements du secrétariat de l'OCDE.

Note : Les données concernant le total de la dette et le total du service de la dette
comprennent la dette à long terme et à court terme ainsi que les crédits du FMI.

29. Debt and debt service ratios

In per cent

Country	1982	1983	1984	1985	1986	Debt/GDP Dette/PIB 1987	1988	1989	1990	1991	1992
Afghanistan	91	122	97	62	76	90	91	66	65	100	110
Bangladesh	38	45	41	43	51	57	58	52	54	53	55
Benin	50	66	60	74	71	71	51	78	75	74	65
Bhutan	2	1	3	5	10	16	32	28	30	37	33
Botswana	35	34	28	39	45	45	30	21	18	17	16
Burkina Faso	28	34	38	44	39	40	37	42	43	42	42
Burundi	27	31	37	41	48	70	76	80	89	92	105
Cambodia	55	50	41	38	37	49	64	99	108	89	89
Cape Verde	67	85	85	101	87	80	61	61	55	51	46
Central African Rep.	36	42	42	50	45	59	58	60	66	74	69
Chad	28	29	24	24	28	37	34	43	47	53	59
Comoros	75	78	97	118	101	102	94	101	86	84	79
Djibouti	15	20	43	70	62	73	65	53	50	49	49
Equatorial Guinea	172	164	87	139	151	145	134	159	169	177	161
Ethiopia	60	73	70	86	92	115	121	117	124	125	178
Gambia	87	87	107	91	96	160	127	105	122	112	123
Guinea	97	87	80	99	84	94	88	87	90	86	96
Guinea-Bissau	105	103	187	241	177	302	290	299	245	267	288
Haiti	40	43	37	36	32	40	39	37	31	30	24
Kiribati	29	29	28	46	48	71	42	46	47	44	47
Lao People's Dem.Rep.	375	219	61	48	67	129	248	200	185	177	167
Lesotho	42	44	49	69	70	70	65	67	78	72	95
Liberia	83	116	118	128	147	167	150	135	142	138	131
Madagascar	47	56	62	75	81	126	132	144	125	143	123
Malawi	80	79	75	91	96	113	101	87	84	76	92
Maldives	101	122	107	70	71	78	61	54	61	56	75
Mali	70	91	106	116	101	103	107	110	106	117	102
Mauritania	155	175	188	215	217	211	205	197	205	181	171
Mozambique	87	105	107	101	138	378	387	369	359	385	387
Myanmar	34	37	37	43	43	42	38	24	20	18	14
Nepal	15	19	18	24	29	38	40	46	53	57	66
Niger	45	54	70	86	78	74	74	77	73	71	72
Rwanda	16	17	19	21	23	29	29	31	35	54	58
Samoa	59	70	74	84	81	78	55	56	64	79	80
Sao Tome and Principe	167	212	256	247	165	215	229	302	302	318	414
Sierra Leone	42	42	58	48	41	128	58	70	83	104	110
Solomon Islands	196	40	76	184	85	80	57	55	72	96	89
Somalia	50	80	58	85	117	143	131	200	208	213	204
Sudan	71	84	81	93	100	87	90	69	47	26	114
Togo	130	123	126	127	102	104	90	97	91	86	89
Tuvalu	-	1	3	3	3	8	2	5	11	-	266
Uganda	43	42	35	28	26	31	31	39	66	86	85
United Rep.of Tanzania	43	49	50	49	76	128	129	153	200	160	206
Vanuatu	14	76	75	108	156	140	157	181	199	161	143
Yemen	65	74	73	83	96	125	135	139	121	102	89
Zaire	37	51	63	81	87	114	99	105	119	117	106
Zambia	90	122	143	201	302	276	148	138	147	161	163
All LDCs	53	63	62	68	75	87	83	77	73	65	76

Source: UNCTAD secretariat, mainly based on information from the OECD secretariat, the World Bank and IMF.

Note: Debt and debt service are defined as in table 28.

a Exports of goods and services (including non-factor services).

Les Pays les moins avancés. Rapport 1995 - Annexe

A-47

29. Rapports de la dette et du service de la dette

En pourcentage

| | | | | | *Debt service/exports* **a** | | | | | | |
| | | | | | *Service de la dette/exportations* **a** | | | | | | |
1982	*1983*	*1984*	*1985*	*1986*	*1987*	*1988*	*1989*	*1990*	*1991*	*1992*	*Pays*
5	5	5	7	8	8	7	15	41	42	4	Afghanistan
23	25	29	31	41	38	32	32	29	25	18	Bangladesh
16	36	18	10	15	9	7	14	12	9	7	Bénin
7	1	1	-	-	1	3	9	5	11	7	Bhoutan
10	4	5	5	5	4	5	3	5	4	4	Botswana
15	17	15	19	18	13	16	21	11	16	11	Burkina Faso
17	27	23	20	24	40	31	37	46	36	38	Burundi
7	6	6	58	57	43	45	40	100	51	44	Cambodge
6	11	24	18	14	16	15	8	11	15	13	Cap-Vert
6	10	25	16	16	12	15	18	17	12	13	Rép. centrafricaine
4	2	9	15	5	4	4	7	5	5	5	Tchad
9	10	27	13	11	6	3	4	8	6	8	Comores
2	4	15	27	22	16	15	16	16	10	6	Djibouti
27	45	47	51	21	19	12	23	17	10	6	Guinée équatoriale
14	20	22	26	25	30	37	38	31	30	27	Ethiopie
20	19	13	15	35	23	18	14	19	15	11	Gambie
24	18	24	16	15	25	23	20	21	17	13	Guinée
22	30	37	94	113	91	82	99	42	59	35	Guinée-Bissau
10	14	13	13	17	17	18	19	14	9	2	Haïti
-	-	-	4	5	5	-	3	3	4	4	Kiribati
4	10	17	19	15	14	18	20	10	6	5	Rép. dém. pop. lao
3	6	6	8	5	4	5	5	6	6	5	Lesotho
23	35	25	19	17	18	14	9	14	13	9	Libéria
38	38	28	41	52	49	54	49	40	33	24	Madagascar
35	32	33	42	49	36	32	41	25	20	22	Malawi
3	9	31	13	12	6	5	5	3	4	4	Maldives
19	10	13	23	24	22	25	26	19	10	13	Mali
21	18	26	29	25	28	32	26	34	22	17	Mauritanie
46	64	70	100	81	42	47	45	39	33	21	Mozambique
42	60	58	72	81	107	125	94	30	23	7	Myanmar
8	9	9	7	10	9	13	20	17	12	10	Népal
39	35	35	39	40	36	43	43	35	45	24	Niger
6	8	13	16	8	13	15	22	21	23	24	Rwanda
17	14	23	26	27	24	19	17	12	11	10	Samoa
4	20	23	42	15	46	23	32	25	22	33	Sao Tomé-et-Principe
32	44	35	27	45	15	18	19	13	10	17	Sierra leone
4	18	6	19	15	10	7	9	12	22	17	Iles Salomon
13	27	68	44	92	59	84	100	39	16	13	Somalie
25	41	44	34	75	60	57	41	46	49	41	Soudan
14	21	29	20	22	19	28	24	21	16	14	Togo
..	..	..	..	..	..	..	..	..	..	..	Tuvalu
22	29	41	45	43	46	74	67	66	71	44	Ouganda
21	35	25	26	36	45	39	35	33	36	21	Rép.-Unie de Tanzanie
4	13	21	20	62	19	18	26	26	23	16	Vanuatu
23	37	60	80	104	105	59	45	17	19	13	Yémen
20	16	25	33	37	36	28	37	47	17	23	Zaïre
44	36	36	25	72	24	17	15	18	53	31	Zambie
22	**24**	**26**	**28**	**34**	**28**	**27**	**28**	**24**	**21**	**16**	**Ensemble des PMA**

Source: Secrétariat de la CNUCED, principalement d'après des renseignements du secrétariat de l'OCDE, de la Banque mondiale et du FMI.

Note: La dette et le service de la dette sont définis comme au tableau 28.

a Exportations de biens et de services (y compris les services non-facteurs).

30. Structure of debt and debt service

Country	Percentage of total debt [a] *Parts en pourcentage de la dette totale* [a]							
	Long-term *A long-terme*		Concessional *Concessionelle*		Non-concessional *Non concessionelle*		Official and off. guaranteed *Publique et guarantie par l'Etat*	
	1982	1992	1982	1992	1982	1992	1982	1992
Afghanistan	100	99	98	99	1	-	1	-
Bangladesh	99	99	83	93	16	6	5	5
Benin	89	89	35	75	55	15	24	7
Bhutan	68	100	36	82	32	17	-	17
Botswana	88	98	30	40	58	58	24	16
Burkina Faso	91	95	67	80	24	15	12	7
Burundi	94	96	72	92	22	4	10	-
Cambodia	99	98	97	98	2	-	-	-
Cape Verde	100	96	47	78	53	18	17	6
Central African Rep.	95	97	45	87	50	10	26	4
Chad	91	96	62	80	29	16	8	4
Comoros	86	97	82	90	4	7	2	-
Djibouti	57	87	35	78	23	10	8	6
Equatorial Guinea	86	75	27	53	59	22	33	15
Ethiopia	99	99	33	35	66	64	4	2
Gambia	92	93	55	79	38	14	10	7
Guinea	91	89	66	77	25	12	11	3
Guinea-Bissau	100	89	46	63	53	26	6	6
Haiti	72	88	50	83	22	5	5	-
Kiribati	100	88	6	44	94	50	-	-
Lao People's Dem.Rep.	100	100	40	100	60	-	-	-
Lesotho	100	81	55	53	45	28	18	19
Liberia	87	81	35	37	52	43	6	-
Madagascar	94	92	45	55	49	36	20	17
Malawi	92	97	41	84	50	13	9	5
Maldives	91	68	73	63	18	5	2	4
Mali	99	98	90	90	9	8	4	-
Mauritania	90	93	64	71	26	21	6	6
Mozambique	89	78	11	55	78	23	33	5
Myanmar	99	92	74	88	25	4	11	3
Nepal	91	100	85	93	7	7	2	4
Niger	88	96	34	67	54	29	23	24
Rwanda	90	97	86	94	5	3	2	2
Samoa	100	100	71	98	29	2	8	-
Sao Tome and Principe	93	94	44	76	49	19	3	9
Sierra Leone	78	84	44	57	34	27	16	15
Solomon Islands	12	85	10	49	2	36	-	32
Somalia	99	92	63	61	36	31	4	4
Sudan	88	83	38	42	50	41	18	17
Togo	88	88	27	64	61	25	42	20
Tuvalu	100	-	-	-	-	-	-	-
Uganda	99	95	28	74	70	22	10	8
United Rep.of Tanzania	92	88	55	64	37	23	15	13
Vanuatu	77	48	28	18	49	31	14	7
Yemen	96	97	89	53	7	44	3	2
Zaire	92	84	22	38	70	46	41	30
Zambia	85	89	28	40	57	49	12	11
All LDCs	**93**	**92**	**52**	**66**	**40**	**26**	**14**	**8**

Source: UNCTAD secretariat calculations, based on information from the OECD secretariat.

  a Debt and debt service are defined as in table 28.

Les Pays les moins avancés. Rapport 1995 - Annexe

A-49

30. Structure de la dette et du service de la dette

Long-term *A long-terme*		Concessional *Concessionelle*		Non-concessional *Non concessionelle*		Official and off. guaranteed *Publique et guarantie par l'Etat*		
1982	1992	1982	1992	1982	1992	1982	1992	*Pays*
98	78	94	78	5	-	3	-	Afghanistan
97	99	44	66	54	32	12	6	Bangladesh
60	97	15	51	46	46	32	17	Bénin
68	100	-	29	67	71	-	57	Bhoutan
98	99	3	16	95	83	3	17	Botswana
97	90	17	54	80	36	43	13	Burkina Faso
90	95	12	67	77	29	18	2	Burundi
100	94	-	31	100	63	-	-	Cambodge
100	88	6	38	94	50	47	25	Cap-Vert
92	92	12	58	81	33	48	12	Rép. centrafricaine
50	93	9	57	41	36	-	14	Tchad
100	100	39	50	61	50	15	-	Comores
91	77	45	77	46	-	28	-	Djibouti
98	100	1	25	97	75	43	-	Guinée équatoriale
97	95	26	26	72	69	28	48	Ethiopie
92	96	10	44	82	52	14	16	Gambie
94	94	45	45	49	49	23	5	Guinée
100	100	24	57	76	43	49	-	Guinée-Bissau
70	80	16	60	55	20	27	-	Haïti
100	100	-	-	100	99	-	-	Kiribati
95	90	87	90	8	-	-	-	Rép. dém. pop. lao
90	91	8	29	82	63	18	17	Lesotho
88	88	5	8	83	79	59	54	Libéria
58	98	9	34	49	64	22	32	Madagascar
92	98	8	24	85	74	25	19	Malawi
95	75	69	63	26	12	19	25	Maldives
30	93	15	66	15	28	6	9	Mali
88	94	32	45	57	49	27	5	Mauritanie
93	123	-	29	93	95	59	32	Mozambique
76	93	19	228	57	-134	35	31	Myanmar
82	100	27	63	54	37	20	25	Népal
95	93	7	20	88	73	50	44	Niger
75	92	61	76	13	16	7	8	Rwanda
100	100	19	60	81	40	22	20	Samoa
71	100	69	67	2	33	66	-	Sao Tomé-et-Principe
65	91	6	41	60	50	25	6	Sierra leone
100	94	21	17	79	78	35	67	Somalie
95	100	27	29	67	71	2	71	Iles Salomon
89	78	16	22	73	56	12	24	Soudan
89	91	5	26	84	65	53	36	Togo
-	100	-	100	-	-	-	-	Tuvalu
97	98	19	27	77	70	5	12	Ouganda
81	97	20	34	61	63	19	22	Rép.-Unie de Tanzanie
83	65	33	6	50	59	17	12	Vanuatu
93	90	65	78	28	12	25	-	Yémen
92	93	7	18	85	76	50	46	Zaïre
74	96	3	10	70	87	16	12	Zambie
85	95	17	39	68	56	28	20	**Ensemble des PMA**

Percentage of total debt service [a]
Parts en pourcentage du service de la dette totale [a]

Source: Secrétariat de la CNUCED, d'après des renseignements du secrétariat de l'OCDE.

a La dette et le service de la dette sont définis comme au tableau 28.

31. ODA debt and debt service payments to OECD countries

$ million

Country	*Debt (at year end)* *Dette (en fin d'année)*										
	1982	*1983*	*1984*	*1985*	*1986*	*1987*	*1988*	*1989*	*1990*	*1991*	*1992*
Afghanistan	157	145	133	141	142	146	132	126	123	115	110
Bangladesh	1783	1755	2093	2559	2922	3747	4280	3630	3798	3683	3662
Benin	45	24	24	40	63	91	94	140	171	172	166
Bhutan	-	-	-	-	-	-	-	-	-	-	-
Botswana	56	49	45	46	46	49	66	73	62	65	66
Burkina Faso	34	44	49	71	100	156	166	202	248	264	257
Burundi	19	24	29	57	81	123	125	144	171	182	176
Cambodia	236	233	230	236	241	249	244	245	249	248	247
Cape Verde	1	0	0	4	6	8	7	7	8	7	6
Central African Rep.	37	42	39	67	96	158	155	173	203	202	191
Chad	5	6	5	11	20	51	65	83	115	130	128
Comoros	2	3	6	12	17	28	30	38	44	43	40
Djibouti	10	10	15	12	13	70	64	7	22	25	23
Equatorial Guinea	-	-	-	-	0	8	17	24	31	33	32
Ethiopia	183	175	187	223	263	323	317	367	417	464	328
Gambia	14	11	14	17	25	33	28	32	35	36	31
Guinea	123	127	132	165	227	319	382	459	528	567	563
Guinea-Bissau	6	6	6	1	1	1	1	1	1	1	1
Haiti	88	99	117	139	134	153	188	169	190	112	107
Kiribati	-	-	-	-	-	-	-	-	-	-	-
Lao People's Dem.Rep.	54	51	44	55	66	79	69	65	69	68	64
Lesotho	3	2	2	3	1	3	4	7	20	29	30
Liberia	197	229	245	280	340	390	369	362	384	383	373
Madagascar	191	222	234	337	482	683	700	729	600	568	443
Malawi	137	123	119	113	137	186	203	199	182	197	196
Maldives	2	2	1	1	2	3	3	4	3	3	3
Mali	26	18	112	255	334	437	426	544	685	710	676
Mauritania	41	46	46	70	109	140	139	150	123	126	132
Mozambique	109	134	153	235	339	466	476	545	512	445	365
Myanmar	855	1011	1005	1463	2049	2747	2813	2606	2869	3056	3054
Nepal	20	25	30	51	85	124	130	145	193	284	319
Niger	77	75	80	123	159	233	205	230	266	269	254
Rwanda	23	22	20	34	55	90	91	101	115	121	121
Samoa	0	0	0	0	0	1	0	0	0	0	0
Sao Tome and Principe	-	-	-	-	-	-	-	3	6	9	10
Sierra Leone	119	123	117	82	101	121	111	133	79	155	167
Solomon Islands	10	9	9	6	7	11	21	25	23	24	24
Somalia	120	150	220	267	334	458	349	351	357	367	338
Sudan	164	169	320	426	510	587	643	631	874	656	627
Togo	149	141	137	43	72	102	135	148	203	211	209
Tuvalu	-	-	-	-	-	-	-	-	-	-	-
Uganda	60	31	29	32	32	43	53	66	67	61	57
United Rep.of Tanzania	310	351	369	464	461	704	580	682	621	557	576
Vanuatu	4	3	2	3	4	7	8	9	12	15	16
Yemen	85	80	89	126	165	232	247	301	332	352	348
Zaire	562	587	640	781	1011	1273	1367	1522	1906	1557	1701
Zambia	510	537	575	677	872	1082	1129	1139	862	857	887
All LDCs	**6628**	**6893**	**7721**	**9727**	**12124**	**15914**	**16632**	**16618**	**17779**	**17429**	**17124**

Source: UNCTAD secretariat calculations, based on information from the OECD secretariat.

31. Dette d'APD et paiements au titre du service de la dette d'APD aux pays de l'OCDE

Millions de dollars

						Debt service Service de la dette					
1982	1983	1984	1985	1986	1987	1988	1989	1990	1991	1992	Pays
10	10	10	5	8	10	10	10	11	8	4	Afghanistan
39	39	49	50	84	85	127	109	106	126	136	Bangladesh
2	1	1	1	2	3	5	9	4	4	6	Bénin
-	-	-	-	-	-	-	-	-	-	-	Bhoutan
1	1	2	2	3	3	5	4	5	5	2	Botswana
1	1	1	2	2	4	5	13	0	5	7	Burkina Faso
0	1	1	1	2	3	7	7	8	3	4	Burundi
-	-	0	0	5	0	0	0	5	5	5	Cambodge
-	-	0	-	0	0	0	0	0	0	0	Cap-Vert
0	1	16	5	6	2	5	7	0	4	4	Rép. centrafricaine
-	0	4	0	0	1	2	2	4	2	3	Tchad
0	0	0	0	0	0	0	1	2	1	1	Comores
2	2	2	12	4	1	2	0	3	0	0	Djibouti
-	-	-	-	-	0	0	0	0	1	1	Guinée équatoriale
9	11	11	11	10	13	16	28	16	5	9	Ethiopie
0	0	1	1	1	3	3	3	4	1	1	Gambie
9	4	4	6	4	12	10	11	12	12	13	Guinée
0	0	0	6	1	0	1	0	0	0	0	Guinée-Bissau
2	2	2	1	3	2	3	1	4	4	2	Haïti
-	-	-	-	-	-	-	-	-	-	-	Kiribati
2	1	2	2	2	4	5	4	4	3	3	Rép. dém. pop. lao
0	0	0	0	0	0	0	0	0	0	1	Lesotho
4	7	10	8	8	7	10	12	5	4	4	Libéria
8	5	10	10	22	23	13	32	12	16	13	Madagascar
4	2	5	9	6	8	10	12	15	10	5	Malawi
1	0	0	0	1	0	-	0	0	0	0	Maldives
1	1	1	4	6	8	2	11	3	13	14	Mali
3	2	1	2	3	3	9	9	7	5	5	Mauritanie
0	1	1	3	5	7	29	17	24	10	12	Mozambique
30	35	48	50	62	78	53	28	28	40	34	Myanmar
1	1	1	1	2	3	4	4	4	5	9	Népal
6	6	6	8	10	10	7	9	5	6	6	Niger
1	1	1	2	2	3	5	4	6	2	3	Rwanda
-	-	0	0	0	0	0	0	0	0	0	Samoa
-	-	-	-	-	-	-	-	0	0	0	Sao Tomé-et-Principe
2	0	1	5	4	4	2	10	3	1	1	Sierra leone
1	0	1	1	0	0	0	1	1	1	1	Iles Salomon
4	4	6	10	3	5	13	20	9	4	4	Somalie
5	2	5	4	13	10	5	10	14	14	10	Soudan
1	8	13	5	8	5	25	9	9	5	6	Togo
-	-	-	-	-	-	-	-	-	-	-	Tuvalu
1	1	2	2	4	2	3	2	4	2	2	Ouganda
3	4	4	8	9	21	17	22	23	11	11	Rép.-Unie de Tanzanie
1	1	0	1	1	1	1	1	3	0	1	Vanuatu
2	2	3	3	6	8	12	14	16	16	13	Yémen
18	32	46	18	68	36	49	60	98	19	19	Zaïre
13	4	4	5	24	11	25	20	16	21	19	Zambie
184	194	276	263	401	399	497	517	494	394	394	**Ensemble des PMA**

Source: Secrétariat de la CNUCED, d'après des renseignements du secrétariat de l'OCDE.

32A. Multilateral debt [a]

Country	\multicolumn{11}{c}{Total multilateral debt ($ million) / Dette multilatérale totale (Millions de dollars)}
	1982	1983	1984	1985	1986	1987	1988	1989	1990	1991	1992
Afghanistan	110	109	109	119	129	139	137	133	131	131	130
Bangladesh	2278	2538	2742	3321	3993	5013	5417	5843	7033	7755	8151
Benin	160	188	202	240	297	370	384	442	546	617	649
Bhutan	1	2	2	5	9	20	25	32	42	48	50
Botswana	116	135	146	213	259	341	327	349	363	423	408
Burkina Faso	222	244	255	308	390	447	465	499	565	649	723
Burundi	132	175	209	258	354	489	550	607	703	768	828
Cambodia	17	16	16	17	19	22	21	23	24	25	15
Cape Verde	31	35	41	55	64	74	76	82	91	95	103
Central African Rep.	97	109	122	160	219	300	338	368	489	532	541
Chad	86	93	90	100	120	159	190	254	350	419	525
Comoros	31	39	51	69	92	109	107	107	114	117	123
Djibouti	6	12	23	39	54	75	80	79	90	100	105
Equatorial Guinea	29	29	22	27	33	50	61	68	72	84	84
Ethiopia	574	596	601	672	773	939	998	1080	1243	1354	1505
Gambia	100	101	104	118	147	197	196	218	250	263	286
Guinea	218	231	255	300	398	499	543	626	730	883	979
Guinea-Bissau	50	61	75	103	125	174	183	209	257	292	296
Haiti	255	320	368	401	421	500	479	487	522	539	552
Kiribati	8	9	8	9	10	12	13	13	14	14	14
Lao People's Dem.Rep.	51	58	66	75	93	108	125	196	283	354	403
Lesotho	75	90	107	145	168	207	222	258	307	327	353
Liberia	371	443	460	551	635	754	727	709	762	766	739
Madagascar	465	517	558	662	837	1119	1157	1214	1379	1517	1497
Malawi	416	473	550	651	773	926	953	1015	1191	1314	1358
Maldives	13	14	15	16	22	27	28	28	32	45	58
Mali	323	387	428	498	603	718	769	816	978	1077	1133
Mauritania	311	365	358	386	466	600	612	639	726	736	772
Mozambique	75	87	88	111	152	256	323	409	542	680	859
Myanmar	568	654	741	802	881	935	991	1060	1234	1258	1306
Nepal	268	320	382	477	581	746	870	1060	1312	1430	1495
Niger	193	259	286	352	466	599	646	680	787	804	793
Rwanda	134	161	188	242	306	398	440	479	542	625	659
Samoa	48	53	60	63	65	67	63	63	82	105	110
Sao Tome and Principe	17	20	20	21	24	32	42	58	76	93	108
Sierra Leone	164	185	194	224	243	277	278	277	290	288	297
Solomon Islands	18	23	27	32	38	46	51	56	63	66	63
Somalia	365	437	448	564	643	784	787	825	913	932	900
Sudan	1369	1511	1545	1698	1895	2189	2279	2364	2679	2816	2813
Togo	180	250	294	367	455	519	548	576	650	690	695
Tuvalu	0	0	0	0	0	0	0	0	0	0	0
Uganda	455	596	651	760	830	1107	1149	1232	1579	1777	1909
United Rep.of Tanzania	874	935	937	1089	1253	1510	1596	1657	1964	2131	2414
Vanuatu	0	0	1	1	2	6	8	13	17	25	27
Yemen	508	614	693	799	864	1259	1346	1446	1025	1042	1011
Zaire	931	1071	1151	1415	1650	2178	2174	2205	2395	2588	2534
Zambia	1157	1197	1237	1533	1846	2223	2146	2140	2366	2432	2435
All LDCs	13873	15759	16926	20073	23700	29519	30919	32994	37803	41026	42808

Source: UNCTAD secretariat calculations, based on information from the OECD secretariat.

a Including use of IMF credit.

32A. Dette multilatérale [a]

1982	1983	1984	1985	1986	1987	1988	1989	1990	1991	1992	Pays
						of which: non-concessional *(In per cent)* *dont: dette non concessionnelle* *(En pourcentage)*					
-	-	-	-	-	-	11	-	-	-	-	Afghanistan
19	18	13	13	13	12	11	8	4	2	-	Bangladesh
17	14	12	11	11	11	10	9	7	6	5	Bénin
-	-	-	-	-	-	-	-	-	-	-	Bhoutan
65	67	68	75	79	80	79	72	68	65	62	Botswana
7	7	7	8	10	12	13	13	14	12	11	Burkina Faso
11	11	11	13	11	10	9	8	7	6	5	Burundi
98	98	98	98	98	98	98	83	88	84	80	Cambodge
23	31	26	24	23	22	19	16	14	12	10	Cap-Vert
27	28	23	23	23	21	15	10	6	5	4	Rép. centrafricaine
9	8	5	9	7	8	6	3	2	2	15	Tchad
4	7	8	10	13	13	12	12	12	12	10	Comores
-	-	-	-	-	-	-	-	-	-	-	Djibouti
75	71	63	51	41	30	24	16	14	10	7	Guinée équatoriale
29	24	19	15	16	14	11	9	7	7	7	Ethiopie
45	38	36	35	25	22	18	14	10	7	5	Gambie
37	35	34	33	31	29	22	16	11	7	7	Guinée
6	4	15	16	14	11	9	7	5	5	5	Guinée-Bissau
19	24	23	20	16	12	7	6	5	4	4	Haïti
94	93	94	93	92	85	83	62	57	57	57	Kiribati
-	-	-	-	-	-	-	-	-	-	-	Rép. dém. pop. lao
2	3	7	15	14	14	13	11	11	9	8	Lesotho
77	76	73	73	72	72	72	71	72	72	72	Libéria
36	32	31	29	28	25	21	16	11	8	6	Madagascar
40	40	35	36	32	29	24	19	15	11	8	Malawi
52	44	40	36	-	-	-	-	-	-	-	Maldives
13	14	17	18	16	12	9	7	5	3	2	Mali
46	46	40	39	40	39	35	28	23	18	18	Mauritanie
23	25	25	36	32	25	20	18	15	13	11	Mozambique
13	14	11	9	5	2	-	-	-	-	-	Myanmar
6	4	2	4	4	5	4	2	1	-	-	Népal
16	29	30	33	31	25	16	13	10	8	7	Niger
-	1	-	-	-	-	-	-	-	-	-	Rwanda
9	11	14	15	14	11	5	2	1	-	-	Samoa
-	-	-	-	-	3	2	2	2	1	-	Sao Tomé-et-Principe
44	48	46	42	36	37	33	31	31	29	24	Sierra leone
15	15	12	9	9	5	3	3	1	-	-	Iles Salomon
20	26	24	27	25	22	20	17	17	16	16	Somalie
50	49	44	45	45	45	41	39	38	36	35	Soudan
24	24	29	30	28	26	22	16	11	8	5	Togo
-	-	-	-	-	-	-	-	-	-	-	Tuvalu
64	64	58	49	41	37	31	21	15	11	8	Ouganda
32	29	24	26	27	27	23	20	16	12	8	Rép.-Unie de Tanzanie
-	-	-	-	-	-	12	8	6	4	4	Vanuatu
18	16	17	16	13	5	5	6	4	1	-	Yémen
58	58	58	59	57	50	46	36	32	34	33	Zaïre
89	88	85	82	78	77	75	75	74	63	57	Zambie
37	**36**	**33**	**32**	**31**	**28**	**25**	**21**	**18**	**15**	**13**	**Ensemble des PMA**

Source: Secrétariat de la CNUCED, d'après des renseignements du secrétariat de l'OCDE.

a Y compris les crédits du FMI.

32B. Multilateral debt service payments [a]

Country	\multicolumn{11}{c}{Multilateral debt service ($ million) / Service de la dette multilatérale (Millions de dollars)}
	1982	1983	1984	1985	1986	1987	1988	1989	1990	1991	1992
Afghanistan	2	0	1	12	3	12	4	5	5	5	3
Bangladesh	98	97	157	178	262	300	220	253	356	286	226
Benin	5	6	7	12	15	14	14	13	33	22	21
Bhutan	-	0	0	0	0	0	0	0	0	3	1
Botswana	10	12	14	20	32	49	48	45	60	59	65
Burkina Faso	6	4	9	8	15	17	25	23	21	37	23
Burundi	3	9	14	12	15	21	19	20	21	22	26
Cambodia	2	1	1	7	1	1	1	0	2	0	10
Cape Verde	0	1	2	2	1	4	4	3	3	6	5
Central African Rep.	3	4	11	16	15	13	18	23	19	13	10
Chad	1	1	5	7	6	4	6	9	9	6	7
Comoros	0	1	1	1	1	0	0	0	0	2	3
Djibouti	0	0	1	1	3	5	6	5	5	5	5
Equatorial Guinea	1	1	7	9	4	4	3	6	5	3	3
Ethiopia	24	42	51	59	65	53	52	60	56	47	41
Gambia	5	10	7	6	27	19	17	14	14	16	12
Guinea	17	14	18	18	38	42	40	46	49	41	47
Guinea-Bissau	1	1	1	2	2	5	5	7	4	4	4
Haiti	6	7	11	23	35	41	38	32	22	15	0
Kiribati	0	-	0	0	-	1	0	1	1	1	1
Lao People's Dem.Rep.	1	1	2	4	5	6	6	5	5	5	6
Lesotho	1	2	3	7	9	10	11	11	12	13	15
Liberia	25	39	57	35	23	3	3	3	1	1	1
Madagascar	19	22	48	58	83	79	93	99	99	80	59
Malawi	34	36	48	44	65	72	71	67	62	64	61
Maldives	0	1	0	1	6	1	1	2	2	2	2
Mali	6	9	15	29	41	41	56	48	47	25	26
Mauritania	19	26	35	63	49	61	88	59	104	64	63
Mozambique	0	-	4	3	5	8	13	16	15	17	22
Myanmar	26	26	28	44	65	65	39	27	27	27	31
Nepal	11	12	14	15	16	20	22	29	36	29	29
Niger	32	9	14	19	28	52	61	38	28	23	18
Rwanda	4	3	5	6	8	10	10	13	10	10	11
Samoa	2	2	3	4	4	6	7	5	4	4	3
Sao Tome and Principe	0	0	0	0	0	2	1	1	1	1	2
Sierra Leone	13	11	25	10	51	5	8	4	9	11	28
Solomon Islands	0	0	1	1	2	3	2	1	2	3	2
Somalia	23	17	17	17	60	35	5	23	10	0	0
Sudan	107	122	96	56	125	48	40	67	25	23	26
Togo	13	9	22	29	28	46	56	55	44	33	27
Tuvalu	-	-	0	0	0	0	-	0	0	0	0
Uganda	33	40	79	113	138	122	119	130	88	80	69
United Rep.of Tanzania	51	66	75	60	105	99	92	89	116	122	79
Vanuatu	-	-	0	0	0	0	0	0	1	1	1
Yemen	19	24	41	62	104	136	108	62	56	90	66
Zaire	80	77	132	204	232	306	252	455	257	131	60
Zambia	201	236	190	105	314	69	45	47	99	516	269
All LDCs	**903**	**1001**	**1270**	**1384**	**2107**	**1911**	**1729**	**1921**	**1845**	**1968**	**1489**

Source: UNCTAD secretariat calculations, based on information from the OECD secretariat.

a Including use of IMF credit.

Les Pays les moins avancés. Rapport 1995 - Annexe

A-55

32B. Paiements au titre du service de la dette multilatérale [a]

				of which: non-concessional (In per cent) dont: service de la dette non concessionnelle (En pourcentage)							
1982	*1983*	*1984*	*1985*	*1986*	*1987*	*1988*	*1989*	*1990*	*1991*	*1992*	*Pays*
-	-	-	-	-	-	-	-	-	-	-	Afghanistan
82	76	76	64	67	67	51	61	71	62	40	Bangladesh
57	58	44	48	40	38	37	48	55	45	48	Bénin
-	-	-	-	-	-	-	-	-	-	-	Bhoutan
92	89	86	86	91	93	92	92	92	90	88	Botswana
38	33	17	35	31	27	21	36	29	51	43	Burkina Faso
62	74	56	26	37	42	38	37	43	41	35	Burundi
100	100	100	14	100	98	100	97	99	-	90	Cambodge
71	45	46	46	-	58	59	50	57	50	40	Cap-Vert
78	75	81	79	66	54	67	76	68	54	50	Rép. centrafricaine
82	46	65	53	21	14	33	57	56	17	14	Tchad
2	21	25	34	-	-	-	-	-	-	67	Comores
-	-	-	-	-	-	-	-	-	-	-	Djibouti
95	93	99	97	63	56	46	76	55	67	67	Guinée équatoriale
67	81	76	72	65	52	46	60	64	47	44	Ethiopie
86	93	70	74	86	56	53	57	64	63	42	Gambie
88	75	72	56	70	71	62	67	73	73	64	Guinée
40	91	80	71	70	67	73	44	43	50	50	Guinée-Bissau
63	61	56	69	72	71	67	62	50	27	-	Haïti
100	-	1	-	-	91	-	94	86	99	99	Kiribati
5	2	2	2	1	-	-	-	-	-	-	Rép. dém. pop. lao
22	15	18	42	43	42	47	47	50	62	53	Lesotho
95	94	93	95	91	91	90	1	99	-	99	Libéria
83	74	80	83	78	70	70	77	73	69	56	Madagascar
88	86	86	81	84	84	81	81	79	75	72	Malawi
-	79	-	60	80	-	-	-	-	-	-	Maldives
44	51	43	41	59	69	46	54	51	56	35	Mali
74	73	78	77	68	61	70	64	78	66	57	Mauritanie
100	-	13	74	81	86	66	61	59	59	55	Mozambique
83	67	49	54	57	54	27	3	-	4	3	Myanmar
62	52	46	33	15	16	15	36	42	21	3	Népal
85	54	65	55	60	75	76	76	71	65	50	Niger
5	13	16	7	7	5	9	4	-	-	-	Rwanda
61	58	49	53	52	57	59	43	23	25	-	Samoa
-	-	-	-	4	-	-	-	-	-	-	Sao Tomé-et-Principe
94	83	84	77	76	63	93	13	56	82	54	Sierra leone
58	59	62	52	66	66	31	22	44	33	-	Iles Salomon
82	65	73	84	89	79	20	61	40	-	100	Somalie
83	80	84	75	20	32	11	24	12	13	8	Soudan
90	61	69	75	66	73	77	76	75	70	63	Togo
-	-	100	-	-	-	-	-	-	-	-	Tuvalu
58	92	95	91	90	86	84	87	80	75	71	Ouganda
85	84	80	74	71	67	65	65	70	68	62	Rép.-Unie de Tanzanie
-	-	-	-	1	-	-	-	-	-	-	Vanuatu
22	31	44	50	52	58	40	13	30	27	18	Yémen
94	89	86	86	85	86	85	93	91	85	65	Zaïre
98	99	97	88	95	86	83	68	87	93	93	Zambie
84	**82**	**79**	**72**	**72**	**68**	**63**	**68**	**69**	**68**	**56**	**Ensemble des PMA**

Source: Secrétariat de la CNUCED, d'après des renseignements du secrétariat de l'OCDE.

a Y compris les crédits du FMI.

33. Debt reschedulings with official creditors, 1988-1994

Country		Date of meeting (month/year)	Cut-off date	Consolidation period (months)	Percentage of principal and interest consolidated	Grace period [a]	Repayment period	Arrears	Rescheduling of previously rescheduled debt	Good-will clause	Estimated amounts rescheduled ($ million)
Benin	I b	06/1989	31/03/1989	13	100	Toronto terms		yes	no	yes	193
	II c	12/1991	31/03/1989	15	100	Enhanced concessional terms		yes	yes	yes	160
	III c	06/1993	31/03/1989	29 e	100	Enhanced concessional terms		yes	no	yes	25
Burkina Faso	I b	03/1991	01/01/1991	15	100	Toronto terms		yes	no	yes	63
	II c	05/1993	01/01/1991	32 e	100	Enhanced concessional terms		yes	no	yes	36
Central African Republic	IV b	12/1988	01/01/1983	18	100	Toronto terms		yes	yes	yes	28
	V b	06/1990	01/01/1983	12	100	Toronto terms		no	yes	no	4
	VI c	04/1994	01/01/1983	12	100	Enhanced concessional terms		yes	yes	yes	89
Chad	I b	10/1989 d	..	15	100	Toronto terms		yes	..	..	38
Ethiopia	I c	12/1992	31/12/1989	37 e	100	Enhanced concessional terms		yes	no	yes	441
Equatorial Guinea	II b	03/1989 d	..	..	..	Toronto terms		yes	no	yes	10
Guinea	II b	04/1989	01/01/1986	12	100	Toronto terms		yes	yes	yes	123
	III c	11/1992	01/01/1986	..	100	Enhanced concessional terms		yes	yes	yes	203
Guinea-Bissau	II b	10/1989	31/12/1986	15	100	Toronto terms		yes	yes	yes	21
Madagascar	VI b	10/1988	01/07/1983	21	100	Toronto terms		yes	yes	yes	254
	VII b	07/1990	01/07/1983	13	100	Toronto terms		no	yes	yes	139
Malawi	III	04/1988	01/01/1982	14	100	9ys 11ms	9ys 6ms	yes	yes	yes	27
Mali	I b	10/1988	01/01/1988	16	100	Toronto terms		yes	no	yes	63
	II b	11/1989	01/01/1988	26 e	100	Toronto terms		yes	no	yes	44
	III c	10/1992	01/01/1988	35 e	100	Enhanced concessional terms		yes	no	yes	20
Mauritania	IV b	06/1989	31/12/1984	12	100	Toronto terms		yes	yes	no	52
	V c	01/1993	31/12/1984	24 e	100	Enhanced concessional terms		yes	yes	yes	218
Mozambique	III b	06/1990	01/02/1984	30 e	100	Toronto terms		yes	yes	yes	719
	IV c	03/1993	01/02/1984	24 e	100	Enhanced concessional terms		yes	yes	yes	440

33. Debt reschedulings with official creditors, 1988-1994 (concluded)

Country	Date of meeting (month/year)	Cut-off date	Consolidation period (months)	Percentage of principal and interest consolidated	Grace period [a]	Repayment period	Arrears	Rescheduling of previously rescheduled debt	Good-will clause	Estimated amounts rescheduled ($ million)
Niger										
V b	04/1988	01/07/1983	13	100, 75 f	10ys 0m	9ys 6ms	no	no	no	37
VI b	12/1988	01/07/1983	12	100	Toronto terms		no	yes	yes	48
VII b	09/1990	01/07/1983	28 e	100	Toronto terms		yes	yes	yes	116
VIII c	03/1994	01/07/1983	15	100	Enhanced concessional terms		yes	yes	yes	160
Sierra Leone										
V c	11/1992	01/07/1983	16	100 g	Enhanced concessional terms h		yes	yes	yes	164
VI c	07/1994	01/07/1983	17	100	Enhanced concessional terms		yes	yes	yes	..
Togo										
VI	03/1988	01/01/1983	16	100	7ys 10ms	7ys 6ms	yes	yes	no	139
VII b	06/1989	01/01/1983	15	100	Toronto terms		no	yes	yes	76
VIII b	07/1990	01/01/1983	24 e	100	Toronto terms		no	yes	no	88
IX c	06/1992	01/01/1983	24 e	100	Enhanced concessional terms		no	yes	yes	52
Uganda										
IV b	01/1989	01/07/1981	18	100	Toronto terms		yes	yes	yes	89
V c	06/1992	01/07/1981	18	100	Enhanced concessional terms		yes	yes	yes	39
United Rep. of Tanzania										
II b	12/1988	30/06/1986	6	100	Toronto terms		yes	yes	yes	377
III b	03/1990	30/06/1986	12	100	Toronto terms		yes	yes	yes	200
IV c	01/1992	30/06/1986	30 e	100	Enhanced concessional terms		yes	yes	yes	691
Zaïre										
X b	06/1989	30/06/1983	13	100	Toronto terms		yes	yes	yes	1530
Zambia										
IV b	07/1990	01/01/1983	18	100	Toronto terms		yes	yes	yes	963
V c	07/1992	01/01/1983	33 e	100	Enhanced concessional terms		yes	yes	yes	917

Source: Paris Club Agreed Minutes.

Note: Roman numerals indicate the number of debt reschedulings for the country since 1976.

a The grace period is defined as starting at the beginning of the consolidation period and running up to the date of the first payment.
b Beneficiary of the concessional debt relief measures agreed upon at the Toronto summit.
c Beneficiary of new terms going beyond the Toronto terms following the Trinidad proposal (1990), and the London Summit recommendations of 1992.
d Dates of informal meeting of creditors on the terms to be applied in the bilateral agreements. Given the very small number of creditors involved, creditors did not call for a full Paris club meeting.
e Multi-year rescheduling.
f The first percentage relates to principal, and the second to interest.
g Including 50% of moratorium interest.
h Does not apply to moratorium interest nor to arrears on short-term debt.

34. Arrangements in support of structural adjustment in the 1980s
(As of July 1994)

Millions of SDRs (except where otherwise indicated)

Country	IMF arrangements				World Bank loans and credits								Purpose
	Stand-by/Extended Facility		SAF/ ESAF		Structural adjustment				Sector and other adjustment				
						Amount				Amount			
	Period	Amount	Period	Amount	Date of approval	IDA	African Facility [1]	Co-financing [2]	Date of approval	IDA	African Facility [1]	Co-financing [2]	
Bangladesh	July 1979-July 1980	85											
	Dec.1980-Dec.1983 [3]	800 [4]											
	March 1983-Aug. 1983	68.4											
	Dec. 1985-June 1987	180	Feb. 1987-Feb. 1990	201.3					June 1987	147.8			Industrial policy reform
									Apr. 1989	137.0		Germany (DM 26 mn.)	Energy sector
			Aug. 1990-Sept.1993	345 [5]					Oct. 1989	1.8 [6]			Idem
									June 1990	132.7		USAID (18.2)	Financial sector
									Nov. 1990	2.5 [6]			Idem
									Nov. 1991	2.2 [6]			Idem
									May 1992	109.3			Public resource Management
									Oct. 1992	72.2			Industry
									Dec. 1992	2.5 [6]			Idem
									Feb. 1994	175.0			Jute Sector
									May 1994	2.4 [6]			Idem
Benin			June 1989-June 1992	21.9 [7]	May 1989	33.5							
			Jan. 1993-Jan. 1996	47.0 [5]	June 1991	41.3			Nov. 1993	3.7		DANIDA (4) ACBF (2)	Economic management
Burkina Faso			Mar. 1991-Mar. 1993	22.1 [8]	June 1991	60.0		EC (30); AfDB (20); France (17); Canada (13); Germany (12)	Feb. 1985	13.8		France/CCCE (3.2); Netherlands (2.1); Germany/GTZ (2); France/FAC (1.7)	Fertilizers
			Mar. 1993-Mar. 1996	48.6 [5]					Feb. 1992	49.6		EDF (99); AfDB (60.6); CIDA (29.8); Germany (28.6); West African Development Fund (10.2); BADEA (8.5); CCCE & FAC (7.8); IsDB (5.5); BOAD (3.1); UNDP (0.6)	Transport sector
									June 1992	20.6		France (21)	Agriculture
									Mar. 1994	18.0		EC (20); AfDB (13)	Economic recovery

Les Pays les moins avancés. Rapport 1995 - Annexe

A-59

34. Arrangements in support of structural adjustment in the 1980s (*continued*)
(As of July 1994)

Millions of SDRs (except where otherwise indicated)

Country	IMF arrangements				World Bank loans and credits								Purpose
	Stand-by/Extended Facility		SAF/ESAF		Structural adjustment		Amount		Sector and other adjustment		Amount		
	Period	Amount	Period	Amount	Date of approval	IDA	African Facility[1]	Co-financing[2]	Date of approval	IDA	African Facility[1]	Co-financing[2]	
Burundi	Aug. 1986-March 1988	21	Aug. 1986-Aug. 1989	29.9	May 1986	13.2	14.3	Japan (11); Switzerland (7.7); Japan (18.1); Germany (6); Saudi Arabia (2.9)					
			Nov. 1991-Nov. 1994	42.7[5]	June 1988	64.9							
					June 1992	22							
Central African Republic	Feb. 1980-Feb. 1981	4	June 1987-May 1990	21.3	Sept. 1986	12.3	14	ADF (25)	July 1987	11.5		Saudi Arabia (2); Japan (6)	Cotton sector
	April 1981-Dec. 1981	10.4[9]			June 1988	28.9							
	April 1983-April 1984	18[10]			June 1990	34.5							
	April 1984-July 1985	15											
	July 1985-Sept. 1985	15[11]											
	Sept. 1985-March 1987												
	June 1987-May 1988	8											
	Mar. 1994-Mar. 1995	16.5											
Chad			Oct. 1987-Oct. 1990	21.4					July 1988	11.9	(16.2)	USAID (23); Germany (22.7); CCCE (13.1); ADF (11.3); BDEAC (10.6); EDF (4.8); OPEC Fund for Int.Dev.(4.5); FAC (3.3); UNDP (0.5)	Public finance and cotton sector
									Apr. 1989	45.4			Transport sector
									Mar. 1994	14.4			Economic recovery
Cambodia	Mar. 1994-Mar. 1995	16.5	May 1994-May 1995	84[5]	July 1988	11.9							

34. Arrangements in support of structural adjustment in the 1980s (continued)
(As of July 1994)

Millions of SDRs (except where otherwise indicated)

Country	IMF arrangements				World Bank loans and credits									
	Stand-by/Extended Facility		SAF/ESAF		Structural adjustment				Sector and other adjustment					
						Amount					Amount			
	Period	Amount	Period	Amount	Date of approval	IDA	African Facility [1]	Co-financing [2]	Date of approval	IDA	African Facility [1]	Co-financing [2]	Purpose
Comoros			June 1991-June 1994	3.2					June 1991	6.0		ADF (17); UNDP (1)	Macroeconomic reform and capacity building
Equatorial Guinea	July 1980-June 1981	5.5	Dec. 1988-Dec. 1991	12.9 [13]									
	June 1985-June 1986	9.2 [12]	Feb. 1993-Feb. 1996	12.9 [5]									
Ethiopia	May 1981-June 1982	67.5	Oct. 1992-Oct. 1995	49.4	June 1993	176.5							
					Jan. 1994	0.3 [6]							
Gambia	Nov. 1979-Nov. 1980	1.6	Sept. 1986-Nov. 1988	12.0 [16]	Aug. 1986	4.3	9.9	United Kingdom (4.5); ADF (9) ADF (6) Netherlands (2.5)					
	Feb. 1982-Feb. 1983	16.9	Nov. 1988-Nov. 1991	20.5 [5]	June 1989	17.9							
	April 1984-July 1985 [15]	12.8 [14]											
	Sept. 1986-Oct. 1987	5.1											

34. Arrangements in support of structural adjustment in the 1980s (*continued*)
(As of July 1994)

Millions of SDRs (except where otherwise indicated)

Country	IMF arrangements				World Bank loans and credits								
	Stand-by/Extended Facility		SAF/ESAF		Structural adjustment				Sector and other adjustment				
						Amount				Amount			
	Period	Amount	Period	Amount	Date of approval	IDA	African Facility [1]	Co-financing [2]	Date of approval	IDA	African Facility [1]	Co-financing [2]	Purpose
Guinea	Dec. 1982-Nov. 1983	25 [17]											
	Feb. 1986-March 1987	33 [18]			Feb. 1986	22.9	15.6	France (26.7); Germany (9.4); Japan (27.8); Switzerland (4.8); ADF (12); Japan (11.2)					
	July 1987-Aug. 1988	11.6	July 1987-July 1990	40.5 [19]	June 1988	47.0							
			Nov. 1991-Nov. 1994	57.9 [5]	Dec. 1992	0.1 [6]			June 1990	15.4			Education Sector
Guinea-Bissau			Oct. 1987-Oct. 1990	5.3 [20]	May 1987	8	4	Switzerland (5.2); Saudi Arabia (3.2); ADF (11.3); IFAD (5.3)	Dec.1984	10.1		Switzerland (SwF 4.5 mn.)	Economic recovery programme [21]
					May 1989	18		Netherlands (4.8) USAID (4.5) ADF (12.0) [22]					
Haiti	Oct. 1978-Oct. 1981 [24]	32.2 [23]											
	Aug. 1982-Sept.1983	34.5											
	Nov. 1983-Sept. 1985	60 [25]	Dec.1986-Dec.1989	30.9 [26]					Mar.1987	32.8			Economic recovery
	Sept. 1989-Dec. 1990	21 [18]											

34. Arrangements in support of structural adjustment in the 1980s (continued)
(As of July 1994)

Millions of SDRs (except where otherwise indicated)

Country	IMF arrangements				World Bank loans and credits								Purpose
	Stand-by/Extended Facility		SAF/ESAF		Structural adjustment				Sector and other adjustment				
						Amount				Amount			
	Period	Amount	Period	Amount	Date of approval	IDA	African Facility[1]	Co-financing[2]	Date of approval	IDA	African Facility[1]	Co-financing[2]	
Lao People's Dem.Rep.	Aug. 1980-Aug. 1981	14	Sept. 1989-Sept. 1992	20.5	June 1989	30.8							
			June 1993-June 1996	35.2[5]	Oct. 1991	30							
Lesotho			June 1988-June 1991	10.6									
			May 1991-Aug. 1994	18.1[5]									
Madagascar	June 1980-June 1982	64.5[27]											
	April 1981-June 1982	76.7[28]											
	July 1982-July 1983	51[14]											
	April 1984-March 1985	33											
	April 1985-April 1986	29.5							May 1986	19		Kfw (4);	Agricultural sector
	Sept. 1986-Feb. 1988	30	Aug. 1987-May 1989	46.5[29]					June 1988	90.5	(33)	Japan (3) ADF (40); Switzerland (8)	Public sector
	Sept. 1988-July 1989	13.3[30]	May 1989-May 1992	76.9[5]					Mar.1989	1.1[6]			Public sector
									Oct.1989	0.9[6]			Idem
									Nov.1990	1.2[6]			Idem
									Nov.1991	1[6]			Idem
									Dec.1992	1[6]			Idem

34. Arrangements in support of structural adjustment in the 1980s (*continued*)
(As of July 1994)
Millions of SDRs (except where otherwise indicated)

Country	IMF arrangements — Stand-by/Extended Facility: Period	Amount	SAF/ESAF: Period	Amount	World Bank loans and credits — Structural adjustment: Date of approval	IDA	African Facility [1]	Co-financing [2]	Sector and other adjustment: Date of approval	IDA	African Facility [1]	Co-financing [2]	Purpose
Malawi	Oct. 1979-Dec. 1981 [31]	26.3											
	May 1980-March 1982	49.9 [32]			June 1981	36.7 [33]							
	Aug. 1982-Aug. 1983	22							Apr. 1983	4.6		IFAD (10.3)	Smallholder fertilizers
	Sept.1983-Sept.1986 [35]	81 [34]			Dec. 1983	51.9		Germany/KfW (6.4); Japan/OECF (22.6); USAID (15)					
	March 1988-May 1989	13.0	July 1988-May 1994	67 [5]	Dec. 1985	28.0	37.3						
					Jan. 1987		8.4	Japan (17.7); United Kingdom (7.5); Germany (5)	June 1988	50.6		OECF (30); USAID (25); ADF (19.5); EEC (16)	Industrial and trade policy adjustment
									Mar. 1989	4 [6]			Idem
									Oct. 1989	3.8 [6]			Idem
									Apr. 1990	52.6		USAID (25); United Kingdom (16.5); Netherlands (5); Germany, EEC and Japan	Agriculture
									Nov. 1990	5.1 [6]			Industry and trade
									Nov. 1991	4 [6]			Agriculture
									June 1992	85.4		AfDB (13.4)	Entrepreneurship dev. & drought recovery
									Dec. 1992	4.3 [6]			Idem
									Jan. 1994	4.1 [6]			Idem
Mali	May 1982-May 1983	30.4											
	May 1983-May 1985	40.5							June 1988	29.4		Japan (38.7); Saudi Arabia (5.9); ADF (45)	Public enterprise sector
	Nov. 1985-March 1987	22.9 [36]											
	Aug. 1988-June 1990	12.7	Aug. 1988-Aug. 1991	35.6 [14]	Dec. 1990	50.3		EC (20); AfDB (18)	June 1990	40.7		FAC/CCCE (50.8); SDC (6.9); Netherlands (5.2); Germany (2.9)	Agricultural sector/investment
			Aug. 1992-Aug. 1995	61.0 [5]					Mar. 1994	18.2			Economic recovery

34. Arrangements in support of structural adjustment in the 1980s (*continued*)
(As of July 1994)

Millions of SDRs (except where otherwise indicated)

Country	IMF arrangements				Structural adjustment				World Bank loans and credits — Sector and other adjustment				
	Stand-by/Extended Facility		SAF/ESAF				Amount				Amount		
	Period	Amount	Period	Amount	Date of approval	IDA	African Facility[1]	Co-financing[2]	Date of approval	IDA	African Facility[1]	Co-financing[2]	Purpose
Mauritania	July 1980-March 1982[38]	29.7[37]	Sept. 1986-May 1989	23.7[39]	June 1987	11.7	21.4	Saudi Arabia (4.8) Germany (2.8)	Feb. 1990	19.4		CCCE (8) Germany (2) WFP (1)	Agricultural sector/investment
	June 1981-March 1982	25.8	May 1989-Dec.1994	50.9[5]					June 1990	30.7		Japan (50) SFD (19.8) KFAED (13.7) AFESD (10.3) Abu Dhabi Fund (6.1) Spain (5) Germany (4)	Public enterprises
	April 1985-April 1986	12	Dec. 1992-Dec. 1994	33.9[5]					Nov. 1990	2.9[6]			Public enterprises
	April 1986-April 1987	12							Nov. 1991	1.9[6]			Idem
	May 1987-May 1988	10							Dec. 1992	1.6[6]			Idem
									Jan. 1994	1.0[6]			Idem
Mozambique			June 1987-June 1990	42.7					May 1985	45.5			Economic rehabilitation programme I
			June 1990-June 1995	130.1[5]					Aug. 1987	54.5	(18.6)	Switzerland (11.2)	Economic rehabilitation programme II
									May 1989	68.2		United Kingdom (17.5) Switzerland (12.8) Germany (10.9) Sweden (9.4) Finland (8.9)	Economic rehabilitation programme III
									June 1992	132		Switzerland (6)	Economic recovery
									June 1994	141.7			Economic recovery II

Les Pays les moins avancés. Rapport 1995 - Annexe

A-65

34. Arrangements in support of structural adjustment in the 1980s (continued)
(As of July 1994)

Millions of SDRs (except where otherwise indicated)

Country	IMF arrangements				World Bank loans and credits										Purpose
	Stand-by/Extended Facility		SAF/ESAF		Structural adjustment				Sector and other adjustment						
						Amount				Amount					
	Period	Amount	Period	Amount	Date of approval	IDA	African Facility[1]	Co-financing[2]	Date of approval	IDA	African Facility[1]	Co-financing[2]			
Myanmar	June 1981-June 1982	27													
Nepal	Dec. 1985-April 1987	18.7	Oct. 1987-Oct. 1990	26.1	March 1987	40.9									
			Oct. 1992-Oct. 1995	33.6[5]	June 1989	46.2		KfW (5)							
Niger	Oct. 1983-Dec. 1984	18													
	Dec. 1984-Dec. 1985	16													
	Dec. 1985-Dec. 1986	13.5	Nov. 1986-Dec. 1988	23.6[40]	Feb. 1986	18.3	36.6								
	Dec. 1986-Dec. 1987	10.1	Dec. 1988-Dec. 1991	47.2[41]					June 1987	46	15.4				Public enterprises
	Mar. 1994-Mar. 1995	18.6							Mar. 1994	18.2					Economic recovery
Rwanda	Oct. 1979-Oct. 1980	5[42]	Apr. 1991-Apr. 1994	30.7	June 1991	67.5		Switzerland (SwF 10); Belgium (BF 400)							
Samoa	Aug. 1979-Aug. 1980	0.7[42]													
	June 1983-June 1984	3.4													
	July 1984-July 1985	3.4													
Sao Tome and Principe			June 1989-June 1992	2.8[43]	June 1987	3.1	2.3								
					June 1990	7.5		ADF (8.5) ADF(12) IMF (2.6)							

34. Arrangements in support of structural adjustment in the 1980s *(continued)*
(As of July 1994)

Millions of SDRs (except where otherwise indicated)

	IMF arrangements				World Bank loans and credits									
	Stand-by/Extended Facility		SAF/ESAF		Structural adjustment				Sector and other adjustment					
						Amount				Amount				
Country	Period	Amount	Period	Amount	Date of approval	IDA	African Facility[1]	Co-financing[2]	Date of approval	IDA	African Facility[1]	Co-financing[2]	Purpose
Sierra Leone	Nov. 1979-Nov. 1980	17											
	March 1981-Feb. 1984[45]	186[44]							June 1984	20.3		IFAD (5.4)	Agriculture
	Feb. 1984-Feb. 1985	50.2[46]	Nov. 1986-Nov. 1989	40.5[47]					April 1992	31.4			Reconstruction Imports
	Nov. 1986-Nov. 1987	23.2							April 1992	0.2[6]			Idem
									Dec. 1992	0.2[6]			Idem
			Mar. 1994-Mar. 1995	27.0	Oct. 1993	35.9[6]							
			Mar. 1994-Mar. 1997	88.5[5]	Jan. 1994	0.1[6]							
Somalia	Feb. 1980-Feb. 1981	11.5[48]											
	July 1981-July 1982	43.1											
	July 1982-Jan. 1984	60											
	Feb. 1985-Sept. 1986	22.1											
	June 1987-Feb. 1989	33.2	June 1987-June 1990	30.9[26]					June 1989	54.2		ADF (25) BITS (0.5)	Agriculture
Sudan	May 1979-May 1982[49]	427											
	Feb. 1982-Feb. 1983	198[50]							June 1983	46.4			Agricultural rehabilitation
	Feb. 1983-March 1984	170											
	June 1984-June 1985	90[51]											

34. Arrangements in support of structural adjustment in the 1980s *(continued)*
(As of July 1994)

Millions of SDRs (except where otherwise indicated)

Country	IMF arrangements				World Bank loans and credits								
	Stand-by/Extended Facility		SAF/ESAF		Structural adjustment				Sector and other adjustment				
						Amount				Amount			
	Period	Amount	Period	Amount	Date of approval	IDA	African Facility[1]	Co-financing[2]	Date of approval	IDA	African Facility[1]	Co-financing[2]	Purpose
Togo	June 1979-Dec. 1980	15 [52]											
	Feb. 1981-Feb. 1983	47.5 [53]											
	March 1983-April 1984	21.4			May 1983	36.9							
	May 1984-May 1985	19											
	May 1985-May 1986	15.4			May 1985	28.1							
	June 1986-April 1988	23.0			Aug. 1985		9.7						
	March 1988-	13.0	March 1988-May 1989	26.9 [54]	Mar. 1988	33.0		ADF (17.3); Japan (20.8)					
			May 1989-May 1993	46.1 [5]	Mar. 1989	0.1 [6]							
					Oct. 1989	0.2 [6]							
					Dec. 1990	39.6			Feb. 1991	10.2			Population and health
Uganda	Jan. 1980-Dec. 1980	12.5											
	June 1981-June 1982	112.5							Feb. 1983	63.5		Italy/DCD (10)	Agricultural rehabilitation
	Aug. 1982-Aug. 1983	112.5							May 1984	47.2			Reconstruction
	Sept. 1983-Sept. 1984	95 [55]	June 1987-April 1989	69.7 [56]					Sept.1987	50.9	18.8	United Kingdom/ODA (16)	Economic recovery
			April 1989-June 1994	219.2 [57]					Mar. 1989	1.3 [6]			*Idem*
									Apr. 1989	19 [6]			*Idem*
									Oct. 1989	1.2 [6]			*Idem*
									Feb. 1990	98.1	(12.8)		*Idem*
									Nov. 1990	1.5 [6]			Agriculture
					Dec. 1991	91.9			Dec. 1990	69.5			Economic Recovery
					Dec. 1992	1.0 [6]			Nov. 1991	1.2 [6]			Finance
					May 1994	57.8			May 1993	72.8			*Idem*
									Jan. 1994	0.8 [6]			

34. Arrangements in support of structural adjustment in the 1980s (continued)
(As of July 1994)

Millions of SDRs (except where otherwise indicated)

Country	IMF arrangements				World Bank loans and credits								
	Stand-by/Extended Facility		SAF/ESAF		Structural adjustment				Sector and other adjustment				
					Date of approval	Amount			Date of approval	Amount			Purpose
	Period	Amount	Period	Amount		IDA	African Facility [1]	Co-financing [2]		IDA	African Facility [1]	Co-financing [2]	
Un.-Rep. of Tanzania	Sept.1980-June 1982	179.6 [58]							Nov. 1986	41.3	38.2	Germany (17.3); Switzerland (9.2); United Kingdom (7.3)	Multi-sector rehabilitation
	Aug. 1986-Feb. 1988	64.2	Oct. 1987-Oct. 1990	74.9					Jan. 1988	22.5	(26.0)	Saudi Arabia (4)	Multi-sector rehabilitation
									Dec. 1988	97.6		ADF (24) United Kingdom (15) Switzerland (14) Netherlands (10)	Industrial rehabilitation and trade adjustment
									Mar. 1989	9.7 [6]			Industrial rehabilitation
									Oct. 1989	8.3 [6]			Industry and trade adjustment
									Mar. 1990	150.4		Netherlands (40) United Kingdom (20)	Agriculture
			July 1991-July 1994	181.9 [5]					Dec. 1990	11.5 [6]			Agriculture
									Nov. 1991	8.6 [6]		United Kingdom (16.8)	Idem
									Nov. 1991	150.2		Switzerland (6.6)	Finance
									Dec. 1992	8.2 [6]			Idem
Zaire	Aug. 1979-Feb. 1981	118 [59]							June 1986	17.6	(60)		Industrial sector
	June 1981-June 1984 [21]	912 [60]							June 1987	42.2	(94.3)	Japan (15.7)	Agricultural and rural dev.
	Dec. 1983-March 1985	228 [61]											
	April 1985-April 1986	162											
	May 1986-March 1988	214.2 [62]	May 1987-May 1990	203.7 [63]									
	May 1987-May 1988	100 [64]											
	June 1989-June 1990	116.4 [65]											

34. Arrangements in support of structural adjustment in the 1980s (concluded)

(As of July 1994)

Millions of SDRs (except where otherwise indicated)

Country	IMF arrangements — Stand-by/Extended Facility		IMF arrangements — SAF/ESAF		Structural adjustment — Date of approval	Structural adjustment — Amount IDA	African Facility [1]	Co-financing [2]	World Bank loans and credits — Sector and other adjustment — Date of approval	IDA	African Facility [1]	Co-financing [2]	Purpose
	Period	Amount	Period	Amount								
Zambia	April 1978-April 1980	250						Jan. 1985	24.7	(10)	AFDB (23.4); CIDA (6.8); USAID (5); Switzerland (4.8); Germany (18.8)	Agricultural rehabilitation
	May 1981-May 1984 [24]	800 [66]						March 1991	149.6			Economic recovery
	April 1983-April 1984	211.5 [67]						March 1991	19.4 [6]			Idem
	July 1984-April 1986	225 [68]						May 1992	7.6 [6]			Idem
	Feb. 1986-Feb. 1988	229.8 [69]						June 1992	146			Privatization and industry
								Dec. 1992	15.1 [6]			Idem
								June 1993	72.1			Idem
								Aug. 1993	7.0 [6]			Idem
								Jan. 1994	12.1 [6]			Idem
								Mar. 1994	108.9			Economic and social adj.

Source: IMF, *Annual Report* (various issues); *IMF Survey* (various issues); World Bank, *Annual Report* (various issues); *World Bank News* (various issues).

1 Special Facility for Sub-Saharan Africa; amounts in parenthesis are expressed in millions of dollars.
2 Including special joint financing and bilateral support; amounts are in millions of dollars.
3 Extended Facility arrangement, cancelled as of June 1982.
4 SDR 580 mn. not purchased.
5 ESAF.
6 Supplemental credit.
7 SDR 6.3 mn. not purchased.
8 SDR 15.8 mn. not purchased.
9 SDR 2.4 mn. not purchased.
10 SDR 13.5 mn. not purchased.
11 SDR 7.5 mn. not purchased.
12 SDR 3.8 mn. not purchased.
13 SDR 3.7 mn. not purchased.
14 SDR 10.2 mn. not purchased.
15 Cancelled as of April 1985.
16 SDR 3.4 mn. not purchased.
17 SDR 13.5 mn. not purchased.
18 SDR 6 mn. not purchased.
19 SDR 11.6 mn. not purchased.
20 SDR 1.5 mn. not purchased.
21 Supported by IMF; (SDR 1.88 mn. purchased in first credit tranche).
22 Additional financing.

23 SDR 21.4 mn. not purchased.
24 Extended Facility arrangement.
25 SDR 39 mn. not purchased.
26 SDR 22.1 mn. not purchased.
27 Cancelled as of April 1981; SDR 54.5 mn. not purchased.
28 Augmented in June 1981 with SDR 32.3 mn.;
29 SDR 33.2 mn. not purchased.
30 Cancelled as of May 1989; SDR 10.5 mn. not purchased.
31 Cancelled as of May 1980; SDR 20.9 mn. not purchased.
32 SDR 9.9 mn. not purchased.
33 IBRD loan.
34 Original amount decreased from SDR 100 mn.;
35 Extended Facility arrangement; cancelled as of August 198
36 SDR 6.6 mn. not purchased.
37 SDR 20.8 mn. not purchased.
38 Cancelled as of May 1981.
39 SDR 6.8 mn. not purchased.
40 SDR 6.7 mn. not purchased.
41 ESAF; original amount decreased from SDR 50.6 mn.;
42 Not purchased.
43 SDR 2 mn. not purchased.
44 Including an increase of SDR 22.3 mn. in June 1981.

45 Extended Facility arrangement; cancelled as of April 1982.
46 SDR 31.2 mn. not purchased.
47 SDR 29 mn. not purchased.
48 SDR 5.5 mn. not purchased.
49 Extended Facility arrangement; cancelled as of February 1982; SDR 176 mn. not purchased.
50 SDR 128 mn. not purchased.
51 SDR 70 mn. not purchased.
52 SDR 1.75 mn. not purchased.
53 SDR 40.3 mn. not purchased.
54 SDR 19.2 mn. not purchased.
55 SDR 30 mn. not purchased.
56 SDR 19.9 mn. not purchased.
57 ESAF; original amount increased from SDR 179.3 mn..
58 SDR 154.6 mn. not purchased.
59 SDR 9 mn. not purchased.
60 Cancelled as of June 1982; SDR 737 mn. not purchased.
61 SDR 30 mn. not purchased.
62 Cancelled as of April 1987; SDR 166.6 mn. not purchased.
63 SDR 58.2 mn. not purchased.
64 SDR 75.5 mn. not purchased.
65 SDR 41.4 mn. not purchased.
66 Cancelled as of July 1982; SDR 500 mn. not purchased.
67 SDR 67.5 mn. not purchased.
68 Cancelled as of Feb. 1986; SDR 145 mn. not purchased.
69 Cancelled as of May 1987; SDR 194.8 mn. not purchased.

35. Indicators on area and population   **35. Indicateurs relatifs à la superficie et à la population**

Country	Area / Superficie — Total / Totale (000 km²)	Area / Superficie — % of arable land and land under permanent crops / % de terres arables et sous cultures permanentes 1992	Population — Density / Densité Pop./km² 1993	Population — Total / Totale (mill.) 1993	Population — Urban / Urbaine % 1992	Population — Activity rate a / Taux d'activité a — M 1985-1990 b	Population — Activity rate a / Taux d'activité a — F 1985-1990 b	Population — Activity rate a / Taux d'activité a — T 1985-1990 b	Pays
Afghanistan	652.1	12.4	27	17.7	19	53	5	30	Afghanistan
Bangladesh	144.0	64.8	800	115.2	18	52	4	29	Bangladesh
Benin	112.6	16.7	45	5.1	40	50	43	46	Bénin
Bhutan	47.0	2.9	34	1.6	6	58	30	44	Bhoutan
Botswana	581.7	2.0	2	1.4	27	45	23	33	Botswana
Burkina Faso	274.0	13.0	36	9.8	17	57	48	53	Burkina Faso
Burundi	27.8	48.9	216	6.0	6	56	48	52	Burundi
Cambodia	181.0	13.3	53	9.7	12	56	35	46	Cambodge
Cape Verde	4.0	11.2	92	0.4	30	58	21	38	Cap-Vert
Central African Rep.	623.0	3.2	5	3.2	48	53	42	48	Rép. Centrafricaine
Chad	1284.0	2.5	5	6.0	34	56	14	35	Tchad
Comoros	2.2	44.8	272	0.6	28 c	54	36	45	Comores
Djibouti	23.2	..	24	0.6	81 c	..	..	..	Djibouti
Equatorial Guinea	28.1	8.2	14	0.4	29 c	51	32	41	Guinée équatoriale
Ethiopia	1221.9	11.4	42	51.9	13	53	32	42	Ethiopie
Gambia	11.3	15.9	92	1.0	23 c	56	37	46	Gambie
Guinea	245.9	3.0	26	6.3	27	55	35	45	Guinée
Guinea Bissau	36.1	9.4	28	1.0	21	56	37	46	Guinée-Bissau
Haiti	27.8	32.8	248	6.9	30	49	34	42	Haïti
Kiribati	0.7	50.7	107	0.1	36 c	..	..	..	Kiribati
Lao People's Dem.Rep.	236.8	3.4	19	4.6	20	53	43	48	Rép.dém.populaire lao
Lesotho	30.4	10.5	64	1.9	21	55	39	47	Lesotho
Liberia	111.4	3.8	26	2.8	47	50	21	35	Libéria
Madagascar	587.0	5.3	24	13.9	25	53	34	43	Madagascar
Malawi	118.5	14.4	89	10.5	12	51	35	43	Malawi
Maldives	0.3	10.0	800	0.2	29 c	..	..	..	Maldives
Mali	1240.2	1.8	8	10.1	25	54	10	32	Mali
Mauritania	1025.5	0.2	2	2.2	49	48	14	31	Mauritanie
Mozambique	801.6	4.0	19	15.1	30	56	50	53	Mozambique
Myanmar	676.6	14.8	66	44.6	25	56	33	45	Myanmar
Nepal	140.8	16.7	148	20.8	12	54	29	42	Népal
Niger	1267.0	2.9	7	8.6	21	55	47	51	Niger
Rwanda	26.3	44.4	287	7.6	6	52	46	49	Rwanda
Samoa	2.8	43.0	59	0.2	22 c	..	..	..	Samoa
Sao Tome & Principe	1.0	38.5	132	0.1	42 c	..	..	..	Sao Tomé-et-Principe
Sierra Leone	71.7	7.5	60	4.3	34	50	23	36	Sierra Leone
Solomon Islands	28.9	2.0	12	0.4	16	..	..	..	Iles Salomon
Somalia	637.7	1.6	14	9.0	25	52	32	41	Somalie
Sudan	2505.8	5.2	11	26.6	23	51	14	32	Soudan
Togo	56.8	11.8	68	3.9	29	52	29	41	Togo
Tuvalu	0.0	..	356	0.0	..	..	..	..	Tuvalu
Uganda	241.0	28.7	83	19.9	12	52	36	44	Ouganda
Un. Rep. of Tanzania	883.7	3.7	32	28.0	22	49	44	47	Rép. Unie de Tanzanie
Vanuatu	12.2	11.8	13	0.2	19 c	..	..	..	Vanuatu
Yemen	528.0	2.8	25	13.2	31	45	6	25	Yémen
Zaire	2344.9	3.4	18	41.2	28	49	26	38	Zaïre
Zambia	752.6	7.0	12	8.9	42	48	19	33	Zambie
ALL LDCs	19858.0	6.0	27	543.6	21	52	25	39	**Ensemble des PMA**
All developing countries	66788.6	10.1	45	3001.4	38	53	21	38	**Ensemble des pays en développement**

Source: United Nations, *Demographic Yearbook, 1992*;
United Nations, *World Population Prospects 1994*;
United Nations, *World Urbanization Prospects 1992*;
UNFPA, *The State of World Population 1994*;
FAO, *Production Yearbook 1993*; and
ILO, *Economically active population 1950-2025*.

a Economically active population as a percentage of total population of sex(es) specified of all ages.
b Projections.
c 1990.

Source: Nations Unies, *Annuaire démographique 1992*;
Nations Unies, *World Population Prospects 1994*;
Nations Unies, *World Urbanization Prospects 1992*;
FNUAP, *Etat de la Population Mondiale 1994*;
FAO, *Annuaire de la production 1993*; et
BIT, *Population active 1950-2025*.

a Population active en pourcentage de la population totale de tous âges du sexe ou des sexes précisés.
b Projections.
c 1990.

36. Indicators on demography

36. Indicateurs relatifs à la démographie

Country	Infant mortality rate (per 1000 live births) Taux de mortalité infantile (pour 1000 naissances (vivantes)		Average life expectancy at birth (years) Espérance de vie moyenne à la naissance (années)						Crude birth rate (per 1000) Taux brut de natalité (pour 1000)		Crude death rate (per 1000) Taux brut de mortalité (pour 1000)		Pays
	1985-90	1992 a	1985-90			1992 a			1985-90	1992	1985-90	1992	
			M	F	T	M	F	T					
Afghanistan	172	165	41	42	42	43	43	43	48	52	23	22	Afghanistan
Bangladesh	119	97	53	53	53	55	56	55	37	39	14	14	Bangladesh
Benin	90	88	44	48	46	49	52	51	49	49	19	18	Bénin
Bhutan	143	131	47	50	48	48	49	48	40	40	17	17	Bhoutan
Botswana	54	45	61	64	62	66	70	68	39	39	18	10	Botswana
Burkina Faso	138	101	45	49	47	47	50	48	47	47	19	18	Burkina Faso
Burundi	111	108	48	51	49	46	50	48	47	46	17	17	Burundi
Cambodia	130	117	48	50	49	49	52	50	47	39	16	14	Cambodge
Cape Verde	58	44	62	64	63	66	68	67	36	41 e	10	8 e	Cap-Vert
Central African Rep.	107	105	46	51	48	45	49	47	41	45	17	18	Rép. centrafricaine
Chad	132	123	44	47	46	46	49	47	44	44	20	18	Tchad
Comoros	99	90	54	55	54	55	56	55	49	47 e	13	12 e	Comores
Djibouti	122	113	45	49	47	47	50	48	42	46 e	18	17 e	Djibouti
Equatorial Guinea	127	118	44	48	46	46	49	47	44	44 e	20	19 e	Guinée équatoriale
Ethiopia	132	123	43	47	45	47	50	49	49	49	20	19	Ethiopie
Gambia	143	133	41	45	43	43	46	44	47	46 e	21	20 e	Gambie
Guinea	145	135	42	43	43	44	44	44	51	51	22	21	Guinée
Guinea-Bissau	151	141	40	43	42	38	39	39	43	43	23	22	Guinée-Bissau
Haiti	97	87	53	56	55	54	58	56	36	35	13	12	Haïti
Kiribati	67 b	60	52 c	52 c	52 c	53	56	58	26 b	33	9 b	11	Kiribati
Lao People's Dem.Rep.	110	98	47	50	49	50	53	51	45	45	17	15	Rép.dém.populaire lao
Lesotho	89	108	56	61	58	58	63	60	39	35	11	10	Lesotho
Liberia	142	146	52	55	54	53	56	55	47	47	16	14	Libéria
Madagascar	112	110	53	56	54	50	53	51	47	45	14	13	Madagascar
Malawi	151	143	46	47	46	44	45	44	52	55	20	21	Malawi
Maldives	82	56	61	58	60	64	61	63	42	42	10	12	Maldives
Mali	169	122	42	46	44	47	50	48	51	51	21	19	Mali
Mauritania	110	118	48	51	50	46	50	48	41	46	16	18	Mauritanie
Mozambique	156	167	44	48	46	43	45	44	46	45	19	18	Mozambique
Myanmar	98	83	54	57	55	58	62	60	34	33	13	11	Myanmar
Nepal	110	90	52	50	51	54	53	54	40	38	15	13	Népal
Niger	135	191	43	46	45	44	48	46	56	51	20	19	Niger
Rwanda	115	131	47	50	48	45	48	46	45	52	17	18	Rwanda
Samoa	72	45	64	67	66	65	70	65	37	32	7	7	Samoa
Sao Tome & Principe	77 b	65	..	..	65 b	..	..	68	44 b	37 f	..	10 e	Sao Tomé-et-Principe
Sierra Leone	179	144	36	39	37	41	45	43	49	48	27	22	Sierra Leone
Solomon Islands	32	27	67	71	69	68	72	70	39	42	5	7	Iles Salomon
Somalia	132	125	43	47	45	47	50	49	50	50	20	19	Somalie
Sudan	85	100	50	52	51	51	53	52	42	42	14	14	Soudan
Togo	94	86	51	55	53	53	57	55	45	45	14	13	Togo
Tuvalu	..	40	..	..	..	..	..	..	24 d	25 e	10 d	11 e	Tuvalu
Uganda	120	111	45	48	47	43	44	43	52	51	18	21	Ouganda
Un.Rep. of Tanzania	89	111	51	54	53	49	52	51	45	48	14	15	Rép.-Unie de Tanzanie
Vanuatu	57	65	61	65	63	57	60	63	37	39 e	10	7 e	Vanuatu
Yemen	131	107	48	48	48	52	53	53	50	49	17	14	Yémen
Zaire	99	121	50	53	52	50	53	52	48	48	15	15	Zaïre
Zambia	109	113	51	53	52	46	49	48	47	47	14	18	Zambie
ALL LDCs	118	112	49	51	50	50	53	51	44	44	16	16	Ensemble des PMA
All developing countries	92	85	58	60	59	59	63	61	35	34	11	10	Ensemble des pays en développement

Source: United Nations, *World Population Prospects 1994*; UNICEF, *The State of the World's Children 1994*; UNDP, *Human Development Report 1994*; ESCAP, *Statistical Yearbook for Asia and the Pacific 1992*; World Bank, *World Development Report 1994*; and AsDB, *Gender Indicators of Developing Asian and Pacific Countries 1993*.

a Or latest year available.
b 1985.   *c* 1988.
d 1983.   *e* 1990.
f 1989.

Source: Nations Unies, *World Population Prospects 1994*; FISE, *La situation des enfants dans le monde 1994*; PNUD, *Rapport Mondial sur Le Développement Humain 1994*; CESAP, *Annuaire statistique pour l'Asie et le Pacifique 1992*; Banque Mondiale, *Rapport sur le développement dans le monde 1994*; et BAsD, *Gender Indicators of Developing Asian and Pacific Countries 1993*.

a Ou année la plus récente disponible.
b 1985.   *c* 1988.
d 1983.   *e* 1990.
f 1989.

37. **Indicators on health**				37. **Indicateurs relatifs à la santé**
Country	*Low-birth-weight infants (in per cent)* *Enfants de poids insuffisant à la naissance (en pourcentage)* 1990 a	*Percentage of women attended during child-birth by trained personnel* *Pourcentage des femmes ayant reçu des soins prodigués par du personnel qualifié pendant l'accouchement* 1983-1992 a	*Percentage of children immunized against DPT (3 doses)* *Pourcentage d'enfants vaccinés DTC (3 doses)* 1992 a	*Pays*
Afghanistan	20	9	23	Afghanistan
Bangladesh	50	5	96	Bangladesh
Benin	10	45	72	Bénin
Bhutan	..	7	72	Bhoutan
Botswana	8	78	59	Botswana
Burkina Faso	21	42	33	Burkina Faso
Burundi	14	19	82	Burundi
Cambodia	..	47	32	Cambodge
Cape Verde	..	49	100	Cap-Vert
Central African Rep.	15	66	52	République centrafricaine
Chad	11	15	10	Tchad
Comoros	13	24	24	Comores
Djibouti	9	79	84	Djibouti
Equatorial Guinea	10	58	75	Guinée équatoriale
Ethiopia	16	14	13	Ethiopie
Gambia	10	65	85	Gambie
Guinea	21	25	52	Guinée
Guinea Bissau	20	27	66	Guinée-Bissau
Haiti	15	20	41	Haïti
Kiribati	..	..	86	Kiribati
Lao People's Dem. Rep.	18	..	22	Rép. dém. pop. lao
Lesotho	11	40	80	Lesotho
Liberia	..	58	28	Libéria
Madagascar	10	58	65	Madagascar
Malawi	20	55	86	Malawi
Maldives	20	61	98	Maldives
Mali	17	32	34	Mali
Mauritania	11	40	32	Mauritanie
Mozambique	20	25	50	Mozambique
Myanmar	16	57	72	Myanmar
Nepal	26	6	72	Népal
Niger	15	15	19	Niger
Rwanda	17	29	85	Rwanda
Samoa	4	52	91	Samoa
Sao Tome and Principe	7	63	78	Sao Tomé-et-Principe
Sierra Leone	17	25	64	Sierra Leone
Solomon Islands	20	85	76	Iles Salomon
Somalia	16	2	18	Somalie
Sudan	15	69	53	Soudan
Togo	20	54	45	Togo
Tuvalu	..	..	69	Tuvalu
Uganda	10	38	71	Ouganda
Un. Rep. of Tanzania	14	53	82	Rép. Unie de Tanzanie
Vanuatu	5	67	77	Vanuatu
Yemen	19	16	50	Yémen
Zaire	15	..	16	Zaïre
Zambia	13	51	57	Zambie
All LDCs	**24**	**28**	**58**	**Ensemble des PMA**
All developing countries	**23**	**38**	**79**	**Ensemble des pays en développpement**

Source: UNICEF, *The State of the World's Children 1994,* UNDP, *Human Development Report 1994* and WHO, *Expanded Program on Immunization 1994.*

a Or latest year available.

Source: FISE, *La situation des enfants dans le monde 1994,* PNUD, *Rapport Mondial sur Le Développement Humain 1994* et OMS, *Expanded Program on Immunization 1994.*

a Ou année la plus récente disponible.

38. Indicators on nutrition and sanitation
38. Indicateurs relatifs à la nutrition et à l'hygiène

Country	Daily calorie intake per capita / Disponibilités alimentaires (calories par personne par jour) — Average/Moyenne		Percentage of population with access to safe water or adequate sanitation / Pourcentage de la population disposant d'eau saine ou de mesures suffisantes d'hygiène du milieu — Urban/Urbaine				Rural/Rurale				Pays
			Water Eau		Sanitation Hygiène du milieu		Water Eau		Sanitation Hygiène du milieu		
	1979-1981	1988-1990	1980	1991 [a]	1980	1991 [a]	1980	1991 [a]	1980	1991 [a]	
Afghanistan	2179	1766	28	79	..	71	8	85	..	..	Afghanistan
Bangladesh	1973	2037	26	82	21	63	40	81	1	26	Bangladesh
Benin	2145	2383	26	73	48	60	15	43	4	35	Bénin
Bhutan	..	..	50	60	..	50	5	30	..	7	Bhoutan
Botswana	2155	2260	..	100	..	100	..	88	..	85	Botswana
Burkina Faso	1815	2219	27	78	38	77	31	70	5	5	Burkina Faso
Burundi	2059	1948	90	99	40	71	20	54	..	47	Burundi
Cambodia	1657	2122	..	65	..	81	..	33	..	8	Cambodge
Cape Verde	2587	2778	100	87	34	35	21	65	10	18	Cap-Vert
Central African Rep.	2136	1846	..	19	..	45	..	26	..	46	Rép. Centrafricaine
Chad	1710	1735	..	25	..	..	..	70	..	..	Tchad
Comoros	1783	1760	..	98	..	90	..	66	..	80	Comores
Djibouti	..	..	50	88	43	64	20	70	20	24	Djibouti
Equatorial Guinea	..	..	..	70	..	95	..	14	..	10	Guinée équatoriale
Ethiopia	1795	1699	..	91	..	76	..	19	..	7	Ethiopie
Gambia	2101	2290	85	100	..	100	..	48	..	27	Gambie
Guinea	2268	2242	69	87	54	84	2	56	1	5	Guinée
Guinea-Bissau	2057	2235	18	56	21	27	8	35	13	32	Guinée-Bissau
Haiti	2051	2005	48	55	39	55	8	33	10	16	Haïti
Kiribati	2731	2517	93	91	87	91	25	63	80	49	Kiribati
Lao People's Dem.Rep.	2365	2465	21	54	..	97	12	33	..	8	Rép.dém.populaire lao
Lesotho	2354	2121	37	59	13	14	11	45	14	23	Lesotho
Liberia	2400	2259	..	35	..	55	..	22	..	55	Libéria
Madagascar	2472	2156	80	55	9	12	7	9	..	3	Madagascar
Malawi	2273	2049	77	97	100	100	37	50	81	81	Malawi
Maldives	2193	2400	11	100	60	100	3	33	1	4	Maldives
Mali	1898	2259	37	53	79	81	0	38	0	10	Mali
Mauritania	2081	2447	80	67	5	34	85	65	..	13	Mauritanie
Mozambique	1951	1805	..	44	..	61	..	17	..	11	Mozambique
Myanmar	2313	2454	38	37	38	39	15	72	15	35	Myanmar
Nepal	1846	2205	83	67	16	52	7	39	1	3	Népal
Niger	2224	2239	41	98	36	71	32	45	3	4	Niger
Rwanda	2064	1913	48	75	60	77	55	65	50	56	Rwanda
Samoa	2557	2695	97	100	86	100	94	77	83	92	Samoa
Sao Tome & Principe	2060	2153	..	33	..	8	..	45	..	13	Sao Tomé-et-Principe
Sierra Leone	2096	1899	50	33	31	92	2	37	6	49	Sierra Leone
Solomon Islands	2287	2278	91	76	82	73	20	58	10	2	Iles Salomon
Somalia	1942	1874	60	7	45	44	20	29	5	5	Somalie
Sudan	2215	2043	100	55	63	89	31	43	0	65	Soudan
Togo	2266	2269	70	77	24	56	31	53	10	10	Togo
Tuvalu	..	..	..	99	..	79	..	100	..	77	Tuvalu
Uganda	2114	2178	45	43	40	63	8	30	10	28	Ouganda
Un. Rep. of Tanzania	2239	2195	..	65	..	74	..	45	..	62	Rép. Unie de Tanzanie
Vanuatu	2565	2736	65	100	95	82	53	64	68	33	Vanuatu
Yemen	2056	2230	93	61	60	87	19	30	..	60	Yémen
Zaire	2133	2130	..	68	..	46	..	24	..	11	Zaïre
Zambia	2186	2016	65	70	100	75	32	28	48	12	Zambie
All LDCs	2060	2074	50	64	39	62	26	50	10	26	Ensemble des PMA
All developing countries b	2333	2412	72	85	50	70	32	63	11	22	Ensemble des pays en développement b

Source: FAO, *Production Yearbook 1992* and
The State of Food and Agriculture 1992;
WHO/UNICEF, *Water Supply and Sanitation Sector Monitoring Report 1993;*
WHO, *The International Drinking Water Supply and Sanitation Decade: End of Decade Review* (as at December 1990); and
UNICEF, *The State of the World's Children 1994.*

a Or latest year available.
b Average of countries for which data are available.

Source: FAO, *Annuaire de la production 1992* et
La situation mondiale de l'alimentation et de l'agriculture 1992; OMS/FISE, *Water Supply and Sanitation Sector Monitoring Report 1993;*
OMS, *The International Drinking Water Supply and Sanitation Decade : End of Decade Review* (as at December 1990); et
FISE, *La situation des enfants dans le monde 1994.*

a Ou année la plus récente disponible.
b Moyenne des pays pour lesquels les données sont disponibles.

39. Indicators on education and literacy   **39. Indicateurs relatifs à l'enseignement et à l'alphabétisme**

	Adult literacy rate Taux d'alphabétisme (adultes) (%) 1990 a			School enrolment ratio (% of relevant age group) Taux d'inscription scolaire (en % du groupe d'âge pertinent) Primary Primaire 1980			Primary Primaire 1991 b			Secondary Secondaire 1980			Secondary Secondaire 1991 b			
Country	M	F	T	M	F	T	M	F	T	M	F	T	M	F	T	Pays
Afghanistan	44	14	29	54	12	34	32	17	24	16	4	10	11	6	9	Afghanistan
Bangladesh	47	22	35	72	46	58	83	71	77	25	9	17	25	12	19	Bangladesh
Benin	32	16	23	87	41	64	78	39	58	24	9	16	17	7	12	Bénin
Bhutan	51	25	38	23	10	17	31	19	25	3	1	2	7	2	5	Bhoutan
Botswana	84	65	74	84	100	92	116	121	119	20	22	21	50	57	54	Botswana
Burkina Faso	28	9	18	23	14	18	46	29	37	4	2	3	10	5	8	Burkina Faso
Burundi	61	40	50	32	21	26	77	63	70	4	2	3	7	4	6	Burundi
Cambodia	48	22	35	..	..	..	..	..	..	..	..	..	..	..	..	Cambodge
Cape Verde	..	..	67	117	111	114	117	113	115	9	7	8	20	19	19	Cap-Vert
Central African Rep.	52	25	38	92	51	71	85	52	68	21	7	14	17	7	12	Rép. centrafricaine
Chad	42	18	30	52	19	36	89	41	65	9	1	5	12	3	7	Tchad
Comoros	49	35	42	99	75	88	82	68	75	30	15	23	20	15	17	Comores
Djibouti	49	35	42	44	26	35	52	37	44	15	9	12	18	12	15	Djibouti
Equatorial Guinea	64	37	50	153	120	136	122	120	121	20	4	12	35	11	23	Guinée équatoriale
Ethiopia	70	35	55	45	25	35	29	21	25	11	6	9	13	11	12	Ethiopie
Gambia	39	16	27	67	35	51	81	56	68	16	7	11	24	12	18	Gambie
Guinea	35	13	24	48	25	36	50	24	37	24	10	17	15	5	10	Guinée
Guinea-Bissau	50	24	37	94	42	68	77	42	60	10	2	6	9	4	7	Guinée-Bissau
Haiti	59	47	53	82	70	76	58	54	56	14	13	14	22	21	22	Haïti
Kiribati	..	..	..	..	..	..	..	..	..	..	..	..	..	..	..	Kiribati
Lao People's Dem. Rep.	92	76	84	123	104	113	112	84	98	25	16	21	27	17	22	Rép.dém.populaire lao
Lesotho	62	85	74	85	120	102	97	116	107	14	21	18	21	30	26	Lesotho
Liberia	50	29	40	62	34	48	45	25	35	31	12	22	22	9	16	Libéria
Madagascar	88	73	80	145	139	142	93	91	92	35	24	29	18	18	18	Madagascar
Malawi	65	34	49	72	48	60	72	60	66	5	2	3	5	3	4	Malawi
Maldives	91	92	91	153	139	146	141	142	142	4	5	4	45	44	44	Maldives
Mali	41	24	32	34	19	27	32	19	25	12	5	9	10	5	7	Mali
Mauritania	46	27	36	47	26	37	63	48	55	17	4	11	19	10	14	Mauritanie
Mozambique	45	21	33	114	84	99	72	53	63	8	3	5	10	5	8	Mozambique
Myanmar	89	72	81	93	89	91	107	100	104	25	19	22	25	23	24	Myanmar
Nepal	38	13	26	122	52	88	108	54	82	33	9	22	43	17	30	Népal
Niger	40	17	28	33	18	25	37	21	29	7	3	5	9	4	7	Niger
Rwanda	64	37	50	66	60	63	72	70	71	4	3	3	9	7	8	Rwanda
Samoa	..	..	..	..	..	..	..	..	..	..	..	..	..	..	..	Samoa
Sao Tome & Principe	76	47	60	..	..	..	..	..	..	..	..	..	..	..	..	Sao Tomé-et-Principe
Sierra Leone	31	11	21	61	43	52	56	39	48	20	8	14	21	12	16	Sierra Leone
Solomon Islands	..	..	..	..	..	..	110	98	104	..	..	..	24	15	19	Iles Salomon
Somalia	36	14	24	24	14	19	15	8	11	11	4	8	9	5	7	Somalie
Sudan	43	12	27	59	41	50	56	43	50	20	12	16	25	20	22	Soudan
Togo	56	31	43	146	91	118	134	87	111	51	16	33	35	12	23	Togo
Tuvalu	..	..	..	..	..	..	..	..	..	..	..	..	..	..	..	Tuvalu
Uganda	62	35	48	56	43	50	78	64	71	7	3	5	16	8	12	Ouganda
Un. Rep. of Tanzania	89	83	87	99	86	93	70	68	69	4	2	3	6	4	5	Rép.-Unie de Tanzanie
Vanuatu	..	..	..	..	..	..	..	..	..	..	..	..	..	..	..	Vanuatu
Yemen	53	26	39	71	16	44	111	43	79	11	3	7	47	10	29	Yémen
Zaire	84	61	72	108	77	92	87	64	76	35	13	24	32	15	24	Zaïre
Zambia	81	65	73	98	82	90	101	92	97	22	11	16	25	14	20	Zambie
All LDCs c	**59**	**36**	**48**	**75**	**52**	**64**	**73**	**58**	**66**	**19**	**9**	**14**	**21**	**12**	**17**	**Ensemble des PMA c**
All developing countries c	**70**	**51**	**61**	**96**	**77**	**87**	**97**	**81**	**89**	**37**	**25**	**31**	**46**	**34**	**40**	**Ensemble des pays en développement c**

Source: UNESCO, *Compendium of Statistics on Illiteracy - 1990 Edition; Statistical Yearbook 1993; Trends and Projections of Enrolment by Level of of Education and by Age, 1960-2025 (as assessed in 1993); and* ECA, *African Socio-economic Indicators, 1990/91.*

a Estimates and projections.
b Or latest year available.
c Average of countries for which data are available.

Source: UNESCO, *Compendium des statistiques relatives à l'analphabétisme - Edition 1990; Annuaire statistique 1993; Trends and Projections of Enrolment by Level of of Education and by Age, 1960-2025 (as assessed in 1993); et* CEA, *Indicateurs Socio-économiques africains, 1990/91.*

a Estimations et projections.
b Ou année la plus récente disponible.
c Moyenne des pays pour lesquels les données sont disponibles.

40. Indicators on communications and media   40. Indicateurs relatifs aux communications et aux médias

Country	Post offices open to the public per 100,000 inhabitants / Bureaux de poste ouverts au public pour 100,000 habitants — Total		of which: urban / dont: urbains		Telephones per 1000 inhabitants / Téléphones pour 1000 habitants		Radio receivers per 1000 inhabitants / Postes récepteurs de radio pour 1000 habitants		Circulation of daily newspapers per 1000 inhabitants / Tirage de journaux quotidiens pour 1000 habitants		Pays
	1980	1992	1980	1992	1980	1992	1980	1991	1980	1990	
Afghanistan	..	2.3 m	..	0.5 m	1.7	2.3 o	75	107	6	11	Afghanistan
Bangladesh	8.2	7.5 m	0.7	0.6 m	1.1	2.2	17	43	3	6	Bangladesh
Benin	..	3.9	..	1.1	4.9 c	3.2	66	90	0.3	3	Bénin
Bhutan	6.3	5.3	..	4.3	..	1.8	6	16	..	..	Bhoutan
Botswana	6.3	12.4	1.3	1.0	13.3 f	26.6	83	122	21	14	Botswana
Burkina Faso	1.2	1.6	0.6	..	1.5 c	2.1	18	26	0.2	0.3	Burkina Faso
Burundi	0.4 g	0.6 o	0.0 g	0.3 o	1.3 h	2.3	39	60	0.2	4	Burundi
Cambodia	..	..	..	..	..	0.6 o	92	112	..	..	Cambodge
Cape Verde	18.7 g	16.2	7.1 g	4.3	5.7 i	31.4	142	164	..	..	Cap-Vert
Central African Rep.	3.0 h	1.8 o	0.2 h	1.9 b	2.1 i	1.7 o	52	68	..	0.7	Rép. Centrafricaine
Chad	0.5 h	1.4	0.1 h	0.6	1.5 i	0.7	168	243	0.2	0.3	Tchad
Comoros	..	11.2	..	7.0	5.0 c	6.6	120	128	..	..	Comores
Djibouti	1.6	1.8 k	0.3	0.6 k	16.8	14.5	69	86	..	..	Djibouti
Equatorial Guinea	4.6 g	5.8 m	4.1 g	5.5 m	..	3.9 l	401	425	7	6	Guinée équatoriale
Ethiopia	1.1 i	1.0	0.1 i	0.9	2.3	2.3	77	189	1	0.8	Ethiopie
Gambia	..	..	..	..	5.4 f	13.3	114	170	..	2	Gambie
Guinea	..	1.3 o	..	0.7 o	1.9 j	1.6 o	30	42	5 f	2 l	Guinée
Guinea-Bissau	..	2.5 o	..	2.5 o	..	7.1 o	31	40	8	6	Guinée-Bissau
Haiti	..	2.0	..	2.0	..	8.2 o	20	47	7	7	Haïti
Kiribati	..	2.0	..	4.2	12.3	19.6	203	207	..	..	Kiribati
Lao People's Dem. Rep.	2.1	2.9	2.0	2.6 o	2.1 i	1.5	109	125	4	3	Rép.dém.populaire lao
Lesotho	9.2	7.9 n	0.8	1.1 n	..	6.9	25	32	33	11	Lesotho
Liberia	2.6	1.9 n	0.5	0.4 n	..	4.0 l	179	225	6	14	Libéria
Madagascar	85.6	70.8	0.7	1.8	4.3	2.9	182	200	6	4	Madagascar
Malawi	3.9	3.6 e	0.6	0.5 e	5.2	3.3	42	220	3	3	Malawi
Maldives	5.8	17.3	1.3	2.6	6.8	37.0	44	118	6	7	Maldives
Mali	1.8 g	1.0	1.1 g	0.6 n	..	1.3	15	44	0.5	1	Mali
Mauritania	3.7	3.0 o	1.3	0.6 o	2.5 g	2.4	97	144	..	0.5	Mauritanie
Mozambique	4.8	1.9	0.2	1.9	4.6 i	3.8	21	47	4	5	Mozambique
Myanmar	3.3	2.8 o	1.8	1.6 n	1.1 f	2.0 l	23	82	10	5	Myanmar
Nepal	9.6	21.2 o	..	0.9 b	1.0 c	3.3	20	33	8	8	Népal
Niger	2.6	3.7 n	0.4	0.6 n	1.6	1.2	45	60	0.5	0.6	Niger
Rwanda	..	0.6 n	..	0.2 n	0.9	1.7	34	64	0.1	0.1	Rwanda
Samoa	..	28.1 o	..	5.6 o	36.9	40.6	206	475	..	..	Samoa
Sao Tome and Principe	..	9.3	..	2.5	15.1 i	19.3	245	269	..	..	Sao Tomé-et-Principe
Sierra Leone	3.3 g	2.0	1.7 g	0.9	..	3.2	138	223	3	2	Sierra Leone
Solomon Islands	..	34.5 o	..	2.7 o	..	13.8 o	88	119	..	..	Iles Salomon
Somalia	..	..	..	..	..	2.0 o	17	37	0.9	1	Somalie
Sudan	4.0	3.2 n	1.4	1.1	3.4	2.4	187	250	6	24	Soudan
Togo	..	11.7 o	..	0.8 o	3.8	4.1	203	211	6	3	Togo
Tuvalu	..	..	..	..	..	14.4	206	229	..	..	Tuvalu
Uganda	..	1.9	..	0.5 o	3.6	1.5	30	109	2	2	Ouganda
Un. Rep. of Tanzania	3.2	3.7	..	0.9	5.0	2.9	16	25	11	7	Rép. Unie de Tanzanie
Vanuatu	5.3	..	1.8	..	23.2 c	18.6 o	198	300	..	..	Vanuatu
Yemen	2.4	3.6 m	1.6	1.8 l	..	11.4	29	27	12	12	Yémen
Zaire	1.3	0.8	0.3	0.2	1.0	1.0 o	56	97	2	1 l	Zaïre
Zambia	7.0 i	5.9 o	1.0 i	1.2 o	10.7	8.8	24	81	19	12	Zambie
All LDCs a	6.8	6.1	0.7	0.9	2.4	3.1	52	95	5	6	Ensemble des PMA a
All developing countries a	13.1	12.6	1.9	2.3	20.8	32.6	115	175	36	62	Ensemble des pays en développement a

Source: UNESCO, *Statistical Yearbook 1993*;
Universal Postal Union, *Statistique des services postaux 1992*; ITU, *Statistical Yearbook 1992* and other international and national sources.

a Average of countries for which data are available.
b 1987. c 1978. d 1986. e 1985. f 1979.
g 1982. h 1983. i 1981. j 1977. k 1984.
l 1988. m 1989. n 1990. o 1991.

Source: UNESCO, *Annuaire statistique 1993*;
Union postale universelle, *Statistique des services postaux 1992*; UIT, *Annuaire statistique 1992* et autres sources internationales et nationales.

a Moyenne des pays pour lesquels les données sont disponibles.
b 1987. c 1978. d 1986. e 1985. f 1979.
g 1982. h 1983. i 1981. j 1977. k 1984.
l 1988. m 1989. n 1990. o 1991.

41. Indicators on transport a   41. Indicateurs relatifs aux transports a

	Road network/Réseau routier			Railways/Chemins de fer				Civil aviation/Aviation civile				
	Total	Paved Pavé	Density Densité	Network Réseau	Density Densité	Freight Frêt	Passenger Passagers	Freight Frêt Total	International	Passenger Passagers Total	International	
Country	km	%	km/ 1000 km²	km	km/ 1000 km²	mio.ton- km	mio.pass- km	thousand tons milliers de tonnes		thousands milliers		Pays
Afghanistan	19010	15.1	29.2	..	..	..	..	9.9	9.5	174	65	Afghanistan
Bangladesh	12960	58.3	90.0	2792	19.4	678	5365	31.4	29.5	1189	846	Bangladesh
Benin	6070	20.0	53.9	579	5.1	211	200	..	..	..	..	Bénin
Botswana	13500	15.0	23.2	714	1.2	1370	..	..	..	236	145	Botswana
Burkina Faso	11231	12.0	41.0	504	1.8	..	..	7.6	7.5	112	85	Burkina Faso
Burundi	14473	7.1	520.0	..	..	..	..	5.3	5.3	68	67	Burundi
Cambodia	17000	15.2	93.9	601	3.3	28	62	..	..	..	..	Cambodge
Cape Verde	1496	26.7	370.9	..	..	..	..	1.2	0.8	173	80	Cap-Vert
Central African Rep.	23738	1.8	38.1	..	..	..	..	13.3	13.3	84	82	Rép. centrafricaine
Chad	27000	1.4	21.0	..	..	..	..	..	..	..	..	Tchad
Comoros	900	67.2	402.7	..	..	..	..	..	..	..	..	Comores
Djibouti	2879	12.6	124.1	100	4.3	..	..	8.4	8.4	126	112	Djibouti
Equatorial Guinea	1326	38.3	47.3	..	..	..	..	..	..	..	..	Guinée équatoriale
Ethiopia	27972	15.0	22.9	681	0.6	149	413	29.0	17.0	480	260	Ethiopie
Gambia	2386	32.0	211.2	..	..	..	..	..	..	..	..	Gambie
Guinea	16051	8.7	65.3	940	3.8	605	..	..	..	..	..	Guinée
Guinea-Bissau	4100	8.3	113.5	..	..	..	..	0.3	0.3	21	21	Guinée-Bissau
Haiti	3700	17.4	133.3	135	4.9	..	..	21.1	21.1	545	525	Haïti
Kiribati	640	..	879.1	..	..	..	..	0.5	0.1	51	16	Kiribati
Lao People's Dem.Rep.	14130	16.0	59.7	..	..	..	..	0.6	0.3	165	59	Rép.dém.populaire lao
Lesotho	5242	16.0	172.7	..	..	..	..	..	..	34	26	Lesotho
Liberia	8064	9.0	72.4	493	4.4	..	..	..	..	..	..	Libéria
Madagascar	34750	15.4	59.2	1030	1.8	125	230	7.8	6.0	340	140	Madagascar
Malawi	27294	..	230.4	782	6.6	113	117	5.1	3.9	226	145	Malawi
Maldives	..	..	..	..	..	..	..	11.5	11.5	623	554	Maldives
Mali	14040	14.8	11.3	642	0.5	202	186	10.2	9.7	176	164	Mali
Mauritania	7300	11.0	7.1	650	0.6	6610	..	1.7	1.6	212	68	Mauritanie
Mozambique	27287	17.2	34.0	3150	3.9	1340	500	18.4	1.9	509	244	Mozambique
Myanmar	23200	17.0	34.3	2775	4.1	458	3920	1.5	1.5	580	100	Myanmar
Nepal	7401	40.8	52.6	52	0.4	.	..	17.5	17.0	800	600	Népal
Niger	11258	29.0	8.9	..	..	.	..	2.8	2.5	78	77	Niger
Rwanda	13173	9.0	500.2	..	..	.	..	7.1	7.1	52	47	Rwanda
Samoa	2088	12.5	737.5	..	..	..	..	..	..	..	..	Samoa
Sao Tome & Principe	240	41.7	249.0	..	..	..	..	0.1	0.1	23	18	Sao Tomé-et-Principe
Sierra Leone	8580	17.6	119.6	84	..	..	..	2.0	2.0	98	98	Sierra Leone
Somalia	21600	28.7	33.9	..	..	..	..	2.0	1.9	136	110	Somalie
Sudan	10270	33.3	4.1	4756	1.9	1920	920	..	..	..	..	Soudan
Togo	7545	24.3	132.9	514	9.1	14	124	4.1	4.1	256	255	Togo
Uganda	27000	6.7	112.0	1100	4.7	82	315	10.0	10.0	122	111	Ouganda
Un.Rep. of Tanzania	55600	37.0	62.9	2600	2.8	1420	3630	7.3	5.5	471	230	Rép.-Unie de Tanzanie
Vanuatu	1341	..	110.0	..	..	..	..	..	..	..	..	Vanuatu
Yemen	51392	9.4	97.3	..	..	..	..	11.3 b	10.5 b	791	b596	bYémen
Zaire	145000	0.0	61.8	5088	2.2	1788	545	44.9	8.4	335	107	Zaïre
Zambia	37359	17.6	49.6	1924	2.6	..	..	9.4	8.8	413	265	Zambie

Source: IRU, *World Transport Data 1990*;
IRF, *World Road Statistics* (various issues);
ICAO Digest of Statistics, *Airport Traffic 1992*;
ESCAP, *Statistical Yearbook for Asia
and the Pacific 1992* and national sources.

a Data refer to 1992 or latest year available.

b Data refer only to the former Democratic Yemen.

Source: IRU, *Statistiques mondiales de Transport 1990*;
IRF, *Statistiques Routières Mondiales* (diverses parutions);
OACI Recueil de statistiques, *Trafic d'aéroport 1992*;
CESAP, *Annuaire statistique pour l'Asie
et le Pacifique 1992* et sources nationales.

a Les données se rapportent à l'année 1992
ou année la plus récente disponible.

b Les données se rapportent seulement
à l'ancien Yémen démocratique.

42. Indicators on energy   42. Indicateurs relatifs à l'énergie

Country	Coal, oil, gas and electricity Charbon, pétrole, gaz et électricité Consummption per capita in kg. of coal equivalent Consommation par habitant en kg. équivalant en charbon 1980	1991	Fuelwood, charcoal and bagasse Bois de chauffage, charbon de bois et bagasse 1980	1991	Installed electricity capacity Puissance électrique installée (kw./1000 inhabitants) (kw./1000 habitants) 1980	1991	Pays
Afghanistan	48	166	99	110	27	31	Afghanistan
Bangladesh	45	77	23	24	11	24	Bangladesh
Benin	52	48	347	344	4	3	Bénin
Bhutan	9	50	777	255	10	230	Bhoutan
Botswana	..	..	..	..	..	..	Botswana
Burkina Faso	29	29	277	312	6	6	Burkina Faso
Burundi	14	22	252	254	2	8	Burundi
Cambodia	22	26	213	201	6	4	Cambodge
Cape Verde	194	110	..	..	10	20	Cap-Vert
Central African Rep.	26	35	358	383	16	14	République centrafricaine
Chad	23	21	206	212	7	5	Tchad
Comoros	48	55	..	..	13	9	Comores
Djibouti	474	375	..	..	125	71	Djibouti
Equatorial Guinea	124	164	645	413	23	14	Guinée équatoriale
Ethiopia	21	27	296	289	9	8	Ethiopie
Gambia	117	106	452	316	17	13	Gambie
Guinea	103	85	246	203	37	30	Guinée
Guinea-Bissau	81	99	177	143	9	11	Guinée-Bissau
Haiti	61	52	322	292	23	23	Haiti
Kiribati	220	139	..	..	34	27	Kiribati
Lao People's Dem. Rep.	34	38	354	303	55	59	Rép. dém. pop. lao
Lesotho	..	..	..	..	..	..	Lesotho
Liberia	500	57	709	621	173	125	Libéria
Madagascar	86	43	194	199	11	17	Madagascar
Malawi	56	37	288	462	24	19	Malawi
Maldives	129	205	..	..	13	63	Maldives
Mali	28	24	196	192	12	9	Mali
Mauritania	188	583	1	1	44	51	Mauritanie
Mozambique	150	34	351	348	156	163	Mozambique
Myanmar	60	55	143	144	20	26	Myanmar
Nepal	17	25	305	277	5	14	Népal
Niger	48	58	191	200	6	8	Niger
Rwanda	28	30	292	251	8	8	Rwanda
Samoa	310	399	145	153	82	116	Samoa
Sao Tome & Principe	213	289	..	..	53	50	Sao Tomé-et-Principe
Sierra Leone	80	76	709	247	31	31	Sierra Leone
Solomon Islands	212	233	..	139	53	36	Iles Salomon
Somalia	36	10	192	277	7	7	Somalie
Sudan	81	62	282	297	16	20	Soudan
Togo	70	78	66	97	12	9	Togo
Tuvalu	..	..	..	..	..	..	Tuvalu
Uganda	27	29	235	247	12	9	Ouganda
Un. Rep. of Tanzania	46	38	331	426	22	17	Rép. Unie de Tanzanie
Vanuatu	248	209	68	52	85	72	Vanuatu
Yemen	187	328	45	39	20	68	Yémen
Zaire	75	65	298	322	64	73	Zaïre
Zambia	396	205	496	526	301	290	Zambie
All LDCs	62	68	209	218	27	33	**Ensemble des PMA**
All developing countries	490	636	177	167	114	177	**Ensemble des pays en développpement**

Source: United Nations, *Energy Statistics Yearbook 1991* and *Statistical Yearbook 1985/86.*

Source: Nations Unies, Annuaire des statistiques de l'énergie 1991 et *Annuaire statistique 1985/86.*

43. Indicators on the status of women in LDCs

Country	Education, training and literacy : Female-male gaps a / Education, formation et alphabétisation : Inégalités entre les femmes et les hommes a				Health, fertility and mortality Santé, fécondité et mortalité		
	Adult literacy rate / Taux d'alphabétisme (adultes)	School enrolment ratio Taux d'inscription scolaire 1991 b			Average age at first marriage / Age moyen au premier mariage	Total fertility rate (births per woman) / Taux de fécondité totale (nombre de naissance par femme)	Maternal mortality (per 100,000 births) / Taux de mortalité maternelle (pour 100.000 naissances)
		Primary Primaire	Secondary Secondaire	Post Secondary Post Secondaire	(years/ années) 1980-1990	1991	1988
	1990 b						
Afghanistan	32	53	55	91	18	7	1000
Bangladesh	47	86	48	22	17	5	650
Benin	49	50	41	15	18	7	800
Bhutan	48	61	29	33	..	6	800
Botswana	78	104	114	81	26	5	300
Burkina Faso	32	63	50	27	18	7	750
Burundi	65	82	57	36	22	7	800
Cambodia	46	..	..	..	21	5	800
Cape Verde	..	97	95	..	24	4	200
Central African Rep.	48	61	41	23	18	6	650
Chad	42	46	25	11	17	6	800
Comoros	72	83	75	..	20	7	500
Djibouti	72	71	67	..	..	7	740
Equatorial Guinea	58	98	31	12	..	6	800
Ethiopia	49	72	85	23	18	7	900
Gambia	41	69	50	..	..	6	1000
Guinea	38	48	33	12	16	7	1000
Guinea-Bissau	48	55	44	17	18	6	1000
Haiti	80	93	95	35	24	5	600
Kiribati	..	..	..	..	..	..	..
Lao People's Dem. Rep.	82	75	63	50	..	7	750
Lesotho	135	120	143	116	21	5	350
Liberia	58	56	41	32	19	7	600
Madagascar	83	98	100	82	20	7	600
Malawi	52	83	60	33	18	8	500
Maldives	100	101	98	..	18	6	..
Mali	59	59	50	14	16	7	850
Mauritania	58	76	53	18	20	7	800
Mozambique	47	74	50	50	18	7	800
Myanmar	81	93	92	137	22	4	600
Nepal	35	50	40	34	18	6	850
Niger	42	57	44	17	16	7	850
Rwanda	58	97	78	20	21	9	700
Samoa	..	..	..	..	23	5	..
Sao Tome & Principe	62	..	..	..	16	5	..
Sierra Leone	37	70	57	20	..	7	1000
Solomon Islands	..	89	63	..	21	6	..
Somalia	39	53	56	24	20	7	900
Sudan	27	77	80	68	21	6	700
Togo	54	65	34	15	19	7	600
Tuvalu	..	..	..	..	..	..	..
Uganda	56	82	50	38	18	7	700
Un. Rep. of Tanzania	93	97	67	25	19	7	600
Vanuatu	..	..	..	..	23	5	..
Yemen	49	39	21	40	18	7	800
Zaire	73	74	47	21	20	7	700
Zambia	81	91	56	37	19	7	600
All LDCs c	**60**	**79**	**58**	**41**	**19**	**6**	**723**

Source: UNDP, *Human Development Report 1994*; United Nations, *The World's Women 1970-1990, Trends and Statistics*; United Nations, *Women's Indicators and Statistics* (Wistat); UNESCO, *Statistical Yearbook 1993*; IFAD, *The State of World Rural Poverty*, and other international sources.

a   Females as percentage of males. All figures are expressed in relation to the male average, which is indexed to equal 100. The smaller the figure the bigger the gap; the closer the figure to 100, the smaller the gap; and a figure above 100 indicates that the female average is higher than the male.

b   Or latest year available.
c   Average of countries for which data are available.

43. Indicateurs relatifs à la condition de la femme dans les PMA

Economic activity, employment / Activité économique, emploi				Political participation / Participation à la vie politique			
Women as a percentage of : / Part en pourcentage de femmes dans :				Female labour force % share in	Legislators	Decision makers in all ministries	
Labour force Main d'oeuvre	Employees Employés	Self-Employed Travailleurs indépendants	Unpaid Family Travailleurs familiaux non-rétribués	agriculture Main d'oeuvre feminine part en % dans l'agriculture	Organes législatifs	Postes de décision dans tous les ministères (%)	Pays
1990-1992 b	1991 b	1991 b	1991 b	1988	1993 b	1994	
8	..	..	..	3	3	-	Afghanistan
41	14	4	6	68	10	8.0	Bangladesh
24	..	..	..	68	6	14.3	Bénin
32	..	..	..	95	2	12.5	Bhoutan
38	36	48	35	79	5	5.9	Botswana
49	13	16	66	85	6	11.1	Burkina Faso
53	13	53	60	98	10	7.1	Burundi
56	..	..	..	..	4	-	Cambodge
37	32	46	54	25	8	12.5	Cap-Vert
47	10	52	55	71	4	5.3	Rép. centrafricaine
17	..	..	..	84	..	5.0	Tchad
41	24	25	..	84	-	-	Comores
40	33	28	22	87	-	-	Djibouti
36	..	..	..	81	3	4.0	Guinée équatoriale
41	..	..	..	82	..	10.0	Ethiopie
41	..	..	..	91	8	-	Gambie
30	..	..	..	83	..	4.2	Guinée
42	..	..	..	90	13	4.2	Guinée-Bissau
40	44	38	37	51	4	20.0	Haïti
14	..	..	..	..	-	..	Kiribati
45	..	..	..	76	9	-	Rép. dém. pop. lao
44	38	24	39	85	2	5.6	Lesotho
31	..	..	..	81	6	5.3	Libéria
40	..	..	..	91	7	-	Madagascar
51	13	57	58	91	12	13.6	Malawi
20	17	22	29	75	4	5.0	Maldives
16	17	15	53	76	2	-	Mali
22	15	23	38	84	-	-	Mauritanie
48	..	..	..	97	16	4.2	Mozambique
37	..	..	..	33	..	-	Myanmar
34	15	36	55	96	3	-	Népal
47	15	17	24	92	6	5.0	Niger
54	15	33	70	97	17	9.1	Rwanda
28	37	9	8	7	4	..	Samoa
36	32	26	54	81	11	-	Sao Tomé-et-Principe
33	20	24	74	78	..	-	Sierra Leone
14	20	39	..	47	-	5.3	Iles Salomon
39	..	..	..	86	4	-	Somalie
29	..	..	..	82	5	3.2	Soudan
37	15	48	54	65	6	4.5	Togo
..	..	..	..	..	..	..	Tuvalu
41	..	..	..	84	13	10.0	Ouganda
48	..	..	..	89	11	9.4	Rép.-Unie de Tanzanie
46	..	..	..	..	4	7.1	Vanuatu
13	8	13	68	48	1	-	Yémen
36	..	..	..	93	5	4.5	Zaïre
29	16	55	54	82	7	5.9	Zambie
39	..	..	..	**79**	**8**	**5.6**	**Ensemble des PMA c**

Source: PNUD, *Rapport Mondial sur Le Développement Humain 1994*; Nations Unies, *Les femmes dans le monde 1970-1990, Des idées et des chiffres*; Nations Unies, *Women's Indicators and Statistics* (Wistat); UNESCO, *Annuaire statistique 1993*; FIDA, *The State of World Rural Poverty*, et autres sources internationales.

a Données pour les femmes exprimées en pourcentage des données concernant les hommes.
Tous les chiffres sont exprimés en fonction de la moyenne concernant les hommes, qui est égale à 100.
Plus le chiffre est faible, plus l'écart est grand; plus le chiffre est près de 100, plus faible est l'écart;
un chiffre supérieur à 100 indique que la moyenne concernant les femmes a dépassé celle des hommes.
b Ou année la plus récente disponible.
c Moyenne des pays pour lesquels les données sont disponibles.